MznLnx

Missing Links Exam Preps

Exam Prep for

The Handbook of Fixed Income Securities

Fabozzi, 7th Edition

The MznLnx Exam Prep is your link from the texbook and lecture to your exams.
The MznLnx Exam Preps are unauthorized and comprehensive reviews of your textbooks.

All material provided by MznLnx and Rico Publications (c) 2010
Textbook publishers and textbook authors do not particpate in or contribute to these reviews.

MznLnx

Rico
Publications

Exam Prep for The Handbook of Fixed Income Securities
7th Edition
Fabozzi

Publisher: Raymond Houge
Assistant Editor: Michael Rouger
Text and Cover Designer: Lisa Buckner
Marketing Manager: Sara Swagger
Project Manager, Editorial Production: Jerry Emerson
Art Director: Vernon Lowerui

Product Manager: Dave Mason
Editorial Assitant: Rachel Guzmanji
Pedagogy: Debra Long
Cover Image: Jim Reed/Getty Images
Text and Cover Printer: City Printing, Inc.
Compositor: Media Mix, Inc.

(c) 2010 Rico Publications
ALL RIGHTS RESERVED. No part of this work covered by the copyright may be reproduced or used in any form or by an means--graphic, electronic, or mechanical, including photocopying, recording, taping, Web distribution, information storage, and retrieval systems, or in any other manner--without the written permission of the publisher.

Printed in the United States
ISBN:

For more information about our products, contact us at:
Dave.Mason@RicoPublications.com

For permission to use material from this text or product, submit a request online to:
Dave.Mason@RicoPublications.com

Contents

CHAPTER 1
Overview of the Types and Features of Fixed Income Securities — 1

CHAPTER 2
Risks Associated with Investing in Fixed Income Securities — 12

CHAPTER 3
The Primary and Secondary Bond Markets — 18

CHAPTER 4
Bond Market Indexes — 25

CHAPTER 5
Bond Pricing, Yield Measures, and Total Return — 28

CHAPTER 6
Calculating Investment Returns — 37

CHAPTER 7
The Structure of Interest Rates — 42

CHAPTER 8
Overview of Forward Rate Analysis — 50

CHAPTER 9
Measuring Interest-Rate Risk — 56

CHAPTER 10
U.S. Treasury and Agency Securities — 61

CHAPTER 11
Municipal Bonds — 67

CHAPTER 12
Private Money Market Instruments — 75

CHAPTER 13
Corporate Bonds — 80

CHAPTER 14
Medium-Term Notes — 88

CHAPTER 15
Inflation-Linked Bonds — 89

CHAPTER 16
Floating-Rate Securities — 94

CHAPTER 17
Nonconvertible Preferred Stock — 97

CHAPTER 18
International Bond Markets and Instruments — 98

CHAPTER 19
The Eurobond Market — 101

CHAPTER 20
Emerging Markets Debt — 105

Contents (Cont.)

CHAPTER 21
Stable Value Investments — 110

CHAPTER 22
An Overview of Mortgages and the Mortgage Market — 114

CHAPTER 23
Agency Mortgage-Backed Securities — 118

CHAPTER 24
Collateralized Mortgage Obligations — 125

CHAPTER 25
Nonagency CMOs — 133

CHAPTER 26
Residential Asset-Backed Securities — 136

CHAPTER 27
Commercial Mortgage-Backed Securities — 141

CHAPTER 28
Credit Card Asset-Backed Securities — 144

CHAPTER 29
Securities Backed by Automobile Loans and Leases — 147

CHAPTER 30
Cash-Collateralized Debt Obligations — 152

CHAPTER 31
Synthetic CDOs — 155

CHAPTER 32
Credit Analysis for Corporate Bonds — 160

CHAPTER 33
Credit Risk Modeling — 168

CHAPTER 34
Guidelines in the Credit Analysis of Municipal General Obligation and Bonds — 171

CHAPTER 35
Rating Agency Approach to Structured Finance — 176

CHAPTER 36
Fixed Income Risk Modeling — 178

CHAPTER 37
Valuation of Bonds with Embedded Options — 182

CHAPTER 38
Valuation of Mortgage-Backed Securities — 186

CHAPTER 39
OAS and Effective Duration — 189

CHAPTER 40
A Framework for Analyzing Yield-Curve Trades — 191

Contents (Cont.)

CHAPTER 41
The Market Yield Curve and Fitting the Term Structure of Interest Rates — 195

CHAPTER 42
Hedging Interest-Rate Risk with Term-Structure Factor Models — 202

CHAPTER 43
Introduction to Bond Portfolio Management — 205

CHAPTER 44
Quantitative Management of Benchmarked Portfolios — 209

CHAPTER 45
Financing Positions in the Bond Market — 215

CHAPTER 46
Global Credit Bond Portfolio Management — 220

CHAPTER 47
Bond Immunization: An Asset/Liability Optimization Strategy — 226

CHAPTER 48
Dedicated Bond Portfolios — 228

CHAPTER 49
International Bond Portfolio Management — 229

CHAPTER 50
Transition Management — 234

CHAPTER 51
Introduction to Interest-Rate Futures and Options Contracts — 237

CHAPTER 52
Pricing Futures and Portfolio Applications — 244

CHAPTER 53
Treasury Bond Futures Mechanics and Basis Valuation — 249

CHAPTER 54
The Basics of Interest-Rate Options — 253

CHAPTER 55
Interest-Rate Swaps and Swaptions — 258

CHAPTER 56
Interest-Rate Caps and Floors and Compound Options — 264

CHAPTER 57
Controlling Interest-Rate Risk with Futures and Options — 266

CHAPTER 58
Introduction to Credit Derivatives — 269

CHAPTER 59
Convertible Securities and Their Investment Characteristics — 274

CHAPTER 60
Convertible Securities and Their Valuation — 278

ANSWER KEY — 285

TO THE STUDENT

COMPREHENSIVE

The *MznLnx* Exam Prep series is designed to help you pass your exams. Editors at MznLnx review your textbooks and then prepare these practice exams to help you master the textbook material. Unlike study guides, workbooks, and practice tests provided by the texbook publisher and textbook authors, *MznLnx* gives you **all** of the material in each chapter in exam form, not just samples, so you can be sure to nail your exam.

MECHANICAL

The MznLnx Exam Prep series creates exams that will help you learn the subject matter as well as test you on your understanding. Each question is designed to help you master the concept. Just working through the exams, you gain an understanding of the subject--its a simple mechanical process that produces success.

INTEGRATED STUDY GUIDE AND REVIEW

MznLnx is not just a set of exams designed to test you, its also a comprehensive review of the subject content. Each exam question is also a review of the concept, making sure that you will get the answer correct without having to go to other sources of material. You learn as you go! Its the easiest way to pass an exam.

HUMOR

Studying can be tedious and dry. MznLnx's instructional design includes moderate humor within the exam questions on occassion, to break the tedium and revitalize the brain

Chapter 1. Overview of the Types and Features of Fixed Income Securities

1. In economics and finance, _____ is the practice of taking advantage of a price differential between two or more markets: striking a combination of matching deals that capitalize upon the imbalance, the profit being the difference between the market prices. When used by academics, an _____ is a transaction that involves no negative cash flow at any probabilistic or temporal state and a positive cash flow in at least one state; in simple terms, a risk-free profit.
    a. Arbitrage
    b. Initial margin
    c. Efficient-market hypothesis
    d. Issuer

2. In finance, a _____ is a debt security, in which the authorized issuer owes the holders a debt and, depending on the terms of the _____, is obliged to pay interest (the coupon) and/or to repay the principal at a later date, termed maturity.

    Thus a _____ is a loan: the issuer is the borrower, the _____ holder is the lender, and the coupon is the interest. _____s provide the borrower with external funds to finance long-term investments, or, in the case of government _____s, to finance current expenditure.

    a. Catastrophe bonds
    b. Puttable bond
    c. Bond
    d. Convertible bond

3. _____ is the investment strategy where an investor buys a financial instrument denominated in a foreign currency, and hedges his foreign exchange risk by selling a forward contract in the amount of the proceeds of the investment back into his base currency. The proceeds of the investment are only known exactly if the financial instrument is risk-free and only pays interest once, on the date of the forward sale of foreign currency. Otherwise, some foreign exchange risk remains.
    a. Floating exchange rate
    b. Covered interest arbitrage
    c. Triangular arbitrage
    d. Currency future

4. _____ is a fee paid on borrowed assets. It is the price paid for the use of borrowed money, or, money earned by deposited funds. Assets that are sometimes lent with _____ include money, shares, consumer goods through hire purchase, major assets such as aircraft, and even entire factories in finance lease arrangements.
    a. AAB
    b. Interest
    c. Insolvency
    d. A Random Walk Down Wall Street

5. _____ are dollar-denominated bonds, issued mostly by Latin American countries in the 1980s, named after U.S. Treasury Secretary Nicholas Brady.

    _____ were created in March 1989 in order to convert bonds issued by mostly Latin American countries into a variety or 'menu' of new bonds after many of those countries defaulted on their debt in the 1980's. At that time, the market for sovereign debt was small and illiquid, and the standardization of emerging-market debt facilitated risk-spreading and trading.

    a. Municipal bond
    b. Coupon rate
    c. Brady bonds
    d. Nominal yield

6. A _____ is an international bond that is denominated in a currency not native to the country where it is issued. It can be categorised according to the currency in which it is issued. London is one of the centers of the _____ market, but _____s may be traded throughout the world - for example in Singapore or Tokyo.

a. Eurobond
b. Education production function
c. Interest rate option
d. Economic entity

7. _____s are deposits denominated in United States dollars at banks outside the United States, and thus are not under the jurisdiction of the Federal Reserve. Consequently, such deposits are subject to much less regulation than similar deposits within the United States, allowing for higher margins. There is nothing 'European' about _____ deposits; a US dollar-denominated deposit in Tokyo or Caracas would likewise be deemed _____ deposits.
   a. ABN Amro
   b. AAB
   c. A Random Walk Down Wall Street
   d. Eurodollar

8. A _____ is a legal pledge in United States municipal finance, in which an entity pledges its full faith and credit to repay its debt, typically a _____ bond.
   a. Covenant
   b. Financial Institutions Reform Recovery and Enforcement Act
   c. Letter of credit
   d. General obligation

9. In finance, a _____ (non-investment grade bond, speculative grade bond or junk bond) is a bond that is rated below investment grade at the time of purchase. These bonds have a higher risk of default or other adverse credit events, but typically pay higher yields than better quality bonds in order to make them attractive to investors.
   a. Volatility
   b. Sharpe ratio
   c. Private equity
   d. High yield bond

10. _____ is a legal entity that develops, registers and sells securities for the purpose of financing its operations. _____s may be domestic or foreign governments, corporations or investment trusts. _____s are legally responsible for the obligations of the issue and for reporting financial conditions, material developments and any other operational activities as required by the regulations of their jurisdictions.
    a. Issuer
    b. Efficient-market hypothesis
    c. Initial margin
    d. Arbitrage

11. In financial accounting, _____s are precautions for which the amount or probability of occurrence are not known. Typical examples are _____s for warranty costs and _____ for taxes the term reserve is used instead of term _____; such a use, however, is inconsistent with the terminology suggested by International Accounting Standards Board.
    a. Provision
    b. Momentum Accounting and Triple-Entry Bookkeeping
    c. Petty cash
    d. Money measurement concept

12. _____ is a life of security. It may also refer to the final payment date of a loan or other financial instrument, at which point all remaining interest and principal is due to be paid.

1, 3, 6 months _____ band can be calculated by using 30-day per month periods.

   a. Replacement cost
   b. False billing
   c. Primary market
   d. Maturity

Chapter 1. Overview of the Types and Features of Fixed Income Securities

13. In finance, _____ occurs when a debtor has not met its legal obligations according to the debt contract, e.g. it has not made a scheduled payment, or has violated a loan covenant (condition) of the debt contract. _____ may occur if the debtor is either unwilling or unable to pay their debt. This can occur with all debt obligations including bonds, mortgages, loans, and promissory notes.

   a. Default   b. Vendor finance
   c. Credit crunch   d. Debt validation

14. The coupon or _____ of a bond is the amount of interest paid per year expressed as a percentage of the face value of the bond.

For example if you hold $10,000 nominal of a bond described as a 4.5% loan stock, you will receive $450 in interest each year (probably in two installments of $225 each.)

Not all bonds have coupons.

   a. Revenue bonds   b. Puttable bond
   c. Zero-coupon bond   d. Coupon rate

15. In economic models, the _____ time frame assumes no fixed factors of production. Firms can enter or leave the marketplace, and the cost (and availability) of land, labor, raw materials, and capital goods can be assumed to vary. In contrast, in the short-run time frame, certain factors are assumed to be fixed, because there is not sufficient time for them to change.

   a. Long-run   b. Short-run
   c. 529 plan   d. 4-4-5 Calendar

16. _____s are financial bonds that mature in installments over a period of time. In effect, a $100,000, 5-year _____ would mature in a $20,000 annuity over a 5-year interval. Bond issues consisting of a series of blocks of securities maturing in sequence, the coupon rate can be different.

   a. Brady bonds   b. Serial bond
   c. Callable bond   d. Bond fund

17. In economics, the concept of the _____ refers to the decision-making time frame of a firm in which at least one factor of production is fixed. Costs which are fixed in the _____ have no impact on a firms decisions. For example a firm can raise output by increasing the amount of labour through overtime.

   a. 4-4-5 Calendar   b. 529 plan
   c. Long-run   d. Short-run

18. _____, in finance and accounting, means stated value or face value. From this comes the expressions at par (at the _____), over par (over _____) and under par (under _____.)

The term '_____' has several meanings depending on context and geography.

   a. FIDC   b. Global Squeeze
   c. Sinking fund   d. Par value

4 *Chapter 1. Overview of the Types and Features of Fixed Income Securities*

19. A _____ is a document that indicates that the bearer of the document has title to property, such as shares or bonds. They differ from normal registered instruments, in that no records are kept of who owns the underlying property, or of the transactions involving transfer of ownership. Whoever physically holds the bearer bond papers owns the property.
   a. Bearer instrument
   b. Marketable
   c. Book entry
   d. Securities lending

20. A _____ is different from normal stock in that it is unregistered - no records are kept of the owner, or the transactions involving ownership. Whoever physically holds the _____ papers owns the stock or corporation. This is useful for investors and corporate officers who wish to retain anonymity.
   a. Revenue bonds
   b. Clean price
   c. Bearer bond
   d. Gilts

21. _____, refers to consumption opportunity gained by an entity within a specified time frame, which is generally expressed in monetary terms. However, for households and individuals, '_____ is the sum of all the wages, salaries, profits, interests payments, rents and other forms of earnings received... in a given period of time.' For firms, _____ generally refers to net-profit: what remains of revenue after expenses have been subtracted.
   a. Accrual
   b. Annual report
   c. OIBDA
   d. Income

22. In economics, _____ is a rise in the general level of prices of goods and services in an economy over a period of time. The term '_____' once referred to increases in the money supply (monetary _____); however, economic debates about the relationship between money supply and price levels have led to its primary use today in describing price _____. _____ can also be described as a decline in the real value of money--a loss of purchasing power in the medium of exchange which is also the monetary unit of account.
   a. ABN Amro
   b. Inflation
   c. A Random Walk Down Wall Street
   d. AAB

23. _____ are bonds where the principal is indexed to inflation. They are thus designed to cut out the inflation risk of an investment. _____ pay a periodic coupon that is equal to the product of the inflation index and the nominal coupon rate. The relationship between coupon payments, breakeven inflation and real interest rates is given by the Fisher equation.
   a. ABN Amro
   b. Inflation-indexed bonds
   c. A Random Walk Down Wall Street
   d. AAB

24. A _____ is a fungible, negotiable instrument representing financial value. They are broadly categorized into debt securities (such as banknotes, bonds and debentures), and equity securities; e.g., common stocks. The company or other entity issuing the _____ is called the issuer.
   a. Securities lending
   b. Security
   c. Book entry
   d. Tracking stock

25. A _____ is a bond bought at a price lower than its face value, with the face value repaid at the time of maturity. It does not make periodic interest payments, or have so-called 'coupons,' hence the term _____. Investors earn return from the compounded interest all paid at maturity plus the difference between the discounted price of the bond and its par value.
   a. Zero-coupon bond
   b. Clean price
   c. Corporate bond
   d. Bond fund

Chapter 1. Overview of the Types and Features of Fixed Income Securities

26. A _____ is a bond issued by a corporation. The term is usually applied to longer-term debt instruments, generally with a maturity date falling at least a year after their issue date. (The term 'commercial paper' is sometimes used for instruments with a shorter maturity.)
    a. Serial bond
    b. Corporate Bond
    c. Brady bonds
    d. Government bond

27. An _____ is a type of bond or other type of debt instrument used in finance whose coupon rate has an inverse relationship to short-term interest rates (or its reference rate.) With an _____, as interest rates rise the coupon rate falls. The basic structure is the same as an ordinary floating rate note except for the direction in which the coupon rate is adjusted.
    a. A Random Walk Down Wall Street
    b. Inverse floater
    c. AAB
    d. ABN Amro

28. _____ are bonds that have a variable coupon, equal to a money market reference rate, like LIBOR or federal funds rate, plus a spread. The spread is a rate that remains constant. Almost all _____ have quarterly coupons, i.e. they pay out interest every three months, though counter examples do exist.
    a. Gordon growth model
    b. CVECAs
    c. Loan participation
    d. Floating rate notes

29. _____ is a type of bond that allows the issuer of the bond to retain the privilege of redeeming the bond at some point before the bond reaches the date of maturity. In other words, on the call dates, the issuer has the right, but not the obligation, to buy back the bonds from the bond holders at the call price. Technically speaking, the bonds are not really bought and held by the issuer but cancelled immediately.
    a. Coupon rate
    b. Callable bond
    c. Bond fund
    d. Gilts

30. A '_____' is a 'Charge' that is paid to obtain the right to delay a payment. Essentially, the payer purchases the right to make a given payment in the future instead of in the Present. The '_____', or 'Charge' that must be paid to delay the payment, is simply the difference between what the payment amount would be if it were paid in the present and what the payment amount would be paid if it were paid in the future.
    a. Value at risk
    b. Risk aversion
    c. Discount
    d. Risk modeling

31. A _____ is a bond bought at a price lower than its face value, with the face value repaid at the time of maturity. It does not make periodic interest payments, or so-called 'coupons,' hence the term zero-coupon bond. Investors earn return from the compounded interest all paid at maturity plus the difference between the discounted price of the bond and its par value.
    a. Municipal bond
    b. Bowie bonds
    c. Callable bond
    d. Zero coupon bond

32. _____ most frequently refers to the standard deviation of the continuously compounded returns of a financial instrument with a specific time horizon. It is often used to quantify the risk of the instrument over that time period. _____ is typically expressed in annualized terms, and it may either be an absolute number ($5) or a fraction of the mean (5%).
    a. Seasoned equity offering
    b. Currency swap
    c. Volatility
    d. Portfolio insurance

Chapter 1. Overview of the Types and Features of Fixed Income Securities

33. In the United States, a _____ is a bond issued by a city or other local government, or their agencies. Potential issuers of these bonds include cities, counties, redevelopment agencies, school districts, publicly owned airports and seaports, and any other governmental entity (or group of governments) below the state level. They may be general obligations of the issuer or secured by specified revenues.
    a. Senior debt
    b. Premium bond
    c. Puttable bond
    d. Municipal bond

34. The _____ is a financial market where participants buy and sell debt securities, usually in the form of bonds. As of 2006, the size of the international _____ is an estimated $45 trillion, of which the size of the outstanding U.S. _____ debt was $25.2 trillion.

    Nearly all of the $923 billion average daily trading volume in the U.S. _____ takes place between broker-dealers and large institutions in a decentralized, over-the-counter market.

    a. 4-4-5 Calendar
    b. Fixed income
    c. 529 plan
    d. Bond market

35. _____ is the provision of resources (such as granting a loan) by one party to another party where that second party does not reimburse the first party immediately, thereby generating a debt, and instead arranges either to repay or return those resources (or material(s) of equal value) at a later date. The first party is called a creditor, also known as a lender, while the second party is called a debtor, also known as a borrower.

    Movements of financial capital are normally dependent on either _____ or equity transfers.

    a. Clearing house
    b. Credit
    c. Warrant
    d. Comparable

36. _____ is the risk of loss due to a debtor's non-payment of a loan or other line of credit (either the principal or interest (coupon) or both)

    Most lenders employ their own models (credit scorecards) to rank potential and existing customers according to risk, and then apply appropriate strategies. With products such as unsecured personal loans or mortgages, lenders charge a higher price for higher risk customers and vice versa. With revolving products such as credit cards and overdrafts, risk is controlled through careful setting of credit limits.

    a. Market risk
    b. Liquidity risk
    c. Transaction risk
    d. Credit risk

37. In finance, a _____ is a type of bond that can be converted into shares of stock in the issuing company, usually at some pre-announced ratio. It is a hybrid security with debt- and equity-like features. Although it typically has a low coupon rate, the holder is compensated with the ability to convert the bond to common stock, usually at a substantial discount to the stock's market value.
    a. Corporate bond
    b. Bond fund
    c. Convertible bond
    d. Gilts

Chapter 1. Overview of the Types and Features of Fixed Income Securities

38. _____ is a combination of straight bond and embedded put option. The holder of the _____ has the right, but not the obligation, to demand early repayment of the principal. The put option is usually exercisable on specified dates.
   a. Brady bonds
   b. Callable bond
   c. Convertible bond
   d. Puttable bond

39. An _____ is a contract written by a seller that conveys to the buyer the right -- but not the obligation -- to buy (in the case of a call _____) or to sell (in the case of a put _____) a particular asset, such as a piece of property such as, among others, a futures contract. In return for granting the _____, the seller collects a payment (the premium) from the buyer.

For example, buying a call _____ provides the right to buy a specified quantity of a security at a set strike price at some time on or before expiration, while buying a put _____ provides the right to sell.

   a. Option
   b. Annuity
   c. AT'T Mobility LLC
   d. Amortization

40. In finance, a _____ is a security that entitles the holder to buy stock of the company that issued it at a specified price, which is usually higher than the stock price at time of issue.

_____s are frequently attached to bonds or preferred stock as a sweetener, allowing the issuer to pay lower interest rates or dividends. They can be used to enhance the yield of the bond, and make them more attractive to potential buyers.

   a. Credit
   b. Clearing
   c. Clearing house
   d. Warrant

41. In finance, the term _____ describes the amount in cash that returns to the owners of a security. Normally it does not include the price variations, at the difference of the total return. _____ applies to various stated rates of return on stocks (common and preferred, and convertible), fixed income instruments (bonds, notes, bills, strips, zero coupon), and some other investment type insurance products (e.g. annuities.)
   a. Macaulay duration
   b. Yield to maturity
   c. Yield
   d. 4-4-5 Calendar

Chapter 1. Overview of the Types and Features of Fixed Income Securities

42. _____ is the process of decreasing an amount over a period of time. The word comes from Middle English amortisen to kill, alienate in mortmain, from Anglo-French amorteser, alteration of amortir, from Vulgar Latin admortire to kill, from Latin ad- + mort-, mors death. Particular instances of the term include:

- _____ (business), the allocation of a lump sum amount to different time periods, particularly for loans and other forms of finance, including related interest or other finance charges.
    - _____ schedule, a table detailing each periodic payment on a loan (typically a mortgage), as generated by an _____ calculator.
    - Negative _____, an _____ schedule where the loan amount actually increases through not paying the full interest
- Amortized analysis, analyzing the execution cost of algorithms over a sequence of operations.
- _____ of capital expenditures of certain assets under accounting rules, particularly intangible assets, in a manner analogous to depreciation.
- _____ (tax law)

_____ is also used in the context of zoning regulations and describes the time in which a property owner has to relocate when the property's use constitutes a preexisting nonconforming use under zoning regulations.

- Depreciation

a. Intrinsic value
b. Option
c. Amortization
d. AT'T Inc.

43. In finance, a _____ is a derivative in which two counterparties agree to exchange one stream of cash flows against another stream. These streams are called the legs of the _____.

The cash flows are calculated over a notional principal amount, which is usually not exchanged between counterparties.

a. Local volatility
b. Volatility arbitrage
c. Swap
d. Volatility swap

44. A _____ is a payment made by a corporation to its shareholder members. When a corporation earns a profit or surplus, that money can be put to two uses: it can either be re-invested in the business (called retained earnings), or it can be paid to the shareholders as a _____. Many corporations retain a portion of their earnings and pay the remainder as a _____.

a. Special dividend
b. Dividend yield
c. Dividend puzzle
d. Dividend

45. _____ is capital stock which provides a specific dividend that is paid before any dividends are paid to common stock holders, and which takes precedence over common stock in the event of a liquidation. This form of financing is used by private equity investors and venture capital firms. Holders of _____ get both their money back (with interest) and the money that is distributable with respect to the percentage of common shares into which their preferred stock can convert.

Chapter 1. Overview of the Types and Features of Fixed Income Securities 9

a. Preferred stock
b. Participating preferred stock
c. Cash is king
d. Shareholder value

46. _____ is typically a higher ranking stock than voting shares, and its terms are negotiated between the corporation and the investor.

_____ usually carry no voting rights, but may carry superior priority over common stock in the payment of dividends and upon liquidation. _____ may carry a dividend that is paid out prior to any dividends to common stock holders.

a. Preferred stock
b. Follow-on offering
c. Trade-off theory
d. Second lien loan

47. A _____ is an asset-backed security whose cash flows are backed by the principal and interest payments of a set of mortgage loans. Payments are typically made monthly over the lifetime of the underlying loans.
a. Conforming loan
b. Mortgage-backed security
c. Home equity line of credit
d. Shared appreciation mortgage

48. _____ is that which is owed; usually referencing assets owed, but the term can cover other obligations. In the case of assets, _____ is a means of using future purchasing power in the present before a summation has been earned. Some companies and corporations use _____ as a part of their overall corporate finance strategy.
a. Cross-collateralization
b. Credit cycle
c. Debt
d. Partial Payment

49. The institution most often referenced by the word '_____' is a public or publicly traded _____, the shares of which are traded on a public stock exchange (e.g., the New York Stock Exchange or Nasdaq in the United States) where shares of stock of _____s are bought and sold by and to the general public. Most of the largest businesses in the world are publicly traded _____s. However, the majority of _____s are said to be closely held, privately held or close _____s, meaning that no ready market exists for the trading of shares.
a. Protect
b. Federal Home Loan Mortgage Corporation
c. Depository Trust Company
d. Corporation

50. The _____ (NYSE: FRE) is an insolvent government sponsored enterprise (GSE) of the United States federal government.

The _____ was created in 1970 to expand the secondary market for mortgages in the US. Along with other GSEs, Freddie Mac buys mortgages on the secondary market, pools them, and sells them as mortgage-backed securities to investors on the open market.

a. Public company
b. The Depository Trust ' Clearing Corporation
c. Governmental Accounting Standards Board
d. Federal Home Loan Mortgage Corporation

51. The _____ is a U.S. government-owned corporation within the Department of Housing and Urban Development

Ginnie Mae provides guarantees on mortgage-backed securities backed by federally insured or guaranteed loans, mainly loans issued by the Federal Housing Administration, Department of Veterans Affairs, Rural Housing Service, and Office of Public and Indian Housing. Ginnie Mae securities are the only MBS that are guaranteed by the United States government.

a. Certified Emission Reductions	b. Cash budget
c. Case-Shiller Home Price Indices	d. GNMA

52. The _____ is a U.S. government-owned corporation within the Department of Housing and Urban Development

Ginnie Mae provides guarantees on mortgage-backed securities backed by federally insured or guaranteed loans, mainly loans issued by the Federal Housing Administration, Department of Veterans Affairs, Rural Housing Service, and Office of Public and Indian Housing. Ginnie Mae securities are the only MBS that are guaranteed by the United States government.

a. Graduated payment mortgage	b. 4-4-5 Calendar
c. Government National Mortgage Association	d. Jumbo mortgage

53. _____ is early repayment of a loan by a borrower.

In the case of a mortgage-backed security (MBS), _____ is perceived as a risk, because mortgage debts are often paid off early in order to incur lower total interest payments through cheaper refinancing. The new financing may be cheaper because the borrower's credit rating has improved or because interest rates are lower, but in either case, the payments that would have been made to the MBS investor would be above market rates.

a. Bankruptcy remote	b. Retention ratio
c. Prepayment	d. Disposal tax effect

54. The _____ (NYSE: FNM), commonly known as Fannie Mae, is a stockholder-owned corporation chartered by Congress in 1968 as a government sponsored enterprise (GSE), but founded in 1938 during the Great Depression. The corporation's purpose is to purchase and securitize mortgages in order to ensure that funds are consistently available to the institutions that lend money to home buyers.

On September 7, 2008, James Lockhart, director of the Federal Housing Finance Agency (FHFA), announced that Fannie Mae and Freddie Mac were being placed into conservatorship of the FHFA.

a. SPDR	b. Federal National Mortgage Association
c. General partnership	d. The Depository Trust ' Clearing Corporation

55. An _____ is a security whose value and income payments are derived from and collateralized (or 'backed') by a specified pool of underlying assets. The pool of assets is typically a group of small and illiquid assets that are unable to be sold individually. Pooling the assets allows them to be sold to general investors, a process called securitization, and allows the risk of investing in the underlying assets to be diversified because each security will represent a fraction of the total value of the diverse pool of underlying assets.

a. A Random Walk Down Wall Street
c. Asset-backed security
b. AAB
d. ABN Amro

56. _____ are a type of bond commonly issued in American security markets. They are a type of mortgage-backed security backed by mortgages on commercial rather than residential real estate. CMBS issues are usually structured as multiple tranches, similar to CMOs, rather than typical residential 'passthroughs.'

Many American CMBSs carry less prepayment risk than other MBS types, thanks to the structure of commercial mortgages.

a. Stop order
c. Contract for difference
b. Stock market index
d. Commercial mortgage-backed securities

Chapter 2. Risks Associated with Investing in Fixed Income Securities

1. _____ is the provision of resources (such as granting a loan) by one party to another party where that second party does not reimburse the first party immediately, thereby generating a debt, and instead arranges either to repay or return those resources (or material(s) of equal value) at a later date. The first party is called a creditor, also known as a lender, while the second party is called a debtor, also known as a borrower.

Movements of financial capital are normally dependent on either _____ or equity transfers.

    a. Comparable
    b. Clearing house
    c. Warrant
    d. Credit

2. _____ is the risk of loss due to a debtor's non-payment of a loan or other line of credit (either the principal or interest (coupon) or both)

Most lenders employ their own models (credit scorecards) to rank potential and existing customers according to risk, and then apply appropriate strategies. With products such as unsecured personal loans or mortgages, lenders charge a higher price for higher risk customers and vice versa. With revolving products such as credit cards and overdrafts, risk is controlled through careful setting of credit limits.

    a. Liquidity risk
    b. Market risk
    c. Transaction risk
    d. Credit risk

3. In finance, the _____ of a financial asset measures the sensitivity of the asset's price to interest rate movements, expressed as a number of years. The reason for expressing this sensitivity in years is that the time that will elapse until a cash flow is received allows more interest to accumulate. Therefore the price of an asset with long term cashflows has more interest rate sensitivity than an asset with cashflows in the near future.

    a. Macaulay duration
    b. 4-4-5 Calendar
    c. Yield to maturity
    d. Duration

4. _____ is the risk that the value of an investment will decrease due to moves in market factors. The five standard _____ factors are:

- Equity risk, the risk that stock prices will change.
- Interest rate risk, the risk that interest rates will change.
- Currency risk, the risk that foreign exchange rates will change.
- Commodity risk, the risk that commodity prices (e.g. grains, metals) will change.

As with other forms of risk, _____ may be measured in a number of ways. Traditionally, this is done using a Value at Risk methodology. Value at risk is well established as a risk management technique, but it contains a number of limiting assumptions that constrain its accuracy.

    a. Market risk
    b. Tracking error
    c. Currency risk
    d. Transaction risk

5. _____ is one of the main genres of financial risk. The term describes the risk that a particular investment might be canceled or stopped somehow, that one may have to find a new place to invest that money with the risk being there might not be a similarly attractive investment available. This primarily occurs if bonds (which are portions of loans to entities) are paid back earlier then expected.

Chapter 2. Risks Associated with Investing in Fixed Income Securities

a. Standard of deferred payment
c. Debt cash flow
b. Biweekly Mortgage
d. Reinvestment risk

6. _____ is early repayment of a loan by a borrower.

In the case of a mortgage-backed security (MBS), _____ is perceived as a risk, because mortgage debts are often paid off early in order to incur lower total interest payments through cheaper refinancing. The new financing may be cheaper because the borrower's credit rating has improved or because interest rates are lower, but in either case, the payments that would have been made to the MBS investor would be above market rates.

a. Bankruptcy remote
c. Prepayment
b. Retention ratio
d. Disposal tax effect

7. In financial accounting, _____s are precautions for which the amount or probability of occurrence are not known. Typical examples are _____s for warranty costs and _____ for taxes the term reserve is used instead of term _____; such a use, however, is inconsistent with the terminology suggested by International Accounting Standards Board.

a. Money measurement concept
c. Petty cash
b. Momentum Accounting and Triple-Entry Bookkeeping
d. Provision

8. The institution most often referenced by the word '_____' is a public or publicly traded _____, the shares of which are traded on a public stock exchange (e.g., the New York Stock Exchange or Nasdaq in the United States) where shares of stock of _____s are bought and sold by and to the general public. Most of the largest businesses in the world are publicly traded _____s. However, the majority of _____s are said to be closely held, privately held or close _____s, meaning that no ready market exists for the trading of shares.

a. Depository Trust Company
c. Federal Home Loan Mortgage Corporation
b. Protect
d. Corporation

9. A _____ assesses the credit worthiness of an individual, corporation, or even a country. _____s are calculated from financial history and current assets and liabilities. Typically, a _____ tells a lender or investor the probability of the subject being able to pay back a loan.

a. Credit rating
c. Debenture
b. Credit report monitoring
d. Credit cycle

10. In finance, _____ occurs when a debtor has not met its legal obligations according to the debt contract, e.g. it has not made a scheduled payment, or has violated a loan covenant (condition) of the debt contract. _____ may occur if the debtor is either unwilling or unable to pay their debt. This can occur with all debt obligations including bonds, mortgages, loans, and promissory notes.

a. Credit crunch
c. Debt validation
b. Vendor finance
d. Default

11. _____ is a life of security. It may also refer to the final payment date of a loan or other financial instrument, at which point all remaining interest and principal is due to be paid.

1, 3, 6 months _____ band can be calculated by using 30-day per month periods.

a. False billing
b. Replacement cost
c. Primary market
d. Maturity

12. In economic models, the _____ time frame assumes no fixed factors of production. Firms can enter or leave the marketplace, and the cost (and availability) of land, labor, raw materials, and capital goods can be assumed to vary. In contrast, in the short-run time frame, certain factors are assumed to be fixed, because there is not sufficient time for them to change.
   a. Short-run
   b. 529 plan
   c. 4-4-5 Calendar
   d. Long-run

13. In economics, the concept of the _____ refers to the decision-making time frame of a firm in which at least one factor of production is fixed. Costs which are fixed in the _____ have no impact on a firms decisions. For example a firm can raise output by increasing the amount of labour through overtime.
   a. 4-4-5 Calendar
   b. Long-run
   c. 529 plan
   d. Short-run

14. In economics, _____ is a rise in the general level of prices of goods and services in an economy over a period of time. The term '_____' once referred to increases in the money supply (monetary _____); however, economic debates about the relationship between money supply and price levels have led to its primary use today in describing price _____. _____ can also be described as a decline in the real value of money--a loss of purchasing power in the medium of exchange which is also the monetary unit of account.
   a. Inflation
   b. A Random Walk Down Wall Street
   c. ABN Amro
   d. AAB

15. _____ is a measure of the ability of a debtor to pay their debts as and when they fall due. It is usually expressed as a ratio or a percentage of current liabilities.

For a corporation with a published balance sheet there are various ratios used to calculate a measure of liquidity.

   a. Operating leverage
   b. Operating profit margin
   c. Invested capital
   d. Accounting liquidity

16. _____ arises from situations in which a party interested in trading an asset cannot do it because nobody in the market wants to trade that asset. _____ becomes particularly important to parties who are about to hold or currently hold an asset, since it affects their ability to trade.

Manifestation of _____ is very different from a drop of price to zero.

   a. Tracking error
   b. Currency risk
   c. Credit risk
   d. Liquidity risk

17. A _____ or market-based mechanism is any of a wide variety of ways to match up buyers and sellers.

An example of a _____ uses announced bid and ask prices. Generally speaking, when two parties wish to engage in a trade, the purchaser will announce a price he is willing to pay (the bid price) and seller will announce a price he is willing to accept (the ask price).

Chapter 2. Risks Associated with Investing in Fixed Income Securities

a. 529 plan
c. 7-Eleven
b. 4-4-5 Calendar
d. Price mechanism

18. The _____ for securities is the difference between the price quoted by a market maker for an immediate sale and an immediate purchase The size of the bid-offer spread in a given commodity is a measure of the liquidity of the market.

The trader initiating the transaction is said to demand liquidity, and the other party to the transaction supplies liquidity.

a. Defined contribution plan
c. Bid/offer spread
b. Capital outflow
d. Trade-off

19. _____ is a form of risk that arises from the change in price of one currency against another. Whenever investors or companies have assets or business operations across national borders, they face _____ if their positions are not hedged.

- Transaction risk is the risk that exchange rates will change unfavourably over time. It can be hedged against using forward currency contracts;
- Translation risk is an accounting risk, proportional to the amount of assets held in foreign currencies. Changes in the exchange rate over time will render a report inaccurate, and so assets are usually balanced by borrowings in that currency.

The exchange risk associated with a foreign denominated instrument is a key element in foreign investment. This risk flows from differential monetary policy and growth in real productivity, which results in differential inflation rates.

a. Tracking error
c. Credit risk
b. Market risk
d. Currency risk

20. In finance, the _____ between two currencies specifies how much one currency is worth in terms of the other. For example an _____ of 102 Japanese yen to the United States dollar means that JPY 102 is worth the same as USD 1. The foreign exchange market is one of the largest markets in the world.

a. Exchange rate
c. AAB
b. A Random Walk Down Wall Street
d. ABN Amro

21. _____: Sometimes governments change the law in a way that adversely affects a bank's position.

The Risk Principle is an area of law closely tied to legal causation in negligence. It provides limits on negligence for harm caused unforeseeably.

a. Legal and regulatory risk
c. Federal Work Study program
b. Flow to Equity-Approach
d. Price channel

Chapter 2. Risks Associated with Investing in Fixed Income Securities

22. In the United States, a _____ is a bond issued by a city or other local government, or their agencies. Potential issuers of these bonds include cities, counties, redevelopment agencies, school districts, publicly owned airports and seaports, and any other governmental entity (or group of governments) below the state level. They may be general obligations of the issuer or secured by specified revenues.

    a. Premium bond
    b. Senior debt
    c. Puttable bond
    d. Municipal bond

23. _____ is a type of risk faced by investors, corporations, and governments. It is a risk that can be understood and managed with proper aforethought and investment.

    Broadly, _____ refers to the complications businesses and governments may face as a result of what are commonly referred to as political decisions--or 'any political change that alters the expected outcome and value of a given economic action by changing the probability of achieving business objectives.' .

    a. Mid price
    b. Capital asset
    c. Political risk
    d. Single-index model

24. _____ most frequently refers to the standard deviation of the continuously compounded returns of a financial instrument with a specific time horizon. It is often used to quantify the risk of the instrument over that time period. _____ is typically expressed in annualized terms, and it may either be an absolute number ($5) or a fraction of the mean (5%).

    a. Seasoned equity offering
    b. Currency swap
    c. Portfolio insurance
    d. Volatility

25. _____ in financial markets is the likelihood of fluctuations in the exchange rate of currencies. Therefore, it is a probability measure of the threat that an exchange rate movement poses to an investor's portfolio in a foreign currency. The volatility of the exchange rate is measured as standard deviation over a dataset of exchange rate movements.

    a. 4-4-5 Calendar
    b. 7-Eleven
    c. 529 plan
    d. Volatility risk

26. In finance, a _____ is a debt security, in which the authorized issuer owes the holders a debt and, depending on the terms of the _____, is obliged to pay interest (the coupon) and/or to repay the principal at a later date, termed maturity.

    Thus a _____ is a loan: the issuer is the borrower, the _____ holder is the lender, and the coupon is the interest. _____s provide the borrower with external funds to finance long-term investments, or, in the case of government _____s, to finance current expenditure.

    a. Puttable bond
    b. Catastrophe bonds
    c. Convertible bond
    d. Bond

27. The _____ is a financial market where participants buy and sell debt securities, usually in the form of bonds. As of 2006, the size of the international _____ is an estimated $45 trillion, of which the size of the outstanding U.S. _____ debt was $25.2 trillion.

    Nearly all of the $923 billion average daily trading volume in the U.S. _____ takes place between broker-dealers and large institutions in a decentralized, over-the-counter market.

Chapter 2. Risks Associated with Investing in Fixed Income Securities

a. 529 plan
c. Fixed income
b. 4-4-5 Calendar
d. Bond market

28. _____ in finance is the risk associated with imperfect hedging using futures. It could arise because of the difference between the asset whose price is to be hedged and the asset underlying the derivative, or because of a mismatch between the expiration date of the futures and the actual selling date of the asset.

Under these conditions, the spot price of the asset, and the futures price, do not converge on the expiration date of the future.

a. Currency risk
c. Credit risk
b. Basis risk
d. Liquidity risk

29. A _____ occurs when a financial sponsor acquires a controlling interest in a company's equity and where a significant percentage of the purchase price is financed through leverage (borrowing.) The assets of the acquired company are used as collateral for the borrowed capital, sometimes with assets of the acquiring company. The bonds or other paper issued for _____s are commonly considered not to be investment grade because of the significant risks involved.

a. Pension fund
c. Leverage
b. Leveraged buyout
d. Limited partnership

Chapter 3. The Primary and Secondary Bond Markets

1. The _____ is that part of the capital markets that deals with the issuance of new securities. Companies, governments or public sector institutions can obtain funding through the sale of a new stock or bond issue. This is typically done through a syndicate of securities dealers.
   a. Primary market
   b. Sector rotation
   c. Peer group analysis
   d. Volatility clustering

2. A _____ is a fungible, negotiable instrument representing financial value. They are broadly categorized into debt securities (such as banknotes, bonds and debentures), and equity securities; e.g., common stocks. The company or other entity issuing the _____ is called the issuer.
   a. Tracking stock
   b. Security
   c. Securities lending
   d. Book entry

3. Congress enacted the _____, in the aftermath of the stock market crash of 1929 and during the ensuing Great Depression. It requires that any offer or sale of securities using the means and instrumentalities of interstate commerce be registered pursuant to the 1933 Act, unless an exemption from registration exists under the law.
   a. 529 plan
   b. 7-Eleven
   c. 4-4-5 Calendar
   d. Securities Act of 1933

4. The U.S. _____ is an independent agency of the United States government which holds primary responsibility for enforcing the federal securities laws and regulating the securities industry, the nation's stock and options exchanges, and other electronic securities markets. The SEC was created by section 4 of the SEC of 1934 (now codified as 15 U.S.C. § 78d and commonly referred to as the 1934 Act.)
   a. 4-4-5 Calendar
   b. 529 plan
   c. Securities and Exchange Commission
   d. 7-Eleven

5. In finance, a _____ is a debt security, in which the authorized issuer owes the holders a debt and, depending on the terms of the _____, is obliged to pay interest (the coupon) and/or to repay the principal at a later date, termed maturity.

   Thus a _____ is a loan: the issuer is the borrower, the _____ holder is the lender, and the coupon is the interest. _____s provide the borrower with external funds to finance long-term investments, or, in the case of government _____s, to finance current expenditure.

   a. Puttable bond
   b. Catastrophe bonds
   c. Convertible bond
   d. Bond

6. _____ refers to the fees that underwriters receive for arranging and underwriting an offering of debt or equity securities. The _____ for an initial public offering (IPO) can be higher than 10% while the _____ on a debt offering can be as low as 0.05%.

   For example, if a company sells $100 million of shares in an IPO and the _____ is 7%, the underwriting syndicate will receive fees of $7 million.

   a. Gross spread
   b. Capital guarantee
   c. Redemption value
   d. Package loan

Chapter 3. The Primary and Secondary Bond Markets

7. A '_____' is a 'Charge' that is paid to obtain the right to delay a payment. Essentially, the payer purchases the right to make a given payment in the future instead of in the Present. The '_____', or 'Charge' that must be paid to delay the payment, is simply the difference between what the payment amount would be if it were paid in the present and what the payment amount would be paid if it were paid in the future.
   - a. Value at risk
   - b. Discount
   - c. Risk aversion
   - d. Risk modeling

8. A _____ occurs when an underwriter, such as an investment bank or a syndicate, purchases securities from an issuer before selling them to the public. The investment bank (or underwriter) acts as principal rather than agent and thus actually 'goes long' in the security. The bank negotiates a price with the issuer (usually at a discount to the current market price, if applicable.)
   - a. Shelf registration
   - b. 4-4-5 Calendar
   - c. Black Sea Trade and Development Bank
   - d. Bought deal

9. _____ is the acquisition of goods and/or services at the best possible total cost of ownership, in the right quantity and quality, at the right time, in the right place and from the right source for the direct benefit or use of corporations or individuals, generally via a contract. Simple _____ may involve nothing more than repeat purchasing. Complex _____ could involve finding long term partners - or even 'co-destiny' suppliers that might fundamentally commit one organization to another.
   - a. Pac-Man defense
   - b. Synthetic CDO
   - c. Market capitalization
   - d. Procurement

10. A _____ is a type of auction where the auctioneer begins with a high asking price which is lowered until some participant is willing to accept the auctioneer's price, or a predetermined reserve price (the seller's minimum acceptable price) is reached. The winning participant pays the last announced price. This is also known as a 'clock auction' or an open-outcry descending-price auction.
    - a. 7-Eleven
    - b. 529 plan
    - c. 4-4-5 Calendar
    - d. Dutch auction

11. A _____ is a bond issued by a corporation. The term is usually applied to longer-term debt instruments, generally with a maturity date falling at least a year after their issue date. (The term 'commercial paper' is sometimes used for instruments with a shorter maturity.)
    - a. Corporate bond
    - b. Brady bonds
    - c. Government bond
    - d. Serial bond

12. In the United States, a _____ is an offering of securities that are not registered with the Securities and Exchange Commission (SEC.) Such offerings exploit an exemption offered by the Securities Act of 1933 that comes with several restrictions, including a prohibition against general solicitation. This exemption allows companies to avoid quarterly reporting requirements and many of the legal liabilities associated with the Sarbanes-Oxley Act.
    - a. 4-4-5 Calendar
    - b. 529 plan
    - c. Private placement
    - d. 7-Eleven

13. In structured finance, a _____ is one of a number of related securities offered as part of the same transaction. The word _____ is French for slice, section, series, or portion. In the financial sense of the word, each bond is a different slice of the deal's risk.

a. 4-4-5 Calendar
c. Credit enhancement
b. Yield curve spread
d. Tranche

14. In business and finance, a _____ (also referred to as equity _____) of stock means a _____ of ownership in a corporation (company.) In the plural, stocks is often used as a synonym for _____s especially in the United States, but it is less commonly used that way outside of North America.

In the United Kingdom, South Africa, and Australia, stock can also refer to completely different financial instruments such as government bonds or, less commonly, to all kinds of marketable securities.

a. Bucket shop
c. Procter ' Gamble
b. Share
d. Margin

15. A _____, in law and finance, is a purchaser of securities that is deemed financially sophisticated and is legally recognized by security market regulators to need less protection from issuers than most public investors.

A _____ is an investing entity owning and investing large amounts of securities on a discretionary basis. The threshold is defined as ownership of at least $100 million of securities not affiliated with the entity and dependent on the type of entity. Additionally, they must be entities that fall under one of several categories including an insurance company, investment company, employee benefit plan, trust fund, Business Development Company, 501(c)(3) not-for-profit organization, corporation , partnership, business trust or investment adviser. An individual cannot be designated as a _____ without first establishing an entity falling under one of the previous categories.

a. Qualified institutional buyer
c. 4-4-5 Calendar
b. 529 plan
d. 7-Eleven

16. _____ is a regulation of the U.S. Securities and Exchange Commission It allows an issuer to sell securities without registering them with the SEC. Rule 501 contains definitions that apply to the rest of _____. Rule 502 contains the general conditions that must be met to take advantage of the exemptions under _____. Generally speaking, these conditions are that all sales within a certain time period that are part of the same Reg D offering must be 'integrated', information and disclosures must be provided, there must be no 'general solicitation', and that the securities being sold contain restrictions on their resale.

a. 529 plan
c. 7-Eleven
b. 4-4-5 Calendar
d. Regulation D

17. _____ are organizations which pool large sums of money and invest those sums in companies. They include banks, insurance companies, retirement or pension funds, hedge funds and mutual funds. Their role in the economy is to act as highly specialized investors on behalf of others.

a. A Random Walk Down Wall Street
c. ABN Amro
b. AAB
d. Institutional investors

Chapter 3. The Primary and Secondary Bond Markets

18. _____, adopted pursuant to the U.S. Securities Act of 1933, as amended (the 'Securities Act') provides a safe harbor from the registration requirements of the Securities Act of 1933 for certain private resales of restricted securities to QIBs (qualified institutional buyers), which generally are large institutional investors with over $100 million in investable assets. When a broker or dealer is selling securities in reliance on _____, it is subject to the condition that it may not make offers to persons other than those it reasonably believes to be QIBs.

Since its adoption, _____ has greatly increased the liquidity of the securities affected.

   a. Securities Investor Protection Corporation
   b. SIPC
   c. Prudent man rule
   d. Rule 144A

19. The _____ is the financial market where previously issued securities and financial instruments such as stock, bonds, options, and futures are bought and sold. The term '_____' is also used refer to the market for any used goods or assets, or an alternative use for an existing product or asset where the customer base is the second market

With primary issuances of securities or financial instruments, or the primary market, investors purchase these securities directly from issuers such as corporations issuing shares in an IPO or private placement, or directly from the federal government in the case of treasuries.

   a. Secondary market
   b. Delta neutral
   c. Performance attribution
   d. Financial market

20. An _____ is the term used in financial circles for a type of computer system that facilitates trading of financial products outside of stock exchanges. The primary products that are traded on an _____ are stocks and currencies. They came into existence in 1998 when the SEC authorized their creation.
   a. Intellidex
   b. Electronic communication network
   c. Insider trading
   d. Open outcry

21. The _____ is an American stock exchange. It is the largest electronic screen-based equity securities trading market in the United States. With approximately 3,200 companies, it has more trading volume per day than any other stock exchange in the world.
   a. 529 plan
   b. 7-Eleven
   c. 4-4-5 Calendar
   d. Nasdaq

22. The _____ is a stock exchange based in New York City, New York. It is the largest stock exchange in the world by dollar value of its listed companies securities. As of October 2008, the combined capitalization of all domestic _____ listed companies was $10.1 trillion.
   a. 7-Eleven
   b. 529 plan
   c. 4-4-5 Calendar
   d. New York Stock Exchange

23. A _____, securities exchange or (in Europe) bourse is a corporation or mutual organization which provides 'trading' facilities for stock brokers and traders, to trade stocks and other securities. _____s also provide facilities for the issue and redemption of securities as well as other financial instruments and capital events including the payment of income and dividends. The securities traded on a _____ include: shares issued by companies, unit trusts and other pooled investment products and bonds.

Chapter 3. The Primary and Secondary Bond Markets

a. 4-4-5 Calendar
b. 7-Eleven
c. 529 plan
d. Stock Exchange

24. _____ refers to any type of investment that yields a regular (or fixed) return.

For example, if you lend money to a borrower and the borrower has to pay interest once a month, you have been issued a fixed-income security. When a company does this, it is often called a bond or corporate bank debt (although preferred stock is also sometimes considered to be _____).

a. Bond market
b. 4-4-5 Calendar
c. Fixed income
d. 529 plan

25. The _____, makes rules regulating broker-dealers and banks that deal in municipal bonds, municipal notes, and other municipal securities in the United States. In addition, the _____ operates the Electronic Municipal Market Access system (http://emma.msrb.org), which provides free on-line access to comprehensive municipal securities disclosure documents and trade price information.

The _____ was established in 1975 by the U.S. Congress to develop rules regulating security firms and banks involved in underwriting, trading, and selling municipal securities -- bonds, notes and other securities issued by states, cities, and counties or their agencies to help finance public projects or for other public policy purposes.

a. Municipal Securities Rulemaking Board
b. World Trade Organization
c. Gamelan Council
d. Public Company Accounting Oversight Board

26. In the United States, the Financial Industry Regulatory Authority (FINRA) is a self-regulatory organization (SRO) under the Securities Exchange Act of 1934, successor to the _____, Inc.

FINRA is responsible for regulatory oversight of all securities firms that do business with the public; professional training, testing and licensing of registered persons; arbitration and mediation; market regulation by contract for The NASDAQ Stock Market, Inc., the American Stock Exchange LLC, and the International Securities Exchange, LLC; and industry utilities, such as Trade Reporting Facilities and other over-the-counter operations.

a. 529 plan
b. National Association of Securities Dealers
c. 4-4-5 Calendar
d. 7-Eleven

27. _____, refers to consumption opportunity gained by an entity within a specified time frame, which is generally expressed in monetary terms. However, for households and individuals, '_____ is the sum of all the wages, salaries, profits, interests payments, rents and other forms of earnings received... in a given period of time.' For firms, _____ generally refers to net-profit: what remains of revenue after expenses have been subtracted.

a. Annual report
b. OIBDA
c. Accrual
d. Income

28. _____ is a system of tracking ownership of securities where no certificate is given to investors. In the case of _____ only issues, while investors do not receive certificates, a custodian holds one or more global certificates. Dematerialized securities, in contrast are ones in which no certificates exist (instead, the security issuer or its agent keeps records, usually electronically, of who holds outstanding securities.)

Chapter 3. The Primary and Secondary Bond Markets

a. Tracking stock
b. Securities lending
c. Marketable
d. Book entry

29. _____ are dollar-denominated bonds, issued mostly by Latin American countries in the 1980s, named after U.S. Treasury Secretary Nicholas Brady.

_____ were created in March 1989 in order to convert bonds issued by mostly Latin American countries into a variety or 'menu' of new bonds after many of those countries defaulted on their debt in the 1980's. At that time, the market for sovereign debt was small and illiquid, and the standardization of emerging-market debt facilitated risk-spreading and trading.

a. Municipal bond
b. Nominal yield
c. Coupon rate
d. Brady bonds

30. A _____ is an international bond that is denominated in a currency not native to the country where it is issued. It can be categorised according to the currency in which it is issued. London is one of the centers of the _____ market, but _____s may be traded throughout the world - for example in Singapore or Tokyo.

a. Education production function
b. Eurobond
c. Economic entity
d. Interest rate option

31. _____s are deposits denominated in United States dollars at banks outside the United States, and thus are not under the jurisdiction of the Federal Reserve. Consequently, such deposits are subject to much less regulation than similar deposits within the United States, allowing for higher margins. There is nothing 'European' about _____ deposits; a US dollar-denominated deposit in Tokyo or Caracas would likewise be deemed _____ deposits.

a. AAB
b. A Random Walk Down Wall Street
c. ABN Amro
d. Eurodollar

32. A _____ is a legal pledge in United States municipal finance, in which an entity pledges its full faith and credit to repay its debt, typically a _____ bond.

a. Financial Institutions Reform Recovery and Enforcement Act
b. Letter of credit
c. Covenant
d. General obligation

33. In finance, a _____ (non-investment grade bond, speculative grade bond or junk bond) is a bond that is rated below investment grade at the time of purchase. These bonds have a higher risk of default or other adverse credit events, but typically pay higher yields than better quality bonds in order to make them attractive to investors.

a. Sharpe ratio
b. High yield bond
c. Private equity
d. Volatility

34. _____ is a nonprofit international trade association representing electronic and physical security product manufacturers, specifiers, and service providers. SIA provides education, research, technical standards and representation and defense of its members'e; interests. SIA is the sole sponsor of the International Security Conference and Exhibitions (ISC EXPOs.)

a. Linear regression
b. Vasicek model
c. The Security Industry Association
d. BootStrap Method

35. In finance, a _____ is a type of bond that can be converted into shares of stock in the issuing company, usually at some pre-announced ratio. It is a hybrid security with debt- and equity-like features. Although it typically has a low coupon rate, the holder is compensated with the ability to convert the bond to common stock, usually at a substantial discount to the stock's market value.
   a. Convertible bond
   b. Corporate bond
   c. Gilts
   d. Bond fund

36. In financial accounting, _____s are precautions for which the amount or probability of occurrence are not known. Typical examples are _____s for warranty costs and _____ for taxes the term reserve is used instead of term _____; such a use, however, is inconsistent with the terminology suggested by International Accounting Standards Board.
   a. Money measurement concept
   b. Petty cash
   c. Provision
   d. Momentum Accounting and Triple-Entry Bookkeeping

Chapter 4. Bond Market Indexes

1. In finance, a _____ is a debt security, in which the authorized issuer owes the holders a debt and, depending on the terms of the _____, is obliged to pay interest (the coupon) and/or to repay the principal at a later date, termed maturity.

Thus a _____ is a loan: the issuer is the borrower, the _____ holder is the lender, and the coupon is the interest. _____s provide the borrower with external funds to finance long-term investments, or, in the case of government _____s, to finance current expenditure.

   a. Bond
   b. Convertible bond
   c. Catastrophe bonds
   d. Puttable bond

2. The _____ is a financial market where participants buy and sell debt securities, usually in the form of bonds. As of 2006, the size of the international _____ is an estimated $45 trillion, of which the size of the outstanding U.S. _____ debt was $25.2 trillion.

Nearly all of the $923 billion average daily trading volume in the U.S. _____ takes place between broker-dealers and large institutions in a decentralized, over-the-counter market.

   a. Bond market
   b. Fixed income
   c. 4-4-5 Calendar
   d. 529 plan

3. A _____ is a listing of bonds or fixed income instruments and a statistic reflecting the composite value of its components. It is used as a tool to represent the characteristics of its component fixed income instruments. They differ from stock market indices in their complexity.

   a. 4-4-5 Calendar
   b. Bond market index
   c. 7-Eleven
   d. 529 plan

4. A _____ is a private or public market for the trading of company stock and derivatives of company stock at an agreed price; these are securities listed on a stock exchange as well as those only traded privately.

The size of the world _____ is estimated at about $36.6 trillion US at the beginning of October 2008. The world derivatives market has been estimated at about $480 trillion face or nominal value, 12 times the size of the entire world economy.

   a. Andrew Tobias
   b. Anton Gelonkin
   c. Adolph Coors
   d. Stock market

5. A _____ is a method of measuring a section of the stock market. Many indices are cited by news or financial services firms and are used to benchmark the performance of portfolios such as mutual funds.

   a. Stop order
   b. Program trading
   c. Trading curb
   d. Stock market index

6. _____ most frequently refers to the standard deviation of the continuously compounded returns of a financial instrument with a specific time horizon. It is often used to quantify the risk of the instrument over that time period. _____ is typically expressed in annualized terms, and it may either be an absolute number ($5) or a fraction of the mean (5%).

Chapter 4. Bond Market Indexes

a. Volatility
b. Portfolio insurance
c. Currency swap
d. Seasoned equity offering

7. The term _____ is used to describe a nation's social, or business activity in the process of rapid industrialization. _____ are generally less-wealthy than the developed world, and are wealthier (or the wealthiest of) the developing world. According to The Economist many people find the term dated, but a new term has yet to gain much traction.
   a. Emerging Markets
   b. A Random Walk Down Wall Street
   c. ABN Amro
   d. AAB

8. A _____ is a bond issued by a national government denominated in the country's own currency. Bonds issued by national governments in foreign currencies are normally referred to as sovereign bonds. The first ever _____ was issued by the British government in 1693 to raise money to fund a war against France.
   a. Collateralized debt obligations
   b. Municipal bond
   c. Zero-coupon bond
   d. Government bond

9. In finance, a _____ (non-investment grade bond, speculative grade bond or junk bond) is a bond that is rated below investment grade at the time of purchase. These bonds have a higher risk of default or other adverse credit events, but typically pay higher yields than better quality bonds in order to make them attractive to investors.
   a. Private equity
   b. Volatility
   c. Sharpe ratio
   d. High yield bond

10. In probability theory and statistics, _____ indicates the strength and direction of a linear relationship between two random variables. That is in contrast with the usage of the term in colloquial speech, which denotes any relationship, not necessarily linear. In general statistical usage, _____ or co-relation refers to the departure of two random variables from independence.
    a. Geometric mean
    b. Probability distribution
    c. Correlation
    d. Variance

11. The _____, in mathematics, is a type of mean or average, which indicates the central tendency or typical value of a set of numbers. It is similar to the arithmetic mean, which is what most people think of with the word 'average,' except that instead of adding the set of numbers and then dividing the sum by the count of numbers in the set, n, the numbers are multiplied and then the nth root of the resulting product is taken.

    For instance, the _____ of two numbers, say 2 and 8, is just the square root (i.e., the second root) of their product, 16, which is 4.

    a. Kurtosis
    b. Statistics
    c. Geometric mean
    d. Standard deviation

12. In statistics, _____ has two related meanings:

    - the arithmetic _____
    - the expected value of a random variable, which is also called the population _____.

Chapter 4. Bond Market Indexes

It is sometimes stated that the '_____' is average. This is incorrect if '_____' is taken in the specific sense of 'arithmetic _____' as there are different types of averages: the _____, median, and mode. Other simple statistical analyses use measures of spread, such as range, interquartile range, or standard deviation. For a real-valued random variable X, the _____ is the expectation of X. Note that not every probability distribution has a defined _____; see the Cauchy distribution for an example.

a. Sample size
b. Probability distribution
c. Harmonic mean
d. Mean

13. In probability and statistics, the _____ of a collection of numbers is a measure of the dispersion of the numbers from their expected (mean) value. It can apply to a probability distribution, a random variable, a population or a data set. The _____ is usually denoted with the letter σ (lowercase sigma.)

a. Mean
b. Standard deviation
c. Sample size
d. Kurtosis

14. _____ is a process of analyzing possible future events by considering alternative possible outcomes (scenarios.) The analysis is designed to allow improved decision-making by allowing consideration of outcomes and their implications.

For example, in economics and finance, a financial institution might attempt to forecast several possible scenarios for the economy (e.g. rapid growth, moderate growth, slow growth) and it might also attempt to forecast financial market returns (for bonds, stocks and cash) in each of those scenarios.

a. 529 plan
b. Detection Risk
c. 4-4-5 Calendar
d. Scenario analysis

Chapter 5. Bond Pricing, Yield Measures, and Total Return

1. In finance, a _____ is a debt security, in which the authorized issuer owes the holders a debt and, depending on the terms of the _____, is obliged to pay interest (the coupon) and/or to repay the principal at a later date, termed maturity.

Thus a _____ is a loan: the issuer is the borrower, the _____ holder is the lender, and the coupon is the interest. _____s provide the borrower with external funds to finance long-term investments, or, in the case of government _____s, to finance current expenditure.

   a. Convertible bond   b. Catastrophe bonds
   c. Puttable bond   d. Bond

2. _____ is the balance of the amounts of cash being received and paid by a business during a defined period of time, sometimes tied to a specific project. Measurement of _____ can be used

- to evaluate the state or performance of a business or project.
- to determine problems with liquidity. Being profitable does not necessarily mean being liquid. A company can fail because of a shortage of cash, even while profitable.
- to generate project rate of returns. The time of _____s into and out of projects are used as inputs to financial models such as internal rate of return, and net present value.
- to examine income or growth of a business when it is believed that accrual accounting concepts do not represent economic realities. Alternately, _____ can be used to 'validate' the net income generated by accrual accounting.

_____ as a generic term may be used differently depending on context, and certain _____ definitions may be adapted by analysts and users for their own uses. Common terms include operating _____ and free _____.

_____s can be classified into:

1. Operational _____s: Cash received or expended as a result of the company's core business activities.
2. Investment _____s: Cash received or expended through capital expenditure, investments or acquisitions.
3. Financing _____s: Cash received or expended as a result of financial activities, such as interests and dividends.

All three together - the net _____ - are necessary to reconcile the beginning cash balance to the ending cash balance. Loan draw downs or equity injections, that is just shifting of capital but no expenditure as such, are not considered in the net _____.

   a. Real option   b. Corporate finance
   c. Shareholder value   d. Cash flow

3. _____ is a fee paid on borrowed assets. It is the price paid for the use of borrowed money, or, money earned by deposited funds. Assets that are sometimes lent with _____ include money, shares, consumer goods through hire purchase, major assets such as aircraft, and even entire factories in finance lease arrangements.

Chapter 5. Bond Pricing, Yield Measures, and Total Return

a. A Random Walk Down Wall Street
c. AAB
b. Interest
d. Insolvency

4. An _____ is the price a borrower pays for the use of money they do not own, and the return a lender receives for deferring the use of funds, by lending it to the borrower. _____s are normally expressed as a percentage rate over the period of one year.

_____s targets are also a vital tool of monetary policy and are used to control variables like investment, inflation, and unemployment.

a. Interest rate
c. A Random Walk Down Wall Street
b. ABN Amro
d. AAB

5. In finance, the term _____ describes the amount in cash that returns to the owners of a security. Normally it does not include the price variations, at the difference of the total return. _____ applies to various stated rates of return on stocks (common and preferred, and convertible), fixed income instruments (bonds, notes, bills, strips, zero coupon), and some other investment type insurance products (e.g. annuities.)

a. 4-4-5 Calendar
c. Macaulay duration
b. Yield to maturity
d. Yield

6. _____ is a life of security. It may also refer to the final payment date of a loan or other financial instrument, at which point all remaining interest and principal is due to be paid.

1, 3, 6 months _____ band can be calculated by using 30-day per month periods.

a. Replacement cost
c. Primary market
b. Maturity
d. False billing

7. The coupon or _____ of a bond is the amount of interest paid per year expressed as a percentage of the face value of the bond.

For example if you hold $10,000 nominal of a bond described as a 4.5% loan stock, you will receive $450 in interest each year (probably in two installments of $225 each.)

Not all bonds have coupons.

a. Puttable bond
c. Coupon rate
b. Revenue bonds
d. Zero-coupon bond

8. A _____ is a bond bought at a price lower than its face value, with the face value repaid at the time of maturity. It does not make periodic interest payments, or have so-called 'coupons,' hence the term _____. Investors earn return from the compounded interest all paid at maturity plus the difference between the discounted price of the bond and its par value.

a. Zero-coupon bond
c. Corporate bond
b. Clean price
d. Bond fund

9. _____ is the concept of adding accumulated interest back to the principal, so that interest is earned on interest from that moment on. The act of declaring interest to be principal is called compounding (i.e., interest is compounded.) A loan, for example, may have its interest compounded every month: in this case, a loan with $100 principal and 1% interest per month would have a balance of $101 at the end of the first month.

   a. 4-4-5 Calendar   b. Risk management

   c. Penny stock   d. Compound interest

10. In finance, _____ is the interest that has accumulated since the principal investment, or since the previous interest payment if there has been one already. For a financial instrument such as a bond, interest is calculated and paid in set intervals.

The primary formula for calculating the interest accrued in a given period is:

$$I_A = T \times P \times R$$

where I_A is the _____, T is the fraction of the year, P is the principal, and R is the annualized interest rate.

   a. A Random Walk Down Wall Street   b. AAB

   c. ABN Amro   d. Accrued interest

11. The _____ of a bond represents the value of a bond, exclusive of any commissions or fees. The _____ is also called the 'full price.'

Bonds, as well as a variety of other fixed income securities, provide for coupon payments to be made to bond holders on a fixed schedule. The _____ of a bond will decrease on the days coupons are paid, resulting in a saw-tooth pattern for the bond value.

   a. Collateralized debt obligations   b. Premium bond

   c. Dirty price   d. Serial bond

12. _____ refers to any type of investment that yields a regular (or fixed) return.

For example, if you lend money to a borrower and the borrower has to pay interest once a month, you have been issued a fixed-income security. When a company does this, it is often called a bond or corporate bank debt (although preferred stock is also sometimes considered to be _____).

   a. Fixed income   b. Bond market

   c. 529 plan   d. 4-4-5 Calendar

13. _____, refers to consumption opportunity gained by an entity within a specified time frame, which is generally expressed in monetary terms. However, for households and individuals, '_____ is the sum of all the wages, salaries, profits, interests payments, rents and other forms of earnings received... in a given period of time.' For firms, _____ generally refers to net-profit: what remains of revenue after expenses have been subtracted.

a. Annual report
b. Income
c. OIBDA
d. Accrual

14. _____ refers to the use of formal econometric techniques to determine the aggregate risk in a financial portfolio. _____ is one of many subtasks within the broader area of financial modeling.

_____ uses a variety of techniques including market risk, Value-at-Risk (VaR), Historical Simulation (HS), or Extreme Value Theory (EVT) in order to analyze a portfolio and make forecasts of the likely losses that would be incurred for a variety of risks.

a. Value at risk
b. Risk adjusted return on capital
c. Risk premium
d. Risk modeling

15. In finance, _____ is the process of estimating the potential market value of a financial asset or liability. they can be done on assets (for example, investments in marketable securities such as stocks, options, business enterprises, or intangible assets such as patents and trademarks) or on liabilities (e.g., Bonds issued by a company.) _____s are required in many contexts including investment analysis, capital budgeting, merger and acquisition transactions, financial reporting, taxable events to determine the proper tax liability, and in litigation.

a. Margin
b. Share
c. Procter ' Gamble
d. Valuation

16. In finance, the _____ is the price of a bond excluding any interest that has accrued since issue or the most recent coupon payment. This is to be compared with the dirty price, which is the price of a bond including the accrued interest.

When bond prices are quoted on a Bloomberg Terminal or Reuters they are quoted using the _____.

a. Bowie bonds
b. Bond valuation
c. Gilts
d. Clean price

17. _____ are dollar-denominated bonds, issued mostly by Latin American countries in the 1980s, named after U.S. Treasury Secretary Nicholas Brady.

_____ were created in March 1989 in order to convert bonds issued by mostly Latin American countries into a variety or 'menu' of new bonds after many of those countries defaulted on their debt in the 1980's. At that time, the market for sovereign debt was small and illiquid, and the standardization of emerging-market debt facilitated risk-spreading and trading.

a. Coupon rate
b. Municipal bond
c. Brady bonds
d. Nominal yield

18. The _____, interest yield, income yield, flat yield or running yield is a financial term used in reference to bonds and other fixed-interest securities such as gilts. It is the ratio of the annual interest payment and the bond's current price.

The _____ only therefore refers to the yield of the bond at the current moment. It does not reflect the total return over the life of the bond. In particular, it takes no account of reinvestment risk (the uncertainty about the rate at which future cashflows can be reinvested) or the fact that bonds usually mature at par value, which can be an important component of a bond's return.

    a. Stochastic volatility
    c. Modified Internal Rate of Return
    b. Perpetuity
    d. Current yield

19. A _____ is an international bond that is denominated in a currency not native to the country where it is issued. It can be categorised according to the currency in which it is issued. London is one of the centers of the _____ market, but _____s may be traded throughout the world - for example in Singapore or Tokyo.
    a. Economic entity
    c. Education production function
    b. Interest rate option
    d. Eurobond

20. _____s are deposits denominated in United States dollars at banks outside the United States, and thus are not under the jurisdiction of the Federal Reserve. Consequently, such deposits are subject to much less regulation than similar deposits within the United States, allowing for higher margins. There is nothing 'European' about _____ deposits; a US dollar-denominated deposit in Tokyo or Caracas would likewise be deemed _____ deposits.
    a. A Random Walk Down Wall Street
    c. AAB
    b. ABN Amro
    d. Eurodollar

21. A _____ is a legal pledge in United States municipal finance, in which an entity pledges its full faith and credit to repay its debt, typically a _____ bond.
    a. Covenant
    b. Financial Institutions Reform Recovery and Enforcement Act
    c. Letter of credit
    d. General obligation

22. In finance, a _____ (non-investment grade bond, speculative grade bond or junk bond) is a bond that is rated below investment grade at the time of purchase. These bonds have a higher risk of default or other adverse credit events, but typically pay higher yields than better quality bonds in order to make them attractive to investors.
    a. Volatility
    c. Sharpe ratio
    b. High yield bond
    d. Private equity

23. In financial accounting, _____s are precautions for which the amount or probability of occurrence are not known. Typical examples are _____s for warranty costs and _____ for taxes the term reserve is used instead of term _____; such a use, however, is inconsistent with the terminology suggested by International Accounting Standards Board.
    a. Momentum Accounting and Triple-Entry Bookkeeping
    b. Petty cash
    c. Money measurement concept
    d. Provision

24. The _____ or redemption yield is the yield promised to the bondholder on the assumption that the bond or other fixed-interest security such as gilts will be held to maturity, that all coupon and principal payments will be made and coupon payments are reinvested at the bond's promised yield at the same rate as invested. It is a measure of the return of the bond. This technique in theory allows investors to calculate the fair value of different financial instruments.

Chapter 5. Bond Pricing, Yield Measures, and Total Return

a. Yield
c. 4-4-5 Calendar
b. Yield to maturity
d. Macaulay duration

25. _____ is one of the main genres of financial risk. The term describes the risk that a particular investment might be canceled or stopped somehow, that one may have to find a new place to invest that money with the risk being there might not be a similarly attractive investment available. This primarily occurs if bonds (which are portions of loans to entities) are paid back earlier then expected.
   a. Debt cash flow
   c. Standard of deferred payment
   b. Reinvestment risk
   d. Biweekly Mortgage

26. The _____ is a capital budgeting metric used by firms to decide whether they should make investments. It is an indicator of the efficiency or quality of an investment, as opposed to net present value (NPV), which indicates value or magnitude.

The IRR is the annualized effective compounded return rate which can be earned on the invested capital, i.e., the yield on the investment.

   a. ABN Amro
   c. A Random Walk Down Wall Street
   b. AAB
   d. Internal rate of return

27. In finance, a _____ is collateral that the holder of a position in securities, options, or futures contracts has to deposit to cover the credit risk of his counterparty (most often his broker.) This risk can arise if the holder has done any of the following:

   - borrowed cash from the counterparty to buy securities or options,
   - sold securities or options short, or
   - entered into a futures contract.

The collateral can be in the form of cash or securities, and it is deposited in a _____ account. On U.S. futures exchanges, '_____' was formally called performance bond.

_____ buying is buying securities with cash borrowed from a broker, using other securities as collateral.

   a. Credit
   c. Procter ' Gamble
   b. Share
   d. Margin

28. In finance, _____, also known as return on investment is the ratio of money gained or lost on an investment relative to the amount of money invested. The amount of money gained or lost may be referred to as interest, profit/loss, gain/loss, or net income/loss. The money invested may be referred to as the asset, capital, principal, or the cost basis of the investment.
   a. Composiition of Creditors
   c. Stock or scrip dividends
   b. Doctrine of the Proper Law
   d. Rate of return

29. A _____ is a fungible, negotiable instrument representing financial value. They are broadly categorized into debt securities (such as banknotes, bonds and debentures), and equity securities; e.g., common stocks. The company or other entity issuing the _____ is called the issuer.

a. Tracking stock
b. Book entry
c. Securities lending
d. Security

30. The _____ on a portfolio of investments takes into account not only the capital appreciation on the portfolio, but also the income received on the portfolio. The income typically consists of interest, dividends, and securities lending fees. This contrasts with the price return, which takes into account only the capital gain on an investment.
    a. Capitalization rate
    b. Global tactical asset allocation
    c. Total return
    d. Profitability index

31. In economics and finance, _____ is the practice of taking advantage of a price differential between two or more markets: striking a combination of matching deals that capitalize upon the imbalance, the profit being the difference between the market prices. When used by academics, an _____ is a transaction that involves no negative cash flow at any probabilistic or temporal state and a positive cash flow in at least one state; in simple terms, a risk-free profit.
    a. Issuer
    b. Initial margin
    c. Efficient-market hypothesis
    d. Arbitrage

32. _____ is a process of analyzing possible future events by considering alternative possible outcomes (scenarios.) The analysis is designed to allow improved decision-making by allowing consideration of outcomes and their implications.

For example, in economics and finance, a financial institution might attempt to forecast several possible scenarios for the economy (e.g. rapid growth, moderate growth, slow growth) and it might also attempt to forecast financial market returns (for bonds, stocks and cash) in each of those scenarios.

    a. Detection Risk
    b. 4-4-5 Calendar
    c. 529 plan
    d. Scenario analysis

33. An _____ is an exchange of tangible assets for intangible assets or vice versa. Since it is a swap of assets, the procedure takes place on the active side of the balance sheet and has no impact on the latter in regards to volume. As an example, a company may sell equity and receive the value in cash thus increasing liquidity.
    a. AAB
    b. A Random Walk Down Wall Street
    c. ABN Amro
    d. Asset swap

34. A _____ is an option granting its owner the right but not the obligation to enter into an underlying swap. Although options can be traded on a variety of swaps, the term '_____' typically refers to options on interest rate swaps.

There are two types of _____ contracts:

- A payer _____ gives the owner of the _____ the right to enter into a swap where they pay the fixed leg and receive the floating leg.
- A receiver _____ gives the owner of the _____ the right to enter into a swap where they will receive the fixed leg, and pay the floating leg.

The buyer and seller of the _____ agree on:

- the premium (price) of the _____
- the strike rate (equal to the fixed rate of the underlying swap)
- length of the option period (which usually ends two business days prior to the start date of the underlying swap),
- the term of the underlying swap,
- notional amount,
- amortization, if any
- frequency of settlement of payments on the underlying swap

The participants in the _____ market are predominantly large corporations, banks, financial institutions and hedge funds. End users such as corporations and banks typically use _____s to manage interest rate risk arising from their core business or from their financing arrangements.

a. Put option
b. Swaption
c. Straddle
d. Bear call spread

35. In finance, a _____ is a derivative in which two counterparties agree to exchange one stream of cash flows against another stream. These streams are called the legs of the _____.

The cash flows are calculated over a notional principal amount, which is usually not exchanged between counterparties.

a. Volatility swap
b. Volatility arbitrage
c. Local volatility
d. Swap

36. In the United States, a _____ is a bond issued by a city or other local government, or their agencies. Potential issuers of these bonds include cities, counties, redevelopment agencies, school districts, publicly owned airports and seaports, and any other governmental entity (or group of governments) below the state level. They may be general obligations of the issuer or secured by specified revenues.

a. Premium bond
b. Municipal bond
c. Puttable bond
d. Senior debt

37. In business and accounting, _____s are everything of value that is owned by a person or company. The balance sheet of a firm records the monetary value of the _____s owned by the firm. The two major _____ classes are tangible _____s and intangible _____s.

a. Income
b. Asset
c. Accounts payable
d. EBITDA

38. A _____ is a bond issued by a corporation. The term is usually applied to longer-term debt instruments, generally with a maturity date falling at least a year after their issue date. (The term 'commercial paper' is sometimes used for instruments with a shorter maturity.)

a. Government bond   b. Corporate bond
c. Brady bonds   d. Serial bond

Chapter 6. Calculating Investment Returns

1. In finance, _____, also known as return on investment is the ratio of money gained or lost on an investment relative to the amount of money invested. The amount of money gained or lost may be referred to as interest, profit/loss, gain/loss, or net income/loss. The money invested may be referred to as the asset, capital, principal, or the cost basis of the investment.
   a. Doctrine of the Proper Law
   b. Rate of return
   c. Composiition of Creditors
   d. Stock or scrip dividends

2. Realization is generally understood in financial circles as the point at which revenue is recognized, typically through a transaction which involves the exchange of an asset, product, or service for cash or its equivalents.

   This approach gives the accounting division a strictly objective basis for changing the books. For example, a homeowner may believe that his house has grown in value during a strong market, or fallen in value during a weak market, but until the house is actually sold for a specific price to a specific buyer, the change in value can only be estimated and is considered _____.

   a. Unrealized
   b. AAB
   c. A Random Walk Down Wall Street
   d. ABN Amro

3. _____ are dollar-denominated bonds, issued mostly by Latin American countries in the 1980s, named after U.S. Treasury Secretary Nicholas Brady.

   _____ were created in March 1989 in order to convert bonds issued by mostly Latin American countries into a variety or 'menu' of new bonds after many of those countries defaulted on their debt in the 1980's. At that time, the market for sovereign debt was small and illiquid, and the standardization of emerging-market debt facilitated risk-spreading and trading.

   a. Nominal yield
   b. Brady bonds
   c. Coupon rate
   d. Municipal bond

4. A _____ is an international bond that is denominated in a currency not native to the country where it is issued. It can be categorised according to the currency in which it is issued. London is one of the centers of the _____ market, but _____s may be traded throughout the world - for example in Singapore or Tokyo.
   a. Interest rate option
   b. Education production function
   c. Economic entity
   d. Eurobond

5. _____s are deposits denominated in United States dollars at banks outside the United States, and thus are not under the jurisdiction of the Federal Reserve. Consequently, such deposits are subject to much less regulation than similar deposits within the United States, allowing for higher margins. There is nothing 'European' about _____ deposits; a US dollar-denominated deposit in Tokyo or Caracas would likewise be deemed _____ deposits.
   a. A Random Walk Down Wall Street
   b. AAB
   c. Eurodollar
   d. ABN Amro

6. A _____ is a legal pledge in United States municipal finance, in which an entity pledges its full faith and credit to repay its debt, typically a _____ bond.
   a. Financial Institutions Reform Recovery and Enforcement Act
   b. Letter of credit
   c. Covenant
   d. General obligation

Chapter 6. Calculating Investment Returns

7. In finance, a _____ (non-investment grade bond, speculative grade bond or junk bond) is a bond that is rated below investment grade at the time of purchase. These bonds have a higher risk of default or other adverse credit events, but typically pay higher yields than better quality bonds in order to make them attractive to investors.

   a. Volatility
   b. Private equity
   c. Sharpe ratio
   d. High yield bond

8. _____ is the price at which an asset would trade in a competitive Walrasian auction setting. _____ is often used interchangeably with open _____, fair value or fair _____, although these terms have distinct definitions in different standards, and may differ in some circumstances.

   International Valuation Standards defines _____ as 'the estimated amount for which a property should exchange on the date of valuation between a willing buyer and a willing seller in an arm'e;s-length transaction after proper marketing wherein the parties had each acted knowledgeably, prudently, and without compulsion.'

   _____ is a concept distinct from market price, which is 'e;the price at which one can transact'e;, while _____ is 'e;the true underlying value'e; according to theoretical standards.

   a. Debt restructuring
   b. Wrap account
   c. T-Model
   d. Market value

9. The _____ on a portfolio of investments takes into account not only the capital appreciation on the portfolio, but also the income received on the portfolio. The income typically consists of interest, dividends, and securities lending fees. This contrasts with the price return, which takes into account only the capital gain on an investment.

   a. Global tactical asset allocation
   b. Capitalization rate
   c. Profitability index
   d. Total return

10. In finance, a _____ is a debt security, in which the authorized issuer owes the holders a debt and, depending on the terms of the _____, is obliged to pay interest (the coupon) and/or to repay the principal at a later date, termed maturity.

    Thus a _____ is a loan: the issuer is the borrower, the _____ holder is the lender, and the coupon is the interest. _____s provide the borrower with external funds to finance long-term investments, or, in the case of government _____s, to finance current expenditure.

    a. Puttable bond
    b. Catastrophe bonds
    c. Convertible bond
    d. Bond

11. _____, refers to consumption opportunity gained by an entity within a specified time frame, which is generally expressed in monetary terms. However, for households and individuals, '_____ is the sum of all the wages, salaries, profits, interests payments, rents and other forms of earnings received... in a given period of time.' For firms, _____ generally refers to net-profit: what remains of revenue after expenses have been subtracted.

    a. Accrual
    b. OIBDA
    c. Annual report
    d. Income

Chapter 6. Calculating Investment Returns

12. In financial accounting, _____s are precautions for which the amount or probability of occurrence are not known. Typical examples are _____s for warranty costs and _____ for taxes the term reserve is used instead of term _____; such a use, however, is inconsistent with the terminology suggested by International Accounting Standards Board.

    a. Petty cash
    b. Momentum Accounting and Triple-Entry Bookkeeping
    c. Money measurement concept
    d. Provision

13. _____ is a term used in accounting relating to the increase in value of an asset. In this sense it is the reverse of depreciation, which measures the fall in value of assets over their normal life-time.

    _____ is a rise of a currency in a floating exchange rate.

    a. Other Comprehensive Basis of Accounting
    b. Operating cash flow
    c. A Random Walk Down Wall Street
    d. Appreciation

14. _____ is the balance of the amounts of cash being received and paid by a business during a defined period of time, sometimes tied to a specific project. Measurement of _____ can be used

    - to evaluate the state or performance of a business or project.
    - to determine problems with liquidity. Being profitable does not necessarily mean being liquid. A company can fail because of a shortage of cash, even while profitable.
    - to generate project rate of returns. The time of _____s into and out of projects are used as inputs to financial models such as internal rate of return, and net present value.
    - to examine income or growth of a business when it is believed that accrual accounting concepts do not represent economic realities. Alternately, _____ can be used to 'validate' the net income generated by accrual accounting.

    _____ as a generic term may be used differently depending on context, and certain _____ definitions may be adapted by analysts and users for their own uses. Common terms include operating _____ and free _____.

    _____s can be classified into:

    1. Operational _____s: Cash received or expended as a result of the company's core business activities.
    2. Investment _____s: Cash received or expended through capital expenditure, investments or acquisitions.
    3. Financing _____s: Cash received or expended as a result of financial activities, such as interests and dividends.

    All three together - the net _____ - are necessary to reconcile the beginning cash balance to the ending cash balance. Loan draw downs or equity injections, that is just shifting of capital but no expenditure as such, are not considered in the net _____.

a. Real option
b. Shareholder value
c. Corporate finance
d. Cash flow

15. A _____ is a professionally managed type of collective investment scheme that pools money from many investors and invests it in stocks, bonds, short-term money market instruments, and/or other securities. The _____ will have a fund manager that trades the pooled money on a regular basis. Currently, the worldwide value of all _____s totals more than $26 trillion.

Since 1940, there have been three basic types of investment companies in the United States: open-end funds, also known in the US as _____s; unit investment trusts (UITs); and closed-end funds.

a. Net asset value
b. Financial intermediary
c. Trust company
d. Mutual fund

16. _____ is the concept of adding accumulated interest back to the principal, so that interest is earned on interest from that moment on. The act of declaring interest to be principal is called compounding (i.e., interest is compounded.) A loan, for example, may have its interest compounded every month: in this case, a loan with $100 principal and 1% interest per month would have a balance of $101 at the end of the first month.

a. Risk management
b. 4-4-5 Calendar
c. Penny stock
d. Compound interest

17. _____ measures the nominal future sum of money that a given sum of money is 'worth' at a specified time in the future assuming a certain interest rate rate of return; it is the present value multiplied by the accumulation function.

The value does not include corrections for inflation or other factors that affect the true value of money in the future. This is used in time value of money calculations.

a. Future-oriented
b. Future value
c. Discounted cash flow
d. Present value of costs

18. In finance, the value of an option consists of two components, its intrinsic value and its _____. Time value is simply the difference between option value and intrinsic value. _____ is also known as theta, extrinsic value, or instrumental value.

a. Debt buyer
b. Global Squeeze
c. Conservatism
d. Time value

19. _____ is the strategy of making buy or sell decisions of financial assets (often stocks) by attempting to predict future market price movements. The prediction may be based on an outlook of market or economic conditions resulting from technical or fundamental analysis. This is an investment strategy based on the outlook for an aggregate market, rather than for a particular financial asset.

a. Late trading
b. Portable alpha
c. Divestment
d. Market timing

20. _____ has many definitions and is not easily analysed. In general, it represents the capital investment necessary for a business to function. Consequently, it is not a measure of assets, but of capital investment: stock or shares and long-term liabilities.

Chapter 6. Calculating Investment Returns

a. PEG ratio
b. Capital employed
c. Times interest earned
d. Return on assets

21. The _____ is a capital budgeting metric used by firms to decide whether they should make investments. It is an indicator of the efficiency or quality of an investment, as opposed to net present value (NPV), which indicates value or magnitude.

The IRR is the annualized effective compounded return rate which can be earned on the invested capital, i.e., the yield on the investment.

a. AAB
b. ABN Amro
c. A Random Walk Down Wall Street
d. Internal rate of return

22. The _____, in mathematics, is a type of mean or average, which indicates the central tendency or typical value of a set of numbers. It is similar to the arithmetic mean, which is what most people think of with the word 'average,' except that instead of adding the set of numbers and then dividing the sum by the count of numbers in the set, n, the numbers are multiplied and then the nth root of the resulting product is taken.

For instance, the _____ of two numbers, say 2 and 8, is just the square root (i.e., the second root) of their product, 16, which is 4.

a. Geometric mean
b. Standard deviation
c. Kurtosis
d. Statistics

23. In statistics, _____ has two related meanings:

- the arithmetic _____
- the expected value of a random variable, which is also called the population _____.

It is sometimes stated that the '_____' is average. This is incorrect if '_____' is taken in the specific sense of 'arithmetic _____' as there are different types of averages: the _____, median, and mode. Other simple statistical analyses use measures of spread, such as range, interquartile range, or standard deviation. For a real-valued random variable X, the _____ is the expectation of X. Note that not every probability distribution has a defined _____; see the Cauchy distribution for an example.

a. Probability distribution
b. Mean
c. Harmonic mean
d. Sample size

Chapter 7. The Structure of Interest Rates

1. In economics and finance, _____ is the practice of taking advantage of a price differential between two or more markets: striking a combination of matching deals that capitalize upon the imbalance, the profit being the difference between the market prices. When used by academics, an _____ is a transaction that involves no negative cash flow at any probabilistic or temporal state and a positive cash flow in at least one state; in simple terms, a risk-free profit.
   a. Efficient-market hypothesis
   b. Initial margin
   c. Arbitrage
   d. Issuer

2. In finance, a _____ is a debt security, in which the authorized issuer owes the holders a debt and, depending on the terms of the _____, is obliged to pay interest (the coupon) and/or to repay the principal at a later date, termed maturity.

   Thus a _____ is a loan: the issuer is the borrower, the _____ holder is the lender, and the coupon is the interest. _____s provide the borrower with external funds to finance long-term investments, or, in the case of government _____s, to finance current expenditure.

   a. Convertible bond
   b. Puttable bond
   c. Catastrophe bonds
   d. Bond

3. _____ is the investment strategy where an investor buys a financial instrument denominated in a foreign currency, and hedges his foreign exchange risk by selling a forward contract in the amount of the proceeds of the investment back into his base currency. The proceeds of the investment are only known exactly if the financial instrument is risk-free and only pays interest once, on the date of the forward sale of foreign currency. Otherwise, some foreign exchange risk remains.
   a. Currency future
   b. Covered interest arbitrage
   c. Floating exchange rate
   d. Triangular arbitrage

4. _____ is a fee paid on borrowed assets. It is the price paid for the use of borrowed money, or, money earned by deposited funds. Assets that are sometimes lent with _____ include money, shares, consumer goods through hire purchase, major assets such as aircraft, and even entire factories in finance lease arrangements.
   a. Insolvency
   b. Interest
   c. AAB
   d. A Random Walk Down Wall Street

5. An _____ is the price a borrower pays for the use of money they do not own, and the return a lender receives for deferring the use of funds, by lending it to the borrower. _____s are normally expressed as a percentage rate over the period of one year.

   _____s targets are also a vital tool of monetary policy and are used to control variables like investment, inflation, and unemployment.

   a. ABN Amro
   b. AAB
   c. A Random Walk Down Wall Street
   d. Interest rate

6. _____ is the provision of resources (such as granting a loan) by one party to another party where that second party does not reimburse the first party immediately, thereby generating a debt, and instead arranges either to repay or return those resources (or material(s) of equal value) at a later date. The first party is called a creditor, also known as a lender, while the second party is called a debtor, also known as a borrower.

   Movements of financial capital are normally dependent on either _____ or equity transfers.

Chapter 7. The Structure of Interest Rates

a. Warrant
b. Credit
c. Comparable
d. Clearing house

7. _____ is the risk of loss due to a debtor's non-payment of a loan or other line of credit (either the principal or interest (coupon) or both)

Most lenders employ their own models (credit scorecards) to rank potential and existing customers according to risk, and then apply appropriate strategies. With products such as unsecured personal loans or mortgages, lenders charge a higher price for higher risk customers and vice versa. With revolving products such as credit cards and overdrafts, risk is controlled through careful setting of credit limits.

a. Liquidity risk
b. Market risk
c. Transaction risk
d. Credit risk

8. In finance, _____ occurs when a debtor has not met its legal obligations according to the debt contract, e.g. it has not made a scheduled payment, or has violated a loan covenant (condition) of the debt contract. _____ may occur if the debtor is either unwilling or unable to pay their debt. This can occur with all debt obligations including bonds, mortgages, loans, and promissory notes.

a. Default
b. Vendor finance
c. Credit crunch
d. Debt validation

9. _____ refers to the use of formal econometric techniques to determine the aggregate risk in a financial portfolio. _____ is one of many subtasks within the broader area of financial modeling.

_____ uses a variety of techniques including market risk, Value-at-Risk (VaR), Historical Simulation (HS), or Extreme Value Theory (EVT) in order to analyze a portfolio and make forecasts of the likely losses that would be incurred for a variety of risks.

a. Risk premium
b. Risk adjusted return on capital
c. Value at risk
d. Risk modeling

10. _____ is a legal entity that develops, registers and sells securities for the purpose of financing its operations. _____s may be domestic or foreign governments, corporations or investment trusts. _____s are legally responsible for the obligations of the issue and for reporting financial conditions, material developments and any other operational activities as required by the regulations of their jurisdictions.

a. Issuer
b. Efficient-market hypothesis
c. Arbitrage
d. Initial margin

11. _____ are dollar-denominated bonds, issued mostly by Latin American countries in the 1980s, named after U.S. Treasury Secretary Nicholas Brady.

_____ were created in March 1989 in order to convert bonds issued by mostly Latin American countries into a variety or 'menu' of new bonds after many of those countries defaulted on their debt in the 1980's. At that time, the market for sovereign debt was small and illiquid, and the standardization of emerging-market debt facilitated risk-spreading and trading.

a. Coupon rate
b. Nominal yield
c. Municipal bond
d. Brady bonds

12. A _____ is an international bond that is denominated in a currency not native to the country where it is issued. It can be categorised according to the currency in which it is issued. London is one of the centers of the _____ market, but _____s may be traded throughout the world - for example in Singapore or Tokyo.
   a. Eurobond
   b. Interest rate option
   c. Economic entity
   d. Education production function

13. _____s are deposits denominated in United States dollars at banks outside the United States, and thus are not under the jurisdiction of the Federal Reserve. Consequently, such deposits are subject to much less regulation than similar deposits within the United States, allowing for higher margins. There is nothing 'European' about _____ deposits; a US dollar-denominated deposit in Tokyo or Caracas would likewise be deemed _____ deposits.
   a. Eurodollar
   b. ABN Amro
   c. A Random Walk Down Wall Street
   d. AAB

14. A _____ is a legal pledge in United States municipal finance, in which an entity pledges its full faith and credit to repay its debt, typically a _____ bond.
   a. Financial Institutions Reform Recovery and Enforcement Act
   b. Covenant
   c. Letter of credit
   d. General obligation

15. In finance, a _____ (non-investment grade bond, speculative grade bond or junk bond) is a bond that is rated below investment grade at the time of purchase. These bonds have a higher risk of default or other adverse credit events, but typically pay higher yields than better quality bonds in order to make them attractive to investors.
   a. High yield bond
   b. Sharpe ratio
   c. Volatility
   d. Private equity

16. _____ is a life of security. It may also refer to the final payment date of a loan or other financial instrument, at which point all remaining interest and principal is due to be paid.

1, 3, 6 months _____ band can be calculated by using 30-day per month periods.

   a. False billing
   b. Replacement cost
   c. Primary market
   d. Maturity

17. _____ on a simple mortgage-backed security (MBS) is the flat spread over the treasury yield curve required in discounting a pre-determined coupon schedule to arrive at its present market price.

That is, the MBS _____ is based on a comparison of the market price to a model of the bond which includes no variability in interest rate or mortgage repayment rates.

For mortgage-backed securities, a model of typical repayment rates tends to be given; the PSA formula for a particular Fannie Mae MBS might equate a particular group of mortgages to an 8 year amortizing bond with a 5% mortality per annum.

Chapter 7. The Structure of Interest Rates

a. Credit enhancement
b. Yield curve spread
c. Tranche
d. 4-4-5 Calendar

18. _____, refers to consumption opportunity gained by an entity within a specified time frame, which is generally expressed in monetary terms. However, for households and individuals, '_____ is the sum of all the wages, salaries, profits, interests payments, rents and other forms of earnings received... in a given period of time.' For firms, _____ generally refers to net-profit: what remains of revenue after expenses have been subtracted.
    a. OIBDA
    b. Annual report
    c. Accrual
    d. Income

19. An _____ is a contract written by a seller that conveys to the buyer the right -- but not the obligation -- to buy (in the case of a call _____) or to sell (in the case of a put _____) a particular asset, such as a piece of property such as, among others, a futures contract. In return for granting the _____, the seller collects a payment (the premium) from the buyer.

For example, buying a call _____ provides the right to buy a specified quantity of a security at a set strike price at some time on or before expiration, while buying a put _____ provides the right to sell.

   a. Amortization
   b. AT'T Mobility LLC
   c. Annuity
   d. Option

20. In financial accounting, _____s are precautions for which the amount or probability of occurrence are not known. Typical examples are _____s for warranty costs and _____ for taxes the term reserve is used instead of term _____; such a use, however, is inconsistent with the terminology suggested by International Accounting Standards Board.
    a. Petty cash
    b. Momentum Accounting and Triple-Entry Bookkeeping
    c. Money measurement concept
    d. Provision

21. In the United States, a _____ is a bond issued by a city or other local government, or their agencies. Potential issuers of these bonds include cities, counties, redevelopment agencies, school districts, publicly owned airports and seaports, and any other governmental entity (or group of governments) below the state level. They may be general obligations of the issuer or secured by specified revenues.
    a. Puttable bond
    b. Premium bond
    c. Senior debt
    d. Municipal bond

22. _____ are government bonds issued by the United States Department of the Treasury through the Bureau of the Public Debt. They are the debt financing instruments of the U.S. Federal government, and they are often referred to simply as Treasuries or Treasurys. There are four types of marketable _____: Treasury bills, Treasury notes, Treasury bonds, and Treasury Inflation Protected Securities (TIPS.)
    a. Treasury Inflation Protected Securities
    b. 4-4-5 Calendar
    c. Treasury Inflation-Protected Securities
    d. Treasury securities

23. A _____ or market-based mechanism is any of a wide variety of ways to match up buyers and sellers.

An example of a _____ uses announced bid and ask prices. Generally speaking, when two parties wish to engage in a trade, the purchaser will announce a price he is willing to pay (the bid price) and seller will announce a price he is willing to accept (the ask price).

a. 7-Eleven
c. 529 plan
b. 4-4-5 Calendar
d. Price mechanism

24. The _____ for securities is the difference between the price quoted by a market maker for an immediate sale and an immediate purchase The size of the bid-offer spread in a given commodity is a measure of the liquidity of the market.

The trader initiating the transaction is said to demand liquidity, and the other party to the transaction supplies liquidity.

a. Defined contribution plan
c. Capital outflow
b. Trade-off
d. Bid/offer spread

25. A _____ is a fungible, negotiable instrument representing financial value. They are broadly categorized into debt securities (such as banknotes, bonds and debentures), and equity securities; e.g., common stocks. The company or other entity issuing the _____ is called the issuer.

a. Tracking stock
c. Security
b. Book entry
d. Securities lending

26. In finance, the term _____ describes the amount in cash that returns to the owners of a security. Normally it does not include the price variations, at the difference of the total return. _____ applies to various stated rates of return on stocks (common and preferred, and convertible), fixed income instruments (bonds, notes, bills, strips, zero coupon), and some other investment type insurance products (e.g. annuities.)

a. Yield to maturity
c. Yield
b. 4-4-5 Calendar
d. Macaulay duration

27. In finance, the _____ is the relation between the interest rate (or cost of borrowing) and the time to maturity of the debt for a given borrower in a given currency. For example, the current U.S. dollar interest rates paid on U.S. Treasury securities for various maturities are closely watched by many traders, and are commonly plotted on a graph such as the one on the right which is informally called 'the _____.' More formal mathematical descriptions of this relation are often called the term structure of interest rates.

The yield of a debt instrument is the annualized percentage increase in the value of the investment.

a. 529 plan
c. 4-4-5 Calendar
b. 7-Eleven
d. Yield curve

28. _____ is a measure of the ability of a debtor to pay their debts as and when they fall due. It is usually expressed as a ratio or a percentage of current liabilities.

For a corporation with a published balance sheet there are various ratios used to calculate a measure of liquidity.

Chapter 7. The Structure of Interest Rates

    a. Accounting liquidity
    b. Operating profit margin
    c. Operating leverage
    d. Invested capital

29. _____ is a method for constructing a (zero-coupon) fixed-income yield curve from the prices of a set of coupon-bearing products by forward substitution.

Using these zero-coupon products it becomes possible to derive par swap rates (forward and spot) for all maturities by making a few assumptions (including linear interpolation.) The term structure of spot returns is recovered from the bond yields by solving for them recursively, this iterative process is called the BootStrap Method.

    a. Reserve requirement
    b. Bullet loan
    c. Bootstrapping
    d. Probability of default

30. The _____ of a commodity, a security or a currency is the price that is quoted for immediate (spot) settlement (payment and delivery.) Spot settlement is normally one or two business days from trade date. This is in contrast with the forward price established in a forward contract or futures contract, where contract terms (price) are set now, but delivery and payment will occur at a future date.
    a. Spot rate
    b. Limits to arbitrage
    c. Long position
    d. Market anomaly

31. The coupon or _____ of a bond is the amount of interest paid per year expressed as a percentage of the face value of the bond.

For example if you hold $10,000 nominal of a bond described as a 4.5% loan stock, you will receive $450 in interest each year (probably in two installments of $225 each.)

Not all bonds have coupons.

    a. Zero-coupon bond
    b. Revenue bonds
    c. Puttable bond
    d. Coupon rate

32. _____ is the difference between price and the costs of bringing to market whatever it is that is accounted as an enterprise (whether by harvest, extraction, manufacture, or purchase) in terms of the component costs of delivered goods and/or services and any operating or other expenses.

A key difficulty in measuring profit is in defining costs. Pure economic monetary profits can be zero or negative even in competitive equilibrium when accounted monetized costs exceed monetized price.

    a. Accounting profit
    b. Economic profit
    c. AAB
    d. A Random Walk Down Wall Street

33. The _____ or forward rate is the agreed upon price of an asset in a forward contract. Using the rational pricing assumption, we can express the _____ in terms of the spot price and any dividends etc., so that there is no possibility for arbitrage.

The _____ is given by:

$$F > $$

where

F is the _____ to be paid at time T
e^x is the exponential function
r is the risk-free interest rate
q is the cost-of-carry
S_0 is the spot price of the asset (i.e. what it would sell for at time 0)
D_i is a dividend which is guaranteed to be paid at time t_i where $0 < t_i < T$.

The two questions here are what price the short position (the seller of the asset) should offer to maximize his gain, and what price the long position (the buyer of the asset) should accept to maximize his gain?

At the very least we know that both do not want to lose any money in the deal.

a. Biweekly Mortgage
c. Financial Gerontology
b. Security interest
d. Forward price

34. In economics, the concept of the _____ refers to the decision-making time frame of a firm in which at least one factor of production is fixed. Costs which are fixed in the _____ have no impact on a firms decisions. For example a firm can raise output by increasing the amount of labour through overtime.
a. 4-4-5 Calendar
c. 529 plan
b. Short-run
d. Long-run

35. In finance, the yield curve is the relation between the interest rate (or cost of borrowing) and the time to maturity of the debt for a given borrower in a given currency. For example, the current U.S. dollar interest rates paid on U.S. Treasury securities for various maturities are closely watched by many traders, and are commonly plotted on a graph such as the one on the right which is informally called 'the yield curve.' More formal mathematical descriptions of this relation are often called the _____.

The yield of a debt instrument is the annualized percentage increase in the value of the investment.

a. 529 plan
c. 4-4-5 Calendar
b. 7-Eleven
d. Term structure of interest rates

36. _____ is one of the main genres of financial risk. The term describes the risk that a particular investment might be canceled or stopped somehow, that one may have to find a new place to invest that money with the risk being there might not be a similarly attractive investment available. This primarily occurs if bonds (which are portions of loans to entities) are paid back earlier then expected.

a. Debt cash flow
c. Biweekly Mortgage
b. Standard of deferred payment
d. Reinvestment risk

Chapter 8. Overview of Forward Rate Analysis

1. The _____ of a commodity, a security or a currency is the price that is quoted for immediate (spot) settlement (payment and delivery.) Spot settlement is normally one or two business days from trade date. This is in contrast with the forward price established in a forward contract or futures contract, where contract terms (price) are set now, but delivery and payment will occur at a future date.
    a. Spot rate
    b. Long position
    c. Limits to arbitrage
    d. Market anomaly

2. The _____ or redemption yield is the yield promised to the bondholder on the assumption that the bond or other fixed-interest security such as gilts will be held to maturity, that all coupon and principal payments will be made and coupon payments are reinvested at the bond's promised yield at the same rate as invested. It is a measure of the return of the bond. This technique in theory allows investors to calculate the fair value of different financial instruments.
    a. Macaulay duration
    b. Yield
    c. 4-4-5 Calendar
    d. Yield to maturity

3. In finance, the term _____ describes the amount in cash that returns to the owners of a security. Normally it does not include the price variations, at the difference of the total return. _____ applies to various stated rates of return on stocks (common and preferred, and convertible), fixed income instruments (bonds, notes, bills, strips, zero coupon), and some other investment type insurance products (e.g. annuities.)
    a. 4-4-5 Calendar
    b. Yield to maturity
    c. Yield
    d. Macaulay duration

4. In finance, the _____ is the relation between the interest rate (or cost of borrowing) and the time to maturity of the debt for a given borrower in a given currency. For example, the current U.S. dollar interest rates paid on U.S. Treasury securities for various maturities are closely watched by many traders, and are commonly plotted on a graph such as the one on the right which is informally called 'the _____.' More formal mathematical descriptions of this relation are often called the term structure of interest rates.

The yield of a debt instrument is the annualized percentage increase in the value of the investment.

    a. 529 plan
    b. 4-4-5 Calendar
    c. 7-Eleven
    d. Yield curve

5. The _____ or forward rate is the agreed upon price of an asset in a forward contract. Using the rational pricing assumption, we can express the _____ in terms of the spot price and any dividends etc., so that there is no possibility for arbitrage.

The _____ is given by:

Chapter 8. Overview of Forward Rate Analysis

where

    F is the _____ to be paid at time T
    e^x is the exponential function
    r is the risk-free interest rate
    q is the cost-of-carry
    S_0 is the spot price of the asset (i.e. what it would sell for at time 0)
    D_i is a dividend which is guaranteed to be paid at time t_i where $0 < t_i < T$.

The two questions here are what price the short position (the seller of the asset) should offer to maximize his gain, and what price the long position (the buyer of the asset) should accept to maximize his gain?

At the very least we know that both do not want to lose any money in the deal.

a. Biweekly Mortgage
c. Financial Gerontology
b. Security interest
d. Forward price

6. In economics and business, specifically cost accounting, the _____ is the point at which cost or expenses and revenue are equal: there is no net loss or gain, and one has 'broken even'. A profit or a loss has not been made, although opportunity costs have been paid, and capital has received the risk-adjusted, expected return.

For example, if the business sells less than 200 tables each month, it will make a loss, if it sells more, it will be a profit.

a. Break-even point
c. Fixed asset turnover
b. Market microstructure
d. Defined contribution plan

7. In finance, a _____ is a debt security, in which the authorized issuer owes the holders a debt and, depending on the terms of the _____, is obliged to pay interest (the coupon) and/or to repay the principal at a later date, termed maturity.

Thus a _____ is a loan: the issuer is the borrower, the _____ holder is the lender, and the coupon is the interest. _____s provide the borrower with external funds to finance long-term investments, or, in the case of government _____s, to finance current expenditure.

a. Bond
c. Catastrophe bonds
b. Convertible bond
d. Puttable bond

8.

In finance, the _____ can be the expected rate of return above the risk-free interest rate. When measuring risk, a common sense approach is to compare the risk-free return on T-bills and the very risky return on other investments. The difference between these two returns can be interpreted as a measure of the excess return on the average risky asset. This excess return is known as the _____.

    a. Risk aversion
    b. Risk adjusted return on capital
    c. Risk modeling
    d. Risk premium

9. _____ are dollar-denominated bonds, issued mostly by Latin American countries in the 1980s, named after U.S. Treasury Secretary Nicholas Brady.

_____ were created in March 1989 in order to convert bonds issued by mostly Latin American countries into a variety or 'menu' of new bonds after many of those countries defaulted on their debt in the 1980's. At that time, the market for sovereign debt was small and illiquid, and the standardization of emerging-market debt facilitated risk-spreading and trading.

    a. Nominal yield
    b. Municipal bond
    c. Coupon rate
    d. Brady bonds

10. A _____ is an international bond that is denominated in a currency not native to the country where it is issued. It can be categorised according to the currency in which it is issued. London is one of the centers of the _____ market, but _____ s may be traded throughout the world - for example in Singapore or Tokyo.

    a. Interest rate option
    b. Education production function
    c. Eurobond
    d. Economic entity

11. _____s are deposits denominated in United States dollars at banks outside the United States, and thus are not under the jurisdiction of the Federal Reserve. Consequently, such deposits are subject to much less regulation than similar deposits within the United States, allowing for higher margins. There is nothing 'European' about _____ deposits; a US dollar-denominated deposit in Tokyo or Caracas would likewise be deemed _____ deposits.

    a. A Random Walk Down Wall Street
    b. AAB
    c. ABN Amro
    d. Eurodollar

12. A _____ is a legal pledge in United States municipal finance, in which an entity pledges its full faith and credit to repay its debt, typically a _____ bond.

    a. General obligation
    b. Covenant
    c. Financial Institutions Reform Recovery and Enforcement Act
    d. Letter of credit

13. In finance, a _____ (non-investment grade bond, speculative grade bond or junk bond) is a bond that is rated below investment grade at the time of purchase. These bonds have a higher risk of default or other adverse credit events, but typically pay higher yields than better quality bonds in order to make them attractive to investors.

    a. Private equity
    b. High yield bond
    c. Sharpe ratio
    d. Volatility

Chapter 8. Overview of Forward Rate Analysis

14. _____ is a measure of the ability of a debtor to pay their debts as and when they fall due. It is usually expressed as a ratio or a percentage of current liabilities.

For a corporation with a published balance sheet there are various ratios used to calculate a measure of liquidity.

a. Accounting liquidity
b. Operating leverage
c. Operating profit margin
d. Invested capital

15. _____ is a term used to explain a difference between two types of financial securities (e.g. stocks), that have all the same qualities except liquidity. For example:

_____ is a segment of a three-part theory that works to explain the behavior of yield curves for interest rates. The upwards-curving component of the interest yield can be explained by the _____.

a. 7-Eleven
b. 4-4-5 Calendar
c. Liquidity premium
d. 529 plan

16. The _____ is the weighted-average most likely outcome in gambling, probability theory, economics or finance.

In gambling and probability theory, there is usually a discrete set of possible outcomes. In this case, _____ is a measure of the relative balance of win or loss weighted by their chances of occurring.

a. A Random Walk Down Wall Street
b. AAB
c. ABN Amro
d. Expected return

17. In economic models, the _____ time frame assumes no fixed factors of production. Firms can enter or leave the marketplace, and the cost (and availability) of land, labor, raw materials, and capital goods can be assumed to vary. In contrast, in the short-run time frame, certain factors are assumed to be fixed, because there is not sufficient time for them to change.

a. Long-run
b. 529 plan
c. 4-4-5 Calendar
d. Short-run

18. In financial accounting, _____s are precautions for which the amount or probability of occurrence are not known. Typical examples are _____s for warranty costs and _____ for taxes the term reserve is used instead of term _____; such a use, however, is inconsistent with the terminology suggested by International Accounting Standards Board.

a. Momentum Accounting and Triple-Entry Bookkeeping
b. Petty cash
c. Provision
d. Money measurement concept

19. In economics and finance, _____ is the practice of taking advantage of a price differential between two or more markets: striking a combination of matching deals that capitalize upon the imbalance, the profit being the difference between the market prices. When used by academics, an _____ is a transaction that involves no negative cash flow at any probabilistic or temporal state and a positive cash flow in at least one state; in simple terms, a risk-free profit.

Chapter 8. Overview of Forward Rate Analysis

a. Initial margin
b. Efficient-market hypothesis
c. Issuer
d. Arbitrage

20. _____ is a life of security. It may also refer to the final payment date of a loan or other financial instrument, at which point all remaining interest and principal is due to be paid.

1, 3, 6 months _____ band can be calculated by using 30-day per month periods.

a. Maturity
b. Primary market
c. False billing
d. Replacement cost

21. In finance, the _____ of a financial asset measures the sensitivity of the asset's price to interest rate movements, expressed as a number of years. The reason for expressing this sensitivity in years is that the time that will elapse until a cash flow is received allows more interest to accumulate. Therefore the price of an asset with long term cashflows has more interest rate sensitivity than an asset with cashflows in the near future.

a. 4-4-5 Calendar
b. Yield to maturity
c. Macaulay duration
d. Duration

22. _____ is a type of bond that allows the issuer of the bond to retain the privilege of redeeming the bond at some point before the bond reaches the date of maturity. In other words, on the call dates, the issuer has the right, but not the obligation, to buy back the bonds from the bond holders at the call price. Technically speaking, the bonds are not really bought and held by the issuer but cancelled immediately.

a. Bond fund
b. Coupon rate
c. Gilts
d. Callable bond

23. _____ are government bonds issued by the United States Department of the Treasury through the Bureau of the Public Debt. They are the debt financing instruments of the U.S. Federal government, and they are often referred to simply as Treasuries or Treasurys. There are four types of marketable _____: Treasury bills, Treasury notes, Treasury bonds, and Treasury Inflation Protected Securities (TIPS.)

a. Treasury Inflation-Protected Securities
b. Treasury Inflation Protected Securities
c. 4-4-5 Calendar
d. Treasury securities

24. A _____ is an exchange of promises between two or more parties to do an act which is enforceable in a court of law. It is where an unqualified offer meets a qualified acceptance and the parties reach Consensus ad Idem. The parties must have the necessary capacity to _____ and the _____ must not be either trifling, indeterminate, impossible or illegal.

a. 4-4-5 Calendar
b. 529 plan
c. 7-Eleven
d. Contract

25. An _____ is a contract written by a seller that conveys to the buyer the right -- but not the obligation -- to buy (in the case of a call _____) or to sell (in the case of a put _____) a particular asset, such as a piece of property such as, among others, a futures contract. In return for granting the _____, the seller collects a payment (the premium) from the buyer.

For example, buying a call _____ provides the right to buy a specified quantity of a security at a set strike price at some time on or before expiration, while buying a put _____ provides the right to sell.

a. AT'T Mobility LLC
b. Annuity
c. Amortization
d. Option

26. A _____ is a fungible, negotiable instrument representing financial value. They are broadly categorized into debt securities (such as banknotes, bonds and debentures), and equity securities; e.g., common stocks. The company or other entity issuing the _____ is called the issuer.

a. Securities lending
b. Book entry
c. Tracking stock
d. Security

Chapter 9. Measuring Interest-Rate Risk

1. _____ are dollar-denominated bonds, issued mostly by Latin American countries in the 1980s, named after U.S. Treasury Secretary Nicholas Brady.

_____ were created in March 1989 in order to convert bonds issued by mostly Latin American countries into a variety or 'menu' of new bonds after many of those countries defaulted on their debt in the 1980's. At that time, the market for sovereign debt was small and illiquid, and the standardization of emerging-market debt facilitated risk-spreading and trading.

   a. Brady bonds
   c. Coupon rate
   b. Municipal bond
   d. Nominal yield

2. A _____ is an international bond that is denominated in a currency not native to the country where it is issued. It can be categorised according to the currency in which it is issued. London is one of the centers of the _____ market, but _____ s may be traded throughout the world - for example in Singapore or Tokyo.

   a. Interest rate option
   c. Economic entity
   b. Education production function
   d. Eurobond

3. _____ s are deposits denominated in United States dollars at banks outside the United States, and thus are not under the jurisdiction of the Federal Reserve. Consequently, such deposits are subject to much less regulation than similar deposits within the United States, allowing for higher margins. There is nothing 'European' about _____ deposits; a US dollar-denominated deposit in Tokyo or Caracas would likewise be deemed _____ deposits.

   a. A Random Walk Down Wall Street
   c. Eurodollar
   b. AAB
   d. ABN Amro

4. A _____ is a legal pledge in United States municipal finance, in which an entity pledges its full faith and credit to repay its debt, typically a _____ bond.

   a. Letter of credit
   b. General obligation
   c. Financial Institutions Reform Recovery and Enforcement Act
   d. Covenant

5. In finance, a _____ (non-investment grade bond, speculative grade bond or junk bond) is a bond that is rated below investment grade at the time of purchase. These bonds have a higher risk of default or other adverse credit events, but typically pay higher yields than better quality bonds in order to make them attractive to investors.

   a. Volatility
   c. Private equity
   b. High yield bond
   d. Sharpe ratio

6. In finance, a _____ is a debt security, in which the authorized issuer owes the holders a debt and, depending on the terms of the _____, is obliged to pay interest (the coupon) and/or to repay the principal at a later date, termed maturity.

Thus a _____ is a loan: the issuer is the borrower, the _____ holder is the lender, and the coupon is the interest. _____ s provide the borrower with external funds to finance long-term investments, or, in the case of government _____ s, to finance current expenditure.

   a. Catastrophe bonds
   c. Bond
   b. Puttable bond
   d. Convertible bond

7. _____ is a type of bond that allows the issuer of the bond to retain the privilege of redeeming the bond at some point before the bond reaches the date of maturity. In other words, on the call dates, the issuer has the right, but not the obligation, to buy back the bonds from the bond holders at the call price. Technically speaking, the bonds are not really bought and held by the issuer but cancelled immediately.
   a. Bond fund   b. Gilts
   c. Coupon rate   d. Callable bond

8. In financial accounting, _____s are precautions for which the amount or probability of occurrence are not known. Typical examples are _____s for warranty costs and _____ for taxes the term reserve is used instead of term _____; such a use, however, is inconsistent with the terminology suggested by International Accounting Standards Board.
   a. Momentum Accounting and Triple-Entry Bookkeeping   b. Petty cash
   c. Money measurement concept   d. Provision

9. _____ most frequently refers to the standard deviation of the continuously compounded returns of a financial instrument with a specific time horizon. It is often used to quantify the risk of the instrument over that time period. _____ is typically expressed in annualized terms, and it may either be an absolute number ($5) or a fraction of the mean (5%).
   a. Seasoned equity offering   b. Currency swap
   c. Portfolio insurance   d. Volatility

10. The coupon or _____ of a bond is the amount of interest paid per year expressed as a percentage of the face value of the bond.

For example if you hold $10,000 nominal of a bond described as a 4.5% loan stock, you will receive $450 in interest each year (probably in two installments of $225 each.)

Not all bonds have coupons.

   a. Zero-coupon bond   b. Puttable bond
   c. Revenue bonds   d. Coupon rate

11. _____ is a life of security. It may also refer to the final payment date of a loan or other financial instrument, at which point all remaining interest and principal is due to be paid.

1, 3, 6 months _____ band can be calculated by using 30-day per month periods.

   a. Maturity   b. Replacement cost
   c. False billing   d. Primary market

12. An _____ is a contract written by a seller that conveys to the buyer the right -- but not the obligation -- to buy (in the case of a call _____) or to sell (in the case of a put _____) a particular asset, such as a piece of property such as, among others, a futures contract. In return for granting the _____, the seller collects a payment (the premium) from the buyer.

For example, buying a call _____ provides the right to buy a specified quantity of a security at a set strike price at some time on or before expiration, while buying a put _____ provides the right to sell.

a. Amortization
b. Annuity
c. AT'T Mobility LLC
d. Option

13. _____ is a combination of straight bond and embedded put option. The holder of the _____ has the right, but not the obligation, to demand early repayment of the principal. The put option is usually exercisable on specified dates.

a. Callable bond
b. Brady bonds
c. Convertible bond
d. Puttable bond

14. A _____ is a fungible, negotiable instrument representing financial value. They are broadly categorized into debt securities (such as banknotes, bonds and debentures), and equity securities; e.g., common stocks. The company or other entity issuing the _____ is called the issuer.

a. Book entry
b. Tracking stock
c. Securities lending
d. Security

15. In finance, the _____ of a financial asset measures the sensitivity of the asset's price to interest rate movements, expressed as a number of years. The reason for expressing this sensitivity in years is that the time that will elapse until a cash flow is received allows more interest to accumulate. Therefore the price of an asset with long term cashflows has more interest rate sensitivity than an asset with cashflows in the near future.

a. 4-4-5 Calendar
b. Yield to maturity
c. Macaulay duration
d. Duration

16. _____ is the weighted average maturity of a bond where the weights are the relative discounted cash flows in each period.

It will be seen that this is the same formula for the duration as given above.

Macaulay showed that an unweighted average maturity is not useful in predicting interest rate risk.

a. Yield to maturity
b. Yield
c. 4-4-5 Calendar
d. Macaulay Duration

17. A _____ is a financial contract whose value is derived from the value of something else (known as the underlying.) The underlying on which a _____ is based can be an asset, weather conditions bonds or other forms of credit.

a. 7-Eleven
b. 4-4-5 Calendar
c. 529 plan
d. Derivative

Chapter 9. Measuring Interest-Rate Risk

18. In economics and finance, _____ is the practice of taking advantage of a price differential between two or more markets: striking a combination of matching deals that capitalize upon the imbalance, the profit being the difference between the market prices. When used by academics, an _____ is a transaction that involves no negative cash flow at any probabilistic or temporal state and a positive cash flow in at least one state; in simple terms, a risk-free profit.
    a. Issuer
    b. Initial margin
    c. Efficient-market hypothesis
    d. Arbitrage

19. In finance, the binomial options pricing model (BOPM) provides a generalisable numerical method for the valuation of options. The _____ was first proposed by Cox, Ross and Rubinstein (1979.) Essentially, the model uses a 'discrete-time' model of the varying price over time of the underlying financial instrument.
    a. Binomial model
    b. Modified Internal Rate of Return
    c. Discount rate
    d. Perpetuity

20. A _____ is a unit that is equal to 1/100th of a percentage point. It is frequently used to express percentage point changes of less than 1%. It avoids the ambiguity between relative and absolute discussions about rates.
    a. Basis point
    b. 4-4-5 Calendar
    c. 529 plan
    d. Bond market

21. _____ is a fee paid on borrowed assets. It is the price paid for the use of borrowed money , or, money earned by deposited funds . Assets that are sometimes lent with _____ include money, shares, consumer goods through hire purchase, major assets such as aircraft, and even entire factories in finance lease arrangements.
    a. A Random Walk Down Wall Street
    b. AAB
    c. Insolvency
    d. Interest

22. An _____ is the price a borrower pays for the use of money they do not own, and the return a lender receives for deferring the use of funds, by lending it to the borrower. _____s are normally expressed as a percentage rate over the period of one year.

    _____s targets are also a vital tool of monetary policy and are used to control variables like investment, inflation, and unemployment.

    a. AAB
    b. ABN Amro
    c. A Random Walk Down Wall Street
    d. Interest rate

23. In finance, the term _____ describes the amount in cash that returns to the owners of a security. Normally it does not include the price variations, at the difference of the total return. _____ applies to various stated rates of return on stocks (common and preferred, and convertible), fixed income instruments (bonds, notes, bills, strips, zero coupon), and some other investment type insurance products (e.g. annuities.)
    a. Yield to maturity
    b. 4-4-5 Calendar
    c. Macaulay duration
    d. Yield

24. In finance, _____ is the process of estimating the potential market value of a financial asset or liability. they can be done on assets (for example, investments in marketable securities such as stocks, options, business enterprises, or intangible assets such as patents and trademarks) or on liabilities (e.g., Bonds issued by a company.) _____s are required in many contexts including investment analysis, capital budgeting, merger and acquisition transactions, financial reporting, taxable events to determine the proper tax liability, and in litigation.

a. Margin
b. Procter ' Gamble
c. Share
d. Valuation

Chapter 10. U.S. Treasury and Agency Securities 61

1. _____ are government bonds issued by the United States Department of the Treasury through the Bureau of the Public Debt. They are the debt financing instruments of the U.S. Federal government, and they are often referred to simply as Treasuries or Treasurys. There are four types of marketable _____: Treasury bills, Treasury notes, Treasury bonds, and Treasury Inflation Protected Securities (TIPS.)
   a. Treasury securities
   c. 4-4-5 Calendar
   b. Treasury Inflation-Protected Securities
   d. Treasury Inflation Protected Securities

2. A _____ or market-based mechanism is any of a wide variety of ways to match up buyers and sellers.

An example of a _____ uses announced bid and ask prices. Generally speaking, when two parties wish to engage in a trade, the purchaser will announce a price he is willing to pay (the bid price) and seller will announce a price he is willing to accept (the ask price).

   a. 4-4-5 Calendar
   c. 529 plan
   b. 7-Eleven
   d. Price mechanism

3. The _____ for securities is the difference between the price quoted by a market maker for an immediate sale and an immediate purchase The size of the bid-offer spread in a given commodity is a measure of the liquidity of the market.

The trader initiating the transaction is said to demand liquidity, and the other party to the transaction supplies liquidity.

   a. Defined contribution plan
   c. Bid/offer spread
   b. Capital outflow
   d. Trade-off

4. A _____ is a fungible, negotiable instrument representing financial value. They are broadly categorized into debt securities (such as banknotes, bonds and debentures), and equity securities; e.g., common stocks. The company or other entity issuing the _____ is called the issuer.
   a. Tracking stock
   c. Securities lending
   b. Book entry
   d. Security

5. The coupon or _____ of a bond is the amount of interest paid per year expressed as a percentage of the face value of the bond.

For example if you hold $10,000 nominal of a bond described as a 4.5% loan stock, you will receive $450 in interest each year (probably in two installments of $225 each.)

Not all bonds have coupons.

   a. Zero-coupon bond
   c. Revenue bonds
   b. Puttable bond
   d. Coupon rate

6. A '_____' is a 'Charge' that is paid to obtain the right to delay a payment. Essentially, the payer purchases the right to make a given payment in the future instead of in the Present. The '_____', or 'Charge' that must be paid to delay the payment, is simply the difference between what the payment amount would be if it were paid in the present and what the payment amount would be paid if it were paid in the future.

Chapter 10. U.S. Treasury and Agency Securities

a. Discount
c. Risk modeling
b. Risk aversion
d. Value at risk

7. _____ mature in one year or less. Like zero-coupon bonds, they do not pay interest prior to maturity; instead they are sold at a discount of the par value to create a positive yield to maturity. Many regard _____ as the least risky investment available to U.S. investors.
   a. Treasury Inflation Protected Securities
   c. Treasury securities
   b. 4-4-5 Calendar
   d. Treasury bills

8. _____ is that which is owed; usually referencing assets owed, but the term can cover other obligations. In the case of assets, _____ is a means of using future purchasing power in the present before a summation has been earned. Some companies and corporations use _____ as a part of their overall corporate finance strategy.
   a. Partial Payment
   c. Debt
   b. Cross-collateralization
   d. Credit cycle

9. The _____ is that part of the capital markets that deals with the issuance of new securities. Companies, governments or public sector institutions can obtain funding through the sale of a new stock or bond issue. This is typically done through a syndicate of securities dealers.
   a. Sector rotation
   c. Peer group analysis
   b. Volatility clustering
   d. Primary market

10. In finance, a _____ is a debt security, in which the authorized issuer owes the holders a debt and, depending on the terms of the _____, is obliged to pay interest (the coupon) and/or to repay the principal at a later date, termed maturity.

    Thus a _____ is a loan: the issuer is the borrower, the _____ holder is the lender, and the coupon is the interest. _____s provide the borrower with external funds to finance long-term investments, or, in the case of government _____s, to finance current expenditure.

    a. Convertible bond
    c. Bond
    b. Puttable bond
    d. Catastrophe bonds

11. _____ are securities that can be easily converted into cash. Such securities will generally have highly liquid markets allowing the security to be sold at a reasonable price very quickly. This is a usual feature in real estate .
    a. Marketable
    c. Tracking stock
    b. Book entry
    d. Securities lending

12. In finance, the term _____ describes the amount in cash that returns to the owners of a security. Normally it does not include the price variations, at the difference of the total return. _____ applies to various stated rates of return on stocks (common and preferred, and convertible), fixed income instruments (bonds, notes, bills, strips, zero coupon), and some other investment type insurance products (e.g. annuities.)
    a. Macaulay duration
    c. Yield
    b. 4-4-5 Calendar
    d. Yield to maturity

Chapter 10. U.S. Treasury and Agency Securities

13. A _____ is a bank or securities broker-dealer that may trade directly with the Federal Reserve System of the United States ('the Fed'.) Such firms are required to make bids or offers when the Fed conducts open market operations, provide information to the Fed's open market trading desk, and to participate actively in U.S. Treasury securities auctions. They consult with both the U.S. Treasury and the Fed about funding the budget deficit and implementing monetary policy.

a. 7-Eleven
b. 4-4-5 Calendar
c. 529 plan
d. Primary dealer

14. The _____ is the financial market where previously issued securities and financial instruments such as stock, bonds, options, and futures are bought and sold. The term '_____' is also used refer to the market for any used goods or assets, or an alternative use for an existing product or asset where the customer base is the second market

With primary issuances of securities or financial instruments, or the primary market, investors purchase these securities directly from issuers such as corporations issuing shares in an IPO or private placement, or directly from the federal government in the case of treasuries.

a. Secondary market
b. Delta neutral
c. Financial market
d. Performance attribution

15. The _____ , a component of the Federal Reserve System, is charged under United States law with overseeing the nation's open market operations. It is the Federal Reserve Committee that makes key decisions about interest rates and the growth jam of the United States money supply. It is the principal organ of United States national monetary policy.

a. Federal Open Market Committee
b. Tax incidence
c. Tax exemption
d. Fiscal policy

16. In financial accounting, the term _____ is most commonly used to describe any part of shareholders' equity, except for basic share capital. Sometimes, the term is used instead of the term provision; such a use, however, is inconsistent with the terminology suggested by International Accounting Standards Board. For more information about provisions, see provision (accounting.)

a. Reserve
b. Treasury stock
c. FIFO and LIFO accounting
d. Closing entries

17. A _____, reserve bank, or monetary authority is the entity responsible for the monetary policy of a country or of a group of member states. It is a bank that can lend money to other banks in times of need. Its primary responsibility is to maintain the stability of the national currency and money supply, but more active duties include controlling subsidized-loan interest rates, and acting as a lender of last resort to the banking sector during times of financial crisis (private banks often being integral to the national financial system.)

a. 529 plan
b. Central bank
c. 7-Eleven
d. 4-4-5 Calendar

18. In the United States, _____ are overnight borrowings by banks to maintain their bank reserves at the Federal Reserve. Banks keep reserves at Federal Reserve Banks to meet their reserve requirements and to clear financial transactions. Transactions in the _____ market enable depository institutions with reserve balances in excess of reserve requirements to lend reserves to institutions with reserve deficiencies.

a. 4-4-5 Calendar
b. Regulation T
c. Federal funds
d. Federal funds rate

Chapter 10. U.S. Treasury and Agency Securities

19. The _____ is an interest rate a central bank charges depository institutions that borrow reserves from it.

The term _____ has two meanings:

- the same as interest rate; the term 'discount' does not refer to the meaning of the word, but to the purpose of using the quantity, such as computations of present value, e.g. net present value / discounted cash flow

- the annual effective _____, which is the annual interest divided by the capital including that interest; this rate is lower than the interest rate; it corresponds to using the value after a year as the nominal value, and seeing the initial value as the nominal value minus a discount; it is used for Treasury Bills and similar financial instruments

The annual effective _____ is the annual interest divided by the capital including that interest, which is the interest rate divided by 100% plus the interest rate. It is the annual discount factor to be applied to the future cash flow, to find the discount, subtracted from a future value to find the value one year earlier.

For example, suppose there is a government bond that sells for $95 and pays $100 in a year's time.

a. Stochastic volatility
c. Fisher equation
b. Black-Scholes
d. Discount rate

20. A _____ is a bond bought at a price lower than its face value, with the face value repaid at the time of maturity. It does not make periodic interest payments, or have so-called 'coupons,' hence the term _____. Investors earn return from the compounded interest all paid at maturity plus the difference between the discounted price of the bond and its par value.
a. Corporate bond
c. Bond fund
b. Clean price
d. Zero-coupon bond

21. _____ is the provision of resources (such as granting a loan) by one party to another party where that second party does not reimburse the first party immediately, thereby generating a debt, and instead arranges either to repay or return those resources (or material(s) of equal value) at a later date. The first party is called a creditor, also known as a lender, while the second party is called a debtor, also known as a borrower.

Movements of financial capital are normally dependent on either _____ or equity transfers.

a. Warrant
c. Credit
b. Comparable
d. Clearing house

22. The _____ (NYSE: FNM), commonly known as Fannie Mae, is a stockholder-owned corporation chartered by Congress in 1968 as a government sponsored enterprise (GSE), but founded in 1938 during the Great Depression. The corporation's purpose is to purchase and securitize mortgages in order to ensure that funds are consistently available to the institutions that lend money to home buyers.

On September 7, 2008, James Lockhart, director of the Federal Housing Finance Agency (FHFA), announced that Fannie Mae and Freddie Mac were being placed into conservatorship of the FHFA.

Chapter 10. U.S. Treasury and Agency Securities

    a. General partnership   b. The Depository Trust ' Clearing Corporation
    c. SPDR   d. Federal National Mortgage Association

23. The _____ is a federally chartered network of borrower-owned lending institutions composed of cooperatives and related service organizations. Cooperatives are organizations that are owned and controlled by their members who use the cooperative'e;s products, supplies or services. The U.S. Congress authorized the creation of the first System institutions in 1916.
    a. 529 plan   b. 4-4-5 Calendar
    c. Farm Credit System   d. 7-Eleven

24. The _____ provide stable, on-demand, low-cost funding to American financial institutions for home mortgage loans, small business, rural, agricultural, and economic development lending. With their members, the _____ank System represents the largest collective source of home mortgage and community credit in the United States. The banks do not provide loans directly to individuals, only to other banks.
    a. 7-Eleven   b. 4-4-5 Calendar
    c. 529 plan   d. Federal Home Loan Banks

25. The institution most often referenced by the word '_____' is a public or publicly traded _____, the shares of which are traded on a public stock exchange (e.g., the New York Stock Exchange or Nasdaq in the United States) where shares of stock of _____s are bought and sold by and to the general public. Most of the largest businesses in the world are publicly traded _____s. However, the majority of _____s are said to be closely held, privately held or close _____s, meaning that no ready market exists for the trading of shares.
    a. Federal Home Loan Mortgage Corporation   b. Depository Trust Company
    c. Corporation   d. Protect

26. The _____ (NYSE: FRE) is an insolvent government sponsored enterprise (GSE) of the United States federal government.

The _____ was created in 1970 to expand the secondary market for mortgages in the US. Along with other GSEs, Freddie Mac buys mortgages on the secondary market, pools them, and sells them as mortgage-backed securities to investors on the open market.

    a. Governmental Accounting Standards Board   b. Public company
    c. Federal Home Loan Mortgage Corporation   d. The Depository Trust ' Clearing Corporation

27. In law, _____ refers to assistance given by a company for the purchase of its own shares or the shares of its holding companies. In many jurisdictions such assistance is prohibited or restricted by law. For example all EU member states are required to prohibit _____ by public companies , although some members go further, for example, France, Belgium and The Netherlands prohibit _____ by all companies.
    a. Cost of living   b. Duration gap
    c. Financial Assistance   d. Decision process tool

28. The _____ is a stockholder-owned, publicly-traded company that was chartered by the United States federal government in 1988 to serve as a secondary market in agricultural loans such as mortgages for agricultural real estate and rural housing. The company purchases loans from agricultural lenders, and sells instruments backed by those loans. The company also works with the United States Department of Agriculture.

a. Public company
c. Limited liability partnership
b. Federal Agricultural Mortgage Corporation
d. Federal Home Loan Mortgage Corporation

29. _____ or financing is to provide capital (funds), which means money for a project, a person, a business or any other private or public institutions.

Those funds can be allocated for either short term or long term purposes. The health fund is a new way of _____ private healthcare centers.

a. Funding
c. Proxy fight
b. Product life cycle
d. Synthetic CDO

Chapter 11. Municipal Bonds

1. In the United States, a _____ is a bond issued by a city or other local government, or their agencies. Potential issuers of these bonds include cities, counties, redevelopment agencies, school districts, publicly owned airports and seaports, and any other governmental entity (or group of governments) below the state level. They may be general obligations of the issuer or secured by specified revenues.

    a. Premium bond
    b. Puttable bond
    c. Senior debt
    d. Municipal bond

2. In finance, a _____ is a debt security, in which the authorized issuer owes the holders a debt and, depending on the terms of the _____, is obliged to pay interest (the coupon) and/or to repay the principal at a later date, termed maturity.

    Thus a _____ is a loan: the issuer is the borrower, the _____ holder is the lender, and the coupon is the interest. _____s provide the borrower with external funds to finance long-term investments, or, in the case of government _____s, to finance current expenditure.

    a. Convertible bond
    b. Bond
    c. Catastrophe bonds
    d. Puttable bond

3. The _____ is a financial market where participants buy and sell debt securities, usually in the form of bonds. As of 2006, the size of the international _____ is an estimated $45 trillion, of which the size of the outstanding U.S. _____ debt was $25.2 trillion.

    Nearly all of the $923 billion average daily trading volume in the U.S. _____ takes place between broker-dealers and large institutions in a decentralized, over-the-counter market.

    a. 4-4-5 Calendar
    b. 529 plan
    c. Bond market
    d. Fixed income

4. _____ is the provision of resources (such as granting a loan) by one party to another party where that second party does not reimburse the first party immediately, thereby generating a debt, and instead arranges either to repay or return those resources (or material(s) of equal value) at a later date. The first party is called a creditor, also known as a lender, while the second party is called a debtor, also known as a borrower.

    Movements of financial capital are normally dependent on either _____ or equity transfers.

    a. Clearing house
    b. Comparable
    c. Warrant
    d. Credit

5. _____ is the risk of loss due to a debtor's non-payment of a loan or other line of credit (either the principal or interest (coupon) or both)

    Most lenders employ their own models (credit scorecards) to rank potential and existing customers according to risk, and then apply appropriate strategies. With products such as unsecured personal loans or mortgages, lenders charge a higher price for higher risk customers and vice versa. With revolving products such as credit cards and overdrafts, risk is controlled through careful setting of credit limits.

Chapter 11. Municipal Bonds

    a. Liquidity risk
    b. Market risk
    c. Transaction risk
    d. Credit risk

6. _____ are bonds that have a variable coupon, equal to a money market reference rate, like LIBOR or federal funds rate, plus a spread. The spread is a rate that remains constant. Almost all _____ have quarterly coupons, i.e. they pay out interest every three months, though counter examples do exist.
    a. Floating rate notes
    b. Loan participation
    c. Gordon growth model
    d. CVECAs

7. In the United States, a _____ is an offering of securities that are not registered with the Securities and Exchange Commission (SEC.) Such offerings exploit an exemption offered by the Securities Act of 1933 that comes with several restrictions, including a prohibition against general solicitation. This exemption allows companies to avoid quarterly reporting requirements and many of the legal liabilities associated with the Sarbanes-Oxley Act.
    a. 7-Eleven
    b. 4-4-5 Calendar
    c. 529 plan
    d. Private placement

8. A _____ is a bond bought at a price lower than its face value, with the face value repaid at the time of maturity. It does not make periodic interest payments, or have so-called 'coupons,' hence the term _____. Investors earn return from the compounded interest all paid at maturity plus the difference between the discounted price of the bond and its par value.
    a. Bond fund
    b. Corporate bond
    c. Clean price
    d. Zero-coupon bond

9. The coupon or _____ of a bond is the amount of interest paid per year expressed as a percentage of the face value of the bond.

For example if you hold $10,000 nominal of a bond described as a 4.5% loan stock, you will receive $450 in interest each year (probably in two installments of $225 each.)

Not all bonds have coupons.

    a. Zero-coupon bond
    b. Puttable bond
    c. Revenue bonds
    d. Coupon rate

10. A '_____' is a 'Charge' that is paid to obtain the right to delay a payment. Essentially, the payer purchases the right to make a given payment in the future instead of in the Present. The '_____', or 'Charge' that must be paid to delay the payment, is simply the difference between what the payment amount would be if it were paid in the present and what the payment amount would be paid if it were paid in the future.
    a. Risk modeling
    b. Risk aversion
    c. Discount
    d. Value at risk

11. A _____ is a bond bought at a price lower than its face value, with the face value repaid at the time of maturity. It does not make periodic interest payments, or so-called 'coupons,' hence the term zero-coupon bond. Investors earn return from the compounded interest all paid at maturity plus the difference between the discounted price of the bond and its par value.

Chapter 11. Municipal Bonds

a. Bowie bonds
c. Callable bond
b. Zero coupon bond
d. Municipal bond

12. In business, _____ is income that a company receives from its normal business activities, usually from the sale of goods and services to customers. Some companies also receive _____ from interest, dividends or royalties paid to them by other companies. _____ may refer to business income in general, or it may refer to the amount, in a monetary unit, received during a period of time, as in 'Last year, Company X had _____ of $32 million.'

In many countries, including the UK, _____ is referred to as turnover.

a. Revenue
c. Furniture, Fixtures and Equipment
b. Matching principle
d. Bottom line

13. _____ are bonds issued by governments, authorities, or public benefit corporations that are guaranteed by the revenue flow of the issuing agency.

The Supreme Court decision of Pollock versus Farmer's Loan and Trust Company of 1895 initiated a wave or series of innovations for the financial services community in both tax-treatment and regulation from government. This specific case, according to a leading investment bank's research, resulted in the 'intergovernmental tax immunity doctrine,' ultimately leading to 'tax-free status.' Municipal bonds are generally exempt from federal tax on their interest payments (not capital gains.)

a. Private activity bond
c. Callable bond
b. Gilts
d. Revenue bonds

14. _____s are financial bonds that mature in installments over a period of time. In effect, a $100,000, 5-year _____ would mature in a $20,000 annuity over a 5-year interval. Bond issues consisting of a series of blocks of securities maturing in sequence, the coupon rate can be different.

a. Bond fund
c. Brady bonds
b. Callable bond
d. Serial bond

15. _____ is a life of security. It may also refer to the final payment date of a loan or other financial instrument, at which point all remaining interest and principal is due to be paid.

1, 3, 6 months _____ band can be calculated by using 30-day per month periods.

a. False billing
c. Primary market
b. Maturity
d. Replacement cost

16. In economics, a _____ is a mechanism that allows people to easily buy and sell (trade) financial securities (such as stocks and bonds), commodities (such as precious metals or agricultural goods), and other fungible items of value at low transaction costs and at prices that reflect the efficient-market hypothesis.

_____s have evolved significantly over several hundred years and are undergoing constant innovation to improve liquidity.

Both general markets (where many commodities are traded) and specialized markets (where only one commodity is traded) exist.

a. Cost of carry
b. Secondary market
c. Financial Market
d. Delta hedging

17. A _____ is a legal pledge in United States municipal finance, in which an entity pledges its full faith and credit to repay its debt, typically a _____ bond.

a. Financial Institutions Reform Recovery and Enforcement Act
b. Covenant
c. Letter of credit
d. General obligation

18. In finance, _____ occurs when a debtor has not met its legal obligations according to the debt contract, e.g. it has not made a scheduled payment, or has violated a loan covenant (condition) of the debt contract. _____ may occur if the debtor is either unwilling or unable to pay their debt. This can occur with all debt obligations including bonds, mortgages, loans, and promissory notes.

a. Vendor finance
b. Default
c. Credit crunch
d. Debt validation

19. A _____ is a fungible, negotiable instrument representing financial value. They are broadly categorized into debt securities (such as banknotes, bonds and debentures), and equity securities; e.g., common stocks. The company or other entity issuing the _____ is called the issuer.

a. Book entry
b. Securities lending
c. Tracking stock
d. Security

20. In economics, _____ is a measure of the relative satisfaction from or desirability of consumption of various goods and services. Given this measure, one may speak meaningfully of increasing or decreasing _____, and thereby explain economic behavior in terms of attempts to increase one's _____. For illustrative purposes, changes in _____ are sometimes expressed in units called utils.

a. A Random Walk Down Wall Street
b. Utility function
c. AAB
d. Utility

21. In finance, the _____ is the global financial market for short-term borrowing and lending. It provides short-term liquidity funding for the global financial system. The _____ is where short-term obligations such as Treasury bills, commercial paper and bankers' acceptances are bought and sold.

a. Money market
b. Cramdown
c. Consumer debt
d. Debt-for-equity swap

22. In the global money market, _____ is an unsecured promissory note with a fixed maturity of one to 270 days. _____ is a money-market security issued (sold) by large banks and corporations to get money to meet short term debt obligations (for example, payroll), and is only backed by an issuing bank or corporation's promise to pay the face amount on the maturity date specified on the note. Since it is not backed by collateral, only firms with excellent credit ratings from a recognized rating agency will be able to sell their _____ at a reasonable price.

Chapter 11. Municipal Bonds

a. Book building
b. Financial distress
c. Trade-off theory
d. Commercial paper

23. A _____ is a financial contract whose value is derived from the value of something else (known as the underlying.) The underlying on which a _____ is based can be an asset, weather conditions bonds or other forms of credit.
   a. 7-Eleven
   b. 529 plan
   c. 4-4-5 Calendar
   d. Derivative

24. An _____ is a type of bond or other type of debt instrument used in finance whose coupon rate has an inverse relationship to short-term interest rates (or its reference rate.) With an _____, as interest rates rise the coupon rate falls. The basic structure is the same as an ordinary floating rate note except for the direction in which the coupon rate is adjusted.
   a. Inverse floater
   b. A Random Walk Down Wall Street
   c. ABN Amro
   d. AAB

25. An _____ is a contract written by a seller that conveys to the buyer the right -- but not the obligation -- to buy (in the case of a call _____) or to sell (in the case of a put _____) a particular asset, such as a piece of property such as, among others, a futures contract. In return for granting the _____, the seller collects a payment (the premium) from the buyer.

For example, buying a call _____ provides the right to buy a specified quantity of a security at a set strike price at some time on or before expiration, while buying a put _____ provides the right to sell.

   a. Amortization
   b. AT'T Mobility LLC
   c. Annuity
   d. Option

26. A _____ assesses the credit worthiness of an individual, corporation, or even a country. _____s are calculated from financial history and current assets and liabilities. Typically, a _____ tells a lender or investor the probability of the subject being able to pay back a loan.
   a. Debenture
   b. Credit report monitoring
   c. Credit cycle
   d. Credit rating

27. _____ is an insurance policy which compensates lenders or investors for losses due to the default of a mortgage loan. _____ can be either public or private depending upon the insurer. The policy is also known as a mortgage indemnity guarantee (Mortgage insuranceG), particularly in the UK.
   a. Reverse mortgage
   b. Subprime lending
   c. Mortgage-backed security
   d. Mortgage insurance

28. _____ is the flat spread over the treasury yield curve required to discount a security payment to match its market price. This concept can be applied to mortgage-backed security (MBS), Options, Bonds and any other interest-rate Derivative.

In contrast to the simple 'yield curve spread' measurement of bond premium over a pre-determined cash-flow model, the _____ describes the market premium over a model including two types of volatility:

- Variable interest rates
- Variable prepayment rates.

Designing such models in the first place is complicated because prepayment variations are a behavioural function of the stochastic interest rate. (They tend to go up as interest rates come down.)

   a. Option adjusted spread   b. ABN Amro
   c. AAB   d. A Random Walk Down Wall Street

29. In finance, _____ is the process of estimating the potential market value of a financial asset or liability. they can be done on assets (for example, investments in marketable securities such as stocks, options, business enterprises, or intangible assets such as patents and trademarks) or on liabilities (e.g., Bonds issued by a company.) _____s are required in many contexts including investment analysis, capital budgeting, merger and acquisition transactions, financial reporting, taxable events to determine the proper tax liability, and in litigation.
   a. Procter ' Gamble   b. Share
   c. Margin   d. Valuation

30. In finance, the term _____ describes the amount in cash that returns to the owners of a security. Normally it does not include the price variations, at the difference of the total return. _____ applies to various stated rates of return on stocks (common and preferred, and convertible), fixed income instruments (bonds, notes, bills, strips, zero coupon), and some other investment type insurance products (e.g. annuities.)
   a. Yield   b. Yield to maturity
   c. Macaulay duration   d. 4-4-5 Calendar

31. _____ is part of the Federal income tax system of the United States. There is an _____ for those who owe personal income tax, and another for corporations owing corporate income tax. Only the _____ for those owing personal income tax is described here.

The _____ operates in effect as a parallel tax system, with its own definition of taxable income, exemptions, and tax rates. Taxpayers compute tax owed under the 'regular' and _____ systems and are liable for whichever is higher.

   a. AAB   b. ABN Amro
   c. A Random Walk Down Wall Street   d. Alternative minimum tax

32. _____, refers to consumption opportunity gained by an entity within a specified time frame, which is generally expressed in monetary terms. However, for households and individuals, '_____ is the sum of all the wages, salaries, profits, interests payments, rents and other forms of earnings received... in a given period of time.' For firms, _____ generally refers to net-profit: what remains of revenue after expenses have been subtracted.
   a. Income   b. Accrual
   c. Annual report   d. OIBDA

Chapter 11. Municipal Bonds

33. _____ is a fee paid on borrowed assets. It is the price paid for the use of borrowed money, or, money earned by deposited funds. Assets that are sometimes lent with _____ include money, shares, consumer goods through hire purchase, major assets such as aircraft, and even entire factories in finance lease arrangements.
   a. Insolvency
   b. A Random Walk Down Wall Street
   c. AAB
   d. Interest

34. _____ is the portion of income that is the subject of taxation according to the laws that determine what is income and the taxation rate for that income. Generally, _____ refers to an individual's (or corporation's) gross income, adjusted for various deductions allowable by statute. The main questions put by most individuals in any jurisdiction are 'what makes up my _____' and what tax rates should be applied such that I can work out my tax liability to the state.
   a. 4-4-5 Calendar
   b. 529 plan
   c. Taxable income
   d. 7-Eleven

35. In finance, the _____ is the relation between the interest rate (or cost of borrowing) and the time to maturity of the debt for a given borrower in a given currency. For example, the current U.S. dollar interest rates paid on U.S. Treasury securities for various maturities are closely watched by many traders, and are commonly plotted on a graph such as the one on the right which is informally called 'the _____.' More formal mathematical descriptions of this relation are often called the term structure of interest rates.

The yield of a debt instrument is the annualized percentage increase in the value of the investment.

   a. 7-Eleven
   b. 4-4-5 Calendar
   c. 529 plan
   d. Yield curve

36. The _____ is that part of the capital markets that deals with the issuance of new securities. Companies, governments or public sector institutions can obtain funding through the sale of a new stock or bond issue. This is typically done through a syndicate of securities dealers.
   a. Peer group analysis
   b. Sector rotation
   c. Volatility clustering
   d. Primary market

37. The _____ is the financial market where previously issued securities and financial instruments such as stock, bonds, options, and futures are bought and sold. The term '_____' is also used refer to the market for any used goods or assets, or an alternative use for an existing product or asset where the customer base is the second market

With primary issuances of securities or financial instruments, or the primary market, investors purchase these securities directly from issuers such as corporations issuing shares in an IPO or private placement, or directly from the federal government in the case of treasuries.

   a. Financial market
   b. Performance attribution
   c. Delta neutral
   d. Secondary market

38. The _____, makes rules regulating broker-dealers and banks that deal in municipal bonds, municipal notes, and other municipal securities in the United States. In addition, the _____ operates the Electronic Municipal Market Access system (http://emma.msrb.org), which provides free on-line access to comprehensive municipal securities disclosure documents and trade price information.

Chapter 11. Municipal Bonds

The _____ was established in 1975 by the U.S. Congress to develop rules regulating security firms and banks involved in underwriting, trading, and selling municipal securities -- bonds, notes and other securities issued by states, cities, and counties or their agencies to help finance public projects or for other public policy purposes.

a. Gamelan Council
b. World Trade Organization
c. Public Company Accounting Oversight Board
d. Municipal Securities Rulemaking Board

39. Congress enacted the _____, in the aftermath of the stock market crash of 1929 and during the ensuing Great Depression. It requires that any offer or sale of securities using the means and instrumentalities of interstate commerce be registered pursuant to the 1933 Act, unless an exemption from registration exists under the law.
a. 529 plan
b. 7-Eleven
c. 4-4-5 Calendar
d. Securities Act of 1933

40. The _____ of 1934 is a law governing the secondary trading of securities (stocks, bonds, and debentures) in the United States of America. The Act, 48 Stat. 881 (enacted June 6, 1934), codified at 15 U.S.C. § 78a et seq., was a sweeping piece of legislation. The Act and related statutes form the basis of regulation of the financial markets and their participants in the United States.
a. 4-4-5 Calendar
b. 7-Eleven
c. 529 plan
d. Securities Exchange Act

41. The U.S. _____ is an independent agency of the United States government which holds primary responsibility for enforcing the federal securities laws and regulating the securities industry, the nation's stock and options exchanges, and other electronic securities markets. The SEC was created by section 4 of the SEC of 1934 (now codified as 15 U.S.C. § 78d and commonly referred to as the 1934 Act.)
a. 4-4-5 Calendar
b. Securities and Exchange Commission
c. 7-Eleven
d. 529 plan

42. In finance, a _____ (non-investment grade bond, speculative grade bond or junk bond) is a bond that is rated below investment grade at the time of purchase. These bonds have a higher risk of default or other adverse credit events, but typically pay higher yields than better quality bonds in order to make them attractive to investors.
a. Private equity
b. Volatility
c. Sharpe ratio
d. High yield bond

Chapter 12. Private Money Market Instruments

1. In the global money market, _____ is an unsecured promissory note with a fixed maturity of one to 270 days. _____ is a money-market security issued (sold) by large banks and corporations to get money to meet short term debt obligations (for example, payroll), and is only backed by an issuing bank or corporation's promise to pay the face amount on the maturity date specified on the note. Since it is not backed by collateral, only firms with excellent credit ratings from a recognized rating agency will be able to sell their _____ at a reasonable price.
   a. Financial distress
   b. Trade-off theory
   c. Book building
   d. Commercial paper

2. In finance, the _____ is the global financial market for short-term borrowing and lending. It provides short-term liquidity funding for the global financial system. The _____ is where short-term obligations such as Treasury bills, commercial paper and bankers' acceptances are bought and sold.
   a. Money market
   b. Debt-for-equity swap
   c. Cramdown
   d. Consumer debt

3. _____ is a measure of the ability of a debtor to pay their debts as and when they fall due. It is usually expressed as a ratio or a percentage of current liabilities.

   For a corporation with a published balance sheet there are various ratios used to calculate a measure of liquidity.
   a. Invested capital
   b. Accounting liquidity
   c. Operating profit margin
   d. Operating leverage

4. _____ is a life of security. It may also refer to the final payment date of a loan or other financial instrument, at which point all remaining interest and principal is due to be paid.

   1, 3, 6 months _____ band can be calculated by using 30-day per month periods.
   a. False billing
   b. Primary market
   c. Replacement cost
   d. Maturity

5. In business and accounting, _____s are everything of value that is owned by a person or company. The balance sheet of a firm records the monetary value of the _____s owned by the firm. The two major _____ classes are tangible _____s and intangible _____s.
   a. EBITDA
   b. Accounts payable
   c. Asset
   d. Income

6. _____ is a form of commercial paper that is collateralised by other financial assets. ABCPs are typically short-term investments that mature between 90 and 180 days and are typically issued by a bank or other financial institution. They are designed to be used for short-term financing needs.
   a. Asset-liability mismatch
   b. Earmark
   c. Amortizing loan
   d. Asset-backed Commercial paper

7. _____ is a legal entity that develops, registers and sells securities for the purpose of financing its operations. _____s may be domestic or foreign governments, corporations or investment trusts. _____s are legally responsible for the obligations of the issue and for reporting financial conditions, material developments and any other operational activities as required by the regulations of their jurisdictions.

Chapter 12. Private Money Market Instruments

a. Efficient-market hypothesis
b. Arbitrage
c. Issuer
d. Initial margin

8. The _____ of 1933 established the Federal Deposit Insurance Corporation (FDIC) in the United States and included banking reforms, some of which were designed to control speculation. Some provisions such as Regulation Q, which allowed the Federal Reserve to regulate interest rates in savings accounts, were repealed by the Depository Institutions Deregulation and Monetary Control Act of 1980. Provisions that prohibit a bank holding company from owning other financial companies were repealed on November 12, 1999, by the Gramm-Leach-Bliley Act.

a. Glass-Steagall Act
b. 529 plan
c. 4-4-5 Calendar
d. 7-Eleven

9. _____ mature in one year or less. Like zero-coupon bonds, they do not pay interest prior to maturity; instead they are sold at a discount of the par value to create a positive yield to maturity. Many regard _____ as the least risky investment available to U.S. investors.

a. Treasury Inflation Protected Securities
b. Treasury bills
c. 4-4-5 Calendar
d. Treasury securities

10. The _____ is the financial market where previously issued securities and financial instruments such as stock, bonds, options, and futures are bought and sold. The term '_____' is also used refer to the market for any used goods or assets, or an alternative use for an existing product or asset where the customer base is the second market

With primary issuances of securities or financial instruments, or the primary market, investors purchase these securities directly from issuers such as corporations issuing shares in an IPO or private placement, or directly from the federal government in the case of treasuries.

a. Secondary market
b. Financial market
c. Delta neutral
d. Performance attribution

11. In finance, the term _____ describes the amount in cash that returns to the owners of a security. Normally it does not include the price variations, at the difference of the total return. _____ applies to various stated rates of return on stocks (common and preferred, and convertible), fixed income instruments (bonds, notes, bills, strips, zero coupon), and some other investment type insurance products (e.g. annuities.)

a. Yield to maturity
b. Macaulay duration
c. 4-4-5 Calendar
d. Yield

12. A _____ or bank is a financial institution whose primary activity is to act as a payment agent for customers and to borrow and lend money.

The first modern bank was founded in Italy in Genoa in 1406, its name was Banco di San Giorgio (Bank of St. George.)

Many other financial activities were added over time.

a. 4-4-5 Calendar
b. Black Sea Trade and Development Bank
c. Bought deal
d. Banker

Chapter 12. Private Money Market Instruments

13. _____ or financing is to provide capital (funds), which means money for a project, a person, a business or any other private or public institutions.

Those funds can be allocated for either short term or long term purposes. The health fund is a new way of _____ private healthcare centers.

   a. Proxy fight
   c. Product life cycle
   b. Synthetic CDO
   d. Funding

14. _____ is the provision of resources (such as granting a loan) by one party to another party where that second party does not reimburse the first party immediately, thereby generating a debt, and instead arranges either to repay or return those resources (or material(s) of equal value) at a later date. The first party is called a creditor, also known as a lender, while the second party is called a debtor, also known as a borrower.

Movements of financial capital are normally dependent on either _____ or equity transfers.

   a. Warrant
   c. Clearing house
   b. Comparable
   d. Credit

15. _____ is the risk of loss due to a debtor's non-payment of a loan or other line of credit (either the principal or interest (coupon) or both)

Most lenders employ their own models (credit scorecards) to rank potential and existing customers according to risk, and then apply appropriate strategies. With products such as unsecured personal loans or mortgages, lenders charge a higher price for higher risk customers and vice versa. With revolving products such as credit cards and overdrafts, risk is controlled through careful setting of credit limits.

   a. Liquidity risk
   c. Market risk
   b. Transaction risk
   d. Credit risk

16. _____ are a type of structured asset-backed security (ABS) whose value and payments are derived from a portfolio of fixed-income underlying assets. _____s are assigned different risk classes, or tranches, whereby 'senior' tranches are considered the safest securities. Interest and principal payments are made in order of seniority, so that junior tranches offer higher coupon payments (and interest rates) or lower prices to compensate for additional default risk.

   a. Collateralized debt obligations
   c. Senior debt
   b. Municipal bond
   d. Zero coupon bond

17. _____s are deposits denominated in United States dollars at banks outside the United States, and thus are not under the jurisdiction of the Federal Reserve. Consequently, such deposits are subject to much less regulation than similar deposits within the United States, allowing for higher margins. There is nothing 'European' about _____ deposits; a US dollar-denominated deposit in Tokyo or Caracas would likewise be deemed _____ deposits.

   a. Eurodollar
   c. A Random Walk Down Wall Street
   b. AAB
   d. ABN Amro

18.

Chapter 12. Private Money Market Instruments

In finance, the _____ can be the expected rate of return above the risk-free interest rate. When measuring risk, a common sense approach is to compare the risk-free return on T-bills and the very risky return on other investments. The difference between these two returns can be interpreted as a measure of the excess return on the average risky asset. This excess return is known as the _____.

a. Risk adjusted return on capital
b. Risk aversion
c. Risk modeling
d. Risk premium

19. A _____ allows a borrower to use a financial security as collateral for a cash loan at a fixed rate of interest. In a repo, the borrower agrees to immediately sell a security to a lender and also agrees to buy the same security from the lender at a fixed price at some later date. A repo is equivalent to a cash transaction combined with a forward contract.

a. Volatility arbitrage
b. Total return swap
c. Contango
d. Repurchase agreement

20. The official bank rate has existing in various forms since 1694 and has ranged from 0.5% to 17%. The name of this key interest rate has changed over the years. The current name 'Official Bank Rate' was introduced in 2006 and replaced the previous title '_____' (repo is short for repurchase agreement) in 1997.

a. London Interbank Offered Rate
b. London Interbank Bid Rate
c. Cash accumulation equation
d. Repo rate

21. _____ is a fee paid on borrowed assets. It is the price paid for the use of borrowed money, or, money earned by deposited funds. Assets that are sometimes lent with _____ include money, shares, consumer goods through hire purchase, major assets such as aircraft, and even entire factories in finance lease arrangements.

a. AAB
b. A Random Walk Down Wall Street
c. Insolvency
d. Interest

22. An _____ is the price a borrower pays for the use of money they do not own, and the return a lender receives for deferring the use of funds, by lending it to the borrower. _____s are normally expressed as a percentage rate over the period of one year.

_____s targets are also a vital tool of monetary policy and are used to control variables like investment, inflation, and unemployment.

a. ABN Amro
b. AAB
c. A Random Walk Down Wall Street
d. Interest rate

23. In financial accounting, the term _____ is most commonly used to describe any part of shareholders' equity, except for basic share capital. Sometimes, the term is used instead of the term provision; such a use, however, is inconsistent with the terminology suggested by International Accounting Standards Board. For more information about provisions, see provision (accounting.)

a. Treasury stock
b. Reserve
c. FIFO and LIFO accounting
d. Closing entries

Chapter 12. Private Money Market Instruments

24. In lending agreements, _____ is a borrower's pledge of specific property to a lender, to secure repayment of a loan. The _____ serves as protection for a lender against a borrower's risk of default - that is, a borrower failing to pay the principal and interest under the terms of a loan obligation. If a borrower does default on a loan (due to insolvency or other event), that borrower forfeits (gives up) the property pledged as _____ ollateral - and the lender then becomes the owner of the _____.
   a. Nominal value
   b. Refinancing risk
   c. Collateral
   d. Future-oriented

25. In the United States, _____ are overnight borrowings by banks to maintain their bank reserves at the Federal Reserve. Banks keep reserves at Federal Reserve Banks to meet their reserve requirements and to clear financial transactions. Transactions in the _____ market enable depository institutions with reserve balances in excess of reserve requirements to lend reserves to institutions with reserve deficiencies.
   a. Federal funds rate
   b. Regulation T
   c. 4-4-5 Calendar
   d. Federal funds

26. A _____ is an exchange of promises between two or more parties to do an act which is enforceable in a court of law. It is where an unqualified offer meets a qualified acceptance and the parties reach Consensus ad Idem. The parties must have the necessary capacity to _____ and the _____ must not be either trifling, indeterminate, impossible or illegal.
   a. 4-4-5 Calendar
   b. 7-Eleven
   c. 529 plan
   d. Contract

27. In finance, a _____ is a standardized contract, to buy or sell a specified commodity of standardized quality at a certain date in the future, at a market determined price (the futures price.)

The price is determined by the instantaneous equilibrium between the forces of supply and demand among competing buy and sell orders on the exchange at the time of the purchase or sale of the contract.

In many cases, the items may be such non-traditional 'commodities' as foreign currencies, commercial or government paper [e.g., bonds], or 'baskets' of corporate equity ['stock indices'] or other financial instruments.

   a. Financial future
   b. Heston model
   c. Repurchase agreement
   d. Futures contract

Chapter 13. Corporate Bonds

1. In business and accounting, _____s are everything of value that is owned by a person or company. The balance sheet of a firm records the monetary value of the _____s owned by the firm. The two major _____ classes are tangible _____s and intangible _____s.

   a. Accounts payable
   c. EBITDA
   b. Income
   d. Asset

2. _____ refers to any type of investment that yields a regular (or fixed) return.

For example, if you lend money to a borrower and the borrower has to pay interest once a month, you have been issued a fixed-income security. When a company does this, it is often called a bond or corporate bank debt (although preferred stock is also sometimes considered to be _____).

   a. 4-4-5 Calendar
   c. 529 plan
   b. Bond market
   d. Fixed Income

3. _____, refers to consumption opportunity gained by an entity within a specified time frame, which is generally expressed in monetary terms. However, for households and individuals, '_____ is the sum of all the wages, salaries, profits, interests payments, rents and other forms of earnings received... in a given period of time.' For firms, _____ generally refers to net-profit: what remains of revenue after expenses have been subtracted.

   a. OIBDA
   c. Income
   b. Accrual
   d. Annual report

4. _____ is that which is owed; usually referencing assets owed, but the term can cover other obligations. In the case of assets, _____ is a means of using future purchasing power in the present before a summation has been earned. Some companies and corporations use _____ as a part of their overall corporate finance strategy.

   a. Credit cycle
   c. Partial Payment
   b. Debt
   d. Cross-collateralization

5. _____ is a legal entity that develops, registers and sells securities for the purpose of financing its operations. _____s may be domestic or foreign governments, corporations or investment trusts. _____s are legally responsible for the obligations of the issue and for reporting financial conditions, material developments and any other operational activities as required by the regulations of their jurisdictions.

   a. Issuer
   c. Efficient-market hypothesis
   b. Initial margin
   d. Arbitrage

6. _____ is a life of security. It may also refer to the final payment date of a loan or other financial instrument, at which point all remaining interest and principal is due to be paid.

1, 3, 6 months _____ band can be calculated by using 30-day per month periods.

   a. Replacement cost
   c. Maturity
   b. Primary market
   d. False billing

7. The coupon or _____ of a bond is the amount of interest paid per year expressed as a percentage of the face value of the bond.

Chapter 13. Corporate Bonds

For example if you hold $10,000 nominal of a bond described as a 4.5% loan stock, you will receive $450 in interest each year (probably in two installments of $225 each.)

Not all bonds have coupons.

- a. Puttable bond
- b. Zero-coupon bond
- c. Revenue bonds
- d. Coupon rate

8. In finance, a _____ is a debt security, in which the authorized issuer owes the holders a debt and, depending on the terms of the _____, is obliged to pay interest (the coupon) and/or to repay the principal at a later date, termed maturity.

Thus a _____ is a loan: the issuer is the borrower, the _____ holder is the lender, and the coupon is the interest. _____s provide the borrower with external funds to finance long-term investments, or, in the case of government _____s, to finance current expenditure.

- a. Catastrophe bonds
- b. Puttable bond
- c. Convertible bond
- d. Bond

9. _____ is a fee paid on borrowed assets. It is the price paid for the use of borrowed money, or, money earned by deposited funds. Assets that are sometimes lent with _____ include money, shares, consumer goods through hire purchase, major assets such as aircraft, and even entire factories in finance lease arrangements.
- a. AAB
- b. Interest
- c. A Random Walk Down Wall Street
- d. Insolvency

10. An _____ is a contract written by a seller that conveys to the buyer the right -- but not the obligation -- to buy (in the case of a call _____) or to sell (in the case of a put _____) a particular asset, such as a piece of property such as, among others, a futures contract. In return for granting the _____, the seller collects a payment (the premium) from the buyer.

For example, buying a call _____ provides the right to buy a specified quantity of a security at a set strike price at some time on or before expiration, while buying a put _____ provides the right to sell.

- a. Amortization
- b. Option
- c. AT'T Mobility LLC
- d. Annuity

11. In finance, the term _____ describes the amount in cash that returns to the owners of a security. Normally it does not include the price variations, at the difference of the total return. _____ applies to various stated rates of return on stocks (common and preferred, and convertible), fixed income instruments (bonds, notes, bills, strips, zero coupon), and some other investment type insurance products (e.g. annuities.)
- a. 4-4-5 Calendar
- b. Yield
- c. Macaulay duration
- d. Yield to maturity

Chapter 13. Corporate Bonds

12. A _____ is a bond bought at a price lower than its face value, with the face value repaid at the time of maturity. It does not make periodic interest payments, or have so-called 'coupons,' hence the term _____. Investors earn return from the compounded interest all paid at maturity plus the difference between the discounted price of the bond and its par value.
   a. Clean price
   b. Bond fund
   c. Corporate bond
   d. Zero-coupon bond

13. A '_____' is a 'Charge' that is paid to obtain the right to delay a payment. Essentially, the payer purchases the right to make a given payment in the future instead of in the Present. The '_____', or 'Charge' that must be paid to delay the payment, is simply the difference between what the payment amount would be if it were paid in the present and what the payment amount would be paid if it were paid in the future.
   a. Risk aversion
   b. Value at risk
   c. Risk modeling
   d. Discount

14. A _____ is a bond bought at a price lower than its face value, with the face value repaid at the time of maturity. It does not make periodic interest payments, or so-called 'coupons,' hence the term zero-coupon bond. Investors earn return from the compounded interest all paid at maturity plus the difference between the discounted price of the bond and its par value.
   a. Zero coupon bond
   b. Callable bond
   c. Municipal bond
   d. Bowie bonds

15. In law, a _____ is a form of security interest granted over an item of property to secure the payment of a debt or performance of some other obligation. The owner of the property, who grants the _____, is referred to as the lienor and the person who has the benefit of the _____ is referred to as the _____ee.

The etymological root is: Anglo-French _____, loyen bond, restraint, from Latin ligamen, from ligare to bind.

   a. Sarbanes-Oxley Act
   b. Family and Medical Leave Act
   c. Lien
   d. Joint venture

16. A _____ is defined as a certificate of agreement of loans which is given under the company's stamp and carries an undertaking that the _____ holder will get a fixed return (fixed on the basis of interest rates) and the principal amount whenever the _____ matures.

In finance, a _____ is a long-term debt instrument used by governments and large companies to obtain funds. It is defined as 'a debt secured only by the debtor's earning power, not by a lien on any specific asset.' It is similar to a bond except the securitization conditions are different.

   a. Partial Payment
   b. Collateral Management
   c. Debenture
   d. Collection agency

17. A _____ is a fungible, negotiable instrument representing financial value. They are broadly categorized into debt securities (such as banknotes, bonds and debentures), and equity securities; e.g., common stocks. The company or other entity issuing the _____ is called the issuer.

Chapter 13. Corporate Bonds

    a. Book entry   b. Securities lending
    c. Security   d. Tracking stock

18.   A _____ is a single mortgage that covers more than one parcel of real estate.
    a. Reverse mortgage   b. Commercial mortgage
    c. Construction loan   d. Blanket mortgage

19.   In lending agreements, _____ is a borrower's pledge of specific property to a lender, to secure repayment of a loan. The _____ serves as protection for a lender against a borrower's risk of default - that is, a borrower failing to pay the principal and interest under the terms of a loan obligation. If a borrower does default on a loan (due to insolvency or other event), that borrower forfeits (gives up) the property pledged as _____ *ollateral* - and the lender then becomes the owner of the _____.
    a. Collateral   b. Future-oriented
    c. Refinancing risk   d. Nominal value

20.   A _____ is a company that owns other companies' outstanding stock. It usually refers to a company which does not produce goods or services itself, rather its only purpose is owning shares of other companies. They allow the reduction of risk for the owners and can allow the ownership and control of a number of different companies.
    a. Federal National Mortgage Association   b. Privately held company
    c. Holding company   d. MRU Holdings

21.   _____ occurs when an entity that has issued callable bonds calls those debt securities from the debt holders with the express purpose of reissuing new debt at a lower coupon rate. In essence, the issue of new, lower-interest debt allows the company to prematurely refund the older, higher-interest debt.

On the contrary, NonRefundable Bonds may be callable but they cannot be re-issued with a lower coupon rate.

    a. No-arbitrage bounds   b. Refunding
    c. Systematic risk   d. Market neutral

22.   An _____ is a financial security used in aircraft finance, most commonly to take advantage of tax benefits in North America.

In a typical _____ transaction, a 'trust certificate' is sold to investors in order to finance the purchase of an aircraft by a trust managed on the investors' behalf. The trust then leases the aircraft to an airline, and the trustee routes payments through the trust to the investors.

    a. ABN Amro   b. Equipment trust certificate
    c. A Random Walk Down Wall Street   d. AAB

23.   In finance, a _____ is a type of bond that can be converted into shares of stock in the issuing company, usually at some pre-announced ratio. It is a hybrid security with debt- and equity-like features. Although it typically has a low coupon rate, the holder is compensated with the ability to convert the bond to common stock, usually at a substantial discount to the stock's market value.

Chapter 13. Corporate Bonds

a. Corporate bond
c. Convertible bond
b. Bond fund
d. Gilts

24. In financial accounting, _____s are precautions for which the amount or probability of occurrence are not known. Typical examples are _____s for warranty costs and _____ for taxes the term reserve is used instead of term _____; such a use, however, is inconsistent with the terminology suggested by International Accounting Standards Board.
   a. Momentum Accounting and Triple-Entry Bookkeeping
   c. Petty cash
   b. Money measurement concept
   d. Provision

25. A _____ is a fund established by a government agency or business for the purpose of reducing debt.

The _____ was first used in Great Britain in the 18th century to reduce national debt. While used by Robert Walpole in 1716 and effectively in the 1720s and early 1730s, it originated in the commercial tax syndicates of the Italian peninsula of the 14th century to retire redeemable public debt of those cities.

   a. Sinking fund
   c. Debtor
   b. Security interest
   d. Modern portfolio theory

26. _____ is a corporate finance term denoting a type of takeover bid. The _____ is a public, open offer or invitation (usually announced in a newspaper advertisement) by a prospective acquirer to all stockholders of a publicly traded corporation (the target corporation) to tender their stock for sale at a specified price during a specified time, subject to the tendering of a minimum and maximum number of shares. In a _____, the bidder contacts shareholders directly; the directors of the company may or may not have endorsed the _____ proposal.
   a. Follow-on offering
   c. Cash is king
   b. Tender offer
   d. Shareholder value

27. The institution most often referenced by the word '_____' is a public or publicly traded _____, the shares of which are traded on a public stock exchange (e.g., the New York Stock Exchange or Nasdaq in the United States) where shares of stock of _____s are bought and sold by and to the general public. Most of the largest businesses in the world are publicly traded _____s. However, the majority of _____s are said to be closely held, privately held or close _____s, meaning that no ready market exists for the trading of shares.
   a. Depository Trust Company
   c. Federal Home Loan Mortgage Corporation
   b. Corporation
   d. Protect

28. _____ is the provision of resources (such as granting a loan) by one party to another party where that second party does not reimburse the first party immediately, thereby generating a debt, and instead arranges either to repay or return those resources (or material(s) of equal value) at a later date. The first party is called a creditor, also known as a lender, while the second party is called a debtor, also known as a borrower.

Movements of financial capital are normally dependent on either _____ or equity transfers.

   a. Comparable
   c. Warrant
   b. Credit
   d. Clearing house

Chapter 13. Corporate Bonds

29. A _____ assesses the credit worthiness of an individual, corporation, or even a country. _____s are calculated from financial history and current assets and liabilities. Typically, a _____ tells a lender or investor the probability of the subject being able to pay back a loan.
   a. Credit report monitoring
   b. Credit rating
   c. Debenture
   d. Credit cycle

30. _____ is the risk of loss due to a debtor's non-payment of a loan or other line of credit (either the principal or interest (coupon) or both)

Most lenders employ their own models (credit scorecards) to rank potential and existing customers according to risk, and then apply appropriate strategies. With products such as unsecured personal loans or mortgages, lenders charge a higher price for higher risk customers and vice versa. With revolving products such as credit cards and overdrafts, risk is controlled through careful setting of credit limits.

   a. Liquidity risk
   b. Transaction risk
   c. Market risk
   d. Credit risk

31. A _____ is a bond issued by a corporation. The term is usually applied to longer-term debt instruments, generally with a maturity date falling at least a year after their issue date. (The term 'commercial paper' is sometimes used for instruments with a shorter maturity.)
   a. Brady bonds
   b. Serial bond
   c. Government bond
   d. Corporate bond

32. In finance, _____ occurs when a debtor has not met its legal obligations according to the debt contract, e.g. it has not made a scheduled payment, or has violated a loan covenant (condition) of the debt contract. _____ may occur if the debtor is either unwilling or unable to pay their debt. This can occur with all debt obligations including bonds, mortgages, loans, and promissory notes.
   a. Vendor finance
   b. Debt validation
   c. Credit crunch
   d. Default

33. In finance, a _____ (non-investment grade bond, speculative grade bond or junk bond) is a bond that is rated below investment grade at the time of purchase. These bonds have a higher risk of default or other adverse credit events, but typically pay higher yields than better quality bonds in order to make them attractive to investors.
   a. High yield bond
   b. Sharpe ratio
   c. Private equity
   d. Volatility

34. A _____ is the financial term used to describe either:

A general default event related to a legal entity's previously agreed financial obligation. In this case, a legal entity fails to meet its obligation on any significant financial transaction (coupon on a bond it issued or interest rate payment on a swap for example.) The marketplace will recognize this as an event related to the legal entity's credit worthiness.

   a. Death spiral financing
   b. Capital surplus
   c. Credit event
   d. No-arbitrage bounds

Chapter 13. Corporate Bonds

35. In business, _____ is the total assets minus total outside liabilities of an individual or a company. For a company, this is called shareholders' equity and may be referred to as book value. _____ is stated as at a particular point in time.
    a. Restructuring
    b. Moneylender
    c. Certified International Investment Analyst
    d. Net worth

36. _____ is a method of financing, used to maintain liquidity while waiting for an anticipated and reasonably expected inflow of cash. _____ is commonly used when the cash flow from a sale of an asset is expected after the cash outlay for the purchase of an asset. For example, when selling a house, the owner may not receive the cash for 90 days, but has already purchased a new home and must pay for it in 30 days.
    a. Real estate investing
    b. Tenancy
    c. Liquidation value
    d. Bridge financing

37. The term _____ is used to describe a nation's social, or business activity in the process of rapid industrialization. _____ are generally less-wealthy than the developed world, and are wealthier (or the wealthiest of) the developing world. According to The Economist many people find the term dated, but a new term has yet to gain much traction.
    a. A Random Walk Down Wall Street
    b. Emerging markets
    c. AAB
    d. ABN Amro

38. The value of speculative bonds is affected to a higher degree than investment grade bonds by the possibility of default. For example, in a recession interest rates may drop, and the drop in interest rates tends to increase the value of investment grade bonds; however, a recession tends to increase the possibility of default in speculative-grade bonds.

    The original speculative grade bonds were bonds that once had been investment grade at time of issue, but where the credit rating of the issuer had slipped and the possibility of default increased significantly. These bonds are called '_____'.

    a. Seed round
    b. Return on capital employed
    c. Sharpe ratio
    d. Fallen angels

39. A _____ occurs when a financial sponsor acquires a controlling interest in a company's equity and where a significant percentage of the purchase price is financed through leverage (borrowing.) The assets of the acquired company are used as collateral for the borrowed capital, sometimes with assets of the acquiring company. The bonds or other paper issued for _____s are commonly considered not to be investment grade because of the significant risks involved.
    a. Pension fund
    b. Limited partnership
    c. Leveraged buyout
    d. Leverage

40. _____ is the corporate management term for the act of reorganizing the legal, ownership, operational, or other structures of a company for the purpose of making it more profitable or better organized for its present needs. Alternate reasons for restructing include a change of ownership or ownership structure, demerger repositioning debt _____ and financial _____.
    a. Concentrated stock
    b. Day trading
    c. Cross-border leasing
    d. Restructuring

41. _____ or financing is to provide capital (funds), which means money for a project, a person, a business or any other private or public institutions.

Chapter 13. Corporate Bonds

Those funds can be allocated for either short term or long term purposes. The health fund is a new way of _____ private healthcare centers.

a. Product life cycle
c. Proxy fight
b. Funding
d. Synthetic CDO

42. _____, in accrual accounting, is any account where the asset or liability is not realized until a future date, e.g. annuities, charges, taxes, income, etc. The _____ item may be carried, dependent on type of deferral, as either an asset or liability. See also: accrual

_____ is also used in the university admissions process. It is the action by which a school rejects a student for early admission but still opts to review that student in the general admissions pool.

a. Revenue
c. Net profit
b. Deferred
d. Current asset

Chapter 14. Medium-Term Notes

1. In finance, a _____ is a debt security, in which the authorized issuer owes the holders a debt and, depending on the terms of the _____, is obliged to pay interest (the coupon) and/or to repay the principal at a later date, termed maturity.

Thus a _____ is a loan: the issuer is the borrower, the _____ holder is the lender, and the coupon is the interest. _____s provide the borrower with external funds to finance long-term investments, or, in the case of government _____s, to finance current expenditure.

   a. Convertible bond
   c. Puttable bond
   b. Bond
   d. Catastrophe bonds

2. A _____ is a bond issued by a corporation. The term is usually applied to longer-term debt instruments, generally with a maturity date falling at least a year after their issue date. (The term 'commercial paper' is sometimes used for instruments with a shorter maturity.)
   a. Serial bond
   c. Government bond
   b. Brady bonds
   d. Corporate bond

3. _____ is a measure of the ability of a debtor to pay their debts as and when they fall due. It is usually expressed as a ratio or a percentage of current liabilities.

For a corporation with a published balance sheet there are various ratios used to calculate a measure of liquidity.

   a. Operating profit margin
   c. Invested capital
   b. Operating leverage
   d. Accounting liquidity

4. _____ exists when sales of identical goods or services are transacted at different prices from the same provider. In a theoretical market with perfect information, no transaction costs or prohibition on secondary exchange (or re-selling) to prevent arbitrage, _____ can only be a feature of monopoly and oligopoly markets, where market power can be exercised. Otherwise, the moment the seller tries to sell the same good at different prices, the buyer at the lower price can arbitrage by selling to the consumer buying at the higher price but with a tiny discount.
   a. Transfer pricing
   c. Price index
   b. Discounts and allowances
   d. Price discrimination

Chapter 15. Inflation-Linked Bonds

1. In economics, _____ is a rise in the general level of prices of goods and services in an economy over a period of time. The term '_____' once referred to increases in the money supply (monetary _____); however, economic debates about the relationship between money supply and price levels have led to its primary use today in describing price _____. _____ can also be described as a decline in the real value of money--a loss of purchasing power in the medium of exchange which is also the monetary unit of account.
   - a. AAB
   - b. A Random Walk Down Wall Street
   - c. ABN Amro
   - d. Inflation

2. A _____ is a fungible, negotiable instrument representing financial value. They are broadly categorized into debt securities (such as banknotes, bonds and debentures), and equity securities; e.g., common stocks. The company or other entity issuing the _____ is called the issuer.
   - a. Security
   - b. Book entry
   - c. Securities lending
   - d. Tracking stock

3. _____ are the inflation-indexed bonds issued by the U.S. Treasury. The principal is adjusted to the Consumer Price Index, the commonly used measure of inflation. The coupon rate is constant, but generates a different amount of interest when multiplied by the inflation-adjusted principal, thus protecting the holder against inflation. _____ are currently offered in 5-year, 10-year and 20-year maturities.
   - a. 4-4-5 Calendar
   - b. Treasury Inflation Protected Securities
   - c. Treasury Inflation-Protected Securities
   - d. Treasury securities

4. _____ is the balance of the amounts of cash being received and paid by a business during a defined period of time, sometimes tied to a specific project. Measurement of _____ can be used

   - to evaluate the state or performance of a business or project.
   - to determine problems with liquidity. Being profitable does not necessarily mean being liquid. A company can fail because of a shortage of cash, even while profitable.
   - to generate project rate of returns. The time of _____s into and out of projects are used as inputs to financial models such as internal rate of return, and net present value.
   - to examine income or growth of a business when it is believed that accrual accounting concepts do not represent economic realities. Alternately, _____ can be used to 'validate' the net income generated by accrual accounting.

   _____ as a generic term may be used differently depending on context, and certain _____ definitions may be adapted by analysts and users for their own uses. Common terms include operating _____ and free _____.

   _____s can be classified into:

   1. Operational _____s: Cash received or expended as a result of the company's core business activities.
   2. Investment _____s: Cash received or expended through capital expenditure, investments or acquisitions.
   3. Financing _____s: Cash received or expended as a result of financial activities, such as interests and dividends.

All three together - the net _____ - are necessary to reconcile the beginning cash balance to the ending cash balance. Loan draw downs or equity injections, that is just shifting of capital but no expenditure as such, are not considered in the net _____.

Chapter 15. Inflation-Linked Bonds

a. Real option
b. Shareholder value
c. Cash flow
d. Corporate finance

5. In finance, the term _____ describes the amount in cash that returns to the owners of a security. Normally it does not include the price variations, at the difference of the total return. _____ applies to various stated rates of return on stocks (common and preferred, and convertible), fixed income instruments (bonds, notes, bills, strips, zero coupon), and some other investment type insurance products (e.g. annuities.)

a. Macaulay duration
b. Yield to maturity
c. 4-4-5 Calendar
d. Yield

6. A _____ is a measure of the average price of consumer goods and services purchased by households. The _____ can be used to index (i.e., adjust for the effects of inflation) wages, salaries, pensions, or regulated or contracted prices. The _____ is, along with the population census and the National Income and Product Accounts, one of the most closely watched national economic statistics.

a. 529 plan
b. Consumer Price Index
c. 4-4-5 Calendar
d. Divisia index

7. A _____ is a normalized average (typically a weighted average) of prices for a given class of goods or services in a given region, during a given interval of time. It is a statistic designed to help to compare how these prices, taken as a whole, differ between time periods or geographical locations.

a. Price Index
b. Discounts and allowances
c. Price discrimination
d. Transfer pricing

8. _____ is a technique to adjust income payments by means of a price index, in order to maintain the purchasing power of the public after inflation.

Applying a cost-of-living escalation COLA clause to a stream of periodic payments protects the real value of those payments and effectively transfers the risk of inflation from the payee to the payor, who must pay more each year to reflect the increases in prices. Thus, inflation _____ is often applied to pension payments, rents and other situations which are not subject to regular re-pricing in the market.

a. ABN Amro
b. A Random Walk Down Wall Street
c. AAB
d. Indexation

9. In economics and business, specifically cost accounting, the _____ is the point at which cost or expenses and revenue are equal: there is no net loss or gain, and one has 'broken even'. A profit or a loss has not been made, although opportunity costs have been paid, and capital has received the risk-adjusted, expected return.

For example, if the business sells less than 200 tables each month, it will make a loss, if it sells more, it will be a profit.

a. Fixed asset turnover
b. Break-even point
c. Market microstructure
d. Defined contribution plan

10. _____ is the coupon rate of a fixed income security, which is a fixed percentage of the par value. Unlike current yield, it does not vary with the market price of the security. .

Chapter 15. Inflation-Linked Bonds

a. Bond valuation
b. Bond fund
c. Zero-coupon bond
d. Nominal yield

11. In finance, the _____ of a financial asset measures the sensitivity of the asset's price to interest rate movements, expressed as a number of years. The reason for expressing this sensitivity in years is that the time that will elapse until a cash flow is received allows more interest to accumulate. Therefore the price of an asset with long term cashflows has more interest rate sensitivity than an asset with cashflows in the near future.
 a. 4-4-5 Calendar
 b. Macaulay duration
 c. Duration
 d. Yield to maturity

12. _____ most frequently refers to the standard deviation of the continuously compounded returns of a financial instrument with a specific time horizon. It is often used to quantify the risk of the instrument over that time period. _____ is typically expressed in annualized terms, and it may either be an absolute number ($5) or a fraction of the mean (5%).
 a. Currency swap
 b. Portfolio insurance
 c. Seasoned equity offering
 d. Volatility

13. _____ is a measure of the ability of a debtor to pay their debts as and when they fall due. It is usually expressed as a ratio or a percentage of current liabilities.

For a corporation with a published balance sheet there are various ratios used to calculate a measure of liquidity.

 a. Accounting liquidity
 b. Operating leverage
 c. Invested capital
 d. Operating profit margin

14. _____ is a business, economics or investment term that refers to an asset's ability to be easily converted through an act of buying or selling without causing a significant movement in the price and with minimum loss of value. Money, or cash on hand, is the most liquid asset. An act of exchange of a less liquid asset with a more liquid asset is called liquidation.
 a. 7-Eleven
 b. 529 plan
 c. 4-4-5 Calendar
 d. Market liquidity

15. In economics, the _____ is a monetary-policy rule that stipulates how much the central bank should change the nominal interest rate in response to divergences of actual GDP from potential GDP and of actual inflation rates from target inflation rates. It was first proposed by the by U.S. economist John B. Taylor in 1993. The rule can be written as follows:

$\square$ >

In this equation, $\square$ > is the target short-term nominal interest rate (e.g. the federal funds rate in the US), $\square$ > is the rate of inflation as measured by the GDP deflator, $\square$ > is the desired rate of inflation, $\square$ > is the assumed equilibrium real interest rate, $\square$ > is the logarithm of real GDP, and $\square$ > is the logarithm of potential output, as determined by a linear trend.

Chapter 15. Inflation-Linked Bonds

a. Regulation T
b. Taylor rule
c. 4-4-5 Calendar
d. Federal funds rate

16. In finance, _____ is the process of estimating the potential market value of a financial asset or liability. they can be done on assets (for example, investments in marketable securities such as stocks, options, business enterprises, or intangible assets such as patents and trademarks) or on liabilities (e.g., Bonds issued by a company.) _____s are required in many contexts including investment analysis, capital budgeting, merger and acquisition transactions, financial reporting, taxable events to determine the proper tax liability, and in litigation.
  a. Margin
  b. Valuation
  c. Share
  d. Procter ' Gamble

17. _____ are bonds where the principal is indexed to inflation. They are thus designed to cut out the inflation risk of an investment. _____ pay a periodic coupon that is equal to the product of the inflation index and the nominal coupon rate. The relationship between coupon payments, breakeven inflation and real interest rates is given by the Fisher equation.
  a. AAB
  b. A Random Walk Down Wall Street
  c. ABN Amro
  d. Inflation-indexed bonds

18. In finance, a _____ is a debt security, in which the authorized issuer owes the holders a debt and, depending on the terms of the _____, is obliged to pay interest (the coupon) and/or to repay the principal at a later date, termed maturity.

Thus a _____ is a loan: the issuer is the borrower, the _____ holder is the lender, and the coupon is the interest. _____s provide the borrower with external funds to finance long-term investments, or, in the case of government _____s, to finance current expenditure.

  a. Catastrophe bonds
  b. Bond
  c. Convertible bond
  d. Puttable bond

19. _____ is a legal entity that develops, registers and sells securities for the purpose of financing its operations. _____s may be domestic or foreign governments, corporations or investment trusts. _____s are legally responsible for the obligations of the issue and for reporting financial conditions, material developments and any other operational activities as required by the regulations of their jurisdictions.
  a. Arbitrage
  b. Initial margin
  c. Issuer
  d. Efficient-market hypothesis

20. _____ is that which is owed; usually referencing assets owed, but the term can cover other obligations. In the case of assets, _____ is a means of using future purchasing power in the present before a summation has been earned. Some companies and corporations use _____ as a part of their overall corporate finance strategy.
  a. Credit cycle
  b. Partial Payment
  c. Cross-collateralization
  d. Debt

21. _____ in economics is a persistent decrease in the general price level of goods and services - a negative inflation rate. When the inflation rate slows down (decreases, but remains positive), this is known as disinflation.

Inflation destroys real value in money.

a. Deflation
b. Recession
c. Mercantilism
d. Fixed exchange rate

Chapter 16. Floating-Rate Securities

1. The coupon or _____ of a bond is the amount of interest paid per year expressed as a percentage of the face value of the bond.

For example if you hold $10,000 nominal of a bond described as a 4.5% loan stock, you will receive $450 in interest each year (probably in two installments of $225 each.)

Not all bonds have coupons.

   a. Coupon rate
   b. Revenue bonds
   c. Puttable bond
   d. Zero-coupon bond

2. A _____ is a fungible, negotiable instrument representing financial value. They are broadly categorized into debt securities (such as banknotes, bonds and debentures), and equity securities; e.g., common stocks. The company or other entity issuing the _____ is called the issuer.
   a. Securities lending
   b. Tracking stock
   c. Book entry
   d. Security

3. _____ is the amount by which a reference rate is multiplied to determine the floating interest rate payable by an inverse floater. Some debt instruments leverage the particular effects of interest rate changes, most commonly in inverse floaters.

As an example, an inverse floater with a multiple may pay interest at the rate of 22 percent minus the product of 2 times the 1-month London Interbank Offered Rate (LIBOR.)

   a. Trade date
   b. Systematic risk
   c. Gross spread
   d. Coupon leverage

4. An _____ is a type of bond or other type of debt instrument used in finance whose coupon rate has an inverse relationship to short-term interest rates (or its reference rate.) With an _____, as interest rates rise the coupon rate falls. The basic structure is the same as an ordinary floating rate note except for the direction in which the coupon rate is adjusted.
   a. A Random Walk Down Wall Street
   b. Inverse floater
   c. AAB
   d. ABN Amro

5. _____ are bonds that have a variable coupon, equal to a money market reference rate, like LIBOR or federal funds rate, plus a spread. The spread is a rate that remains constant. Almost all _____ have quarterly coupons, i.e. they pay out interest every three months, though counter examples do exist.
   a. CVECAs
   b. Loan participation
   c. Gordon growth model
   d. Floating rate notes

6. In finance, _____ (or gearing) is borrowing money to supplement existing funds for investment in such a way that the potential positive or negative outcome is magnified and/or enhanced. It generally refers to using borrowed funds, or debt, so as to attempt to increase the returns to equity. Deleveraging is the action of reducing borrowings.
   a. Limited partnership
   b. Pension fund
   c. Financial endowment
   d. Leverage

Chapter 16. Floating-Rate Securities

7. An _____ is a contract written by a seller that conveys to the buyer the right -- but not the obligation -- to buy (in the case of a call _____) or to sell (in the case of a put _____) a particular asset, such as a piece of property such as, among others, a futures contract. In return for granting the _____, the seller collects a payment (the premium) from the buyer.

For example, buying a call _____ provides the right to buy a specified quantity of a security at a set strike price at some time on or before expiration, while buying a put _____ provides the right to sell.

a. AT'T Mobility LLC
c. Annuity

b. Amortization
d. Option

8. _____ is early repayment of a loan by a borrower.

In the case of a mortgage-backed security (MBS), _____ is perceived as a risk, because mortgage debts are often paid off early in order to incur lower total interest payments through cheaper refinancing. The new financing may be cheaper because the borrower's credit rating has improved or because interest rates are lower, but in either case, the payments that would have been made to the MBS investor would be above market rates.

a. Bankruptcy remote
c. Retention ratio

b. Prepayment
d. Disposal tax effect

9. In finance, a _____ is collateral that the holder of a position in securities, options, or futures contracts has to deposit to cover the credit risk of his counterparty (most often his broker.) This risk can arise if the holder has done any of the following:

- borrowed cash from the counterparty to buy securities or options,
- sold securities or options short, or
- entered into a futures contract.

The collateral can be in the form of cash or securities, and it is deposited in a _____ account. On U.S. futures exchanges, '_____' was formally called performance bond.

_____ buying is buying securities with cash borrowed from a broker, using other securities as collateral.

a. Share
c. Procter ' Gamble

b. Margin
d. Credit

10. In financial accounting, _____s are precautions for which the amount or probability of occurrence are not known. Typical examples are _____s for warranty costs and _____ for taxes the term reserve is used instead of term _____; such a use, however, is inconsistent with the terminology suggested by International Accounting Standards Board.

a. Money measurement concept
c. Provision

b. Momentum Accounting and Triple-Entry Bookkeeping
d. Petty cash

Chapter 16. Floating-Rate Securities

11. A '_____' is a 'Charge' that is paid to obtain the right to delay a payment. Essentially, the payer purchases the right to make a given payment in the future instead of in the Present. The '_____', or 'Charge' that must be paid to delay the payment, is simply the difference between what the payment amount would be if it were paid in the present and what the payment amount would be paid if it were paid in the future.
    a. Risk modeling
    b. Discount
    c. Risk aversion
    d. Value at risk

12. _____ most frequently refers to the standard deviation of the continuously compounded returns of a financial instrument with a specific time horizon. It is often used to quantify the risk of the instrument over that time period. _____ is typically expressed in annualized terms, and it may either be an absolute number ($5) or a fraction of the mean (5%).
    a. Portfolio insurance
    b. Seasoned equity offering
    c. Currency swap
    d. Volatility

13. In finance, the _____ of a financial asset measures the sensitivity of the asset's price to interest rate movements, expressed as a number of years. The reason for expressing this sensitivity in years is that the time that will elapse until a cash flow is received allows more interest to accumulate. Therefore the price of an asset with long term cashflows has more interest rate sensitivity than an asset with cashflows in the near future.
    a. Yield to maturity
    b. Macaulay duration
    c. Duration
    d. 4-4-5 Calendar

Chapter 17. Nonconvertible Preferred Stock

1. _____ is typically a higher ranking stock than voting shares, and its terms are negotiated between the corporation and the investor.

_____ usually carry no voting rights, but may carry superior priority over common stock in the payment of dividends and upon liquidation. _____ may carry a dividend that is paid out prior to any dividends to common stock holders.

   a. Follow-on offering
   c. Second lien loan

   b. Trade-off theory
   d. Preferred stock

2. A _____ is a payment made by a corporation to its shareholder members. When a corporation earns a profit or surplus, that money can be put to two uses: it can either be re-invested in the business (called retained earnings), or it can be paid to the shareholders as a _____. Many corporations retain a portion of their earnings and pay the remainder as a _____.

   a. Special dividend
   c. Dividend puzzle

   b. Dividend yield
   d. Dividend

Chapter 18. International Bond Markets and Instruments

1. In finance, a _____ is a debt security, in which the authorized issuer owes the holders a debt and, depending on the terms of the _____, is obliged to pay interest (the coupon) and/or to repay the principal at a later date, termed maturity.

   Thus a _____ is a loan: the issuer is the borrower, the _____ holder is the lender, and the coupon is the interest. _____s provide the borrower with external funds to finance long-term investments, or, in the case of government _____s, to finance current expenditure.

   a. Puttable bond
   b. Convertible bond
   c. Catastrophe bonds
   d. Bond

2. _____ is that which is owed; usually referencing assets owed, but the term can cover other obligations. In the case of assets, _____ is a means of using future purchasing power in the present before a summation has been earned. Some companies and corporations use _____ as a part of their overall corporate finance strategy.

   a. Cross-collateralization
   b. Credit cycle
   c. Debt
   d. Partial Payment

3. In finance, _____, also known as return on investment is the ratio of money gained or lost on an investment relative to the amount of money invested. The amount of money gained or lost may be referred to as interest, profit/loss, gain/loss, or net income/loss. The money invested may be referred to as the asset, capital, principal, or the cost basis of the investment.

   a. Composiition of Creditors
   b. Stock or scrip dividends
   c. Rate of return
   d. Doctrine of the Proper Law

4. _____s are deposits denominated in United States dollars at banks outside the United States, and thus are not under the jurisdiction of the Federal Reserve. Consequently, such deposits are subject to much less regulation than similar deposits within the United States, allowing for higher margins. There is nothing 'European' about _____ deposits; a US dollar-denominated deposit in Tokyo or Caracas would likewise be deemed _____ deposits.

   a. ABN Amro
   b. AAB
   c. A Random Walk Down Wall Street
   d. Eurodollar

5. The _____ of 1933 established the Federal Deposit Insurance Corporation (FDIC) in the United States and included banking reforms, some of which were designed to control speculation. Some provisions such as Regulation Q, which allowed the Federal Reserve to regulate interest rates in savings accounts, were repealed by the Depository Institutions Deregulation and Monetary Control Act of 1980. Provisions that prohibit a bank holding company from owning other financial companies were repealed on November 12, 1999, by the Gramm-Leach-Bliley Act.

   a. 4-4-5 Calendar
   b. 529 plan
   c. 7-Eleven
   d. Glass-Steagall Act

6. _____ is a fee paid on borrowed assets. It is the price paid for the use of borrowed money , or, money earned by deposited funds . Assets that are sometimes lent with _____ include money, shares, consumer goods through hire purchase, major assets such as aircraft, and even entire factories in finance lease arrangements.

   a. Interest
   b. AAB
   c. Insolvency
   d. A Random Walk Down Wall Street

7. An _____ is the price a borrower pays for the use of money they do not own, and the return a lender receives for deferring the use of funds, by lending it to the borrower. _____s are normally expressed as a percentage rate over the period of one year.

Chapter 18. International Bond Markets and Instruments

_____s targets are also a vital tool of monetary policy and are used to control variables like investment, inflation, and unemployment.

a. AAB
b. ABN Amro
c. A Random Walk Down Wall Street
d. Interest rate

8. _____, adopted pursuant to the U.S. Securities Act of 1933, as amended (the 'Securities Act') provides a safe harbor from the registration requirements of the Securities Act of 1933 for certain private resales of restricted securities to QIBs (qualified institutional buyers), which generally are large institutional investors with over $100 million in investable assets. When a broker or dealer is selling securities in reliance on _____, it is subject to the condition that it may not make offers to persons other than those it reasonably believes to be QIBs.

Since its adoption, _____ has greatly increased the liquidity of the securities affected.

a. SIPC
b. Prudent man rule
c. Securities Investor Protection Corporation
d. Rule 144A

9. A _____ is a bond issued by a corporation. The term is usually applied to longer-term debt instruments, generally with a maturity date falling at least a year after their issue date. (The term 'commercial paper' is sometimes used for instruments with a shorter maturity.)

a. Corporate bond
b. Government bond
c. Brady bonds
d. Serial bond

10. _____ are dollar-denominated bonds, issued mostly by Latin American countries in the 1980s, named after U.S. Treasury Secretary Nicholas Brady.

_____ were created in March 1989 in order to convert bonds issued by mostly Latin American countries into a variety or 'menu' of new bonds after many of those countries defaulted on their debt in the 1980's. At that time, the market for sovereign debt was small and illiquid, and the standardization of emerging-market debt facilitated risk-spreading and trading.

a. Nominal yield
b. Coupon rate
c. Municipal bond
d. Brady bonds

11. The term _____ is used to describe a nation's social, or business activity in the process of rapid industrialization. _____ are generally less-wealthy than the developed world, and are wealthier (or the wealthiest of) the developing world. According to The Economist many people find the term dated, but a new term has yet to gain much traction.

a. ABN Amro
b. A Random Walk Down Wall Street
c. AAB
d. Emerging markets

12. A _____ is an international bond that is denominated in a currency not native to the country where it is issued. It can be categorised according to the currency in which it is issued. London is one of the centers of the _____ market, but _____s may be traded throughout the world - for example in Singapore or Tokyo.

Chapter 18. International Bond Markets and Instruments

a. Education production function
b. Eurobond
c. Economic entity
d. Interest rate option

13. In finance, the term _____ describes the amount in cash that returns to the owners of a security. Normally it does not include the price variations, at the difference of the total return. _____ applies to various stated rates of return on stocks (common and preferred, and convertible), fixed income instruments (bonds, notes, bills, strips, zero coupon), and some other investment type insurance products (e.g. annuities.)

a. 4-4-5 Calendar
b. Macaulay duration
c. Yield to maturity
d. Yield

14. In finance, the _____ between two currencies specifies how much one currency is worth in terms of the other. For example an _____ of 102 Japanese yen to the United States dollar means that JPY 102 is worth the same as USD 1. The foreign exchange market is one of the largest markets in the world.

a. A Random Walk Down Wall Street
b. ABN Amro
c. Exchange rate
d. AAB

Chapter 19. The Eurobond Market

1. A _____ is an international bond that is denominated in a currency not native to the country where it is issued. It can be categorised according to the currency in which it is issued. London is one of the centers of the _____ market, but _____s may be traded throughout the world - for example in Singapore or Tokyo.
   - a. Education production function
   - b. Economic entity
   - c. Interest rate option
   - d. Eurobond

2. _____ is a United States government regulation that put a limit on the interest rates that banks could pay, including a rate of zero on demand deposits (checking accounts.) Section 11 of the Banking Act of 1933 (12 U.S.C. 371a) prohibits member banks from paying interest on demand deposits, which is implemented by _____
   - a. Fair Credit Billing Act
   - b. Truth in Lending Act
   - c. Fair Credit Reporting Act
   - d. Regulation Q

3. In business and accounting, _____s are everything of value that is owned by a person or company. The balance sheet of a firm records the monetary value of the _____s owned by the firm. The two major _____ classes are tangible _____s and intangible _____s.
   - a. Accounts payable
   - b. Asset
   - c. Income
   - d. EBITDA

4. In finance, a _____ is the party in a loan agreement which receives money or other instrument from a lender and promises to repay the lender in a specified time.
   - a. Cash credit
   - b. Borrower
   - c. Line of credit
   - d. Debt management plan

5. In finance, the term _____ describes the amount in cash that returns to the owners of a security. Normally it does not include the price variations, at the difference of the total return. _____ applies to various stated rates of return on stocks (common and preferred, and convertible), fixed income instruments (bonds, notes, bills, strips, zero coupon), and some other investment type insurance products (e.g. annuities.)
   - a. Yield to maturity
   - b. 4-4-5 Calendar
   - c. Macaulay duration
   - d. Yield

6. In finance, a _____ (non-investment grade bond, speculative grade bond or junk bond) is a bond that is rated below investment grade at the time of purchase. These bonds have a higher risk of default or other adverse credit events, but typically pay higher yields than better quality bonds in order to make them attractive to investors.
   - a. Sharpe ratio
   - b. Private equity
   - c. High yield bond
   - d. Volatility

7. In finance, a _____ is a debt security, in which the authorized issuer owes the holders a debt and, depending on the terms of the _____, is obliged to pay interest (the coupon) and/or to repay the principal at a later date, termed maturity.

   Thus a _____ is a loan: the issuer is the borrower, the _____ holder is the lender, and the coupon is the interest. _____s provide the borrower with external funds to finance long-term investments, or, in the case of government _____s, to finance current expenditure.

   - a. Puttable bond
   - b. Catastrophe bonds
   - c. Convertible bond
   - d. Bond

Chapter 19. The Eurobond Market

8. The _____ is a financial market where participants buy and sell debt securities, usually in the form of bonds. As of 2006, the size of the international _____ is an estimated $45 trillion, of which the size of the outstanding U.S. _____ debt was $25.2 trillion.

Nearly all of the $923 billion average daily trading volume in the U.S. _____ takes place between broker-dealers and large institutions in a decentralized, over-the-counter market.

   a. Fixed income
   c. Bond market
   b. 4-4-5 Calendar
   d. 529 plan

9. _____ are a type of structured asset-backed security (ABS) whose value and payments are derived from a portfolio of fixed-income underlying assets. _____s are assigned different risk classes, or tranches, whereby 'senior' tranches are considered the safest securities. Interest and principal payments are made in order of seniority, so that junior tranches offer higher coupon payments (and interest rates) or lower prices to compensate for additional default risk.

   a. Zero coupon bond
   c. Municipal bond
   b. Collateralized debt obligations
   d. Senior debt

10. _____ is that which is owed; usually referencing assets owed, but the term can cover other obligations. In the case of assets, _____ is a means of using future purchasing power in the present before a summation has been earned. Some companies and corporations use _____ as a part of their overall corporate finance strategy.

   a. Cross-collateralization
   c. Partial Payment
   b. Credit cycle
   d. Debt

11. _____ is a measure of the ability of a debtor to pay their debts as and when they fall due. It is usually expressed as a ratio or a percentage of current liabilities.

For a corporation with a published balance sheet there are various ratios used to calculate a measure of liquidity.

   a. Invested capital
   c. Accounting liquidity
   b. Operating leverage
   d. Operating profit margin

12. _____ is a business, economics or investment term that refers to an asset's ability to be easily converted through an act of buying or selling without causing a significant movement in the price and with minimum loss of value. Money, or cash on hand, is the most liquid asset. An act of exchange of a less liquid asset with a more liquid asset is called liquidation.

   a. 4-4-5 Calendar
   c. 529 plan
   b. 7-Eleven
   d. Market liquidity

13. _____ is the provision of resources (such as granting a loan) by one party to another party where that second party does not reimburse the first party immediately, thereby generating a debt, and instead arranges either to repay or return those resources (or material(s) of equal value) at a later date. The first party is called a creditor, also known as a lender, while the second party is called a debtor, also known as a borrower.

Movements of financial capital are normally dependent on either _____ or equity transfers.

Chapter 19. The Eurobond Market

a. Clearing house
b. Comparable
c. Warrant
d. Credit

14. A _____ is a credit derivative contract between two counterparties. The buyer makes periodic payments (premium leg) to the seller, and in return receives a payoff (protection or default leg) if an underlying financial instrument defaults. _____ contracts have been incorrectly compared with insurance, because the buyer pays a premium and, in return, receives a sum of money if a specified event occurs.

a. Stock market index future
b. Commodity tick
c. Futures contract
d. Credit default swap

15. A _____ is a collateralized debt obligation (CDO) in which the underlying credit exposures are taken on using a credit default swap rather than by having a vehicle buy physical assets. _____s can either be single tranche CDOs or fully distributed CDOs. _____s are also commonly divided into balance sheet and arbitrage CDOs, although it is often impossible to distinguish in practice between the two types.

a. Market capitalization
b. Planning horizon
c. Counting house
d. Synthetic CDO

16. In finance, _____ occurs when a debtor has not met its legal obligations according to the debt contract, e.g. it has not made a scheduled payment, or has violated a loan covenant (condition) of the debt contract. _____ may occur if the debtor is either unwilling or unable to pay their debt. This can occur with all debt obligations including bonds, mortgages, loans, and promissory notes.

a. Default
b. Vendor finance
c. Debt validation
d. Credit crunch

17. In finance, a _____ is a derivative in which two counterparties agree to exchange one stream of cash flows against another stream. These streams are called the legs of the _____.

The cash flows are calculated over a notional principal amount, which is usually not exchanged between counterparties.

a. Swap
b. Volatility arbitrage
c. Volatility swap
d. Local volatility

18. The _____ is that part of the capital markets that deals with the issuance of new securities. Companies, governments or public sector institutions can obtain funding through the sale of a new stock or bond issue. This is typically done through a syndicate of securities dealers.

a. Volatility clustering
b. Sector rotation
c. Peer group analysis
d. Primary market

19. A _____, in its most general sense, is a solemn promise to engage in or refrain from a specified action.

More specifically, a _____, in contrast to a contract, is a one-way agreement whereby the _____er is the only party bound by the promise. A _____ may have conditions and prerequisites that qualify the undertaking, including the actions of second or third parties, but there is no inherent agreement by such other parties to fulfill those requirements.

a. Federal Trade Commission Act
b. Partnership
c. Clayton Antitrust Act
d. Covenant

20. The _____ is applied in the choice of law stage of a lawsuit involving the Conflict of Laws.

In a Conflicts lawsuit, one or more state laws will be relevant to the decision-making process. If the laws are the same, this will cause no problems, but if there are substantive differences, the choice of which law to apply will produce a different judgment.

a. Voluntary Emissions Reductions
b. Doctrine of the Proper Law
c. Mitigating Control
d. Green Shoe

21. A _____ is a fungible, negotiable instrument representing financial value. They are broadly categorized into debt securities (such as banknotes, bonds and debentures), and equity securities; e.g., common stocks. The company or other entity issuing the _____ is called the issuer.

a. Tracking stock
b. Securities lending
c. Book entry
d. Security

22. _____s are deposits denominated in United States dollars at banks outside the United States, and thus are not under the jurisdiction of the Federal Reserve. Consequently, such deposits are subject to much less regulation than similar deposits within the United States, allowing for higher margins. There is nothing 'European' about _____ deposits; a US dollar-denominated deposit in Tokyo or Caracas would likewise be deemed _____ deposits.

a. AAB
b. Eurodollar
c. ABN Amro
d. A Random Walk Down Wall Street

23. _____ or financing is to provide capital (funds), which means money for a project, a person, a business or any other private or public institutions.

Those funds can be allocated for either short term or long term purposes. The health fund is a new way of _____ private healthcare centers.

a. Proxy fight
b. Funding
c. Product life cycle
d. Synthetic CDO

24. _____ is a legal entity that develops, registers and sells securities for the purpose of financing its operations. _____s may be domestic or foreign governments, corporations or investment trusts. _____s are legally responsible for the obligations of the issue and for reporting financial conditions, material developments and any other operational activities as required by the regulations of their jurisdictions.

a. Arbitrage
b. Initial margin
c. Efficient-market hypothesis
d. Issuer

Chapter 20. Emerging Markets Debt

1. The term _____ is used to describe a nation's social, or business activity in the process of rapid industrialization. _____ are generally less-wealthy than the developed world, and are wealthier (or the wealthiest of) the developing world. According to The Economist many people find the term dated, but a new term has yet to gain much traction.
   - a. AAB
   - b. A Random Walk Down Wall Street
   - c. ABN Amro
   - d. Emerging markets

2. In finance, a _____ is a debt security, in which the authorized issuer owes the holders a debt and, depending on the terms of the _____, is obliged to pay interest (the coupon) and/or to repay the principal at a later date, termed maturity.

   Thus a _____ is a loan: the issuer is the borrower, the _____ holder is the lender, and the coupon is the interest. _____s provide the borrower with external funds to finance long-term investments, or, in the case of government _____s, to finance current expenditure.
   - a. Convertible bond
   - b. Bond
   - c. Puttable bond
   - d. Catastrophe bonds

3. _____ is that which is owed; usually referencing assets owed, but the term can cover other obligations. In the case of assets, _____ is a means of using future purchasing power in the present before a summation has been earned. Some companies and corporations use _____ as a part of their overall corporate finance strategy.
   - a. Credit cycle
   - b. Debt
   - c. Partial Payment
   - d. Cross-collateralization

4. A _____ is an international bond that is denominated in a currency not native to the country where it is issued. It can be categorised according to the currency in which it is issued. London is one of the centers of the _____ market, but _____s may be traded throughout the world - for example in Singapore or Tokyo.
   - a. Eurobond
   - b. Interest rate option
   - c. Economic entity
   - d. Education production function

5. _____ is a legal entity that develops, registers and sells securities for the purpose of financing its operations. _____s may be domestic or foreign governments, corporations or investment trusts. _____s are legally responsible for the obligations of the issue and for reporting financial conditions, material developments and any other operational activities as required by the regulations of their jurisdictions.
   - a. Initial margin
   - b. Arbitrage
   - c. Efficient-market hypothesis
   - d. Issuer

6. _____ is the provision of resources (such as granting a loan) by one party to another party where that second party does not reimburse the first party immediately, thereby generating a debt, and instead arranges either to repay or return those resources (or material(s)) of equal value) at a later date. The first party is called a creditor, also known as a lender, while the second party is called a debtor, also known as a borrower.

   Movements of financial capital are normally dependent on either _____ or equity transfers.
   - a. Warrant
   - b. Credit
   - c. Comparable
   - d. Clearing house

Chapter 20. Emerging Markets Debt

7. _____ are dollar-denominated bonds, issued mostly by Latin American countries in the 1980s, named after U.S. Treasury Secretary Nicholas Brady.

_____ were created in March 1989 in order to convert bonds issued by mostly Latin American countries into a variety or 'menu' of new bonds after many of those countries defaulted on their debt in the 1980's. At that time, the market for sovereign debt was small and illiquid, and the standardization of emerging-market debt facilitated risk-spreading and trading.

a. Municipal bond
c. Nominal yield
b. Coupon rate
d. Brady bonds

8. The _____ is a measure of the excess return (or Risk Premium) per unit of risk in an investment asset or a trading strategy it is defined as:

$$S = \frac{R - R_f}{\sigma} = \frac{E[R - R_f]}{\sqrt{\text{var}[R - R_f]}},$$

where R is the asset return, R_f is the return on a benchmark asset, such as the risk free rate of return, $E[R - R_f]$ is the expected value of the excess of the asset return over the benchmark return, and σ is the standard deviation of the asset excess return.

Note, if R_f is a constant risk free return throughout the period,

$$\sqrt{\text{var}[R - R_f]} = \sqrt{\text{var}[R]}.$$

The _____ is used to characterize how well the return of an asset compensates the investor for the risk taken. When comparing two assets each with the expected return E[R] against the same benchmark with return R_f, the asset with the higher _____ gives more return for the same risk.

a. P/E ratio
c. Sharpe ratio
b. Current ratio
d. Receivables turnover ratio

9. _____ are government bonds issued by the United States Department of the Treasury through the Bureau of the Public Debt. They are the debt financing instruments of the U.S. Federal government, and they are often referred to simply as Treasuries or Treasurys. There are four types of marketable _____: Treasury bills, Treasury notes, Treasury bonds, and Treasury Inflation Protected Securities (TIPS.)

a. Treasury Inflation-Protected Securities
c. Treasury Inflation Protected Securities
b. 4-4-5 Calendar
d. Treasury securities

10. A _____ is a government debt issued by the United States Department of the Treasury through the Bureau of the Public Debt. They are the debt financing instruments of the United States Federal government, and they are often referred to simply as Treasuries. There are four types of marketable treasury securities: Treasury bills, Treasury notes, Treasury bonds, and Treasury Inflation Protected Securities (TIPS.)

Chapter 20. Emerging Markets Debt

a. International trade
c. United States Treasury security
b. OTC Bulletin Board
d. Insolvency

11. _____ most frequently refers to the standard deviation of the continuously compounded returns of a financial instrument with a specific time horizon. It is often used to quantify the risk of the instrument over that time period. _____ is typically expressed in annualized terms, and it may either be an absolute number ($5) or a fraction of the mean (5%).
   a. Volatility
   c. Portfolio insurance
   b. Currency swap
   d. Seasoned equity offering

12. In probability theory and statistics, _____ indicates the strength and direction of a linear relationship between two random variables. That is in contrast with the usage of the term in colloquial speech, which denotes any relationship, not necessarily linear. In general statistical usage, _____ or co-relation refers to the departure of two random variables from independence.
   a. Geometric mean
   c. Probability distribution
   b. Variance
   d. Correlation

13. _____ is a measure of the ability of a debtor to pay their debts as and when they fall due. It is usually expressed as a ratio or a percentage of current liabilities.

For a corporation with a published balance sheet there are various ratios used to calculate a measure of liquidity.

   a. Operating profit margin
   c. Invested capital
   b. Accounting liquidity
   d. Operating leverage

14. In finance, _____ is the process of estimating the potential market value of a financial asset or liability. they can be done on assets (for example, investments in marketable securities such as stocks, options, business enterprises, or intangible assets such as patents and trademarks) or on liabilities (e.g., Bonds issued by a company.) _____s are required in many contexts including investment analysis, capital budgeting, merger and acquisition transactions, financial reporting, taxable events to determine the proper tax liability, and in litigation.
   a. Margin
   c. Share
   b. Procter ' Gamble
   d. Valuation

15. _____ is a fee paid on borrowed assets. It is the price paid for the use of borrowed money , or, money earned by deposited funds . Assets that are sometimes lent with _____ include money, shares, consumer goods through hire purchase, major assets such as aircraft, and even entire factories in finance lease arrangements.
   a. AAB
   c. Insolvency
   b. A Random Walk Down Wall Street
   d. Interest

16. In finance, _____ occurs when a debtor has not met its legal obligations according to the debt contract, e.g. it has not made a scheduled payment, or has violated a loan covenant (condition) of the debt contract. _____ may occur if the debtor is either unwilling or unable to pay their debt. This can occur with all debt obligations including bonds, mortgages, loans, and promissory notes.
   a. Vendor finance
   c. Credit crunch
   b. Debt validation
   d. Default

Chapter 20. Emerging Markets Debt

17. _____ is the corporate management term for the act of reorganizing the legal, ownership, operational, or other structures of a company for the purpose of making it more profitable or better organized for its present needs. Alternate reasons for restructing include a change of ownership or ownership structure, demerger repositioning debt _____ and financial _____.
   a. Cross-border leasing
   b. Concentrated stock
   c. Day trading
   d. Restructuring

18. A _____ is an exchange of promises between two or more parties to do an act which is enforceable in a court of law. It is where an unqualified offer meets a qualified acceptance and the parties reach Consensus ad Idem. The parties must have the necessary capacity to _____ and the _____ must not be either trifling, indeterminate, impossible or illegal.
   a. 4-4-5 Calendar
   b. 529 plan
   c. 7-Eleven
   d. Contract

19. _____ is a legally declared inability or impairment of ability of an individual or organization to pay their creditors. Creditors may file a _____ petition against a debtor ('involuntary _____') in an effort to recoup a portion of what they are owed or initiate a restructuring. In the majority of cases, however, _____ is initiated by the debtor (a 'voluntary _____' that is filed by the bankrupt individual or organization.)
   a. Debt settlement
   b. 4-4-5 Calendar
   c. Bankruptcy
   d. 529 plan

20. In finance, a _____ is a derivative whose value derives from the credit risk on an underlying bond, loan or other financial asset. In this way, the credit risk is on an entity other than the counterparties to the transaction itself. This entity is known as the reference entity and may be a corporate, a sovereign or any other form of legal entity which has incurred debt.
   a. Futures contract
   b. Derivatives markets
   c. STIRT
   d. Credit derivative

21. A _____ is a financial contract whose value is derived from the value of something else (known as the underlying.) The underlying on which a _____ is based can be an asset, weather conditions bonds or other forms of credit.
   a. 4-4-5 Calendar
   b. 7-Eleven
   c. 529 plan
   d. Derivative

22. A _____ is a credit derivative contract between two counterparties. The buyer makes periodic payments (premium leg) to the seller, and in return receives a payoff (protection or default leg) if an underlying financial instrument defaults. _____ contracts have been incorrectly compared with insurance, because the buyer pays a premium and, in return, receives a sum of money if a specified event occurs.
   a. Futures contract
   b. Stock market index future
   c. Commodity tick
   d. Credit default swap

23. _____ are a type of structured asset-backed security (ABS) whose value and payments are derived from a portfolio of fixed-income underlying assets. _____s are assigned different risk classes, or tranches, whereby 'senior' tranches are considered the safest securities. Interest and principal payments are made in order of seniority, so that junior tranches offer higher coupon payments (and interest rates) or lower prices to compensate for additional default risk.

Chapter 20. Emerging Markets Debt

    a. Zero coupon bond
    b. Municipal bond
    c. Senior debt
    d. Collateralized debt obligations

24. In finance, a _____ is a derivative in which two counterparties agree to exchange one stream of cash flows against another stream. These streams are called the legs of the _____.

The cash flows are calculated over a notional principal amount, which is usually not exchanged between counterparties.

    a. Swap
    b. Volatility arbitrage
    c. Local volatility
    d. Volatility swap

25. A _____ (sometimes, especially in Europe, 'special purpose vehicle' or simply SPV) is a legal entity (usually a limited company of some type or, sometimes, a limited partnership) created to fulfill narrow, specific or temporary objectives. _____'s are typically used by companies to isolate the firm from financial risk. A company will transfer assets to the _____ for management or use the _____ to finance a large project thereby achieving a narrow set of goals without putting the entire firm at risk.

    a. Follow-on offering
    b. Rights issue
    c. Real option
    d. Special purpose entity

26. _____ is the risk of loss due to a debtor's non-payment of a loan or other line of credit (either the principal or interest (coupon) or both)

Most lenders employ their own models (credit scorecards) to rank potential and existing customers according to risk, and then apply appropriate strategies. With products such as unsecured personal loans or mortgages, lenders charge a higher price for higher risk customers and vice versa. With revolving products such as credit cards and overdrafts, risk is controlled through careful setting of credit limits.

    a. Transaction risk
    b. Market risk
    c. Credit risk
    d. Liquidity risk

27. _____ is a legal term for a type of debt which is overdue after missing an expected payment. It is also used (in the form in _____) for payments that occur at the end of a period.

_____ accrue from the date on the first missed payment was due.

    a. A Random Walk Down Wall Street
    b. AAB
    c. Interest
    d. Arrears

Chapter 21. Stable Value Investments

1. In accounting, _____ or *Carrying value* is the value of an asset according to its balance sheet account balance. For assets, the value is based on the original cost of the asset less any depreciation, amortization or impairment costs made against the asset. A company's _____ is its total assets minus intangible assets and liabilities.
   a. Current liabilities
   b. Pro forma
   c. Retained earnings
   d. Book value

2. A _____ is an exchange of promises between two or more parties to do an act which is enforceable in a court of law. It is where an unqualified offer meets a qualified acceptance and the parties reach Consensus ad Idem. The parties must have the necessary capacity to _____ and the _____ must not be either trifling, indeterminate, impossible or illegal.
   a. 529 plan
   b. 7-Eleven
   c. 4-4-5 Calendar
   d. Contract

3. _____ are similar to certificates of deposit that can be purchased at banks; however, they are sold by insurance companies. Like money market funds, they're very safe investments; and like all investments that are considered to be 'very safe', they won't make you very much money. Also known by other names - fixed-income fund, stable value fund, capital-preservation fund, or guaranteed fund, for example -- they generally pay interest from one- to five years.
   a. Reputational risk
   b. CODA plc
   c. Vati-Con
   d. Guaranteed investment contracts

4. In finance, a _____ is a debt security, in which the authorized issuer owes the holders a debt and, depending on the terms of the _____, is obliged to pay interest (the coupon) and/or to repay the principal at a later date, termed maturity.

Thus a _____ is a loan: the issuer is the borrower, the _____ holder is the lender, and the coupon is the interest. _____s provide the borrower with external funds to finance long-term investments, or, in the case of government _____s, to finance current expenditure.

   a. Convertible bond
   b. Catastrophe bonds
   c. Bond
   d. Puttable bond

5. _____ is the concept of adding accumulated interest back to the principal, so that interest is earned on interest from that moment on. The act of declaring interest to be principal is called compounding (i.e., interest is compounded.) A loan, for example, may have its interest compounded every month: in this case, a loan with $100 principal and 1% interest per month would have a balance of $101 at the end of the first month.
   a. Penny stock
   b. 4-4-5 Calendar
   c. Risk management
   d. Compound interest

6. A _____ is a way of investing money with other people to participate in a wider range of investments than those feasible for most individual investors, and to share the costs of doing so.

Terminology varies with country but _____s are often referred to as investment funds, managed funds, mutual funds or simply funds (note: mutual fund has a specific meaning in the US.) Around the world large markets have developed around collective investment and these account for a substantial portion of all trading on major stock exchanges.

Chapter 21. Stable Value Investments

a. Collective investment scheme
b. Net asset value
c. Savings and loan association
d. Person-to-person lending

7. An _____ can be defined as a contract which provides an income stream in return for an initial payment.

An immediate _____ is an _____ for which the time between the contract date and the date of the first payment is not longer than the time interval between payments. A common use for an immediate _____ is to provide a pension to a retired person or persons.

a. AT'T Inc.
b. Intrinsic value
c. Amortization
d. Annuity

8. A _____ is a professionally managed type of collective investment scheme that pools money from many investors and invests it in stocks, bonds, short-term money market instruments, and/or other securities. The _____ will have a fund manager that trades the pooled money on a regular basis. Currently, the worldwide value of all _____s totals more than $26 trillion.

Since 1940, there have been three basic types of investment companies in the United States: open-end funds, also known in the US as _____s; unit investment trusts (UITs); and closed-end funds.

a. Financial intermediary
b. Trust company
c. Net asset value
d. Mutual fund

9. A _____ or bank is a financial institution whose primary activity is to act as a payment agent for customers and to borrow and lend money.

The first modern bank was founded in Italy in Genoa in 1406, its name was Banco di San Giorgio (Bank of St. George.)

Many other financial activities were added over time.

a. 4-4-5 Calendar
b. Bought deal
c. Black Sea Trade and Development Bank
d. Banker

10. A _____ is a fungible, negotiable instrument representing financial value. They are broadly categorized into debt securities (such as banknotes, bonds and debentures), and equity securities; e.g., common stocks. The company or other entity issuing the _____ is called the issuer.

a. Tracking stock
b. Book entry
c. Securities lending
d. Security

11. _____ is a legal entity that develops, registers and sells securities for the purpose of financing its operations. _____s may be domestic or foreign governments, corporations or investment trusts. _____s are legally responsible for the obligations of the issue and for reporting financial conditions, material developments and any other operational activities as required by the regulations of their jurisdictions.

a. Efficient-market hypothesis	b. Arbitrage
c. Initial margin	d. Issuer

12. A _____ is a pool of assets forming an independent legal entity that are bought with the contributions to a pension plan for the exclusive purpose of financing pension plan benefits.

_____s are important shareholders of listed and private companies. They are especially important to the stock market where large institutional investors like the Ontario Teachers' Pension Plan dominate.

a. Limited liability company	b. Leveraged buyout
c. Leverage	d. Pension fund

13. _____ is the provision of resources (such as granting a loan) by one party to another party where that second party does not reimburse the first party immediately, thereby generating a debt, and instead arranges either to repay or return those resources (or material(s) of equal value) at a later date. The first party is called a creditor, also known as a lender, while the second party is called a debtor, also known as a borrower.

Movements of financial capital are normally dependent on either _____ or equity transfers.

a. Warrant	b. Clearing house
c. Comparable	d. Credit

14. _____ in finance is a risk management technique, related to hedging, that mixes a wide variety of investments within a portfolio. Because the fluctuations of a single security have less impact on a diverse portfolio, _____ minimizes the risk from any one investment.

A simple example of _____ is the following: On a particular island the entire economy consists of two companies: one that sells umbrellas and another that sells sunscreen.

a. 529 plan	b. 4-4-5 Calendar
c. Diversification	d. 7-Eleven

15. _____ is a life of security. It may also refer to the final payment date of a loan or other financial instrument, at which point all remaining interest and principal is due to be paid.

1, 3, 6 months _____ band can be calculated by using 30-day per month periods.

a. False billing	b. Primary market
c. Maturity	d. Replacement cost

16. In business and accounting, _____s are everything of value that is owned by a person or company. The balance sheet of a firm records the monetary value of the _____s owned by the firm. The two major _____ classes are tangible _____s and intangible _____s.

a. Income	b. Accounts payable
c. EBITDA	d. Asset

Chapter 21. Stable Value Investments

17. _____ is a term used to refer to how an investor distributes his or her investments among various classes of investment vehicles (e.g., stocks and bonds.)

A large part of financial planning is finding an _____ that is appropriate for a given person in terms of their appetite for and ability to shoulder risk. This can depend on various factors; see investor profile.

a. Investment performance
b. Asset allocation
c. Investing online
d. Alternative investment

18. In finance, the _____ of a financial asset measures the sensitivity of the asset's price to interest rate movements, expressed as a number of years. The reason for expressing this sensitivity in years is that the time that will elapse until a cash flow is received allows more interest to accumulate. Therefore the price of an asset with long term cashflows has more interest rate sensitivity than an asset with cashflows in the near future.

a. Macaulay duration
b. 4-4-5 Calendar
c. Duration
d. Yield to maturity

19. _____ is a step in a risk management process. _____ is the determination of quantitative or qualitative value of risk related to a concrete situation and a recognized threat (also called hazard.) Quantitative _____ requires calculations of two components of risk: R, the magnitude of the potential loss L, and the probability p that the loss will occur.

a. 4-4-5 Calendar
b. 7-Eleven
c. 529 plan
d. Risk assessment

Chapter 22. An Overview of Mortgages and the Mortgage Market

1. _____ is early repayment of a loan by a borrower.

In the case of a mortgage-backed security (MBS), _____ is perceived as a risk, because mortgage debts are often paid off early in order to incur lower total interest payments through cheaper refinancing. The new financing may be cheaper because the borrower's credit rating has improved or because interest rates are lower, but in either case, the payments that would have been made to the MBS investor would be above market rates.

a. Bankruptcy remote
b. Prepayment
c. Disposal tax effect
d. Retention ratio

2. In law, a _____ is a form of security interest granted over an item of property to secure the payment of a debt or performance of some other obligation. The owner of the property, who grants the _____, is referred to as the lienor and the person who has the benefit of the _____ is referred to as the _____ee.

The etymological root is: Anglo-French _____, loyen bond, restraint, from Latin ligamen, from ligare to bind.

a. Lien
b. Family and Medical Leave Act
c. Sarbanes-Oxley Act
d. Joint venture

3. An _____ is a mortgage loan where the interest rate on the note is periodically adjusted based on a variety of indices. Among the most common indices are the rates on 1-year constant-maturity Treasury (CMT) securities, the Cost of Funds Index (COFI), and the London Interbank Offered Rate (LIBOR.) A few lenders use their own cost of funds as an index, rather than using other indices.

a. ABN Amro
b. AAB
c. Adjustable rate mortgage
d. A Random Walk Down Wall Street

4. _____ is the provision of resources (such as granting a loan) by one party to another party where that second party does not reimburse the first party immediately, thereby generating a debt, and instead arranges either to repay or return those resources (or material(s) of equal value) at a later date. The first party is called a creditor, also known as a lender, while the second party is called a debtor, also known as a borrower.

Movements of financial capital are normally dependent on either _____ or equity transfers.

a. Warrant
b. Clearing house
c. Comparable
d. Credit

5. _____ is the risk of loss due to a debtor's non-payment of a loan or other line of credit (either the principal or interest (coupon) or both)

Most lenders employ their own models (credit scorecards) to rank potential and existing customers according to risk, and then apply appropriate strategies. With products such as unsecured personal loans or mortgages, lenders charge a higher price for higher risk customers and vice versa. With revolving products such as credit cards and overdrafts, risk is controlled through careful setting of credit limits.

Chapter 22. An Overview of Mortgages and the Mortgage Market

a. Credit risk
c. Transaction risk
b. Market risk
d. Liquidity risk

6. The institution most often referenced by the word '_____' is a public or publicly traded _____, the shares of which are traded on a public stock exchange (e.g., the New York Stock Exchange or Nasdaq in the United States) where shares of stock of _____s are bought and sold by and to the general public. Most of the largest businesses in the world are publicly traded _____s. However, the majority of _____s are said to be closely held, privately held or close _____s, meaning that no ready market exists for the trading of shares.

a. Protect
c. Federal Home Loan Mortgage Corporation
b. Corporation
d. Depository Trust Company

7. The _____ (NYSE: FRE) is an insolvent government sponsored enterprise (GSE) of the United States federal government.

The _____ was created in 1970 to expand the secondary market for mortgages in the US. Along with other GSEs, Freddie Mac buys mortgages on the secondary market, pools them, and sells them as mortgage-backed securities to investors on the open market.

a. The Depository Trust ' Clearing Corporation
c. Public company
b. Federal Home Loan Mortgage Corporation
d. Governmental Accounting Standards Board

8. The _____ is a U.S. government-owned corporation within the Department of Housing and Urban Development

Ginnie Mae provides guarantees on mortgage-backed securities backed by federally insured or guaranteed loans, mainly loans issued by the Federal Housing Administration, Department of Veterans Affairs, Rural Housing Service, and Office of Public and Indian Housing. Ginnie Mae securities are the only MBS that are guaranteed by the United States government.

a. Certified Emission Reductions
c. Cash budget
b. Case-Shiller Home Price Indices
d. GNMA

9. The _____ is a U.S. government-owned corporation within the Department of Housing and Urban Development

Ginnie Mae provides guarantees on mortgage-backed securities backed by federally insured or guaranteed loans, mainly loans issued by the Federal Housing Administration, Department of Veterans Affairs, Rural Housing Service, and Office of Public and Indian Housing. Ginnie Mae securities are the only MBS that are guaranteed by the United States government.

a. Graduated payment mortgage
c. Jumbo mortgage
b. 4-4-5 Calendar
d. Government National Mortgage Association

10. _____ consists of the sale of goods or merchandise from a fixed location, such as a department store, boutique or kiosk in small or individual lots for direct consumption by the purchaser. _____ may include subordinated services, such as delivery. Purchasers may be individuals or businesses.

a. 529 plan
b. 4-4-5 Calendar
c. Retailing
d. 7-Eleven

11. A _____ assesses the credit worthiness of an individual, corporation, or even a country. _____s are calculated from financial history and current assets and liabilities. Typically, a _____ tells a lender or investor the probability of the subject being able to pay back a loan.
   a. Credit report monitoring
   b. Debenture
   c. Credit cycle
   d. Credit rating

12. A _____ is a numerical expression based on a statistical analysis of a person's credit files, to represent the creditworthiness of that person. A _____ is primarily based on credit report information, typically sourced from credit bureaus.

Lenders, such as banks and credit card companies, use _____s to evaluate the potential risk posed by lending money to consumers and to mitigate losses due to bad debt.

   a. Credit freeze
   b. Credit report monitoring
   c. Paydex
   d. Credit score

13. A _____ is an asset-backed security whose cash flows are backed by the principal and interest payments of a set of mortgage loans. Payments are typically made monthly over the lifetime of the underlying loans.
   a. Conforming loan
   b. Shared appreciation mortgage
   c. Mortgage-backed security
   d. Home equity line of credit

14. The coupon or _____ of a bond is the amount of interest paid per year expressed as a percentage of the face value of the bond.

For example if you hold $10,000 nominal of a bond described as a 4.5% loan stock, you will receive $450 in interest each year (probably in two installments of $225 each.)

Not all bonds have coupons.

   a. Revenue bonds
   b. Zero-coupon bond
   c. Puttable bond
   d. Coupon rate

15. _____ is a methodology adopted by many lenders in the mortgage and financial services industries. It has been in use for many years as lenders try to measure loan risk in terms of interest rates and other fees. The interest rate on a loan is determined not only by the time value of money, but also by the lender's estimate of the probability that the borrower will default on the loan.
   a. Conforming loan
   b. Blanket mortgage
   c. Chain of Blame
   d. Risk-based pricing

16. A _____ is a fungible, negotiable instrument representing financial value. They are broadly categorized into debt securities (such as banknotes, bonds and debentures), and equity securities; e.g., common stocks. The company or other entity issuing the _____ is called the issuer.

Chapter 22. An Overview of Mortgages and the Mortgage Market

a. Tracking stock
b. Security
c. Book entry
d. Securities lending

17. An _____ is a contract written by a seller that conveys to the buyer the right -- but not the obligation -- to buy (in the case of a call _____) or to sell (in the case of a put _____) a particular asset, such as a piece of property such as, among others, a futures contract. In return for granting the _____, the seller collects a payment (the premium) from the buyer.

For example, buying a call _____ provides the right to buy a specified quantity of a security at a set strike price at some time on or before expiration, while buying a put _____ provides the right to sell.

a. Option
b. AT'T Mobility LLC
c. Amortization
d. Annuity

18. _____ is a measure of the rate of payments from a bond that pays principal payments in excess of scheduled payments (so-called prepayments.) Such bonds include mortgage-backed securities, CMOs, and ABS, which prepay at some rate usually dependent on the level of interest rates.

_____ is defined as the annualized rate of principal payments beyond the regularly scheduled payments, and is stated as a percentage of outstanding amount of the security or loan minus the scheduled payments.

a. Conditional prepayment rate
b. Profitability index
c. Cash management
d. Total return

19. The _____, an agency of the United States Department of the Treasury, is the primary regulator of federal savings associations (sometimes referred to as federal thrifts.) Federal savings associations include both federal savings banks and federal savings and loans. The OTS is also responsible for supervising savings and loan holding companies (SLHCs) and some state-chartered institutions.

a. ABN Amro
b. Office of Thrift Supervision
c. A Random Walk Down Wall Street
d. AAB

20. _____ is the legal and professional proceeding in which a mortgagee usually a lender, obtains a court ordered termination of a mortgagor's equitable right of redemption. Usually a lender obtains a security interest from a borrower who mortgages or pledges an asset like a house to secure the loan. If the borrower defaults and the lender tries to repossess the property, courts of equity can grant the borrower the equitable right of redemption if the borrower repays the debt.

a. Liability
b. Federal Acquisition Regulations
c. Letter of credit
d. Foreclosure

21. In finance, _____ occurs when a debtor has not met its legal obligations according to the debt contract, e.g. it has not made a scheduled payment, or has violated a loan covenant (condition) of the debt contract. _____ may occur if the debtor is either unwilling or unable to pay their debt. This can occur with all debt obligations including bonds, mortgages, loans, and promissory notes.

a. Default
b. Debt validation
c. Vendor finance
d. Credit crunch

Chapter 23. Agency Mortgage-Backed Securities

1. An _____ is a mortgage loan where the interest rate on the note is periodically adjusted based on a variety of indices. Among the most common indices are the rates on 1-year constant-maturity Treasury (CMT) securities, the Cost of Funds Index (COFI), and the London Interbank Offered Rate (LIBOR.) A few lenders use their own cost of funds as an index, rather than using other indices.

   a. A Random Walk Down Wall Street
   c. AAB
   b. ABN Amro
   d. Adjustable rate mortgage

2. _____ is that which is owed; usually referencing assets owed, but the term can cover other obligations. In the case of assets, _____ is a means of using future purchasing power in the present before a summation has been earned. Some companies and corporations use _____ as a part of their overall corporate finance strategy.

   a. Debt
   c. Credit cycle
   b. Partial Payment
   d. Cross-collateralization

3. In the United States, a _____ is a mortgage loan that conforms to GSE guidelines.

   In general, any loan which does not meet guidelines is a non-_____. A loan which does not meet guidelines specifically because the loan amount exceeds the guideline limits is known as a jumbo loan.

   a. Blanket mortgage
   c. Mortgage insurance
   b. Home equity line of credit
   d. Conforming loan

4. A '_____' is a 'Charge' that is paid to obtain the right to delay a payment. Essentially, the payer purchases the right to make a given payment in the future instead of in the Present. The '_____', or 'Charge' that must be paid to delay the payment, is simply the difference between what the payment amount would be if it were paid in the present and what the payment amount would be paid if it were paid in the future.

   a. Value at risk
   c. Risk modeling
   b. Risk aversion
   d. Discount

5. The terms _____ , nominal _____, and effective _____ describe the interest rate for a whole year (annualized), rather than just a monthly fee/rate, as applied on a loan, mortgage, credit card, etc. Those terms have formal, legal definitions in some countries or legal jurisdictions, but in general:

   - The nominal _____ is the simple-interest rate (for a year.)
   - The effective _____ is the fee+compound interest rate (calculated across a year.)

   The nominal _____ is calculated as: the rate, for a payment period, multiplied by the number of payment periods in a year. However, the exact legal definition of 'effective _____' can vary greatly in each jurisdiction, depending on the type of fees included, such as participation fees, loan origination fees, monthly service charges, or late fees. The effective _____ has been called the 'mathematically-true' interest rate for each year. The computation for the effective _____, as the fee+compound interest rate, can also vary depending on whether the up-front fees, such as origination or participation fees, are added to the entire amount, or treated as a short-term loan due in the first payment.

   a. Annual percentage rate
   c. ABN Amro
   b. A Random Walk Down Wall Street
   d. AAB

Chapter 23. Agency Mortgage-Backed Securities

6. The _____ is the market for the sale of securities or bonds collateralized by the value of mortgage loans. The mortgage lender, commercial banks, or specialized firm will group together many loans and sell grouped loans as securities called collateralized mortgage obligations (CMOs.) The risk of the individual loans is reduced by that aggregation process.
   a. 4-4-5 Calendar
   b. Secondary mortgage market
   c. 7-Eleven
   d. 529 plan

7. _____ is the increase in the amount of the goods and services produced by an economy over time. It is conventionally measured as the percent rate of increase in real gross domestic product, or real GDP. Growth is usually calculated in real terms, i.e. inflation-adjusted terms, in order to net out the effect of inflation on the price of the goods and services produced.
   a. Economic growth
   b. ABN Amro
   c. A Random Walk Down Wall Street
   d. AAB

8. The _____ (NYSE: FRE) is an insolvent government sponsored enterprise (GSE) of the United States federal government.

The _____ was created in 1970 to expand the secondary market for mortgages in the US. Along with other GSEs, Freddie Mac buys mortgages on the secondary market, pools them, and sells them as mortgage-backed securities to investors on the open market.

   a. The Depository Trust ' Clearing Corporation
   b. Federal Home Loan Mortgage Corporation
   c. Governmental Accounting Standards Board
   d. Public company

9. The _____ is a U.S. government-owned corporation within the Department of Housing and Urban Development

Ginnie Mae provides guarantees on mortgage-backed securities backed by federally insured or guaranteed loans, mainly loans issued by the Federal Housing Administration, Department of Veterans Affairs, Rural Housing Service, and Office of Public and Indian Housing. Ginnie Mae securities are the only MBS that are guaranteed by the United States government.

   a. Certified Emission Reductions
   b. Cash budget
   c. Case-Shiller Home Price Indices
   d. GNMA

10. A _____ is an asset-backed security whose cash flows are backed by the principal and interest payments of a set of mortgage loans. Payments are typically made monthly over the lifetime of the underlying loans.
    a. Mortgage-backed security
    b. Shared appreciation mortgage
    c. Conforming loan
    d. Home equity line of credit

11. A _____ is a fungible, negotiable instrument representing financial value. They are broadly categorized into debt securities (such as banknotes, bonds and debentures), and equity securities; e.g., common stocks. The company or other entity issuing the _____ is called the issuer.
    a. Book entry
    b. Tracking stock
    c. Securities lending
    d. Security

Chapter 23. Agency Mortgage-Backed Securities

12. The _____ (NYSE: FNM), commonly known as Fannie Mae, is a stockholder-owned corporation chartered by Congress in 1968 as a government sponsored enterprise (GSE), but founded in 1938 during the Great Depression. The corporation's purpose is to purchase and securitize mortgages in order to ensure that funds are consistently available to the institutions that lend money to home buyers.

On September 7, 2008, James Lockhart, director of the Federal Housing Finance Agency (FHFA), announced that Fannie Mae and Freddie Mac were being placed into conservatorship of the FHFA.

   a. General partnership   b. The Depository Trust ' Clearing Corporation
   c. SPDR   d. Federal National Mortgage Association

13. The coupon or _____ of a bond is the amount of interest paid per year expressed as a percentage of the face value of the bond.

For example if you hold $10,000 nominal of a bond described as a 4.5% loan stock, you will receive $450 in interest each year (probably in two installments of $225 each.)

Not all bonds have coupons.

   a. Revenue bonds   b. Zero-coupon bond
   c. Puttable bond   d. Coupon rate

14. In finance, a _____ is a debt security, in which the authorized issuer owes the holders a debt and, depending on the terms of the _____, is obliged to pay interest (the coupon) and/or to repay the principal at a later date, termed maturity.

Thus a _____ is a loan: the issuer is the borrower, the _____ holder is the lender, and the coupon is the interest. _____s provide the borrower with external funds to finance long-term investments, or, in the case of government _____s, to finance current expenditure.

   a. Puttable bond   b. Convertible bond
   c. Catastrophe bonds   d. Bond

15. _____ is a life of security. It may also refer to the final payment date of a loan or other financial instrument, at which point all remaining interest and principal is due to be paid.

1, 3, 6 months _____ band can be calculated by using 30-day per month periods.

   a. Maturity   b. False billing
   c. Primary market   d. Replacement cost

Chapter 23. Agency Mortgage-Backed Securities

16. _____ is the balance of the amounts of cash being received and paid by a business during a defined period of time, sometimes tied to a specific project. Measurement of _____ can be used

- to evaluate the state or performance of a business or project.
- to determine problems with liquidity. Being profitable does not necessarily mean being liquid. A company can fail because of a shortage of cash, even while profitable.
- to generate project rate of returns. The time of _____s into and out of projects are used as inputs to financial models such as internal rate of return, and net present value.
- to examine income or growth of a business when it is believed that accrual accounting concepts do not represent economic realities. Alternately, _____ can be used to 'validate' the net income generated by accrual accounting.

_____ as a generic term may be used differently depending on context, and certain _____ definitions may be adapted by analysts and users for their own uses. Common terms include operating _____ and free _____.

_____s can be classified into:

1. Operational _____s: Cash received or expended as a result of the company's core business activities.
2. Investment _____s: Cash received or expended through capital expenditure, investments or acquisitions.
3. Financing _____s: Cash received or expended as a result of financial activities, such as interests and dividends.

All three together - the net _____ - are necessary to reconcile the beginning cash balance to the ending cash balance. Loan draw downs or equity injections, that is just shifting of capital but no expenditure as such, are not considered in the net _____.

a. Real option
b. Corporate finance
c. Shareholder value
d. Cash flow

17. Accrual, in accounting, describes the accounting method known as _____, whereby revenues and expenses are recognized when they are accrued, i.e. accumulated (earned or incurred), regardless when the actual cash is received or paid out.

E.g. a company delivers a product to a customer who will pay for it 30 days later in the next fiscal year starting a week after the delivery. The company recognizes the proceeds as a revenue in its current income statement still for the fiscal year of the delivery, even though it will get paid in cash during the following accounting period.

a. AAB
b. ABN Amro
c. A Random Walk Down Wall Street
d. Accrual basis

18. _____ is a fee paid on borrowed assets. It is the price paid for the use of borrowed money , or, money earned by deposited funds . Assets that are sometimes lent with _____ include money, shares, consumer goods through hire purchase, major assets such as aircraft, and even entire factories in finance lease arrangements.

a. A Random Walk Down Wall Street b. AAB
c. Insolvency d. Interest

19. The _____ is a financial market where participants buy and sell debt securities, usually in the form of bonds. As of 2006, the size of the international _____ is an estimated $45 trillion, of which the size of the outstanding U.S. _____ debt was $25.2 trillion.

Nearly all of the $923 billion average daily trading volume in the U.S. _____ takes place between broker-dealers and large institutions in a decentralized, over-the-counter market.

a. 4-4-5 Calendar b. 529 plan
c. Bond Market d. Fixed income

20. _____ is early repayment of a loan by a borrower.

In the case of a mortgage-backed security (MBS), _____ is perceived as a risk, because mortgage debts are often paid off early in order to incur lower total interest payments through cheaper refinancing. The new financing may be cheaper because the borrower's credit rating has improved or because interest rates are lower, but in either case, the payments that would have been made to the MBS investor would be above market rates.

a. Disposal tax effect b. Prepayment
c. Bankruptcy remote d. Retention ratio

21. In probability theory and statistics, the _____ of a random variable, probability distribution averaging the squared distance of its possible values from the expected value (mean.) Whereas the mean is a way to describe the location of a distribution, the _____ is a way to capture its scale or degree of being spread out. The unit of _____ is the square of the unit of the original variable.

a. Variance b. Semivariance
c. Harmonic mean d. Monte Carlo methods

22. _____ refinancing (in the case of real property) occurs when a loan is taken out on property already owned, and the loan amount is above and beyond the cost of transaction, payoff of existing liens, and related expenses.

Strictly speaking all refinancing of debt is '_____', when funds retrieved are utilized for anything other than repaying an existing lien.

In the case of common usage of the term, _____ refinancing refers to when equity is liquidated from a property above and beyond sum of the payoff of existing loans held in lien on the property, loan fees, costs associated with the loan, taxes, insurance, tax reserves, insurance reserves, and in the past any other non-lien debt held in the name of the owner being paid by loan proceeds.

a. Fixed rate mortgage b. Home equity line of credit
c. Cash-out d. Conforming loan

Chapter 23. Agency Mortgage-Backed Securities

23. _____ is the provision of resources (such as granting a loan) by one party to another party where that second party does not reimburse the first party immediately, thereby generating a debt, and instead arranges either to repay or return those resources (or material(s) of equal value) at a later date. The first party is called a creditor, also known as a lender, while the second party is called a debtor, also known as a borrower.

Movements of financial capital are normally dependent on either _____ or equity transfers.

a. Comparable
b. Warrant
c. Clearing house
d. Credit

24. A _____ is a clause in a loan or promissory note that stipulates that the full balance may be called due upon sale or transfer of ownership of the property used to secure the note. The lender has the right, but not the obligation, to call the note due in such a circumstance.

Virtually all recent mortgages made in the United States contain a _____.

a. Due-on-sale clause
b. 4-4-5 Calendar
c. 529 plan
d. Defeasance

25. In finance, the term _____ describes the amount in cash that returns to the owners of a security. Normally it does not include the price variations, at the difference of the total return. _____ applies to various stated rates of return on stocks (common and preferred, and convertible), fixed income instruments (bonds, notes, bills, strips, zero coupon), and some other investment type insurance products (e.g. annuities.)

a. Yield
b. Yield to maturity
c. Macaulay duration
d. 4-4-5 Calendar

26. In finance, the _____ is the relation between the interest rate (or cost of borrowing) and the time to maturity of the debt for a given borrower in a given currency. For example, the current U.S. dollar interest rates paid on U.S. Treasury securities for various maturities are closely watched by many traders, and are commonly plotted on a graph such as the one on the right which is informally called 'the _____.' More formal mathematical descriptions of this relation are often called the term structure of interest rates.

The yield of a debt instrument is the annualized percentage increase in the value of the investment.

a. Yield curve
b. 529 plan
c. 7-Eleven
d. 4-4-5 Calendar

27. In probability theory and statistics, a _____ is described as the number separating the higher half of a sample, a population, or a probability distribution from the lower half. The _____ of a finite list of numbers can be found by arranging all the observations from lowest value to highest value and picking the middle one. If there is an even number of observations, the _____ is not unique, so one often takes the mean of the two middle values.

a. Variance
b. Median
c. Geometric mean
d. Standard deviation

Chapter 23. Agency Mortgage-Backed Securities

28. In finance, _____ is the process of estimating the potential market value of a financial asset or liability. they can be done on assets (for example, investments in marketable securities such as stocks, options, business enterprises, or intangible assets such as patents and trademarks) or on liabilities (e.g., Bonds issued by a company.) _____s are required in many contexts including investment analysis, capital budgeting, merger and acquisition transactions, financial reporting, taxable events to determine the proper tax liability, and in litigation.

   a. Share
   b. Margin
   c. Procter ' Gamble
   d. Valuation

29. _____ is the flat spread over the treasury yield curve required to discount a security payment to match its market price. This concept can be applied to mortgage-backed security (MBS), Options, Bonds and any other interest-rate Derivative.

In contrast to the simple 'yield curve spread' measurement of bond premium over a pre-determined cash-flow model, the _____ describes the market premium over a model including two types of volatility:

- Variable interest rates
- Variable prepayment rates.

Designing such models in the first place is complicated because prepayment variations are a behavioural function of the stochastic interest rate. (They tend to go up as interest rates come down.)

   a. AAB
   b. ABN Amro
   c. A Random Walk Down Wall Street
   d. Option adjusted spread

30. In finance, the _____ of a financial asset measures the sensitivity of the asset's price to interest rate movements, expressed as a number of years. The reason for expressing this sensitivity in years is that the time that will elapse until a cash flow is received allows more interest to accumulate. Therefore the price of an asset with long term cashflows has more interest rate sensitivity than an asset with cashflows in the near future.

   a. Yield to maturity
   b. 4-4-5 Calendar
   c. Duration
   d. Macaulay duration

Chapter 24. Collateralized Mortgage Obligations

1. _____ is the process of decreasing an amount over a period of time. The word comes from Middle English amortisen to kill, alienate in mortmain, from Anglo-French amorteser, alteration of amortir, from Vulgar Latin admortire to kill, from Latin ad- + mort-, mors death. Particular instances of the term include:

- _____ (business), the allocation of a lump sum amount to different time periods, particularly for loans and other forms of finance, including related interest or other finance charges.
    - _____ schedule, a table detailing each periodic payment on a loan (typically a mortgage), as generated by an _____ calculator.
    - Negative _____, an _____ schedule where the loan amount actually increases through not paying the full interest
- Amortized analysis, analyzing the execution cost of algorithms over a sequence of operations.
- _____ of capital expenditures of certain assets under accounting rules, particularly intangible assets, in a manner analogous to depreciation.
- _____ (tax law)

_____ is also used in the context of zoning regulations and describes the time in which a property owner has to relocate when the property's use constitutes a preexisting nonconforming use under zoning regulations.

- Depreciation

a. AT'T Inc.
c. Intrinsic value
b. Amortization
d. Option

2. In finance, a _____ is a debt security, in which the authorized issuer owes the holders a debt and, depending on the terms of the _____, is obliged to pay interest (the coupon) and/or to repay the principal at a later date, termed maturity.

Thus a _____ is a loan: the issuer is the borrower, the _____ holder is the lender, and the coupon is the interest. _____s provide the borrower with external funds to finance long-term investments, or, in the case of government _____s, to finance current expenditure.

a. Catastrophe bonds
c. Convertible bond
b. Puttable bond
d. Bond

3. _____ is a measure of the ability of a debtor to pay their debts as and when they fall due. It is usually expressed as a ratio or a percentage of current liabilities.

For a corporation with a published balance sheet there are various ratios used to calculate a measure of liquidity.

a. Operating leverage
c. Accounting liquidity
b. Operating profit margin
d. Invested capital

4. The _____ is that part of the capital markets that deals with the issuance of new securities. Companies, governments or public sector institutions can obtain funding through the sale of a new stock or bond issue. This is typically done through a syndicate of securities dealers.

a. Peer group analysis
b. Volatility clustering
c. Sector rotation
d. Primary market

5. The _____ is the financial market where previously issued securities and financial instruments such as stock, bonds, options, and futures are bought and sold. The term '_____' is also used refer to the market for any used goods or assets, or an alternative use for an existing product or asset where the customer base is the second market

With primary issuances of securities or financial instruments, or the primary market, investors purchase these securities directly from issuers such as corporations issuing shares in an IPO or private placement, or directly from the federal government in the case of treasuries.

a. Delta neutral
b. Secondary market
c. Financial market
d. Performance attribution

6. _____ is a fee paid on borrowed assets. It is the price paid for the use of borrowed money, or, money earned by deposited funds. Assets that are sometimes lent with _____ include money, shares, consumer goods through hire purchase, major assets such as aircraft, and even entire factories in finance lease arrangements.
a. Insolvency
b. A Random Walk Down Wall Street
c. AAB
d. Interest

7. A _____ is a fungible, negotiable instrument representing financial value. They are broadly categorized into debt securities (such as banknotes, bonds and debentures), and equity securities; e.g., common stocks. The company or other entity issuing the _____ is called the issuer.
a. Security
b. Tracking stock
c. Securities lending
d. Book entry

8. _____ is the balance of the amounts of cash being received and paid by a business during a defined period of time, sometimes tied to a specific project. Measurement of _____ can be used

- to evaluate the state or performance of a business or project.
- to determine problems with liquidity. Being profitable does not necessarily mean being liquid. A company can fail because of a shortage of cash, even while profitable.
- to generate project rate of returns. The time of _____s into and out of projects are used as inputs to financial models such as internal rate of return, and net present value.
- to examine income or growth of a business when it is believed that accrual accounting concepts do not represent economic realities. Alternately, _____ can be used to 'validate' the net income generated by accrual accounting.

_____ as a generic term may be used differently depending on context, and certain _____ definitions may be adapted by analysts and users for their own uses. Common terms include operating _____ and free _____.

Chapter 24. Collateralized Mortgage Obligations 127

_____s can be classified into:

1. Operational _____s: Cash received or expended as a result of the company's core business activities.
2. Investment _____s: Cash received or expended through capital expenditure, investments or acquisitions.
3. Financing _____s: Cash received or expended as a result of financial activities, such as interests and dividends.

All three together - the net _____ - are necessary to reconcile the beginning cash balance to the ending cash balance. Loan draw downs or equity injections, that is just shifting of capital but no expenditure as such, are not considered in the net _____.

a. Corporate finance
b. Real option
c. Shareholder value
d. Cash flow

9. In lending agreements, _____ is a borrower's pledge of specific property to a lender, to secure repayment of a loan. The _____ serves as protection for a lender against a borrower's risk of default - that is, a borrower failing to pay the principal and interest under the terms of a loan obligation. If a borrower does default on a loan (due to insolvency or other event), that borrower forfeits (gives up) the property pledged as _____ *ollateral* - and the lender then becomes the owner of the _____.

a. Nominal value
b. Refinancing risk
c. Future-oriented
d. Collateral

10. In structured finance, a _____ is one of a number of related securities offered as part of the same transaction. The word _____ is French for slice, section, series, or portion. In the financial sense of the word, each bond is a different slice of the deal's risk.

a. Yield curve spread
b. 4-4-5 Calendar
c. Credit enhancement
d. Tranche

11. The coupon or _____ of a bond is the amount of interest paid per year expressed as a percentage of the face value of the bond.

For example if you hold $10,000 nominal of a bond described as a 4.5% loan stock, you will receive $450 in interest each year (probably in two installments of $225 each.)

Not all bonds have coupons.

a. Puttable bond
b. Revenue bonds
c. Coupon rate
d. Zero-coupon bond

12. A _____ is a collateralized debt obligation (CDO) in which the underlying credit exposures are taken on using a credit default swap rather than by having a vehicle buy physical assets. _____s can either be single tranche CDOs or fully distributed CDOs. _____s are also commonly divided into balance sheet and arbitrage CDOs, although it is often impossible to distinguish in practice between the two types.

a. Counting house
b. Planning horizon
c. Synthetic CDO
d. Market capitalization

13. _____ is a life of security. It may also refer to the final payment date of a loan or other financial instrument, at which point all remaining interest and principal is due to be paid.

1, 3, 6 months _____ band can be calculated by using 30-day per month periods.

a. False billing
b. Replacement cost
c. Primary market
d. Maturity

14. _____ are bonds that have a variable coupon, equal to a money market reference rate, like LIBOR or federal funds rate, plus a spread. The spread is a rate that remains constant. Almost all _____ have quarterly coupons, i.e. they pay out interest every three months, though counter examples do exist.

a. CVECAs
b. Gordon growth model
c. Loan participation
d. Floating rate notes

15. A '_____' is a 'Charge' that is paid to obtain the right to delay a payment. Essentially, the payer purchases the right to make a given payment in the future instead of in the Present. The '_____', or 'Charge' that must be paid to delay the payment, is simply the difference between what the payment amount would be if it were paid in the present and what the payment amount would be paid if it were paid in the future.

a. Risk aversion
b. Risk modeling
c. Discount
d. Value at risk

16. An _____ is a type of bond or other type of debt instrument used in finance whose coupon rate has an inverse relationship to short-term interest rates (or its reference rate.) With an _____, as interest rates rise the coupon rate falls. The basic structure is the same as an ordinary floating rate note except for the direction in which the coupon rate is adjusted.

a. ABN Amro
b. Inverse floater
c. AAB
d. A Random Walk Down Wall Street

17. In finance, a _____ is collateral that the holder of a position in securities, options, or futures contracts has to deposit to cover the credit risk of his counterparty (most often his broker.) This risk can arise if the holder has done any of the following:

- borrowed cash from the counterparty to buy securities or options,
- sold securities or options short, or
- entered into a futures contract.

The collateral can be in the form of cash or securities, and it is deposited in a _____ account. On U.S. futures exchanges, '_____' was formally called performance bond.

_____ buying is buying securities with cash borrowed from a broker, using other securities as collateral.

a. Share
b. Credit
c. Procter ' Gamble
d. Margin

Chapter 24. Collateralized Mortgage Obligations

18. In finance, the _____ of a financial asset measures the sensitivity of the asset's price to interest rate movements, expressed as a number of years. The reason for expressing this sensitivity in years is that the time that will elapse until a cash flow is received allows more interest to accumulate. Therefore the price of an asset with long term cashflows has more interest rate sensitivity than an asset with cashflows in the near future.
   a. Macaulay duration
   b. Yield to maturity
   c. 4-4-5 Calendar
   d. Duration

19. The _____ or forward rate is the agreed upon price of an asset in a forward contract. Using the rational pricing assumption, we can express the _____ in terms of the spot price and any dividends etc., so that there is no possibility for arbitrage.

The _____ is given by:

where

   F is the _____ to be paid at time T
   e^x is the exponential function
   r is the risk-free interest rate
   q is the cost-of-carry
   S_0 is the spot price of the asset (i.e. what it would sell for at time 0)
   D_i is a dividend which is guaranteed to be paid at time t_i where $0 < t_i < T$.

The two questions here are what price the short position (the seller of the asset) should offer to maximize his gain, and what price the long position (the buyer of the asset) should accept to maximize his gain?

At the very least we know that both do not want to lose any money in the deal.

   a. Financial Gerontology
   b. Biweekly Mortgage
   c. Security interest
   d. Forward price

20. A _____ is a financial debt vehicle that was first created in June 1983 by investment banks Salomon Brothers and First Boston for Freddie Mac. (The First Boston team was led by Dexter Senft.) Legally, a _____ is a special purpose entity that is wholly separate from the institution(s) that create it.
   a. Tranche
   b. 4-4-5 Calendar
   c. Yield curve spread
   d. Collateralized mortgage obligation

21. _____ is a legally declared inability or impairment of ability of an individual or organization to pay their creditors. Creditors may file a _____ petition against a debtor ('involuntary _____') in an effort to recoup a portion of what they are owed or initiate a restructuring. In the majority of cases, however, _____ is initiated by the debtor (a 'voluntary _____' that is filed by the bankrupt individual or organization.)

a. 529 plan
b. Debt settlement
c. 4-4-5 Calendar
d. Bankruptcy

22. _____ is the provision of resources (such as granting a loan) by one party to another party where that second party does not reimburse the first party immediately, thereby generating a debt, and instead arranges either to repay or return those resources (or material(s) of equal value) at a later date. The first party is called a creditor, also known as a lender, while the second party is called a debtor, also known as a borrower.

Movements of financial capital are normally dependent on either _____ or equity transfers.

a. Warrant
b. Credit
c. Comparable
d. Clearing house

23. _____ is the risk of loss due to a debtor's non-payment of a loan or other line of credit (either the principal or interest (coupon) or both)

Most lenders employ their own models (credit scorecards) to rank potential and existing customers according to risk, and then apply appropriate strategies. With products such as unsecured personal loans or mortgages, lenders charge a higher price for higher risk customers and vice versa. With revolving products such as credit cards and overdrafts, risk is controlled through careful setting of credit limits.

a. Liquidity risk
b. Transaction risk
c. Market risk
d. Credit risk

24. A standard, commercial _____ is a document issued mostly by a financial institution, used primarily in trade finance, which usually provides an irrevocable payment undertaking.

The _____ can also be the source of payment for a transaction, meaning that redeeming the _____ will pay an exporter. Letters of credit are used primarily in international trade transactions of significant value, for deals between a supplier in one country and a customer in another.

a. Duty of loyalty
b. McFadden Act
c. Bond indenture
d. Letter of credit

25. In financial accounting, the term _____ is most commonly used to describe any part of shareholders' equity, except for basic share capital. Sometimes, the term is used instead of the term provision; such a use, however, is inconsistent with the terminology suggested by International Accounting Standards Board. For more information about provisions, see provision (accounting.)

a. Closing entries
b. Reserve
c. FIFO and LIFO accounting
d. Treasury stock

26. _____ is a key part of the securitization transaction in structured finance, and is important for credit rating agencies when rating a securitization. The credit crisis of 2007-2008 has discredited the process of _____ of structured securities as a legitimate financial practice.

There are two primary types of _____: Internal and External.

Chapter 24. Collateralized Mortgage Obligations

a. Yield curve spread
c. Tranche

b. 4-4-5 Calendar
d. Credit enhancement

27. An _____ is a future interest, held by a third party transferee (i.e. someone other than the grantee), which either cuts off another's interest or begins after the natural termination of a preceding estate. It differs from a remainder.

There are two different types of _____s: shifting and springing.

a. Express warranty
c. Economic depreciation

b. Executory Interest
d. Articles of incorporation

28. _____ is early repayment of a loan by a borrower.

In the case of a mortgage-backed security (MBS), _____ is perceived as a risk, because mortgage debts are often paid off early in order to incur lower total interest payments through cheaper refinancing. The new financing may be cheaper because the borrower's credit rating has improved or because interest rates are lower, but in either case, the payments that would have been made to the MBS investor would be above market rates.

a. Retention ratio
c. Bankruptcy remote

b. Disposal tax effect
d. Prepayment

29. _____ is the flat spread over the treasury yield curve required to discount a security payment to match its market price. This concept can be applied to mortgage-backed security (MBS), Options, Bonds and any other interest-rate Derivative.

In contrast to the simple 'yield curve spread' measurement of bond premium over a pre-determined cash-flow model, the _____ describes the market premium over a model including two types of volatility:

- Variable interest rates
- Variable prepayment rates.

Designing such models in the first place is complicated because prepayment variations are a behavioural function of the stochastic interest rate. (They tend to go up as interest rates come down.)

a. Option adjusted spread
c. A Random Walk Down Wall Street

b. AAB
d. ABN Amro

30. In finance, a _____ is a position established in one market in an attempt to offset exposure to the price risk of an equal but opposite obligation or position in another market -- usually, but not always, in the context of one's commercial activity. Hedging is a strategy designed to minimize exposure to such business risks as a sharp contraction in demand for one's inventory, while still allowing the business to profit from producing and maintaining that inventory. A typical hedger might be a farmer with 2000 acres of unharvested wheat in the ground, who would rather tend his crop without the distraction of uncertain prices.

a. Hedge
c. 7-Eleven

b. 4-4-5 Calendar
d. 529 plan

Chapter 24. Collateralized Mortgage Obligations

31. A _____ is a private investment fund open to a limited range of investors that is permitted by regulators to undertake a wider range of activities than other investment funds and also pays a performance fee to its investment manager. Each fund will have its own strategy which determines the type of investments and the methods of investment it undertakes. _____s as a class invest in a broad range of investments extending over shares, debt, commodities and beyond.
   a. 529 plan
   c. 7-Eleven
   b. 4-4-5 Calendar
   d. Hedge fund

32. A _____ is a pool of assets forming an independent legal entity that are bought with the contributions to a pension plan for the exclusive purpose of financing pension plan benefits.

   _____s are important shareholders of listed and private companies. They are especially important to the stock market where large institutional investors like the Ontario Teachers' Pension Plan dominate.

   a. Leveraged buyout
   c. Limited liability company
   b. Leverage
   d. Pension fund

33. _____ consists of the sale of goods or merchandise from a fixed location, such as a department store, boutique or kiosk in small or individual lots for direct consumption by the purchaser. _____ may include subordinated services, such as delivery. Purchasers may be individuals or businesses.
   a. 7-Eleven
   c. 4-4-5 Calendar
   b. Retailing
   d. 529 plan

34. In finance, a _____ is a type of bond that can be converted into shares of stock in the issuing company, usually at some pre-announced ratio. It is a hybrid security with debt- and equity-like features. Although it typically has a low coupon rate, the holder is compensated with the ability to convert the bond to common stock, usually at a substantial discount to the stock's market value.
   a. Bond fund
   c. Corporate bond
   b. Gilts
   d. Convertible bond

Chapter 25. Nonagency CMOs

1. _____ is the value of a homeowner's unencumbered interest in their property, i.e. the difference between the home's fair market value and the unpaid balance of the mortgage and any outstanding debt over the home. _____ increases as the mortgage is paid or as the property enjoys appreciation. This is sometimes called real property value in economics.

   a. Home equity
   c. REIT
   b. Real Estate Investment Trust
   d. Liquidation value

2. In lending agreements, _____ is a borrower's pledge of specific property to a lender, to secure repayment of a loan. The _____ serves as protection for a lender against a borrower's risk of default - that is, a borrower failing to pay the principal and interest under the terms of a loan obligation. If a borrower does default on a loan (due to insolvency or other event), that borrower forfeits (gives up) the property pledged as _____ *ollateral* - and the lender then becomes the owner of the _____.

   a. Refinancing risk
   c. Nominal value
   b. Future-oriented
   d. Collateral

3. _____ is early repayment of a loan by a borrower.

   In the case of a mortgage-backed security (MBS), _____ is perceived as a risk, because mortgage debts are often paid off early in order to incur lower total interest payments through cheaper refinancing. The new financing may be cheaper because the borrower's credit rating has improved or because interest rates are lower, but in either case, the payments that would have been made to the MBS investor would be above market rates.

   a. Prepayment
   c. Disposal tax effect
   b. Bankruptcy remote
   d. Retention ratio

4. _____ is the provision of resources (such as granting a loan) by one party to another party where that second party does not reimburse the first party immediately, thereby generating a debt, and instead arranges either to repay or return those resources (or material(s) of equal value) at a later date. The first party is called a creditor, also known as a lender, while the second party is called a debtor, also known as a borrower.

   Movements of financial capital are normally dependent on either _____ or equity transfers.

   a. Comparable
   c. Clearing house
   b. Warrant
   d. Credit

5. _____ is a key part of the securitization transaction in structured finance, and is important for credit rating agencies when rating a securitization. The credit crisis of 2007-2008 has discredited the process of _____ of structured securities as a legitimate financial practice.

   There are two primary types of _____: Internal and External.

   a. Credit enhancement
   c. 4-4-5 Calendar
   b. Tranche
   d. Yield curve spread

6. In financial accounting, the term _____ is most commonly used to describe any part of shareholders' equity, except for basic share capital. Sometimes, the term is used instead of the term provision; such a use, however, is inconsistent with the terminology suggested by International Accounting Standards Board. For more information about provisions, see provision (accounting.)
    a. Closing entries
    b. Treasury stock
    c. FIFO and LIFO accounting
    d. Reserve

7. _____ is a fee paid on borrowed assets. It is the price paid for the use of borrowed money , or, money earned by deposited funds . Assets that are sometimes lent with _____ include money, shares, consumer goods through hire purchase, major assets such as aircraft, and even entire factories in finance lease arrangements.
    a. AAB
    b. Interest
    c. A Random Walk Down Wall Street
    d. Insolvency

8. An _____ is a future interest, held by a third party transferee (i.e. someone other than the grantee), which either cuts off another's interest or begins after the natural termination of a preceding estate. It differs from a remainder.

There are two different types of _____s: shifting and springing.

    a. Economic depreciation
    b. Executory Interest
    c. Express warranty
    d. Articles of incorporation

9. The _____ (NYSE: FRE) is an insolvent government sponsored enterprise (GSE) of the United States federal government.

The _____ was created in 1970 to expand the secondary market for mortgages in the US. Along with other GSEs, Freddie Mac buys mortgages on the secondary market, pools them, and sells them as mortgage-backed securities to investors on the open market.

    a. Federal Home Loan Mortgage Corporation
    b. Public company
    c. Governmental Accounting Standards Board
    d. The Depository Trust ' Clearing Corporation

10. In finance, a _____ is a debt security, in which the authorized issuer owes the holders a debt and, depending on the terms of the _____, is obliged to pay interest (the coupon) and/or to repay the principal at a later date, termed maturity.

Thus a _____ is a loan: the issuer is the borrower, the _____ holder is the lender, and the coupon is the interest. _____s provide the borrower with external funds to finance long-term investments, or, in the case of government _____s, to finance current expenditure.

    a. Convertible bond
    b. Catastrophe bonds
    c. Bond
    d. Puttable bond

11. The coupon or _____ of a bond is the amount of interest paid per year expressed as a percentage of the face value of the bond.

For example if you hold $10,000 nominal of a bond described as a 4.5% loan stock, you will receive $450 in interest each year (probably in two installments of $225 each.)

Not all bonds have coupons.

a. Zero-coupon bond
c. Revenue bonds
b. Puttable bond
d. Coupon rate

12. In financial accounting, _____s are precautions for which the amount or probability of occurrence are not known. Typical examples are _____s for warranty costs and _____ for taxes the term reserve is used instead of term _____; such a use, however, is inconsistent with the terminology suggested by International Accounting Standards Board.

a. Momentum Accounting and Triple-Entry Bookkeeping
c. Money measurement concept
b. Petty cash
d. Provision

Chapter 26. Residential Asset-Backed Securities

1. An _____ is a security whose value and income payments are derived from and collateralized (or 'backed') by a specified pool of underlying assets. The pool of assets is typically a group of small and illiquid assets that are unable to be sold individually. Pooling the assets allows them to be sold to general investors, a process called securitization, and allows the risk of investing in the underlying assets to be diversified because each security will represent a fraction of the total value of the diverse pool of underlying assets.
    a. AAB
    b. ABN Amro
    c. A Random Walk Down Wall Street
    d. Asset-backed security

2. _____ is the increase in the amount of the goods and services produced by an economy over time. It is conventionally measured as the percent rate of increase in real gross domestic product, or real GDP. Growth is usually calculated in real terms, i.e. inflation-adjusted terms, in order to net out the effect of inflation on the price of the goods and services produced.
    a. ABN Amro
    b. A Random Walk Down Wall Street
    c. AAB
    d. Economic growth

3. A _____ is a fungible, negotiable instrument representing financial value. They are broadly categorized into debt securities (such as banknotes, bonds and debentures), and equity securities; e.g., common stocks. The company or other entity issuing the _____ is called the issuer.
    a. Tracking stock
    b. Securities lending
    c. Book entry
    d. Security

4. _____ is the value of a homeowner's unencumbered interest in their property, i.e. the difference between the home's fair market value and the unpaid balance of the mortgage and any outstanding debt over the home. _____ increases as the mortgage is paid or as the property enjoys appreciation. This is sometimes called real property value in economics.
    a. Home equity
    b. REIT
    c. Real Estate Investment Trust
    d. Liquidation value

5. In lending agreements, _____ is a borrower's pledge of specific property to a lender, to secure repayment of a loan. The _____ serves as protection for a lender against a borrower's risk of default - that is, a borrower failing to pay the principal and interest under the terms of a loan obligation. If a borrower does default on a loan (due to insolvency or other event), that borrower forfeits (gives up) the property pledged as _____ *ollateral* - and the lender then becomes the owner of the _____.
    a. Future-oriented
    b. Refinancing risk
    c. Nominal value
    d. Collateral

6. In finance, a _____ is the party in a loan agreement which receives money or other instrument from a lender and promises to repay the lender in a specified time.
    a. Debt management plan
    b. Line of credit
    c. Cash credit
    d. Borrower

7. _____ is a legal entity that develops, registers and sells securities for the purpose of financing its operations. _____s may be domestic or foreign governments, corporations or investment trusts. _____s are legally responsible for the obligations of the issue and for reporting financial conditions, material developments and any other operational activities as required by the regulations of their jurisdictions.

Chapter 26. Residential Asset-Backed Securities

a. Efficient-market hypothesis
b. Initial margin
c. Arbitrage
d. Issuer

8. The institution most often referenced by the word '_____' is a public or publicly traded _____, the shares of which are traded on a public stock exchange (e.g., the New York Stock Exchange or Nasdaq in the United States) where shares of stock of _____s are bought and sold by and to the general public. Most of the largest businesses in the world are publicly traded _____s. However, the majority of _____s are said to be closely held, privately held or close _____s, meaning that no ready market exists for the trading of shares.

a. Protect
b. Corporation
c. Depository Trust Company
d. Federal Home Loan Mortgage Corporation

9. _____ or financing is to provide capital (funds), which means money for a project, a person, a business or any other private or public institutions.

Those funds can be allocated for either short term or long term purposes. The health fund is a new way of _____ private healthcare centers.

a. Synthetic CDO
b. Proxy fight
c. Product life cycle
d. Funding

10. _____ is the provision of resources (such as granting a loan) by one party to another party where that second party does not reimburse the first party immediately, thereby generating a debt, and instead arranges either to repay or return those resources (or material(s) of equal value) at a later date. The first party is called a creditor, also known as a lender, while the second party is called a debtor, also known as a borrower.

Movements of financial capital are normally dependent on either _____ or equity transfers.

a. Warrant
b. Clearing house
c. Comparable
d. Credit

11. An _____ is a mortgage loan where the interest rate on the note is periodically adjusted based on a variety of indices. Among the most common indices are the rates on 1-year constant-maturity Treasury (CMT) securities, the Cost of Funds Index (COFI), and the London Interbank Offered Rate (LIBOR.) A few lenders use their own cost of funds as an index, rather than using other indices.

a. AAB
b. ABN Amro
c. A Random Walk Down Wall Street
d. Adjustable rate mortgage

12. _____ is early repayment of a loan by a borrower.

In the case of a mortgage-backed security (MBS), _____ is perceived as a risk, because mortgage debts are often paid off early in order to incur lower total interest payments through cheaper refinancing. The new financing may be cheaper because the borrower's credit rating has improved or because interest rates are lower, but in either case, the payments that would have been made to the MBS investor would be above market rates.

a. Prepayment
c. Bankruptcy remote
b. Disposal tax effect
d. Retention ratio

13. _____ refers to the replacement of an existing debt obligation with a debt obligation bearing different terms. The most common consumer _____ is for a home mortgage.

_____ may be undertaken to reduce interest rate/interest costs (by _____ at a lower rate), to extend the repayment time, to pay off other debt(s), to reduce one's periodic payment obligations (sometimes by taking a longer-term loan), to reduce or alter risk (such as by _____ from a variable-rate to a fixed-rate loan), and/or to raise cash for investment, consumption, or the payment of a dividend.

a. 529 plan
c. 4-4-5 Calendar
b. 7-Eleven
d. Refinancing

14. _____ is the risk of loss due to a debtor's non-payment of a loan or other line of credit (either the principal or interest (coupon) or both)

Most lenders employ their own models (credit scorecards) to rank potential and existing customers according to risk, and then apply appropriate strategies. With products such as unsecured personal loans or mortgages, lenders charge a higher price for higher risk customers and vice versa. With revolving products such as credit cards and overdrafts, risk is controlled through careful setting of credit limits.

a. Transaction risk
c. Credit risk
b. Market risk
d. Liquidity risk

15. _____ is the method by which one calculates the creditworthiness of a business or organization. The audited financial statements of a large company might be analyzed when it issues or has issued bonds. Or, a bank may analyze the financial statements of a small business before making or renewing a commercial loan.

a. Credit analysis
c. Credit crunch
b. Capital note
d. Credit report monitoring

16. In law, a _____ is a form of security interest granted over an item of property to secure the payment of a debt or performance of some other obligation. The owner of the property, who grants the _____, is referred to as the lienor and the person who has the benefit of the _____ is referred to as the _____ee.

The etymological root is: Anglo-French _____, loyen bond, restraint, from Latin ligamen, from ligare to bind.

a. Sarbanes-Oxley Act
c. Family and Medical Leave Act
b. Lien
d. Joint venture

17. In finance, a _____ is a debt security, in which the authorized issuer owes the holders a debt and, depending on the terms of the _____, is obliged to pay interest (the coupon) and/or to repay the principal at a later date, termed maturity.

Chapter 26. Residential Asset-Backed Securities

Thus a _____ is a loan: the issuer is the borrower, the _____ holder is the lender, and the coupon is the interest. _____s provide the borrower with external funds to finance long-term investments, or, in the case of government _____s, to finance current expenditure.

a. Convertible bond
b. Catastrophe bonds
c. Bond
d. Puttable bond

18. The _____ is a financial market where participants buy and sell debt securities, usually in the form of bonds. As of 2006, the size of the international _____ is an estimated $45 trillion, of which the size of the outstanding U.S. _____ debt was $25.2 trillion.

Nearly all of the $923 billion average daily trading volume in the U.S. _____ takes place between broker-dealers and large institutions in a decentralized, over-the-counter market.

a. Bond market
b. Fixed income
c. 529 plan
d. 4-4-5 Calendar

19. A _____ is a listing of bonds or fixed income instruments and a statistic reflecting the composite value of its components. It is used as a tool to represent the characteristics of its component fixed income instruments. They differ from stock market indices in their complexity.

a. 7-Eleven
b. 4-4-5 Calendar
c. 529 plan
d. Bond market index

20. An _____ is a future interest, held by a third party transferee (i.e. someone other than the grantee), which either cuts off another's interest or begins after the natural termination of a preceding estate. It differs from a remainder.

There are two different types of _____s: shifting and springing.

a. Economic depreciation
b. Express warranty
c. Articles of incorporation
d. Executory Interest

21. _____ is a fee paid on borrowed assets. It is the price paid for the use of borrowed money, or, money earned by deposited funds. Assets that are sometimes lent with _____ include money, shares, consumer goods through hire purchase, major assets such as aircraft, and even entire factories in finance lease arrangements.

a. AAB
b. Interest
c. Insolvency
d. A Random Walk Down Wall Street

22. In finance, _____ occurs when a debtor has not met its legal obligations according to the debt contract, e.g. it has not made a scheduled payment, or has violated a loan covenant (condition) of the debt contract. _____ may occur if the debtor is either unwilling or unable to pay their debt. This can occur with all debt obligations including bonds, mortgages, loans, and promissory notes.

a. Vendor finance
b. Debt validation
c. Credit crunch
d. Default

23. _____ is an insurance policy which compensates lenders or investors for losses due to the default of a mortgage loan. _____ can be either public or private depending upon the insurer. The policy is also known as a mortgage indemnity guarantee (Mortgage insuranceG), particularly in the UK.

a. Reverse mortgage
c. Subprime lending
b. Mortgage-backed security
d. Mortgage insurance

24. The coupon or _____ of a bond is the amount of interest paid per year expressed as a percentage of the face value of the bond.

For example if you hold $10,000 nominal of a bond described as a 4.5% loan stock, you will receive $450 in interest each year (probably in two installments of $225 each.)

Not all bonds have coupons.

a. Zero-coupon bond
c. Revenue bonds
b. Puttable bond
d. Coupon rate

Chapter 27. Commercial Mortgage-Backed Securities

1. _____ are a type of bond commonly issued in American security markets. They are a type of mortgage-backed security backed by mortgages on commercial rather than residential real estate. CMBS issues are usually structured as multiple tranches, similar to CMOs, rather than typical residential 'passthroughs.'

Many American CMBSs carry less prepayment risk than other MBS types, thanks to the structure of commercial mortgages.

   a. Commercial mortgage-backed securities
   b. Stop order
   c. Contract for difference
   d. Stock market index

2. A _____ is an asset-backed security whose cash flows are backed by the principal and interest payments of a set of mortgage loans. Payments are typically made monthly over the lifetime of the underlying loans.
   a. Home equity line of credit
   b. Conforming loan
   c. Shared appreciation mortgage
   d. Mortgage-backed security

3. A _____ is a fungible, negotiable instrument representing financial value. They are broadly categorized into debt securities (such as banknotes, bonds and debentures), and equity securities; e.g., common stocks. The company or other entity issuing the _____ is called the issuer.
   a. Securities lending
   b. Tracking stock
   c. Security
   d. Book entry

4. The institution most often referenced by the word '_____' is a public or publicly traded _____, the shares of which are traded on a public stock exchange (e.g., the New York Stock Exchange or Nasdaq in the United States) where shares of stock of _____s are bought and sold by and to the general public. Most of the largest businesses in the world are publicly traded _____s. However, the majority of _____s are said to be closely held, privately held or close _____s, meaning that no ready market exists for the trading of shares.
   a. Federal Home Loan Mortgage Corporation
   b. Protect
   c. Depository Trust Company
   d. Corporation

5. _____ is the provision of resources (such as granting a loan) by one party to another party where that second party does not reimburse the first party immediately, thereby generating a debt, and instead arranges either to repay or return those resources (or material(s) of equal value) at a later date. The first party is called a creditor, also known as a lender, while the second party is called a debtor, also known as a borrower.

Movements of financial capital are normally dependent on either _____ or equity transfers.

   a. Warrant
   b. Clearing house
   c. Credit
   d. Comparable

6. A _____ assesses the credit worthiness of an individual, corporation, or even a country. _____s are calculated from financial history and current assets and liabilities. Typically, a _____ tells a lender or investor the probability of the subject being able to pay back a loan.
   a. Credit report monitoring
   b. Debenture
   c. Credit cycle
   d. Credit rating

Chapter 27. Commercial Mortgage-Backed Securities

7. A _____, in law, is an instrument which defeats the force or operation of some other deed or estate; as distinguished from a condition-- that which in the same deed is called a condition is a _____ in another deed. A _____ should recite the deed to be defeated and its date, and it must be made between the same parties as are interested in the deed.
   a. 4-4-5 Calendar
   b. Due-on-sale clause
   c. 529 plan
   d. Defeasance

8. In finance, the term _____ describes the amount in cash that returns to the owners of a security. Normally it does not include the price variations, at the difference of the total return. _____ applies to various stated rates of return on stocks (common and preferred, and convertible), fixed income instruments (bonds, notes, bills, strips, zero coupon), and some other investment type insurance products (e.g. annuities.)
   a. Yield
   b. 4-4-5 Calendar
   c. Macaulay duration
   d. Yield to maturity

9. _____ is early repayment of a loan by a borrower.

In the case of a mortgage-backed security (MBS), _____ is perceived as a risk, because mortgage debts are often paid off early in order to incur lower total interest payments through cheaper refinancing. The new financing may be cheaper because the borrower's credit rating has improved or because interest rates are lower, but in either case, the payments that would have been made to the MBS investor would be above market rates.

   a. Disposal tax effect
   b. Retention ratio
   c. Prepayment
   d. Bankruptcy remote

10. In finance, _____ occurs when a debtor has not met its legal obligations according to the debt contract, e.g. it has not made a scheduled payment, or has violated a loan covenant (condition) of the debt contract. _____ may occur if the debtor is either unwilling or unable to pay their debt. This can occur with all debt obligations including bonds, mortgages, loans, and promissory notes.
    a. Default
    b. Vendor finance
    c. Debt validation
    d. Credit crunch

11. _____ is the risk of loss due to a debtor's non-payment of a loan or other line of credit (either the principal or interest (coupon) or both)

Most lenders employ their own models (credit scorecards) to rank potential and existing customers according to risk, and then apply appropriate strategies. With products such as unsecured personal loans or mortgages, lenders charge a higher price for higher risk customers and vice versa. With revolving products such as credit cards and overdrafts, risk is controlled through careful setting of credit limits.

   a. Liquidity risk
   b. Transaction risk
   c. Market risk
   d. Credit risk

12. _____ in finance is a risk management technique, related to hedging, that mixes a wide variety of investments within a portfolio. Because the fluctuations of a single security have less impact on a diverse portfolio, _____ minimizes the risk from any one investment.

Chapter 27. Commercial Mortgage-Backed Securities

A simple example of _____ is the following: On a particular island the entire economy consists of two companies: one that sells umbrellas and another that sells sunscreen.

a. 529 plan
c. 4-4-5 Calendar
b. 7-Eleven
d. Diversification

13. In lending agreements, _____ is a borrower's pledge of specific property to a lender, to secure repayment of a loan. The _____ serves as protection for a lender against a borrower's risk of default - that is, a borrower failing to pay the principal and interest under the terms of a loan obligation. If a borrower does default on a loan (due to insolvency or other event), that borrower forfeits (gives up) the property pledged as _____ ollateral - and the lender then becomes the owner of the _____.

a. Collateral
c. Refinancing risk
b. Future-oriented
d. Nominal value

14. _____ is a term used when the collateral for one loan is also used as collateral for another loan. If a person has borrowed from the same bank a home loan secured by the house, a car loan secured by the car, and so on, these assets can be used as cross-collaterals for all the loans. If the person pays off the car loan and wants to sell the car, the bank may veto the deal because the car is still used to secure the home loan and other loans.

a. Credit freeze
c. Credit score
b. Collection agency
d. Cross-collateralization

Chapter 28. Credit Card Asset-Backed Securities

1. _____ is the provision of resources (such as granting a loan) by one party to another party where that second party does not reimburse the first party immediately, thereby generating a debt, and instead arranges either to repay or return those resources (or material(s) of equal value) at a later date. The first party is called a creditor, also known as a lender, while the second party is called a debtor, also known as a borrower.

Movements of financial capital are normally dependent on either _____ or equity transfers.

a. Comparable
b. Clearing house
c. Credit
d. Warrant

2. _____ is a structured finance process that involves pooling and repackaging of cash-flow-producing financial assets into securities, which are then sold to investors. The term '_____' is derived from the fact that the form of financial instruments used to obtain funds from the investors are securities. As a portfolio risk backed by amortizing cash flows - and unlike general corporate debt - the credit quality of securitized debt is non-stationary due to changes in volatility that are time- and structure-dependent.

a. Special journals
b. Securitization
c. The Glass-Steagall Act of 1933
d. Reputational risk

3. _____ is the process of decreasing an amount over a period of time. The word comes from Middle English amortisen to kill, alienate in mortmain, from Anglo-French amorteser, alteration of amortir, from Vulgar Latin admortire to kill, from Latin ad- + mort-, mors death. Particular instances of the term include:

- _____ (business), the allocation of a lump sum amount to different time periods, particularly for loans and other forms of finance, including related interest or other finance charges.
    - _____ schedule, a table detailing each periodic payment on a loan (typically a mortgage), as generated by an _____ calculator.
    - Negative _____, an _____ schedule where the loan amount actually increases through not paying the full interest
- Amortized analysis, analyzing the execution cost of algorithms over a sequence of operations.
- _____ of capital expenditures of certain assets under accounting rules, particularly intangible assets, in a manner analogous to depreciation.
- _____ (tax law)

_____ is also used in the context of zoning regulations and describes the time in which a property owner has to relocate when the property's use constitutes a preexisting nonconforming use under zoning regulations.

- Depreciation

a. Intrinsic value
b. Option
c. AT'T Inc.
d. Amortization

4. _____ is a fee paid on borrowed assets. It is the price paid for the use of borrowed money , or, money earned by deposited funds . Assets that are sometimes lent with _____ include money, shares, consumer goods through hire purchase, major assets such as aircraft, and even entire factories in finance lease arrangements.

Chapter 28. Credit Card Asset-Backed Securities

a. AAB
c. Insolvency

b. A Random Walk Down Wall Street
d. Interest

5. In finance, the term _____ describes the amount in cash that returns to the owners of a security. Normally it does not include the price variations, at the difference of the total return. _____ applies to various stated rates of return on stocks (common and preferred, and convertible), fixed income instruments (bonds, notes, bills, strips, zero coupon), and some other investment type insurance products (e.g. annuities.)

a. 4-4-5 Calendar
c. Macaulay duration

b. Yield to maturity
d. Yield

6. _____ is a key part of the securitization transaction in structured finance, and is important for credit rating agencies when rating a securitization. The credit crisis of 2007-2008 has discredited the process of _____ of structured securities as a legitimate financial practice.

There are two primary types of _____: Internal and External.

a. Tranche
c. 4-4-5 Calendar

b. Yield curve spread
d. Credit enhancement

7. In lending agreements, _____ is a borrower's pledge of specific property to a lender, to secure repayment of a loan. The _____ serves as protection for a lender against a borrower's risk of default - that is, a borrower failing to pay the principal and interest under the terms of a loan obligation. If a borrower does default on a loan (due to insolvency or other event), that borrower forfeits (gives up) the property pledged as _____ *ollateral* - and the lender then becomes the owner of the _____.

a. Future-oriented
c. Collateral

b. Nominal value
d. Refinancing risk

8. _____, in bookkeeping, refers to assets, liabilities, income, and expenses recorded on individual pages of the so called book of final entry or ledger. Changes in _____ value are made by chronologically posting debit (DR) and credit (CR) entries to its page. Examples of _____s are cash, _____s receivable, mortgages, loans, land and buildings, common stock, sales, services provided, wages, and payroll overhead.

a. Accretion
c. Alpha

b. Option
d. Account

9. _____ is the increase in the amount of the goods and services produced by an economy over time. It is conventionally measured as the percent rate of increase in real gross domestic product, or real GDP. Growth is usually calculated in real terms, i.e. inflation-adjusted terms, in order to net out the effect of inflation on the price of the goods and services produced.

a. A Random Walk Down Wall Street
c. ABN Amro

b. AAB
d. Economic growth

10. _____ or amalgamation is the act of merging many things into one. In business, it often refers to the mergers or acquisitions of many smaller companies into much larger ones. The financial accounting term of _____ refers to the aggregated financial statements of a group company as consolidated account.

a. Retained earnings
b. Cost of goods sold
c. Write-off
d. Consolidation

11. _____ is a legal entity that develops, registers and sells securities for the purpose of financing its operations. _____s may be domestic or foreign governments, corporations or investment trusts. _____s are legally responsible for the obligations of the issue and for reporting financial conditions, material developments and any other operational activities as required by the regulations of their jurisdictions.

a. Arbitrage
b. Initial margin
c. Issuer
d. Efficient-market hypothesis

Chapter 29. Securities Backed by Automobile Loans and Leases

1. The institution most often referenced by the word '_____' is a public or publicly traded _____, the shares of which are traded on a public stock exchange (e.g., the New York Stock Exchange or Nasdaq in the United States) where shares of stock of _____s are bought and sold by and to the general public. Most of the largest businesses in the world are publicly traded _____s. However, the majority of _____s are said to be closely held, privately held or close _____s, meaning that no ready market exists for the trading of shares.
   a. Federal Home Loan Mortgage Corporation
   b. Protect
   c. Depository Trust Company
   d. Corporation

2. _____ or financing is to provide capital (funds), which means money for a project, a person, a business or any other private or public institutions.

   Those funds can be allocated for either short term or long term purposes. The health fund is a new way of _____ private healthcare centers.

   a. Proxy fight
   b. Product life cycle
   c. Synthetic CDO
   d. Funding

3. In finance, a _____ is the party in a loan agreement which receives money or other instrument from a lender and promises to repay the lender in a specified time.
   a. Line of credit
   b. Debt management plan
   c. Cash credit
   d. Borrower

4. Leasing is a process by which a firm can obtain the use of a certain fixed assets for which it must pay a series of contractual, periodic, tax deductable payments. The lessee is the receiver of the services or the assets under the lease contract and the lessor is the owner of the assets. The relationship between the tenant and the landlord is called a _____, and can be for a fixed or an indefinite period of time (called the term of the lease.)
   a. REIT
   b. Real Estate Investment Trust
   c. Real estate investing
   d. Tenancy

5. In lending agreements, _____ is a borrower's pledge of specific property to a lender, to secure repayment of a loan. The _____ serves as protection for a lender against a borrower's risk of default - that is, a borrower failing to pay the principal and interest under the terms of a loan obligation. If a borrower does default on a loan (due to insolvency or other event), that borrower forfeits (gives up) the property pledged as _____ _ollateral_ - and the lender then becomes the owner of the _____.
   a. Nominal value
   b. Collateral
   c. Refinancing risk
   d. Future-oriented

6. An _____ is a security whose value and income payments are derived from and collateralized (or 'backed') by a specified pool of underlying assets. The pool of assets is typically a group of small and illiquid assets that are unable to be sold individually. Pooling the assets allows them to be sold to general investors, a process called securitization, and allows the risk of investing in the underlying assets to be diversified because each security will represent a fraction of the total value of the diverse pool of underlying assets.
   a. A Random Walk Down Wall Street
   b. ABN Amro
   c. AAB
   d. Asset-backed security

7. _____ is early repayment of a loan by a borrower.

In the case of a mortgage-backed security (MBS), _____ is perceived as a risk, because mortgage debts are often paid off early in order to incur lower total interest payments through cheaper refinancing. The new financing may be cheaper because the borrower's credit rating has improved or because interest rates are lower, but in either case, the payments that would have been made to the MBS investor would be above market rates.

a. Retention ratio
b. Disposal tax effect
c. Bankruptcy remote
d. Prepayment

8. A _____ is a fungible, negotiable instrument representing financial value. They are broadly categorized into debt securities (such as banknotes, bonds and debentures), and equity securities; e.g., common stocks. The company or other entity issuing the _____ is called the issuer.

a. Tracking stock
b. Securities lending
c. Book entry
d. Security

9. _____ is a measure of the rate of payments from a bond that pays principal payments in excess of scheduled payments (so-called prepayments.) Such bonds include mortgage-backed securities, CMOs, and ABS, which prepay at some rate usually dependent on the level of interest rates.

_____ is defined as the annualized rate of principal payments beyond the regularly scheduled payments, and is stated as a percentage of outstanding amount of the security or loan minus the scheduled payments.

a. Total return
b. Conditional prepayment rate
c. Cash management
d. Profitability index

10. The _____ is one of a number of uniform acts that have been promulgated in conjunction with efforts to harmonize the law of sales and other commercial transactions in all 50 states within the United States of America. This objective is deemed important because of the prevalence today of commercial transactions that extend beyond one state (for example, where the goods are manufactured in state A, warehoused in state B, sold from state C and delivered in state D.) The _____ deals primarily with transactions involving personal property (movable property), not real property (immovable property.)

a. Executory Interest
b. Assumption of risk
c. Uniform Commercial Code
d. External risks

11.

In contract law, _____ are risks that are produced by a non-human source and are beyond human control. They are unexpected but happen regularly enough in a general population to be broadly predictable, and may be the subject of casualty insurance. Good examples of _____ are natural disasters such as earthquakes and volcanoes.

a. Express warranty
b. External risks
c. Economies of scale
d. Uniform Securities Act

Chapter 29. Securities Backed by Automobile Loans and Leases

12. _____ is the provision of resources (such as granting a loan) by one party to another party where that second party does not reimburse the first party immediately, thereby generating a debt, and instead arranges either to repay or return those resources (or material(s) of equal value) at a later date. The first party is called a creditor, also known as a lender, while the second party is called a debtor, also known as a borrower.

Movements of financial capital are normally dependent on either _____ or equity transfers.

- a. Comparable
- b. Credit
- c. Clearing house
- d. Warrant

13. _____ is a key part of the securitization transaction in structured finance, and is important for credit rating agencies when rating a securitization. The credit crisis of 2007-2008 has discredited the process of _____ of structured securities as a legitimate financial practice.

There are two primary types of _____: Internal and External.

- a. 4-4-5 Calendar
- b. Tranche
- c. Yield curve spread
- d. Credit enhancement

14. _____ is a structured finance process that involves pooling and repackaging of cash-flow-producing financial assets into securities, which are then sold to investors. The term '_____' is derived from the fact that the form of financial instruments used to obtain funds from the investors are securities. As a portfolio risk backed by amortizing cash flows - and unlike general corporate debt - the credit quality of securitized debt is non-stationary due to changes in volatility that are time- and structure-dependent.

- a. Securitization
- b. Reputational risk
- c. The Glass-Steagall Act of 1933
- d. Special journals

15. _____ means the inability to pay one's debts as they fall due. Usually used in Business terms, _____ refers to the inability for a 'limited liability' company to pay off debts.

This is defined in two different ways:

Cash flow _____ -
    Unable to pay debts as they fall due.
Balance sheet _____ -
    Having negative net assets: liabilities exceed assets; or net liabilities.

- a. Insolvency
- b. A Random Walk Down Wall Street
- c. AAB
- d. Interest

16. In the most general sense, a _____ is anything that is a hindrance, or puts individuals at a disadvantage.

Before we discuss the financial terms, we should note that a _____ can also have a much more important slang meaning.

This is best described in an example.

a. Limited liability
c. Liability
b. McFadden Act
d. Covenant

17. _____ is a term used in accounting, economics and finance to spread the cost of an asset over the span of several years.

In simple words we can say that _____ is the reduction in the value of an asset due to usage, passage of time, wear and tear, technological outdating or obsolescence, depletion or other such factors.

In accounting, _____ is a term used to describe any method of attributing the historical or purchase cost of an asset across its useful life, roughly corresponding to normal wear and tear.

a. Matching principle
c. Bottom line
b. Deferred financing costs
d. Depreciation

18. _____ is the price at which an asset would trade in a competitive Walrasian auction setting. _____ is often used interchangeably with open _____, fair value or fair _____, although these terms have distinct definitions in different standards, and may differ in some circumstances.

International Valuation Standards defines _____ as 'the estimated amount for which a property should exchange on the date of valuation between a willing buyer and a willing seller in an arm'e;s-length transaction after proper marketing wherein the parties had each acted knowledgeably, prudently, and without compulsion.'

_____ is a concept distinct from market price, which is 'e;the price at which one can transact'e;, while _____ is 'e;the true underlying value'e; according to theoretical standards.

a. T-Model
c. Debt restructuring
b. Wrap account
d. Market value

19. A _____ assesses the credit worthiness of an individual, corporation, or even a country. _____s are calculated from financial history and current assets and liabilities. Typically, a _____ tells a lender or investor the probability of the subject being able to pay back a loan.

a. Credit report monitoring
c. Credit cycle
b. Debenture
d. Credit rating

20. _____ is a measure of the ability of a debtor to pay their debts as and when they fall due. It is usually expressed as a ratio or a percentage of current liabilities.

For a corporation with a published balance sheet there are various ratios used to calculate a measure of liquidity.

a. Operating profit margin
c. Operating leverage
b. Invested capital
d. Accounting liquidity

21. In finance, _____ is the process of estimating the potential market value of a financial asset or liability. they can be done on assets (for example, investments in marketable securities such as stocks, options, business enterprises, or intangible assets such as patents and trademarks) or on liabilities (e.g., Bonds issued by a company.) _____s are required in many contexts including investment analysis, capital budgeting, merger and acquisition transactions, financial reporting, taxable events to determine the proper tax liability, and in litigation.
   a. Procter ' Gamble   b. Margin
   c. Valuation   d. Share

22. In finance, the term _____ describes the amount in cash that returns to the owners of a security. Normally it does not include the price variations, at the difference of the total return. _____ applies to various stated rates of return on stocks (common and preferred, and convertible), fixed income instruments (bonds, notes, bills, strips, zero coupon), and some other investment type insurance products (e.g. annuities.)
   a. 4-4-5 Calendar   b. Yield to maturity
   c. Macaulay duration   d. Yield

Chapter 30. Cash-Collateralized Debt Obligations

1. _____ are a type of structured asset-backed security (ABS) whose value and payments are derived from a portfolio of fixed-income underlying assets. _____s are assigned different risk classes, or tranches, whereby 'senior' tranches are considered the safest securities. Interest and principal payments are made in order of seniority, so that junior tranches offer higher coupon payments (and interest rates) or lower prices to compensate for additional default risk.
   a. Municipal bond
   b. Collateralized debt obligations
   c. Senior debt
   d. Zero coupon bond

2. _____ is that which is owed; usually referencing assets owed, but the term can cover other obligations. In the case of assets, _____ is a means of using future purchasing power in the present before a summation has been earned. Some companies and corporations use _____ as a part of their overall corporate finance strategy.
   a. Credit cycle
   b. Partial Payment
   c. Cross-collateralization
   d. Debt

3. In economics and finance, _____ is the practice of taking advantage of a price differential between two or more markets: striking a combination of matching deals that capitalize upon the imbalance, the profit being the difference between the market prices. When used by academics, an _____ is a transaction that involves no negative cash flow at any probabilistic or temporal state and a positive cash flow in at least one state; in simple terms, a risk-free profit.
   a. Arbitrage
   b. Efficient-market hypothesis
   c. Initial margin
   d. Issuer

4. In structured finance, a _____ is one of a number of related securities offered as part of the same transaction. The word _____ is French for slice, section, series, or portion. In the financial sense of the word, each bond is a different slice of the deal's risk.
   a. 4-4-5 Calendar
   b. Credit enhancement
   c. Yield curve spread
   d. Tranche

5. In finance, a _____ is a derivative in which two counterparties agree to exchange one stream of cash flows against another stream. These streams are called the legs of the _____.

The cash flows are calculated over a notional principal amount, which is usually not exchanged between counterparties.

   a. Volatility swap
   b. Volatility arbitrage
   c. Local volatility
   d. Swap

6. _____, refers to consumption opportunity gained by an entity within a specified time frame, which is generally expressed in monetary terms. However, for households and individuals, '_____ is the sum of all the wages, salaries, profits, interests payments, rents and other forms of earnings received... in a given period of time.' For firms, _____ generally refers to net-profit: what remains of revenue after expenses have been subtracted.
   a. Annual report
   b. OIBDA
   c. Accrual
   d. Income

7. _____ is a fee paid on borrowed assets. It is the price paid for the use of borrowed money, or, money earned by deposited funds. Assets that are sometimes lent with _____ include money, shares, consumer goods through hire purchase, major assets such as aircraft, and even entire factories in finance lease arrangements.

Chapter 30. Cash-Collateralized Debt Obligations

a. Interest
c. Insolvency
b. A Random Walk Down Wall Street
d. AAB

8. _____ in finance is a risk management technique, related to hedging, that mixes a wide variety of investments within a portfolio. Because the fluctuations of a single security have less impact on a diverse portfolio, _____ minimizes the risk from any one investment.

A simple example of _____ is the following: On a particular island the entire economy consists of two companies: one that sells umbrellas and another that sells sunscreen.

a. 4-4-5 Calendar
c. 7-Eleven
b. 529 plan
d. Diversification

9. _____ is the provision of resources (such as granting a loan) by one party to another party where that second party does not reimburse the first party immediately, thereby generating a debt, and instead arranges either to repay or return those resources (or material(s) of equal value) at a later date. The first party is called a creditor, also known as a lender, while the second party is called a debtor, also known as a borrower.

Movements of financial capital are normally dependent on either _____ or equity transfers.

a. Warrant
c. Clearing house
b. Comparable
d. Credit

10. A _____ is a credit derivative contract between two counterparties. The buyer makes periodic payments (premium leg) to the seller, and in return receives a payoff (protection or default leg) if an underlying financial instrument defaults. _____ contracts have been incorrectly compared with insurance, because the buyer pays a premium and, in return, receives a sum of money if a specified event occurs.

a. Futures contract
c. Commodity tick
b. Credit default swap
d. Stock market index future

11. In finance, _____ occurs when a debtor has not met its legal obligations according to the debt contract, e.g. it has not made a scheduled payment, or has violated a loan covenant (condition) of the debt contract. _____ may occur if the debtor is either unwilling or unable to pay their debt. This can occur with all debt obligations including bonds, mortgages, loans, and promissory notes.

a. Debt validation
c. Default
b. Credit crunch
d. Vendor finance

12. The _____ is the financial market where previously issued securities and financial instruments such as stock, bonds, options, and futures are bought and sold. The term '_____' is also used refer to the market for any used goods or assets, or an alternative use for an existing product or asset where the customer base is the second market

With primary issuances of securities or financial instruments, or the primary market, investors purchase these securities directly from issuers such as corporations issuing shares in an IPO or private placement, or directly from the federal government in the case of treasuries.

a. Performance attribution
b. Delta neutral
c. Secondary market
d. Financial market

13. A _____ is a collateralized debt obligation (CDO) in which the underlying credit exposures are taken on using a credit default swap rather than by having a vehicle buy physical assets. _____s can either be single tranche CDOs or fully distributed CDOs. _____s are also commonly divided into balance sheet and arbitrage CDOs, although it is often impossible to distinguish in practice between the two types.

a. Synthetic CDO
b. Market capitalization
c. Counting house
d. Planning horizon

14. A _____ is a situation that involves losing one quality or aspect of something in return for gaining another quality or aspect. It implies a decision to be made with full comprehension of both the upside and downside of a particular choice.

In economics the term is expressed as opportunity cost, referring the most preferred alternative given up.

a. Total revenue
b. Trade-off
c. Break-even point
d. Capital outflow

15. _____ is early repayment of a loan by a borrower.

In the case of a mortgage-backed security (MBS), _____ is perceived as a risk, because mortgage debts are often paid off early in order to incur lower total interest payments through cheaper refinancing. The new financing may be cheaper because the borrower's credit rating has improved or because interest rates are lower, but in either case, the payments that would have been made to the MBS investor would be above market rates.

a. Disposal tax effect
b. Prepayment
c. Bankruptcy remote
d. Retention ratio

Chapter 31. Synthetic CDOs

1. A _____ is a collateralized debt obligation (CDO) in which the underlying credit exposures are taken on using a credit default swap rather than by having a vehicle buy physical assets. _____s can either be single tranche CDOs or fully distributed CDOs. _____s are also commonly divided into balance sheet and arbitrage CDOs, although it is often impossible to distinguish in practice between the two types.
   a. Market capitalization
   b. Synthetic CDO
   c. Counting house
   d. Planning horizon

2. In economics and finance, _____ is the practice of taking advantage of a price differential between two or more markets: striking a combination of matching deals that capitalize upon the imbalance, the profit being the difference between the market prices. When used by academics, an _____ is a transaction that involves no negative cash flow at any probabilistic or temporal state and a positive cash flow in at least one state; in simple terms, a risk-free profit.
   a. Initial margin
   b. Arbitrage
   c. Issuer
   d. Efficient-market hypothesis

3. _____ are a type of structured asset-backed security (ABS) whose value and payments are derived from a portfolio of fixed-income underlying assets. _____s are assigned different risk classes, or tranches, whereby 'senior' tranches are considered the safest securities. Interest and principal payments are made in order of seniority, so that junior tranches offer higher coupon payments (and interest rates) or lower prices to compensate for additional default risk.
   a. Senior debt
   b. Municipal bond
   c. Zero coupon bond
   d. Collateralized debt obligations

4. _____ is the provision of resources (such as granting a loan) by one party to another party where that second party does not reimburse the first party immediately, thereby generating a debt, and instead arranges either to repay or return those resources (or material(s) of equal value) at a later date. The first party is called a creditor, also known as a lender, while the second party is called a debtor, also known as a borrower.

   Movements of financial capital are normally dependent on either _____ or equity transfers.

   a. Comparable
   b. Credit
   c. Clearing house
   d. Warrant

5. A _____ is a credit derivative contract between two counterparties. The buyer makes periodic payments (premium leg) to the seller, and in return receives a payoff (protection or default leg) if an underlying financial instrument defaults. _____ contracts have been incorrectly compared with insurance, because the buyer pays a premium and, in return, receives a sum of money if a specified event occurs.
   a. Futures contract
   b. Commodity tick
   c. Stock market index future
   d. Credit default swap

6. In finance, _____ occurs when a debtor has not met its legal obligations according to the debt contract, e.g. it has not made a scheduled payment, or has violated a loan covenant (condition) of the debt contract. _____ may occur if the debtor is either unwilling or unable to pay their debt. This can occur with all debt obligations including bonds, mortgages, loans, and promissory notes.
   a. Default
   b. Credit crunch
   c. Vendor finance
   d. Debt validation

7. _____ is the increase in the amount of the goods and services produced by an economy over time. It is conventionally measured as the percent rate of increase in real gross domestic product, or real GDP. Growth is usually calculated in real terms, i.e. inflation-adjusted terms, in order to net out the effect of inflation on the price of the goods and services produced.

    a. A Random Walk Down Wall Street   b. Economic growth
    c. ABN Amro   d. AAB

8. In finance, a _____ is a derivative in which two counterparties agree to exchange one stream of cash flows against another stream. These streams are called the legs of the _____.

The cash flows are calculated over a notional principal amount, which is usually not exchanged between counterparties.

    a. Volatility arbitrage   b. Volatility swap
    c. Swap   d. Local volatility

9. _____ is that which is owed; usually referencing assets owed, but the term can cover other obligations. In the case of assets, _____ is a means of using future purchasing power in the present before a summation has been earned. Some companies and corporations use _____ as a part of their overall corporate finance strategy.

    a. Cross-collateralization   b. Partial Payment
    c. Credit cycle   d. Debt

10. _____ is the risk of loss due to a debtor's non-payment of a loan or other line of credit (either the principal or interest (coupon) or both)

Most lenders employ their own models (credit scorecards) to rank potential and existing customers according to risk, and then apply appropriate strategies. With products such as unsecured personal loans or mortgages, lenders charge a higher price for higher risk customers and vice versa. With revolving products such as credit cards and overdrafts, risk is controlled through careful setting of credit limits.

    a. Liquidity risk   b. Market risk
    c. Transaction risk   d. Credit risk

11. In structured finance, a _____ is one of a number of related securities offered as part of the same transaction. The word _____ is French for slice, section, series, or portion. In the financial sense of the word, each bond is a different slice of the deal's risk.

    a. Tranche   b. 4-4-5 Calendar
    c. Credit enhancement   d. Yield curve spread

12. In finance, a _____ is a derivative whose value derives from the credit risk on an underlying bond, loan or other financial asset. In this way, the credit risk is on an entity other than the counterparties to the transaction itself. This entity is known as the reference entity and may be a corporate, a sovereign or any other form of legal entity which has incurred debt.

    a. Derivatives markets   b. STIRT
    c. Futures contract   d. Credit derivative

13. A _____ is the financial term used to describe either:

A general default event related to a legal entity's previously agreed financial obligation. In this case, a legal entity fails to meet its obligation on any significant financial transaction (coupon on a bond it issued or interest rate payment on a swap for example.) The marketplace will recognize this as an event related to the legal entity's credit worthiness.

    a. Capital surplus   b. Credit event
    c. No-arbitrage bounds   d. Death spiral financing

14. A _____ is a financial contract whose value is derived from the value of something else (known as the underlying.) The underlying on which a _____ is based can be an asset, weather conditions bonds or other forms of credit.

    a. 4-4-5 Calendar   b. Derivative
    c. 529 plan   d. 7-Eleven

15. _____ is a legally declared inability or impairment of ability of an individual or organization to pay their creditors. Creditors may file a _____ petition against a debtor ('involuntary _____') in an effort to recoup a portion of what they are owed or initiate a restructuring. In the majority of cases, however, _____ is initiated by the debtor (a 'voluntary _____' that is filed by the bankrupt individual or organization.)

    a. Debt settlement   b. Bankruptcy
    c. 529 plan   d. 4-4-5 Calendar

16. _____ is the corporate management term for the act of reorganizing the legal, ownership, operational, or other structures of a company for the purpose of making it more profitable or better organized for its present needs. Alternate reasons for restructing include a change of ownership or ownership structure, demerger repositioning debt _____ and financial _____.

    a. Restructuring   b. Concentrated stock
    c. Day trading   d. Cross-border leasing

17. In finance, a _____ is a debt security, in which the authorized issuer owes the holders a debt and, depending on the terms of the _____, is obliged to pay interest (the coupon) and/or to repay the principal at a later date, termed maturity.

Thus a _____ is a loan: the issuer is the borrower, the _____ holder is the lender, and the coupon is the interest. _____s provide the borrower with external funds to finance long-term investments, or, in the case of government _____s, to finance current expenditure.

    a. Catastrophe bonds   b. Bond
    c. Puttable bond   d. Convertible bond

18. A _____ is a bond issued by a corporation. The term is usually applied to longer-term debt instruments, generally with a maturity date falling at least a year after their issue date. (The term 'commercial paper' is sometimes used for instruments with a shorter maturity.)

    a. Corporate bond   b. Serial bond
    c. Brady bonds   d. Government bond

19. _____ is a measure of the ability of a debtor to pay their debts as and when they fall due. It is usually expressed as a ratio or a percentage of current liabilities.

For a corporation with a published balance sheet there are various ratios used to calculate a measure of liquidity.

a. Operating leverage
b. Operating profit margin
c. Accounting liquidity
d. Invested capital

20. _____ is early repayment of a loan by a borrower.

In the case of a mortgage-backed security (MBS), _____ is perceived as a risk, because mortgage debts are often paid off early in order to incur lower total interest payments through cheaper refinancing. The new financing may be cheaper because the borrower's credit rating has improved or because interest rates are lower, but in either case, the payments that would have been made to the MBS investor would be above market rates.

a. Bankruptcy remote
b. Retention ratio
c. Disposal tax effect
d. Prepayment

21. In economics, business, and accounting, a _____ is the value of money that has been used up to produce something, and hence is not available for use anymore. In business, the _____ may be one of acquisition, in which case the amount of money expended to acquire it is counted as _____. In this case, money is the input that is gone in order to acquire the thing.

a. Cost
b. Fixed costs
c. Marginal cost
d. Sliding scale fees

22. In business and accounting, _____s are everything of value that is owned by a person or company. The balance sheet of a firm records the monetary value of the _____s owned by the firm. The two major _____ classes are tangible _____s and intangible _____s.

a. Accounts payable
b. Income
c. EBITDA
d. Asset

23. In probability theory and statistics, _____ indicates the strength and direction of a linear relationship between two random variables. That is in contrast with the usage of the term in colloquial speech, which denotes any relationship, not necessarily linear. In general statistical usage, _____ or co-relation refers to the departure of two random variables from independence.

a. Correlation
b. Probability distribution
c. Variance
d. Geometric mean

24. _____ in finance is a risk management technique, related to hedging, that mixes a wide variety of investments within a portfolio. Because the fluctuations of a single security have less impact on a diverse portfolio, _____ minimizes the risk from any one investment.

A simple example of _____ is the following: On a particular island the entire economy consists of two companies: one that sells umbrellas and another that sells sunscreen.

a. 7-Eleven
c. Diversification
b. 529 plan
d. 4-4-5 Calendar

25. _____ are similar to certificates of deposit that can be purchased at banks; however, they are sold by insurance companies. Like money market funds, they're very safe investments; and like all investments that are considered to be 'very safe', they won't make you very much money. Also known by other names - fixed-income fund, stable value fund, capital-preservation fund, or guaranteed fund, for example -- they generally pay interest from one- to five years.
   a. CODA plc
   c. Reputational risk
   b. Vati-Con
   d. Guaranteed investment contracts

26. A _____ is an exchange of promises between two or more parties to do an act which is enforceable in a court of law. It is where an unqualified offer meets a qualified acceptance and the parties reach Consensus ad Idem. The parties must have the necessary capacity to _____ and the _____ must not be either trifling, indeterminate, impossible or illegal.
   a. Contract
   c. 4-4-5 Calendar
   b. 7-Eleven
   d. 529 plan

27. The _____ or cash market is a commodities or securities market in which goods are sold for cash and delivered immediately. Contracts bought and sold on these markets are immediately effective. _____s can operate wherever the infrastructure exists to conduct the transaction.
   a. Spot market
   c. Currency swap
   b. Non-deliverable forward
   d. Foreign exchange controls

Chapter 32. Credit Analysis for Corporate Bonds

1. _____ refers to an assessment of the viability, stability and profitability of a business, sub-business or project.

It is performed by professionals who prepare reports using ratios that make use of information taken from financial statements and other reports. These reports are usually presented to top management as one of their bases in making business decisions.

   a. 4-4-5 Calendar
   b. 529 plan
   c. Value investing
   d. Financial analysis

2. _____ is the provision of resources (such as granting a loan) by one party to another party where that second party does not reimburse the first party immediately, thereby generating a debt, and instead arranges either to repay or return those resources (or material(s) of equal value) at a later date. The first party is called a creditor, also known as a lender, while the second party is called a debtor, also known as a borrower.

Movements of financial capital are normally dependent on either _____ or equity transfers.

   a. Clearing house
   b. Warrant
   c. Comparable
   d. Credit

3. _____ is the risk of loss due to a debtor's non-payment of a loan or other line of credit (either the principal or interest (coupon) or both)

Most lenders employ their own models (credit scorecards) to rank potential and existing customers according to risk, and then apply appropriate strategies. With products such as unsecured personal loans or mortgages, lenders charge a higher price for higher risk customers and vice versa. With revolving products such as credit cards and overdrafts, risk is controlled through careful setting of credit limits.

   a. Market risk
   b. Credit risk
   c. Liquidity risk
   d. Transaction risk

4. _____ refers to the use of formal econometric techniques to determine the aggregate risk in a financial portfolio. _____ is one of many subtasks within the broader area of financial modeling.

_____ uses a variety of techniques including market risk, Value-at-Risk (VaR), Historical Simulation (HS), or Extreme Value Theory (EVT) in order to analyze a portfolio and make forecasts of the likely losses that would be incurred for a variety of risks.

   a. Value at risk
   b. Risk modeling
   c. Risk adjusted return on capital
   d. Risk premium

5. _____ is the standard framework of guidelines for financial accounting used in the United States of America. It includes the standards, conventions, and rules accountants follow in recording and summarizing transactions, and in the preparation of financial statements. _____ are now issued by the Financial Accounting Standards Board (FASB).
   a. Revenue
   b. Net income
   c. Depreciation
   d. Generally accepted accounting principles

Chapter 32. Credit Analysis for Corporate Bonds

6. In business and accounting, _____s are everything of value that is owned by a person or company. The balance sheet of a firm records the monetary value of the _____s owned by the firm. The two major _____ classes are tangible _____s and intangible _____s.
   a. Asset
   b. Income
   c. Accounts payable
   d. EBITDA

7. _____ is a fee paid on borrowed assets. It is the price paid for the use of borrowed money , or, money earned by deposited funds . Assets that are sometimes lent with _____ include money, shares, consumer goods through hire purchase, major assets such as aircraft, and even entire factories in finance lease arrangements.
   a. AAB
   b. Interest
   c. A Random Walk Down Wall Street
   d. Insolvency

8. _____ relates to the cost of borrowing money. It is the price that a lender charges a borrower for the use of the lender's money. _____ is different from OPEX and CAPEX, for it relates to the capital structure of a company.
   a. ABN Amro
   b. Interest expense
   c. A Random Walk Down Wall Street
   d. AAB

9. In economic models, the _____ time frame assumes no fixed factors of production. Firms can enter or leave the marketplace, and the cost (and availability) of land, labor, raw materials, and capital goods can be assumed to vary. In contrast, in the short-run time frame, certain factors are assumed to be fixed, because there is not sufficient time for them to change.
   a. 4-4-5 Calendar
   b. 529 plan
   c. Short-run
   d. Long-run

10. _____ is the difference between operating revenues and operating expenses, but it is also sometimes used as a synonym for EBIT and operating profit. This is true if the firm has no non-_____.

A professional investor contemplating a change to the capital structure of a firm (e.g., through a leveraged buyout) first evaluates a firm's fundamental earnings potential (reflected by Earnings Before Interest, Taxes, Depreciation and Amortization EBITDA and EBIT), and then determines the optimal use of debt vs. equity.

   a. AAB
   b. ABN Amro
   c. A Random Walk Down Wall Street
   d. Operating income

11. _____ is that which is owed; usually referencing assets owed, but the term can cover other obligations. In the case of assets, _____ is a means of using future purchasing power in the present before a summation has been earned. Some companies and corporations use _____ as a part of their overall corporate finance strategy.
   a. Debt
   b. Partial Payment
   c. Credit cycle
   d. Cross-collateralization

12. _____, refers to consumption opportunity gained by an entity within a specified time frame, which is generally expressed in monetary terms. However, for households and individuals, '_____ is the sum of all the wages, salaries, profits, interests payments, rents and other forms of earnings received... in a given period of time.' For firms, _____ generally refers to net-profit: what remains of revenue after expenses have been subtracted.

a. Annual report
b. Accrual
c. OIBDA
d. Income

13. In finance, _____ (or gearing) is borrowing money to supplement existing funds for investment in such a way that the potential positive or negative outcome is magnified and/or enhanced. It generally refers to using borrowed funds, or debt, so as to attempt to increase the returns to equity. Deleveraging is the action of reducing borrowings.

   a. Financial endowment
   b. Limited partnership
   c. Leverage
   d. Pension fund

14. _____ is the balance of the amounts of cash being received and paid by a business during a defined period of time, sometimes tied to a specific project. Measurement of _____ can be used

   - to evaluate the state or performance of a business or project.
   - to determine problems with liquidity. Being profitable does not necessarily mean being liquid. A company can fail because of a shortage of cash, even while profitable.
   - to generate project rate of returns. The time of _____s into and out of projects are used as inputs to financial models such as internal rate of return, and net present value.
   - to examine income or growth of a business when it is believed that accrual accounting concepts do not represent economic realities. Alternately, _____ can be used to 'validate' the net income generated by accrual accounting.

_____ as a generic term may be used differently depending on context, and certain _____ definitions may be adapted by analysts and users for their own uses. Common terms include operating _____ and free _____.

_____s can be classified into:

   1. Operational _____s: Cash received or expended as a result of the company's core business activities.
   2. Investment _____s: Cash received or expended through capital expenditure, investments or acquisitions.
   3. Financing _____s: Cash received or expended as a result of financial activities, such as interests and dividends.

All three together - the net _____ - are necessary to reconcile the beginning cash balance to the ending cash balance. Loan draw downs or equity injections, that is just shifting of capital but no expenditure as such, are not considered in the net _____.

   a. Shareholder value
   b. Cash flow
   c. Corporate finance
   d. Real option

15. In finance, a _____ is a debt security, in which the authorized issuer owes the holders a debt and, depending on the terms of the _____, is obliged to pay interest (the coupon) and/or to repay the principal at a later date, termed maturity.

Thus a _____ is a loan: the issuer is the borrower, the _____ holder is the lender, and the coupon is the interest. _____s provide the borrower with external funds to finance long-term investments, or, in the case of government _____s, to finance current expenditure.

a. Puttable bond
b. Catastrophe bonds
c. Bond
d. Convertible bond

16. _____ are sometimes the same as net worth, or shareholders' equity - assets minus liabilities. The term _____ is commonly used with charities or not for profit entities. Although these entities don't make money, it is important to maintain reasonable reserves to help future growth.

a. Net assets
b. Sustainable growth rate
c. Cash conversion cycle
d. Sharpe ratio

17. A _____ is a fungible, negotiable instrument representing financial value. They are broadly categorized into debt securities (such as banknotes, bonds and debentures), and equity securities; e.g., common stocks. The company or other entity issuing the _____ is called the issuer.

a. Security
b. Book entry
c. Securities lending
d. Tracking stock

18. _____ are defined as identifiable non-monetary assets that cannot be seen, touched or physically measured, which are created through time and/or effort and that are identifiable as a separate asset. There are two primary forms of intangibles - legal intangibles (such as trade secrets (e.g., customer lists), copyrights, patents, trademarks, and goodwill) and competitive intangibles (such as knowledge activities (know-how, knowledge), collaboration activities, leverage activities, and structural activities.) Legal intangibles generate legal property rights defensible in a court of law.

a. ABN Amro
b. A Random Walk Down Wall Street
c. Intangible assets
d. AAB

19. _____ is a financial metric which represents operating liquidity available to a business. Along with fixed assets such as plant and equipment, _____ is considered a part of operating capital. It is calculated as current assets minus current liabilities.

a. 529 plan
b. 4-4-5 Calendar
c. Working capital management
d. Working capital

20. _____ measures the rate of return on the ownership interest (shareholders' equity) of the common stock owners. _____ is viewed as one of the most important financial ratios. It measures a firm's efficiency at generating profits from every dollar of shareholders' equity (also known as net assets or assets minus liabilities.)

a. Return on equity
b. Return on sales
c. Diluted Earnings Per Share
d. Return of capital

21. _____ is the set of processes, customs, policies, laws and institutions affecting the way a corporation is directed, administered or controlled. _____ also includes the relationships among the many stakeholders involved and the goals for which the corporation is governed. The principal stakeholders are the shareholders, management and the board of directors.

Chapter 32. Credit Analysis for Corporate Bonds

- a. Patent
- b. Due diligence
- c. Foreign Corrupt Practices Act
- d. Corporate governance

22. In economics, _____ is a measure of the relative satisfaction from or desirability of consumption of various goods and services. Given this measure, one may speak meaningfully of increasing or decreasing _____, and thereby explain economic behavior in terms of attempts to increase one's _____. For illustrative purposes, changes in _____ are sometimes expressed in units called utils.
    - a. Utility function
    - b. Utility
    - c. AAB
    - d. A Random Walk Down Wall Street

23. In financial accounting, _____s are precautions for which the amount or probability of occurrence are not known. Typical examples are _____s for warranty costs and _____ for taxes the term reserve is used instead of term _____; such a use, however, is inconsistent with the terminology suggested by International Accounting Standards Board.
    - a. Momentum Accounting and Triple-Entry Bookkeeping
    - b. Provision
    - c. Petty cash
    - d. Money measurement concept

24. _____ short for sale-and-_____ is a financial transaction, where one sells an asset and leases it back for a long-term: thus one continues to be able to use the asset, but no longer owns it.

This is generally done for fixed assets, notably real estate and planes, and the purposes are varied, but include financing, accounting, and tax reasons.

After purchasing an asset, the owner enters a long-term agreement by which the property is leased back to the seller, at an agreed-to rate.

- a. Leaseback,
- b. 529 plan
- c. 7-Eleven
- d. 4-4-5 Calendar

25. A _____ is a fund established by a government agency or business for the purpose of reducing debt.

The _____ was first used in Great Britain in the 18th century to reduce national debt. While used by Robert Walpole in 1716 and effectively in the 1720s and early 1730s, it originated in the commercial tax syndicates of the Italian peninsula of the 14th century to retire redeemable public debt of those cities.

- a. Modern portfolio theory
- b. Sinking fund
- c. Security interest
- d. Debtor

26. A _____ is a payment made by a corporation to its shareholder members. When a corporation earns a profit or surplus, that money can be put to two uses: it can either be re-invested in the business (called retained earnings), or it can be paid to the shareholders as a _____. Many corporations retain a portion of their earnings and pay the remainder as a _____.

- a. Special dividend
- b. Dividend yield
- c. Dividend
- d. Dividend puzzle

Chapter 32. Credit Analysis for Corporate Bonds

27. In law, a _____ is a form of security interest granted over an item of property to secure the payment of a debt or performance of some other obligation. The owner of the property, who grants the _____, is referred to as the lienor and the person who has the benefit of the _____ is referred to as the _____ee.

The etymological root is: Anglo-French _____, loyen bond, restraint, from Latin ligamen, from ligare to bind.

   a. Family and Medical Leave Act
   c. Lien
   b. Sarbanes-Oxley Act
   d. Joint venture

28. The _____ is a financial market where participants buy and sell debt securities, usually in the form of bonds. As of 2006, the size of the international _____ is an estimated $45 trillion, of which the size of the outstanding U.S. _____ debt was $25.2 trillion.

Nearly all of the $923 billion average daily trading volume in the U.S. _____ takes place between broker-dealers and large institutions in a decentralized, over-the-counter market.

   a. Bond Market
   c. Fixed income
   b. 529 plan
   d. 4-4-5 Calendar

29. A _____ is a company that owns other companies' outstanding stock. It usually refers to a company which does not produce goods or services itself, rather its only purpose is owning shares of other companies. They allow the reduction of risk for the owners and can allow the ownership and control of a number of different companies.

   a. MRU Holdings
   c. Privately held company
   b. Federal National Mortgage Association
   d. Holding Company

30. The _____ of 1935 was a law that was passed by the United States Congress to facilitate regulation of electric utilities, by either limiting their operations to a single state, and thus subjecting them to effective state regulation, or forcing divestitures so that each became a single integrated system serving a limited geographic area. Another purpose of _____ was to keep utility holding companies engaged in regulated businesses from engaging in unregulated businesses. _____ required that Securities and Exchange Commission (SEC) approval be obtained by a holding company prior to engaging in a non-utility business and that such businesses be kept separate from the regulated business(es.)

   a. Public Utility Holding Company Act
   c. 4-4-5 Calendar
   b. Garn-St. Germain Depository Institutions Act
   d. 529 plan

31. In finance, _____ refers to the way a corporation finances its assets through some combination of equity, debt, or hybrid securities. A firm's _____ is then the composition or 'structure' of its liabilities. For example, a firm that sells $20 billion in equity and $80 billion in debt is said to be 20% equity-financed and 80% debt-financed.

   a. Rights issue
   c. Book building
   b. Market for corporate control
   d. Capital structure

Chapter 32. Credit Analysis for Corporate Bonds

32. The institution most often referenced by the word '_____' is a public or publicly traded _____, the shares of which are traded on a public stock exchange (e.g., the New York Stock Exchange or Nasdaq in the United States) where shares of stock of _____s are bought and sold by and to the general public. Most of the largest businesses in the world are publicly traded _____s. However, the majority of _____s are said to be closely held, privately held or close _____s, meaning that no ready market exists for the trading of shares.
   a. Depository Trust Company
   b. Protect
   c. Corporation
   d. Federal Home Loan Mortgage Corporation

33. _____ is a measure of the ability of a debtor to pay their debts as and when they fall due. It is usually expressed as a ratio or a percentage of current liabilities.

For a corporation with a published balance sheet there are various ratios used to calculate a measure of liquidity.

   a. Accounting liquidity
   b. Invested capital
   c. Operating leverage
   d. Operating profit margin

34. In finance, a _____ (non-investment grade bond, speculative grade bond or junk bond) is a bond that is rated below investment grade at the time of purchase. These bonds have a higher risk of default or other adverse credit events, but typically pay higher yields than better quality bonds in order to make them attractive to investors.
   a. Volatility
   b. Sharpe ratio
   c. Private equity
   d. High yield bond

35. _____ is the method by which one calculates the creditworthiness of a business or organization. The audited financial statements of a large company might be analyzed when it issues or has issued bonds. Or, a bank may analyze the financial statements of a small business before making or renewing a commercial loan.
   a. Capital note
   b. Credit report monitoring
   c. Credit crunch
   d. Credit analysis

36. _____ is a legal entity that develops, registers and sells securities for the purpose of financing its operations. _____s may be domestic or foreign governments, corporations or investment trusts. _____s are legally responsible for the obligations of the issue and for reporting financial conditions, material developments and any other operational activities as required by the regulations of their jurisdictions.
   a. Arbitrage
   b. Initial margin
   c. Issuer
   d. Efficient-market hypothesis

37. The U.S. Securities and Exchange Commission's (SEC's) Regulation Fair Disclosure, also commonly referred to as _____ was an SEC ruling implemented in October 2000 (.) It mandated that all publicly traded companies must disclose material information to all investors at the same time.

The regulation sought to stamp out selective disclosure, in which some investors (often large institutional investors) received market moving information before others (often smaller, individual investors.)

   a. Regulation Fair Disclosure
   b. Commodity Pool Operator
   c. Regulation FD
   d. Revenue recognition

Chapter 32. Credit Analysis for Corporate Bonds

38. Earnings before interest, taxes, depreciation and amortization (_____) is a non-GAAP metric that can be used to evaluate a company's profitability.

_____ = Operating Revenue - Operating Expenses + Other Revenue

Its name comes from the fact that Operating Expenses do not include interest, taxes, or amortization. _____ is not a defined measure according to Generally Accepted Accounting Principles (GAAP), and thus can be calculated however a company wishes.

a. Accounts payable
b. Invoice processing
c. EBITDA
d. Accrual

39. A _____, in its most general sense, is a solemn promise to engage in or refrain from a specified action.

More specifically, a _____, in contrast to a contract, is a one-way agreement whereby the _____er is the only party bound by the promise. A _____ may have conditions and prerequisites that qualify the undertaking, including the actions of second or third parties, but there is no inherent agreement by such other parties to fulfill those requirements.

a. Federal Trade Commission Act
b. Partnership
c. Clayton Antitrust Act
d. Covenant

40. _____ and the related Fisher's linear discriminant are methods used in statistics and machine learning to find the linear combination of features which best separate two or more classes of objects or events. The resulting combination may be used as a linear classifier, or, more commonly, for dimensionality reduction before later classification.

_____ is closely related to ANOVA (analysis of variance) and regression analysis, which also attempt to express one dependent variable as a linear combination of other features or measurements.

a. 529 plan
b. Linear discriminant analysis
c. 7-Eleven
d. 4-4-5 Calendar

41. In statistics, a _____ is a dimensionless quantity derived by subtracting the population mean from an individual raw score and then dividing the difference by the population standard deviation. This conversion process is called standardizing or normalizing; however, 'normalizing' can refer to many types of ratios; see normalization (statistics) for more.

_____s are also called z-values, z-scores, normal scores, and standardized variables; the use of 'Z' is because the normal distribution is also known as the 'Z distribution'.

a. Normal distribution
b. Standard score
c. Monte Carlo methods
d. Semivariance

Chapter 33. Credit Risk Modeling

1. _____ is the provision of resources (such as granting a loan) by one party to another party where that second party does not reimburse the first party immediately, thereby generating a debt, and instead arranges either to repay or return those resources (or material(s) of equal value) at a later date. The first party is called a creditor, also known as a lender, while the second party is called a debtor, also known as a borrower.

Movements of financial capital are normally dependent on either _____ or equity transfers.

   a. Comparable   b. Warrant
   c. Clearing house   d. Credit

2. _____ is the risk of loss due to a debtor's non-payment of a loan or other line of credit (either the principal or interest (coupon) or both)

Most lenders employ their own models (credit scorecards) to rank potential and existing customers according to risk, and then apply appropriate strategies. With products such as unsecured personal loans or mortgages, lenders charge a higher price for higher risk customers and vice versa. With revolving products such as credit cards and overdrafts, risk is controlled through careful setting of credit limits.

   a. Liquidity risk   b. Market risk
   c. Transaction risk   d. Credit risk

3. In finance, _____ occurs when a debtor has not met its legal obligations according to the debt contract, e.g. it has not made a scheduled payment, or has violated a loan covenant (condition) of the debt contract. _____ may occur if the debtor is either unwilling or unable to pay their debt. This can occur with all debt obligations including bonds, mortgages, loans, and promissory notes.

   a. Vendor finance   b. Credit crunch
   c. Debt validation   d. Default

4. _____ is a parameter used in the calculation of economic capital or regulatory capital under Basel II for a banking institution. This is an attribute of a bank's client.

The _____ is the likelihood that a loan will not be repaid and will fall into default.

   a. Probability of default   b. Deposit insurance
   c. Credit bureau   d. Variable rate mortgage

5. _____ is one of the authors of the Black-Scholes equation. In 1997 he was awarded the Nobel Memorial Prize in Economic Sciences for 'a new method to determine the value of derivatives'. The model provides the fundamental conceptual framework for valuing options, such as calls or puts, and is referred to as the Black-Scholes model, which has become the standard in financial markets globally.

   a. Robert James Shiller   b. Adolph Coors
   c. Andrew Tobias   d. Myron Samuel Scholes

6. _____ refers to an assessment of the viability, stability and profitability of a business, sub-business or project.

It is performed by professionals who prepare reports using ratios that make use of information taken from financial statements and other reports. These reports are usually presented to top management as one of their bases in making business decisions.

a. Financial analysis
b. Value investing
c. 529 plan
d. 4-4-5 Calendar

7.

In finance, the _____ can be the expected rate of return above the risk-free interest rate. When measuring risk, a common sense approach is to compare the risk-free return on T-bills and the very risky return on other investments. The difference between these two returns can be interpreted as a measure of the excess return on the average risky asset. This excess return is known as the _____.

a. Risk premium
b. Risk adjusted return on capital
c. Risk aversion
d. Risk modeling

8. A _____ is a fungible, negotiable instrument representing financial value. They are broadly categorized into debt securities (such as banknotes, bonds and debentures), and equity securities; e.g., common stocks. The company or other entity issuing the _____ is called the issuer.

a. Book entry
b. Security
c. Securities lending
d. Tracking stock

9. _____ refers to the use of formal econometric techniques to determine the aggregate risk in a financial portfolio. _____ is one of many subtasks within the broader area of financial modeling.

_____ uses a variety of techniques including market risk, Value-at-Risk (VaR), Historical Simulation (HS), or Extreme Value Theory (EVT) in order to analyze a portfolio and make forecasts of the likely losses that would be incurred for a variety of risks.

a. Risk modeling
b. Value at risk
c. Risk adjusted return on capital
d. Risk premium

10. _____ is the price at which an asset would trade in a competitive Walrasian auction setting. _____ is often used interchangeably with open _____, fair value or fair _____, although these terms have distinct definitions in different standards, and may differ in some circumstances.

International Valuation Standards defines _____ as 'the estimated amount for which a property should exchange on the date of valuation between a willing buyer and a willing seller in an arm'e;s-length transaction after proper marketing wherein the parties had each acted knowledgeably, prudently, and without compulsion.'

_____ is a concept distinct from market price, which is 'e;the price at which one can transact'e;, while _____ is 'e;the true underlying value'e; according to theoretical standards.

a. Debt restructuring
c. Wrap account
b. Market value
d. T-Model

11. In probability theory and statistics, _____ indicates the strength and direction of a linear relationship between two random variables. That is in contrast with the usage of the term in colloquial speech, which denotes any relationship, not necessarily linear. In general statistical usage, _____ or co-relation refers to the departure of two random variables from independence.
   a. Probability distribution
   c. Variance
   b. Geometric mean
   d. Correlation

12. In finance, _____ is the process of estimating the potential market value of a financial asset or liability. they can be done on assets (for example, investments in marketable securities such as stocks, options, business enterprises, or intangible assets such as patents and trademarks) or on liabilities (e.g., Bonds issued by a company.) _____s are required in many contexts including investment analysis, capital budgeting, merger and acquisition transactions, financial reporting, taxable events to determine the proper tax liability, and in litigation.
   a. Valuation
   c. Margin
   b. Share
   d. Procter ' Gamble

Chapter 34. Guidelines in the Credit Analysis of Municipal General Obligation and Bonds

1. In the United States, a _____ is a bond issued by a city or other local government, or their agencies. Potential issuers of these bonds include cities, counties, redevelopment agencies, school districts, publicly owned airports and seaports, and any other governmental entity (or group of governments) below the state level. They may be general obligations of the issuer or secured by specified revenues.
   - a. Premium bond
   - b. Puttable bond
   - c. Municipal bond
   - d. Senior debt

2. _____ is a legally declared inability or impairment of ability of an individual or organization to pay their creditors. Creditors may file a _____ petition against a debtor ('involuntary _____') in an effort to recoup a portion of what they are owed or initiate a restructuring. In the majority of cases, however, _____ is initiated by the debtor (a 'voluntary _____' that is filed by the bankrupt individual or organization.)
   - a. 529 plan
   - b. Debt settlement
   - c. 4-4-5 Calendar
   - d. Bankruptcy

3. In finance, a _____ is a debt security, in which the authorized issuer owes the holders a debt and, depending on the terms of the _____, is obliged to pay interest (the coupon) and/or to repay the principal at a later date, termed maturity.

   Thus a _____ is a loan: the issuer is the borrower, the _____ holder is the lender, and the coupon is the interest. _____s provide the borrower with external funds to finance long-term investments, or, in the case of government _____s, to finance current expenditure.
   - a. Puttable bond
   - b. Convertible bond
   - c. Bond
   - d. Catastrophe bonds

4. In finance, _____ occurs when a debtor has not met its legal obligations according to the debt contract, e.g. it has not made a scheduled payment, or has violated a loan covenant (condition) of the debt contract. _____ may occur if the debtor is either unwilling or unable to pay their debt. This can occur with all debt obligations including bonds, mortgages, loans, and promissory notes.
   - a. Credit crunch
   - b. Debt validation
   - c. Vendor finance
   - d. Default

5. _____ refers to an assessment of the viability, stability and profitability of a business, sub-business or project.

   It is performed by professionals who prepare reports using ratios that make use of information taken from financial statements and other reports. These reports are usually presented to top management as one of their bases in making business decisions.
   - a. Value investing
   - b. 529 plan
   - c. 4-4-5 Calendar
   - d. Financial analysis

6. In business, _____ is income that a company receives from its normal business activities, usually from the sale of goods and services to customers. Some companies also receive _____ from interest, dividends or royalties paid to them by other companies. _____ may refer to business income in general, or it may refer to the amount, in a monetary unit, received during a period of time, as in 'Last year, Company X had _____ of $32 million.'

   In many countries, including the UK, _____ is referred to as turnover.

Chapter 34. Guidelines in the Credit Analysis of Municipal General Obligation and Bonds

a. Matching principle
c. Furniture, Fixtures and Equipment
b. Bottom line
d. Revenue

7. _____ are bonds issued by governments, authorities, or public benefit corporations that are guaranteed by the revenue flow of the issuing agency.

The Supreme Court decision of Pollock versus Farmer's Loan and Trust Company of 1895 initiated a wave or series of innovations for the financial services community in both tax-treatment and regulation from government. This specific case, according to a leading investment bank's research, resulted in the 'intergovernmental tax immunity doctrine,' ultimately leading to 'tax-free status.' Municipal bonds are generally exempt from federal tax on their interest payments (not capital gains.)

a. Gilts
c. Callable bond
b. Private activity bond
d. Revenue bonds

8. A _____ is a legal pledge in United States municipal finance, in which an entity pledges its full faith and credit to repay its debt, typically a _____ bond.

a. Financial Institutions Reform Recovery and Enforcement Act
b. Letter of credit
c. Covenant
d. General obligation

9. A _____ is a fungible, negotiable instrument representing financial value. They are broadly categorized into debt securities (such as banknotes, bonds and debentures), and equity securities; e.g., common stocks. The company or other entity issuing the _____ is called the issuer.

a. Security
c. Book entry
b. Tracking stock
d. Securities lending

10. A _____, in its most general sense, is a solemn promise to engage in or refrain from a specified action.

More specifically, a _____, in contrast to a contract, is a one-way agreement whereby the _____er is the only party bound by the promise. A _____ may have conditions and prerequisites that qualify the undertaking, including the actions of second or third parties, but there is no inherent agreement by such other parties to fulfill those requirements.

a. Partnership
c. Clayton Antitrust Act
b. Federal Trade Commission Act
d. Covenant

11. _____ or financing is to provide capital (funds), which means money for a project, a person, a business or any other private or public institutions.

Those funds can be allocated for either short term or long term purposes. The health fund is a new way of _____ private healthcare centers.

a. Proxy fight
c. Product life cycle
b. Synthetic CDO
d. Funding

Chapter 34. Guidelines in the Credit Analysis of Municipal General Obligation and Bonds   173

12. _____ is a legal entity that develops, registers and sells securities for the purpose of financing its operations. _____s may be domestic or foreign governments, corporations or investment trusts. _____s are legally responsible for the obligations of the issue and for reporting financial conditions, material developments and any other operational activities as required by the regulations of their jurisdictions.

　　a. Efficient-market hypothesis   b. Issuer
　　c. Arbitrage   d. Initial margin

13.   Unemployment occurs when a person is available to work and currently seeking work, but the person is without work. The prevalence of unemployment is usually measured using the _____, which is defined as the percentage of those in the labor force who are unemployed. The _____ is also used in economic studies and economic indexes such as the United States' Conference Board's Index of Leading Indicators as a measure of the state of the macroeconomics.

　　a. ABN Amro   b. Unemployment rate
　　c. A Random Walk Down Wall Street   d. AAB

14. _____ is the provision of resources (such as granting a loan) by one party to another party where that second party does not reimburse the first party immediately, thereby generating a debt, and instead arranges either to repay or return those resources (or material(s) of equal value) at a later date. The first party is called a creditor, also known as a lender, while the second party is called a debtor, also known as a borrower.

Movements of financial capital are normally dependent on either _____ or equity transfers.

　　a. Clearing house   b. Warrant
　　c. Comparable   d. Credit

15. _____ is the method by which one calculates the creditworthiness of a business or organization. The audited financial statements of a large company might be analyzed when it issues or has issued bonds. Or, a bank may analyze the financial statements of a small business before making or renewing a commercial loan.

　　a. Credit report monitoring   b. Credit analysis
　　c. Credit crunch   d. Capital note

16. _____ is that which is owed; usually referencing assets owed, but the term can cover other obligations. In the case of assets, _____ is a means of using future purchasing power in the present before a summation has been earned. Some companies and corporations use _____ as a part of their overall corporate finance strategy.

　　a. Cross-collateralization   b. Partial Payment
　　c. Credit cycle   d. Debt

17. _____ is a financial ratio that indicates the percentage of a company's assets are provided via debt. It is the ratio of total debt (the sum of current liabilities and long-term liabilities) and total assets (the sum of current assets, fixed assets, and other assets such as 'goodwill'.)

or alternatively:

174   Chapter 34. Guidelines in the Credit Analysis of Municipal General Obligation and Bonds

For example, a company with $2 million in total assets and $500,000 in total liabilities would have a _____ of 25%

Like all financial ratios, a company's _____ should be compared with their industry average or other competing firms.

- a. Cash management
- b. Cash concentration
- c. Capitalization rate
- d. Debt ratio

18. In economics, _____ is the analysis of the effect of a particular tax on the distribution of economic welfare. _____ is said to 'fall' upon the group that, at the end of the day, bears the burden of the tax. The key concept is that the _____ or tax burden does not depend on where the revenue is collected, but on the price elasticity of demand and price elasticity of supply.
- a. Tax incidence
- b. Tax compliance solution
- c. Monetary policy
- d. Qualified residence interest

19. _____ is an area of finance dealing with the financial decisions corporations make and the tools and analysis used to make these decisions. The primary goal of _____ is to maximize corporate value while managing the firm's financial risks. Although it is in principle different from managerial finance which studies the financial decisions of all firms, rather than corporations alone, the main concepts in the study of _____ are applicable to the financial problems of all kinds of firms.
- a. Gross profit
- b. Special purpose entity
- c. Corporate finance
- d. Cash flow

20. _____ is the process of decreasing an amount over a period of time. The word comes from Middle English amortisen to kill, alienate in mortmain, from Anglo-French amorteser, alteration of amortir, from Vulgar Latin admortire to kill, from Latin ad- + mort-, mors death. Particular instances of the term include:

- _____ (business), the allocation of a lump sum amount to different time periods, particularly for loans and other forms of finance, including related interest or other finance charges.
  - _____ schedule, a table detailing each periodic payment on a loan (typically a mortgage), as generated by an _____ calculator.
  - Negative _____, an _____ schedule where the loan amount actually increases through not paying the full interest
- Amortized analysis, analyzing the execution cost of algorithms over a sequence of operations.
- _____ of capital expenditures of certain assets under accounting rules, particularly intangible assets, in a manner analogous to depreciation.
- _____ (tax law)

_____ is also used in the context of zoning regulations and describes the time in which a property owner has to relocate when the property's use constitutes a preexisting nonconforming use under zoning regulations.

- Depreciation

a. Option
c. AT'T Inc.
b. Intrinsic value
d. Amortization

Chapter 35. Rating Agency Approach to Structured Finance

1. In lending agreements, _____ is a borrower's pledge of specific property to a lender, to secure repayment of a loan. The _____ serves as protection for a lender against a borrower's risk of default - that is, a borrower failing to pay the principal and interest under the terms of a loan obligation. If a borrower does default on a loan (due to insolvency or other event), that borrower forfeits (gives up) the property pledged as _____ *ollateral* - and the lender then becomes the owner of the _____.
   - a. Nominal value
   - b. Collateral
   - c. Refinancing risk
   - d. Future-oriented

2. _____ is the provision of resources (such as granting a loan) by one party to another party where that second party does not reimburse the first party immediately, thereby generating a debt, and instead arranges either to repay or return those resources (or material(s) of equal value) at a later date. The first party is called a creditor, also known as a lender, while the second party is called a debtor, also known as a borrower.

   Movements of financial capital are normally dependent on either _____ or equity transfers.
   - a. Credit
   - b. Comparable
   - c. Warrant
   - d. Clearing house

3. _____ are a type of structured asset-backed security (ABS) whose value and payments are derived from a portfolio of fixed-income underlying assets. _____s are assigned different risk classes, or tranches, whereby 'senior' tranches are considered the safest securities. Interest and principal payments are made in order of seniority, so that junior tranches offer higher coupon payments (and interest rates) or lower prices to compensate for additional default risk.
   - a. Senior debt
   - b. Municipal bond
   - c. Zero coupon bond
   - d. Collateralized debt obligations

4. In finance, _____ occurs when a debtor has not met its legal obligations according to the debt contract, e.g. it has not made a scheduled payment, or has violated a loan covenant (condition) of the debt contract. _____ may occur if the debtor is either unwilling or unable to pay their debt. This can occur with all debt obligations including bonds, mortgages, loans, and promissory notes.
   - a. Credit crunch
   - b. Debt validation
   - c. Vendor finance
   - d. Default

5. _____ is a key part of the securitization transaction in structured finance, and is important for credit rating agencies when rating a securitization. The credit crisis of 2007-2008 has discredited the process of _____ of structured securities as a legitimate financial practice.

   There are two primary types of _____: Internal and External.
   - a. Tranche
   - b. Yield curve spread
   - c. 4-4-5 Calendar
   - d. Credit enhancement

6. _____ refers to an assessment of the viability, stability and profitability of a business, sub-business or project.

It is performed by professionals who prepare reports using ratios that make use of information taken from financial statements and other reports. These reports are usually presented to top management as one of their bases in making business decisions.

Chapter 35. Rating Agency Approach to Structured Finance

a. 529 plan
c. Value investing
b. 4-4-5 Calendar
d. Financial analysis

7. In finance, a _____ is a debt security, in which the authorized issuer owes the holders a debt and, depending on the terms of the _____, is obliged to pay interest (the coupon) and/or to repay the principal at a later date, termed maturity.

Thus a _____ is a loan: the issuer is the borrower, the _____ holder is the lender, and the coupon is the interest. _____s provide the borrower with external funds to finance long-term investments, or, in the case of government _____s, to finance current expenditure.

a. Puttable bond
c. Catastrophe bonds
b. Convertible bond
d. Bond

8. The _____ is a financial market where participants buy and sell debt securities, usually in the form of bonds. As of 2006, the size of the international _____ is an estimated $45 trillion, of which the size of the outstanding U.S. _____ debt was $25.2 trillion.

Nearly all of the $923 billion average daily trading volume in the U.S. _____ takes place between broker-dealers and large institutions in a decentralized, over-the-counter market.

a. Bond market
c. Fixed income
b. 4-4-5 Calendar
d. 529 plan

9. A _____ is a listing of bonds or fixed income instruments and a statistic reflecting the composite value of its components. It is used as a tool to represent the characteristics of its component fixed income instruments. They differ from stock market indices in their complexity.

a. 7-Eleven
c. 4-4-5 Calendar
b. 529 plan
d. Bond market index

10. A standard, commercial _____ is a document issued mostly by a financial institution, used primarily in trade finance, which usually provides an irrevocable payment undertaking.

The _____ can also be the source of payment for a transaction, meaning that redeeming the _____ will pay an exporter. Letters of credit are used primarily in international trade transactions of significant value, for deals between a supplier in one country and a customer in another.

a. McFadden Act
c. Duty of loyalty
b. Bond indenture
d. Letter of credit

11. In business and accounting, _____s are everything of value that is owned by a person or company. The balance sheet of a firm records the monetary value of the _____s owned by the firm. The two major _____ classes are tangible _____s and intangible _____s.

a. Income
c. Accounts payable
b. Asset
d. EBITDA

Chapter 36. Fixed Income Risk Modeling

1. _____ refers to any type of investment that yields a regular (or fixed) return.

For example, if you lend money to a borrower and the borrower has to pay interest once a month, you have been issued a fixed-income security. When a company does this, it is often called a bond or corporate bank debt (although preferred stock is also sometimes considered to be _____).

   a. 4-4-5 Calendar
   b. 529 plan
   c. Bond market
   d. Fixed income

2. In finance, a _____ (non-investment grade bond, speculative grade bond or junk bond) is a bond that is rated below investment grade at the time of purchase. These bonds have a higher risk of default or other adverse credit events, but typically pay higher yields than better quality bonds in order to make them attractive to investors.

   a. High yield bond
   b. Sharpe ratio
   c. Private equity
   d. Volatility

3. In finance, a _____ is a debt security, in which the authorized issuer owes the holders a debt and, depending on the terms of the _____, is obliged to pay interest (the coupon) and/or to repay the principal at a later date, termed maturity.

Thus a _____ is a loan: the issuer is the borrower, the _____ holder is the lender, and the coupon is the interest. _____s provide the borrower with external funds to finance long-term investments, or, in the case of government _____s, to finance current expenditure.

   a. Convertible bond
   b. Puttable bond
   c. Catastrophe bonds
   d. Bond

4. _____, refers to consumption opportunity gained by an entity within a specified time frame, which is generally expressed in monetary terms. However, for households and individuals, '_____ is the sum of all the wages, salaries, profits, interests payments, rents and other forms of earnings received... in a given period of time.' For firms, _____ generally refers to net-profit: what remains of revenue after expenses have been subtracted.

   a. Accrual
   b. Annual report
   c. OIBDA
   d. Income

5. _____ refers to the use of formal econometric techniques to determine the aggregate risk in a financial portfolio. _____ is one of many subtasks within the broader area of financial modeling.

_____ uses a variety of techniques including market risk, Value-at-Risk (VaR), Historical Simulation (HS), or Extreme Value Theory (EVT) in order to analyze a portfolio and make forecasts of the likely losses that would be incurred for a variety of risks.

   a. Risk modeling
   b. Risk premium
   c. Value at risk
   d. Risk adjusted return on capital

Chapter 36. Fixed Income Risk Modeling

6. In finance, _____ is the process of estimating the potential market value of a financial asset or liability. they can be done on assets (for example, investments in marketable securities such as stocks, options, business enterprises, or intangible assets such as patents and trademarks) or on liabilities (e.g., Bonds issued by a company.) _____s are required in many contexts including investment analysis, capital budgeting, merger and acquisition transactions, financial reporting, taxable events to determine the proper tax liability, and in litigation.
   a. Share
   b. Procter ' Gamble
   c. Valuation
   d. Margin

7. An _____ is a contract written by a seller that conveys to the buyer the right -- but not the obligation -- to buy (in the case of a call _____) or to sell (in the case of a put _____) a particular asset, such as a piece of property such as, among others, a futures contract. In return for granting the _____, the seller collects a payment (the premium) from the buyer.

For example, buying a call _____ provides the right to buy a specified quantity of a security at a set strike price at some time on or before expiration, while buying a put _____ provides the right to sell.

   a. Option
   b. AT'T Mobility LLC
   c. Amortization
   d. Annuity

8. _____ means regulating, adapting or settling in a variety of contexts:

In commercial law, _____ means the settlement of a loss incurred on insured goods. The calculation of the amounts of compensation to be paid by or to the several interests is a complicated matter. It involves much detail and arithmetic, and requires a full and accurate knowledge of the principles of the subject.

   a. Equity method
   b. Intelligent investor
   c. Asset recovery
   d. Adjustment

9. In finance, the term _____ describes the amount in cash that returns to the owners of a security. Normally it does not include the price variations, at the difference of the total return. _____ applies to various stated rates of return on stocks (common and preferred, and convertible), fixed income instruments (bonds, notes, bills, strips, zero coupon), and some other investment type insurance products (e.g. annuities.)
   a. 4-4-5 Calendar
   b. Macaulay duration
   c. Yield to maturity
   d. Yield

10. In finance, the _____ is the difference between the quoted rates of return on two different investments, usually of different credit quality.

It is a compound of yield and spread.

The '_____ of X over Y' is simply the percentage return on investment (ROI) from financial instrument X minus the percentage return on investment from financial instrument Y (per annum.)

   a. Yield spread
   b. Duty of loyalty
   c. Portfolio insurance
   d. Debtor-in-possession financing

Chapter 36. Fixed Income Risk Modeling

11. In finance, a _____ is a risk that affects a very small number of assets. This is sometimes referred to as 'unsystematic risk'. In a balanced portfolio of assets there'd be a spread between general market risk and risks specific to individual components of that portfolio.

   a. Bonus share
   b. Credit event
   c. Consolidated financial statements
   d. Specific risk

12. In finance, the yield curve is the relation between the interest rate (or cost of borrowing) and the time to maturity of the debt for a given borrower in a given currency. For example, the current U.S. dollar interest rates paid on U.S. Treasury securities for various maturities are closely watched by many traders, and are commonly plotted on a graph such as the one on the right which is informally called 'the yield curve.' More formal mathematical descriptions of this relation are often called the _____.

The yield of a debt instrument is the annualized percentage increase in the value of the investment.

   a. 4-4-5 Calendar
   b. 7-Eleven
   c. 529 plan
   d. Term structure of interest rates

13. _____ is a fee paid on borrowed assets. It is the price paid for the use of borrowed money , or, money earned by deposited funds . Assets that are sometimes lent with _____ include money, shares, consumer goods through hire purchase, major assets such as aircraft, and even entire factories in finance lease arrangements.

   a. A Random Walk Down Wall Street
   b. AAB
   c. Insolvency
   d. Interest

14. An _____ is the price a borrower pays for the use of money they do not own, and the return a lender receives for deferring the use of funds, by lending it to the borrower. _____s are normally expressed as a percentage rate over the period of one year.

_____s targets are also a vital tool of monetary policy and are used to control variables like investment, inflation, and unemployment.

   a. ABN Amro
   b. A Random Walk Down Wall Street
   c. AAB
   d. Interest rate

15. _____ are dollar-denominated bonds, issued mostly by Latin American countries in the 1980s, named after U.S. Treasury Secretary Nicholas Brady.

_____ were created in March 1989 in order to convert bonds issued by mostly Latin American countries into a variety or 'menu' of new bonds after many of those countries defaulted on their debt in the 1980's. At that time, the market for sovereign debt was small and illiquid, and the standardization of emerging-market debt facilitated risk-spreading and trading.

   a. Nominal yield
   b. Municipal bond
   c. Coupon rate
   d. Brady bonds

Chapter 36. Fixed Income Risk Modeling

16. A _____ is an international bond that is denominated in a currency not native to the country where it is issued. It can be categorised according to the currency in which it is issued. London is one of the centers of the _____ market, but _____s may be traded throughout the world - for example in Singapore or Tokyo.
   a. Education production function
   b. Economic entity
   c. Eurobond
   d. Interest rate option

17. _____s are deposits denominated in United States dollars at banks outside the United States, and thus are not under the jurisdiction of the Federal Reserve. Consequently, such deposits are subject to much less regulation than similar deposits within the United States, allowing for higher margins. There is nothing 'European' about _____ deposits; a US dollar-denominated deposit in Tokyo or Caracas would likewise be deemed _____ deposits.
   a. AAB
   b. A Random Walk Down Wall Street
   c. ABN Amro
   d. Eurodollar

18. A _____ is a legal pledge in United States municipal finance, in which an entity pledges its full faith and credit to repay its debt, typically a _____ bond.
   a. Financial Institutions Reform Recovery and Enforcement Act
   b. Covenant
   c. Letter of credit
   d. General obligation

19. In financial accounting, _____s are precautions for which the amount or probability of occurrence are not known. Typical examples are _____s for warranty costs and _____ for taxes the term reserve is used instead of term _____; such a use, however, is inconsistent with the terminology suggested by International Accounting Standards Board.
   a. Momentum Accounting and Triple-Entry Bookkeeping
   b. Money measurement concept
   c. Petty cash
   d. Provision

Chapter 37. Valuation of Bonds with Embedded Options

1. _____ are dollar-denominated bonds, issued mostly by Latin American countries in the 1980s, named after U.S. Treasury Secretary Nicholas Brady.

_____ were created in March 1989 in order to convert bonds issued by mostly Latin American countries into a variety or 'menu' of new bonds after many of those countries defaulted on their debt in the 1980's. At that time, the market for sovereign debt was small and illiquid, and the standardization of emerging-market debt facilitated risk-spreading and trading.

   a. Nominal yield
   b. Municipal bond
   c. Coupon rate
   d. Brady bonds

2. A _____ is an international bond that is denominated in a currency not native to the country where it is issued. It can be categorised according to the currency in which it is issued. London is one of the centers of the _____ market, but _____s may be traded throughout the world - for example in Singapore or Tokyo.

   a. Eurobond
   b. Economic entity
   c. Interest rate option
   d. Education production function

3. _____s are deposits denominated in United States dollars at banks outside the United States, and thus are not under the jurisdiction of the Federal Reserve. Consequently, such deposits are subject to much less regulation than similar deposits within the United States, allowing for higher margins. There is nothing 'European' about _____ deposits; a US dollar-denominated deposit in Tokyo or Caracas would likewise be deemed _____ deposits.

   a. ABN Amro
   b. A Random Walk Down Wall Street
   c. AAB
   d. Eurodollar

4. A _____ is a legal pledge in United States municipal finance, in which an entity pledges its full faith and credit to repay its debt, typically a _____ bond.

   a. Letter of credit
   b. General obligation
   c. Covenant
   d. Financial Institutions Reform Recovery and Enforcement Act

5. In finance, a _____ (non-investment grade bond, speculative grade bond or junk bond) is a bond that is rated below investment grade at the time of purchase. These bonds have a higher risk of default or other adverse credit events, but typically pay higher yields than better quality bonds in order to make them attractive to investors.

   a. Sharpe ratio
   b. Volatility
   c. Private equity
   d. High yield bond

6. In finance, a _____ is a debt security, in which the authorized issuer owes the holders a debt and, depending on the terms of the _____, is obliged to pay interest (the coupon) and/or to repay the principal at a later date, termed maturity.

Thus a _____ is a loan: the issuer is the borrower, the _____ holder is the lender, and the coupon is the interest. _____s provide the borrower with external funds to finance long-term investments, or, in the case of government _____s, to finance current expenditure.

   a. Puttable bond
   b. Bond
   c. Convertible bond
   d. Catastrophe bonds

Chapter 37. Valuation of Bonds with Embedded Options

7. An _____ is a contract written by a seller that conveys to the buyer the right -- but not the obligation -- to buy (in the case of a call _____) or to sell (in the case of a put _____) a particular asset, such as a piece of property such as, among others, a futures contract. In return for granting the _____, the seller collects a payment (the premium) from the buyer.

For example, buying a call _____ provides the right to buy a specified quantity of a security at a set strike price at some time on or before expiration, while buying a put _____ provides the right to sell.

  a. Option
  c. AT'T Mobility LLC

  b. Amortization
  d. Annuity

8. In financial accounting, _____s are precautions for which the amount or probability of occurrence are not known. Typical examples are _____s for warranty costs and _____ for taxes the term reserve is used instead of term _____; such a use, however, is inconsistent with the terminology suggested by International Accounting Standards Board.

  a. Momentum Accounting and Triple-Entry Bookkeeping
  c. Money measurement concept

  b. Petty cash
  d. Provision

9. In finance, _____ is the process of estimating the potential market value of a financial asset or liability. they can be done on assets (for example, investments in marketable securities such as stocks, options, business enterprises, or intangible assets such as patents and trademarks) or on liabilities (e.g., Bonds issued by a company.) _____s are required in many contexts including investment analysis, capital budgeting, merger and acquisition transactions, financial reporting, taxable events to determine the proper tax liability, and in litigation.

  a. Margin
  c. Share

  b. Procter ' Gamble
  d. Valuation

10. In finance, the term _____ describes the amount in cash that returns to the owners of a security. Normally it does not include the price variations, at the difference of the total return. _____ applies to various stated rates of return on stocks (common and preferred, and convertible), fixed income instruments (bonds, notes, bills, strips, zero coupon), and some other investment type insurance products (e.g. annuities.)

  a. 4-4-5 Calendar
  c. Yield to maturity

  b. Yield
  d. Macaulay duration

11. In finance, the _____ is the relation between the interest rate (or cost of borrowing) and the time to maturity of the debt for a given borrower in a given currency. For example, the current U.S. dollar interest rates paid on U.S. Treasury securities for various maturities are closely watched by many traders, and are commonly plotted on a graph such as the one on the right which is informally called 'the _____.' More formal mathematical descriptions of this relation are often called the term structure of interest rates.

The yield of a debt instrument is the annualized percentage increase in the value of the investment.

  a. 529 plan
  c. 7-Eleven

  b. Yield curve
  d. 4-4-5 Calendar

Chapter 37. Valuation of Bonds with Embedded Options

12. _____ is a type of bond that allows the issuer of the bond to retain the privilege of redeeming the bond at some point before the bond reaches the date of maturity. In other words, on the call dates, the issuer has the right, but not the obligation, to buy back the bonds from the bond holders at the call price. Technically speaking, the bonds are not really bought and held by the issuer but cancelled immediately.
    a. Gilts
    b. Coupon rate
    c. Callable bond
    d. Bond fund

13. _____ most frequently refers to the standard deviation of the continuously compounded returns of a financial instrument with a specific time horizon. It is often used to quantify the risk of the instrument over that time period. _____ is typically expressed in annualized terms, and it may either be an absolute number ($5) or a fraction of the mean (5%).
    a. Portfolio insurance
    b. Seasoned equity offering
    c. Currency swap
    d. Volatility

14. A _____ is a financial contract between two parties, the buyer and the seller of this type of option. Often it is simply labeled a 'call'. The buyer of the option has the right, but not the obligation to buy an agreed quantity of a particular commodity or financial instrument (the underlying instrument) from the seller of the option at a certain time (the expiration date) for a certain price (the strike price.)
    a. Bear call spread
    b. Bear spread
    c. Call option
    d. Bull spread

15. _____ is a combination of straight bond and embedded put option. The holder of the _____ has the right, but not the obligation, to demand early repayment of the principal. The put option is usually exercisable on specified dates.
    a. Convertible bond
    b. Callable bond
    c. Brady bonds
    d. Puttable bond

16. _____ is the flat spread over the treasury yield curve required to discount a security payment to match its market price. This concept can be applied to mortgage-backed security (MBS), Options, Bonds and any other interest-rate Derivative.

In contrast to the simple 'yield curve spread' measurement of bond premium over a pre-determined cash-flow model, the _____ describes the market premium over a model including two types of volatility:

- Variable interest rates
- Variable prepayment rates.

Designing such models in the first place is complicated because prepayment variations are a behavioural function of the stochastic interest rate. (They tend to go up as interest rates come down.)

    a. Option adjusted spread
    b. A Random Walk Down Wall Street
    c. AAB
    d. ABN Amro

17. In finance, the _____ of a financial asset measures the sensitivity of the asset's price to interest rate movements, expressed as a number of years. The reason for expressing this sensitivity in years is that the time that will elapse until a cash flow is received allows more interest to accumulate. Therefore the price of an asset with long term cashflows has more interest rate sensitivity than an asset with cashflows in the near future.

a. 4-4-5 Calendar
c. Yield to maturity

b. Macaulay duration
d. Duration

Chapter 38. Valuation of Mortgage-Backed Securities

1. _____ is the flat spread over the treasury yield curve required to discount a security payment to match its market price. This concept can be applied to mortgage-backed security (MBS), Options, Bonds and any other interest-rate Derivative.

In contrast to the simple 'yield curve spread' measurement of bond premium over a pre-determined cash-flow model, the _____ describes the market premium over a model including two types of volatility:

- Variable interest rates
- Variable prepayment rates.

Designing such models in the first place is complicated because prepayment variations are a behavioural function of the stochastic interest rate. (They tend to go up as interest rates come down.)

a. A Random Walk Down Wall Street
b. AAB
c. ABN Amro
d. Option adjusted spread

2. In finance, a _____ is a debt security, in which the authorized issuer owes the holders a debt and, depending on the terms of the _____, is obliged to pay interest (the coupon) and/or to repay the principal at a later date, termed maturity.

Thus a _____ is a loan: the issuer is the borrower, the _____ holder is the lender, and the coupon is the interest. _____ s provide the borrower with external funds to finance long-term investments, or, in the case of government _____ s, to finance current expenditure.

a. Convertible bond
b. Puttable bond
c. Catastrophe bonds
d. Bond

3. In finance, _____ is the process of estimating the potential market value of a financial asset or liability. they can be done on assets (for example, investments in marketable securities such as stocks, options, business enterprises, or intangible assets such as patents and trademarks) or on liabilities (e.g., Bonds issued by a company.) _____ s are required in many contexts including investment analysis, capital budgeting, merger and acquisition transactions, financial reporting, taxable events to determine the proper tax liability, and in litigation.

a. Margin
b. Share
c. Procter ' Gamble
d. Valuation

4. A _____ is an asset-backed security whose cash flows are backed by the principal and interest payments of a set of mortgage loans. Payments are typically made monthly over the lifetime of the underlying loans.

a. Shared appreciation mortgage
b. Home equity line of credit
c. Mortgage-backed security
d. Conforming loan

5. A _____ is a fungible, negotiable instrument representing financial value. They are broadly categorized into debt securities (such as banknotes, bonds and debentures), and equity securities; e.g., common stocks. The company or other entity issuing the _____ is called the issuer.

a. Securities lending
b. Tracking stock
c. Security
d. Book entry

Chapter 38. Valuation of Mortgage-Backed Securities 187

6. In finance, the term _____ describes the amount in cash that returns to the owners of a security. Normally it does not include the price variations, at the difference of the total return. _____ applies to various stated rates of return on stocks (common and preferred, and convertible), fixed income instruments (bonds, notes, bills, strips, zero coupon), and some other investment type insurance products (e.g. annuities.)

    a. 4-4-5 Calendar   b. Yield to maturity
    c. Macaulay duration   d. Yield

7. In finance, the _____ is the relation between the interest rate (or cost of borrowing) and the time to maturity of the debt for a given borrower in a given currency. For example, the current U.S. dollar interest rates paid on U.S. Treasury securities for various maturities are closely watched by many traders, and are commonly plotted on a graph such as the one on the right which is informally called 'the _____.' More formal mathematical descriptions of this relation are often called the term structure of interest rates.

The yield of a debt instrument is the annualized percentage increase in the value of the investment.

    a. 7-Eleven   b. 4-4-5 Calendar
    c. 529 plan   d. Yield curve

8. An _____ is a contract written by a seller that conveys to the buyer the right -- but not the obligation -- to buy (in the case of a call _____) or to sell (in the case of a put _____) a particular asset, such as a piece of property such as, among others, a futures contract. In return for granting the _____, the seller collects a payment (the premium) from the buyer.

For example, buying a call _____ provides the right to buy a specified quantity of a security at a set strike price at some time on or before expiration, while buying a put _____ provides the right to sell.

    a. Amortization   b. Option
    c. AT'T Mobility LLC   d. Annuity

9. _____ refers to the replacement of an existing debt obligation with a debt obligation bearing different terms. The most common consumer _____ is for a home mortgage.

_____ may be undertaken to reduce interest rate/interest costs (by _____ at a lower rate), to extend the repayment time, to pay off other debt(s), to reduce one's periodic payment obligations (sometimes by taking a longer-term loan), to reduce or alter risk (such as by _____ from a variable-rate to a fixed-rate loan), and/or to raise cash for investment, consumption, or the payment of a dividend.

    a. 4-4-5 Calendar   b. 7-Eleven
    c. Refinancing   d. 529 plan

10. _____ is the value on a given date of a future payment or series of future payments, discounted to reflect the time value of money and other factors such as investment risk. _____ calculations are widely used in business and economics to provide a means to compare cash flows at different times on a meaningful 'like to like' basis.

The most commonly applied model of the time value of money is compound interest.

a. Net present value
b. Present value
c. Present value of benefits
d. Negative gearing

11. In economics, business, and accounting, a _____ is the value of money that has been used up to produce something, and hence is not available for use anymore. In business, the _____ may be one of acquisition, in which case the amount of money expended to acquire it is counted as _____. In this case, money is the input that is gone in order to acquire the thing.
    a. Fixed costs
    b. Cost
    c. Sliding scale fees
    d. Marginal cost

12. In probability theory and statistics, the _____ of a random variable, probability distribution averaging the squared distance of its possible values from the expected value (mean.) Whereas the mean is a way to describe the location of a distribution, the _____ is a way to capture its scale or degree of being spread out. The unit of _____ is the square of the unit of the original variable.
    a. Variance
    b. Harmonic mean
    c. Semivariance
    d. Monte Carlo methods

13. In mathematics, more specifically in the theory of Monte Carlo methods, _____ is a procedure used to increase the precision of the estimates that can be obtained for a given number of iterations. Every output random variable from the simulation is associated with a variance which limits the precision of the simulation results. In order to make a simulation statistically efficient, i.e., to obtain a greater precision and smaller confidence intervals for the output random variable of interest, _____ techniques can be used.
    a. 4-4-5 Calendar
    b. 529 plan
    c. 7-Eleven
    d. Variance reduction

14. In finance, the _____ of a financial asset measures the sensitivity of the asset's price to interest rate movements, expressed as a number of years. The reason for expressing this sensitivity in years is that the time that will elapse until a cash flow is received allows more interest to accumulate. Therefore the price of an asset with long term cashflows has more interest rate sensitivity than an asset with cashflows in the near future.
    a. Macaulay duration
    b. 4-4-5 Calendar
    c. Yield to maturity
    d. Duration

15. _____ is a type of bond that allows the issuer of the bond to retain the privilege of redeeming the bond at some point before the bond reaches the date of maturity. In other words, on the call dates, the issuer has the right, but not the obligation, to buy back the bonds from the bond holders at the call price. Technically speaking, the bonds are not really bought and held by the issuer but cancelled immediately.
    a. Coupon rate
    b. Gilts
    c. Bond fund
    d. Callable bond

Chapter 39. OAS and Effective Duration

1. In finance, a _____ is a debt security, in which the authorized issuer owes the holders a debt and, depending on the terms of the _____, is obliged to pay interest (the coupon) and/or to repay the principal at a later date, termed maturity.

   Thus a _____ is a loan: the issuer is the borrower, the _____ holder is the lender, and the coupon is the interest. _____s provide the borrower with external funds to finance long-term investments, or, in the case of government _____s, to finance current expenditure.

   a. Convertible bond
   b. Puttable bond
   c. Catastrophe bonds
   d. Bond

2. _____ is a type of bond that allows the issuer of the bond to retain the privilege of redeeming the bond at some point before the bond reaches the date of maturity. In other words, on the call dates, the issuer has the right, but not the obligation, to buy back the bonds from the bond holders at the call price. Technically speaking, the bonds are not really bought and held by the issuer but cancelled immediately.

   a. Callable bond
   b. Gilts
   c. Coupon rate
   d. Bond fund

3. In finance, the _____ of a financial asset measures the sensitivity of the asset's price to interest rate movements, expressed as a number of years. The reason for expressing this sensitivity in years is that the time that will elapse until a cash flow is received allows more interest to accumulate. Therefore the price of an asset with long term cashflows has more interest rate sensitivity than an asset with cashflows in the near future.

   a. Macaulay duration
   b. Duration
   c. 4-4-5 Calendar
   d. Yield to maturity

4. _____ is a combination of straight bond and embedded put option. The holder of the _____ has the right, but not the obligation, to demand early repayment of the principal. The put option is usually exercisable on specified dates.

   a. Callable bond
   b. Convertible bond
   c. Brady bonds
   d. Puttable bond

5. _____ most frequently refers to the standard deviation of the continuously compounded returns of a financial instrument with a specific time horizon. It is often used to quantify the risk of the instrument over that time period. _____ is typically expressed in annualized terms, and it may either be an absolute number ($5) or a fraction of the mean (5%).

   a. Seasoned equity offering
   b. Currency swap
   c. Volatility
   d. Portfolio insurance

6. _____ is a life of security. It may also refer to the final payment date of a loan or other financial instrument, at which point all remaining interest and principal is due to be paid.

   1, 3, 6 months _____ band can be calculated by using 30-day per month periods.

   a. Replacement cost
   b. False billing
   c. Primary market
   d. Maturity

7. _____ is the flat spread over the treasury yield curve required to discount a security payment to match its market price. This concept can be applied to mortgage-backed security (MBS), Options, Bonds and any other interest-rate Derivative.

Chapter 39. OAS and Effective Duration

In contrast to the simple 'yield curve spread' measurement of bond premium over a pre-determined cash-flow model, the _____ describes the market premium over a model including two types of volatility:

- Variable interest rates
- Variable prepayment rates.

Designing such models in the first place is complicated because prepayment variations are a behavioural function of the stochastic interest rate. (They tend to go up as interest rates come down.)

a. AAB
c. ABN Amro
b. A Random Walk Down Wall Street
d. Option adjusted spread

Chapter 40. A Framework for Analyzing Yield-Curve Trades

1. In finance, the term _____ describes the amount in cash that returns to the owners of a security. Normally it does not include the price variations, at the difference of the total return. _____ applies to various stated rates of return on stocks (common and preferred, and convertible), fixed income instruments (bonds, notes, bills, strips, zero coupon), and some other investment type insurance products (e.g. annuities.)

   a. Yield to maturity
   b. 4-4-5 Calendar
   c. Macaulay duration
   d. Yield

2. In finance, a _____ is a debt security, in which the authorized issuer owes the holders a debt and, depending on the terms of the _____, is obliged to pay interest (the coupon) and/or to repay the principal at a later date, termed maturity.

Thus a _____ is a loan: the issuer is the borrower, the _____ holder is the lender, and the coupon is the interest. _____s provide the borrower with external funds to finance long-term investments, or, in the case of government _____s, to finance current expenditure.

   a. Puttable bond
   b. Convertible bond
   c. Catastrophe bonds
   d. Bond

3. The _____ or forward rate is the agreed upon price of an asset in a forward contract. Using the rational pricing assumption, we can express the _____ in terms of the spot price and any dividends etc., so that there is no possibility for arbitrage.

The _____ is given by:

where

      F is the _____ to be paid at time T
      e^x is the exponential function
      r is the risk-free interest rate
      q is the cost-of-carry
      S_0 is the spot price of the asset (i.e. what it would sell for at time 0)
      D_i is a dividend which is guaranteed to be paid at time t_i where $0 < t_i < T$.

The two questions here are what price the short position (the seller of the asset) should offer to maximize his gain, and what price the long position (the buyer of the asset) should accept to maximize his gain?

At the very least we know that both do not want to lose any money in the deal.

   a. Forward price
   b. Financial Gerontology
   c. Security interest
   d. Biweekly Mortgage

4. In finance, the yield curve is the relation between the interest rate (or cost of borrowing) and the time to maturity of the debt for a given borrower in a given currency. For example, the current U.S. dollar interest rates paid on U.S. Treasury securities for various maturities are closely watched by many traders, and are commonly plotted on a graph such as the one on the right which is informally called 'the yield curve.' More formal mathematical descriptions of this relation are often called the _____.

The yield of a debt instrument is the annualized percentage increase in the value of the investment.

a. 7-Eleven
b. Term structure of interest rates
c. 4-4-5 Calendar
d. 529 plan

5. _____ is a type of bond that allows the issuer of the bond to retain the privilege of redeeming the bond at some point before the bond reaches the date of maturity. In other words, on the call dates, the issuer has the right, but not the obligation, to buy back the bonds from the bond holders at the call price. Technically speaking, the bonds are not really bought and held by the issuer but cancelled immediately.

a. Coupon rate
b. Callable bond
c. Bond fund
d. Gilts

6. _____ is a fee paid on borrowed assets. It is the price paid for the use of borrowed money, or, money earned by deposited funds. Assets that are sometimes lent with _____ include money, shares, consumer goods through hire purchase, major assets such as aircraft, and even entire factories in finance lease arrangements.

a. Insolvency
b. AAB
c. A Random Walk Down Wall Street
d. Interest

7. An _____ is the price a borrower pays for the use of money they do not own, and the return a lender receives for deferring the use of funds, by lending it to the borrower. _____s are normally expressed as a percentage rate over the period of one year.

_____s targets are also a vital tool of monetary policy and are used to control variables like investment, inflation, and unemployment.

a. AAB
b. A Random Walk Down Wall Street
c. ABN Amro
d. Interest rate

8.

In finance, the _____ can be the expected rate of return above the risk-free interest rate. When measuring risk, a common sense approach is to compare the risk-free return on T-bills and the very risky return on other investments. The difference between these two returns can be interpreted as a measure of the excess return on the average risky asset. This excess return is known as the _____.

a. Risk aversion
b. Risk modeling
c. Risk adjusted return on capital
d. Risk premium

Chapter 40. A Framework for Analyzing Yield-Curve Trades   193

9. A _____ is a bond bought at a price lower than its face value, with the face value repaid at the time of maturity. It does not make periodic interest payments, or have so-called 'coupons,' hence the term _____. Investors earn return from the compounded interest all paid at maturity plus the difference between the discounted price of the bond and its par value.

   a. Corporate bond
   b. Bond fund
   c. Zero-coupon bond
   d. Clean price

10. A _____ or stock divide increases or decreases the number of shares in a public company. The price is adjusted such that the before and after market capitalization of the company remains the same and dilution does not occur. Options and warrants are included.

    a. Stock split
    b. Stop price
    c. Stop order
    d. Contract for difference

11. _____ (or spoilage) refers to the process by which tissues of dead organisms break down into simpler forms of matter. Such a breakdown of dead organisms is essential for new growth and development of living organisms because it recycles the finite chemical constituents and frees up the limited physical space in the biome. Bodies of living organisms begin to decompose shortly after death.

    a. 529 plan
    b. 7-Eleven
    c. Decomposition
    d. 4-4-5 Calendar

12. The _____ is the weighted-average most likely outcome in gambling, probability theory, economics or finance.

    In gambling and probability theory, there is usually a discrete set of possible outcomes. In this case, _____ is a measure of the relative balance of win or loss weighted by their chances of occurring.

    a. Expected return
    b. ABN Amro
    c. AAB
    d. A Random Walk Down Wall Street

13. _____, refers to consumption opportunity gained by an entity within a specified time frame, which is generally expressed in monetary terms. However, for households and individuals, '_____ is the sum of all the wages, salaries, profits, interests payments, rents and other forms of earnings received... in a given period of time.' For firms, _____ generally refers to net-profit: what remains of revenue after expenses have been subtracted.

    a. OIBDA
    b. Annual report
    c. Accrual
    d. Income

14. In economics and business, specifically cost accounting, the _____ is the point at which cost or expenses and revenue are equal: there is no net loss or gain, and one has 'broken even'. A profit or a loss has not been made, although opportunity costs have been paid, and capital has received the risk-adjusted, expected return.

    For example, if the business sells less than 200 tables each month, it will make a loss, if it sells more, it will be a profit.

    a. Fixed asset turnover
    b. Market microstructure
    c. Break-even point
    d. Defined contribution plan

15. In finance, the _____ is the relation between the interest rate (or cost of borrowing) and the time to maturity of the debt for a given borrower in a given currency. For example, the current U.S. dollar interest rates paid on U.S. Treasury securities for various maturities are closely watched by many traders, and are commonly plotted on a graph such as the one on the right which is informally called 'the _____.' More formal mathematical descriptions of this relation are often called the term structure of interest rates.

The yield of a debt instrument is the annualized percentage increase in the value of the investment.

a. 529 plan
b. 7-Eleven
c. Yield curve
d. 4-4-5 Calendar

16. In economics and finance, _____ is the practice of taking advantage of a price differential between two or more markets: striking a combination of matching deals that capitalize upon the imbalance, the profit being the difference between the market prices. When used by academics, an _____ is a transaction that involves no negative cash flow at any probabilistic or temporal state and a positive cash flow in at least one state; in simple terms, a risk-free profit.

a. Issuer
b. Efficient-market hypothesis
c. Arbitrage
d. Initial margin

17. _____ is a method for constructing a (zero-coupon) fixed-income yield curve from the prices of a set of coupon-bearing products by forward substitution.

Using these zero-coupon products it becomes possible to derive par swap rates (forward and spot) for all maturities by making a few assumptions (including linear interpolation.) The term structure of spot returns is recovered from the bond yields by solving for them recursively, this iterative process is called the BootStrap Method.

a. Reserve requirement
b. Bullet loan
c. Probability of default
d. Bootstrapping

Chapter 41. The Market Yield Curve and Fitting the Term Structure of Interest Rates

1. The coupon or _____ of a bond is the amount of interest paid per year expressed as a percentage of the face value of the bond.

For example if you hold $10,000 nominal of a bond described as a 4.5% loan stock, you will receive $450 in interest each year (probably in two installments of $225 each.)

Not all bonds have coupons.

a. Zero-coupon bond
c. Revenue bonds
b. Puttable bond
d. Coupon rate

2. A '_____' is a 'Charge' that is paid to obtain the right to delay a payment. Essentially, the payer purchases the right to make a given payment in the future instead of in the Present. The '_____', or 'Charge' that must be paid to delay the payment, is simply the difference between what the payment amount would be if it were paid in the present and what the payment amount would be paid if it were paid in the future.

a. Risk aversion
c. Discount
b. Value at risk
d. Risk modeling

3. A _____ is a bond bought at a price lower than its face value, with the face value repaid at the time of maturity. It does not make periodic interest payments, or so-called 'coupons,' hence the term zero-coupon bond. Investors earn return from the compounded interest all paid at maturity plus the difference between the discounted price of the bond and its par value.

a. Bowie bonds
c. Callable bond
b. Municipal bond
d. Zero coupon bond

4. In finance, the term _____ describes the amount in cash that returns to the owners of a security. Normally it does not include the price variations, at the difference of the total return. _____ applies to various stated rates of return on stocks (common and preferred, and convertible), fixed income instruments (bonds, notes, bills, strips, zero coupon), and some other investment type insurance products (e.g. annuities.)

a. Yield
c. Macaulay duration
b. 4-4-5 Calendar
d. Yield to maturity

5. In finance, the _____ is the relation between the interest rate (or cost of borrowing) and the time to maturity of the debt for a given borrower in a given currency. For example, the current U.S. dollar interest rates paid on U.S. Treasury securities for various maturities are closely watched by many traders, and are commonly plotted on a graph such as the one on the right which is informally called 'the _____.' More formal mathematical descriptions of this relation are often called the term structure of interest rates.

The yield of a debt instrument is the annualized percentage increase in the value of the investment.

a. 529 plan
c. 7-Eleven
b. 4-4-5 Calendar
d. Yield curve

6. A _____ is a bond bought at a price lower than its face value, with the face value repaid at the time of maturity. It does not make periodic interest payments, or have so-called 'coupons,' hence the term _____. Investors earn return from the compounded interest all paid at maturity plus the difference between the discounted price of the bond and its par value.

Chapter 41. The Market Yield Curve and Fitting the Term Structure of Interest Rates

   a. Bond fund
   c. Corporate bond
   b. Clean price
   d. Zero-coupon bond

7. In finance, a _____ is a debt security, in which the authorized issuer owes the holders a debt and, depending on the terms of the _____, is obliged to pay interest (the coupon) and/or to repay the principal at a later date, termed maturity.

Thus a _____ is a loan: the issuer is the borrower, the _____ holder is the lender, and the coupon is the interest. _____s provide the borrower with external funds to finance long-term investments, or, in the case of government _____s, to finance current expenditure.

   a. Catastrophe bonds
   c. Bond
   b. Puttable bond
   d. Convertible bond

8. _____ is a method for constructing a (zero-coupon) fixed-income yield curve from the prices of a set of coupon-bearing products by forward substitution.

Using these zero-coupon products it becomes possible to derive par swap rates (forward and spot) for all maturities by making a few assumptions (including linear interpolation.) The term structure of spot returns is recovered from the bond yields by solving for them recursively, this iterative process is called the BootStrap Method.

   a. Bullet loan
   c. Reserve requirement
   b. Bootstrapping
   d. Probability of default

9. The _____, interest yield, income yield, flat yield or running yield is a financial term used in reference to bonds and other fixed-interest securities such as gilts. It is the ratio of the annual interest payment and the bond's current price.

The _____ only therefore refers to the yield of the bond at the current moment. It does not reflect the total return over the life of the bond. In particular, it takes no account of reinvestment risk (the uncertainty about the rate at which future cashflows can be reinvested) or the fact that bonds usually mature at par value, which can be an important component of a bond's return.

   a. Modified Internal Rate of Return
   c. Perpetuity
   b. Stochastic volatility
   d. Current yield

10. The _____ or redemption yield is the yield promised to the bondholder on the assumption that the bond or other fixed-interest security such as gilts will be held to maturity, that all coupon and principal payments will be made and coupon payments are reinvested at the bond's promised yield at the same rate as invested. It is a measure of the return of the bond. This technique in theory allows investors to calculate the fair value of different financial instruments.
   a. 4-4-5 Calendar
   c. Macaulay duration
   b. Yield
   d. Yield to maturity

Chapter 41. The Market Yield Curve and Fitting the Term Structure of Interest Rates

11. In finance, the yield curve is the relation between the interest rate (or cost of borrowing) and the time to maturity of the debt for a given borrower in a given currency. For example, the current U.S. dollar interest rates paid on U.S. Treasury securities for various maturities are closely watched by many traders, and are commonly plotted on a graph such as the one on the right which is informally called 'the yield curve.' More formal mathematical descriptions of this relation are often called the _____.

The yield of a debt instrument is the annualized percentage increase in the value of the investment.

a. Term structure of interest rates
b. 7-Eleven
c. 4-4-5 Calendar
d. 529 plan

12. _____ is a fee paid on borrowed assets. It is the price paid for the use of borrowed money, or, money earned by deposited funds. Assets that are sometimes lent with _____ include money, shares, consumer goods through hire purchase, major assets such as aircraft, and even entire factories in finance lease arrangements.

a. AAB
b. A Random Walk Down Wall Street
c. Insolvency
d. Interest

13. An _____ is the price a borrower pays for the use of money they do not own, and the return a lender receives for deferring the use of funds, by lending it to the borrower. _____s are normally expressed as a percentage rate over the period of one year.

_____s targets are also a vital tool of monetary policy and are used to control variables like investment, inflation, and unemployment.

a. Interest rate
b. AAB
c. ABN Amro
d. A Random Walk Down Wall Street

14. The _____ or forward rate is the agreed upon price of an asset in a forward contract. Using the rational pricing assumption, we can express the _____ in terms of the spot price and any dividends etc., so that there is no possibility for arbitrage.

The _____ is given by:

where

    F is the _____ to be paid at time T
    e^x is the exponential function
    r is the risk-free interest rate
    q is the cost-of-carry
    S_0 is the spot price of the asset (i.e. what it would sell for at time 0)
    D_i is a dividend which is guaranteed to be paid at time t_i where $0 < t_i < T$.

Chapter 41. The Market Yield Curve and Fitting the Term Structure of Interest Rates

The two questions here are what price the short position (the seller of the asset) should offer to maximize his gain, and what price the long position (the buyer of the asset) should accept to maximize his gain?

At the very least we know that both do not want to lose any money in the deal.

a. Security interest
b. Forward price
c. Biweekly Mortgage
d. Financial Gerontology

15. The _____, P(T), is the number which a future cash flow, to be received at time T, must be multiplied by in order to obtain the current present value. Thus, a fixed annually compounded discount rate is

$$P(T) = \frac{1}{(1+r)^T}$$

For fixed continuously compounded discount rate we have

$$P(T) = e^{-rT}$$

For discounts in marketing, see discounts and allowances, sales promotion, and pricing.

a. Risk premium
b. Risk modeling
c. Discount
d. Discount factor

16. The _____ of a commodity, a security or a currency is the price that is quoted for immediate (spot) settlement (payment and delivery.) Spot settlement is normally one or two business days from trade date. This is in contrast with the forward price established in a forward contract or futures contract, where contract terms (price) are set now, but delivery and payment will occur at a future date.

a. Spot rate
b. Market anomaly
c. Long position
d. Limits to arbitrage

17. The arithmetic _____ over n periods is defined as:

The geometric _____, also known as the time-weighted rate of return, over n periods is defined as:

The geometric _____ calculated over n years is also known as the annualized return.

Chapter 41. The Market Yield Curve and Fitting the Term Structure of Interest Rates

The internal rate of return, also known as the dollar-weighted rate of return, is defined as the value(s) of r that satisfies the following equation:

$$NPV$$

where:

- NPV = net present value of the investment

For both arithmetic returns and logarithmic returns, an investment is profitable when either r_a or r_l > 0, and unprofitable when either r_a or r_l < 0.

The value of an investment is doubled over a year if the annual ROR r_a or r_l. The value falls to zero when r_a or r_l.

a. Average rate of return
b. Earnings yield
c. Assets turnover
d. Inventory turnover

18. In finance, _____, also known as return on investment is the ratio of money gained or lost on an investment relative to the amount of money invested. The amount of money gained or lost may be referred to as interest, profit/loss, gain/loss, or net income/loss. The money invested may be referred to as the asset, capital, principal, or the cost basis of the investment.

a. Doctrine of the Proper Law
b. Composiition of Creditors
c. Stock or scrip dividends
d. Rate of return

19. _____ are government bonds issued by the United States Department of the Treasury through the Bureau of the Public Debt. They are the debt financing instruments of the U.S. Federal government, and they are often referred to simply as Treasuries or Treasurys. There are four types of marketable _____: Treasury bills, Treasury notes, Treasury bonds, and Treasury Inflation Protected Securities (TIPS.)

a. Treasury Inflation-Protected Securities
b. Treasury Inflation Protected Securities
c. 4-4-5 Calendar
d. Treasury securities

20. A _____ or market-based mechanism is any of a wide variety of ways to match up buyers and sellers.

An example of a _____ uses announced bid and ask prices. Generally speaking, when two parties wish to engage in a trade, the purchaser will announce a price he is willing to pay (the bid price) and seller will announce a price he is willing to accept (the ask price).

Chapter 41. The Market Yield Curve and Fitting the Term Structure of Interest Rates

a. 7-Eleven
b. 529 plan
c. 4-4-5 Calendar
d. Price mechanism

21. The _____ for securities is the difference between the price quoted by a market maker for an immediate sale and an immediate purchase The size of the bid-offer spread in a given commodity is a measure of the liquidity of the market.

The trader initiating the transaction is said to demand liquidity, and the other party to the transaction supplies liquidity.

a. Capital outflow
b. Defined contribution plan
c. Trade-off
d. Bid/offer spread

22. A _____ is a fungible, negotiable instrument representing financial value. They are broadly categorized into debt securities (such as banknotes, bonds and debentures), and equity securities; e.g., common stocks. The company or other entity issuing the _____ is called the issuer.

a. Securities lending
b. Tracking stock
c. Security
d. Book entry

23. A _____ is used in economic models to describe the weights placed on rewards received at different points in time. For example, if time is discrete and utility is time-separable, with the _____

$f(t)$

total utility is given by

$$\boxed{} >.$$

Total utility in the continuous-time case is given by

$$\boxed{} >$$

provided that this integral exists.

a. 529 plan
b. Discount function
c. 7-Eleven
d. 4-4-5 Calendar

24. The method of least squares or _____ is used to approximately solve overdetermined systems. Least squares is often applied in statistical contexts, particularly regression analysis.

Least squares can be interpreted as a method of fitting data.

a. A Random Walk Down Wall Street
b. ABN Amro
c. Ordinary least squares
d. AAB

25. In statistics and image processing, to smooth a data set is to create an approximating function that attempts to capture important patterns in the data, while leaving out noise or other fine-scale structures/rapid phenomena. Many different algorithms are used in _____. One of the most common algorithms is the 'moving average', often used to try to capture important trends in repeated statistical surveys.

   a. 4-4-5 Calendar   b. 529 plan

   c. 7-Eleven   d. Smoothing

26. _____ mature in one year or less. Like zero-coupon bonds, they do not pay interest prior to maturity; instead they are sold at a discount of the par value to create a positive yield to maturity. Many regard _____ as the least risky investment available to U.S. investors.

   a. 4-4-5 Calendar   b. Treasury Inflation Protected Securities

   c. Treasury securities   d. Treasury bills

Chapter 42. Hedging Interest-Rate Risk with Term-Structure Factor Models

1. _____ is the provision of resources (such as granting a loan) by one party to another party where that second party does not reimburse the first party immediately, thereby generating a debt, and instead arranges either to repay or return those resources (or material(s) of equal value) at a later date. The first party is called a creditor, also known as a lender, while the second party is called a debtor, also known as a borrower.

Movements of financial capital are normally dependent on either _____ or equity transfers.

   a. Warrant   b. Credit
   c. Clearing house   d. Comparable

2. _____ is the risk of loss due to a debtor's non-payment of a loan or other line of credit (either the principal or interest (coupon) or both)

Most lenders employ their own models (credit scorecards) to rank potential and existing customers according to risk, and then apply appropriate strategies. With products such as unsecured personal loans or mortgages, lenders charge a higher price for higher risk customers and vice versa. With revolving products such as credit cards and overdrafts, risk is controlled through careful setting of credit limits.

   a. Credit risk   b. Liquidity risk
   c. Market risk   d. Transaction risk

3. In finance, the _____ of a financial asset measures the sensitivity of the asset's price to interest rate movements, expressed as a number of years. The reason for expressing this sensitivity in years is that the time that will elapse until a cash flow is received allows more interest to accumulate. Therefore the price of an asset with long term cashflows has more interest rate sensitivity than an asset with cashflows in the near future.
   a. Macaulay duration   b. 4-4-5 Calendar
   c. Duration   d. Yield to maturity

4. A _____ is a variable associated with an increased risk of disease or infection. They are correlational and not necessarily causal, because correlation does not imply causation. For example, being young cannot be said to cause measles, but young people are more at risk as they are less likely to have developed immunity during a previous epidemic.
   a. 529 plan   b. Risk factor
   c. 7-Eleven   d. 4-4-5 Calendar

5. In finance, the yield curve is the relation between the interest rate (or cost of borrowing) and the time to maturity of the debt for a given borrower in a given currency. For example, the current U.S. dollar interest rates paid on U.S. Treasury securities for various maturities are closely watched by many traders, and are commonly plotted on a graph such as the one on the right which is informally called 'the yield curve.' More formal mathematical descriptions of this relation are often called the _____.

The yield of a debt instrument is the annualized percentage increase in the value of the investment.

   a. 7-Eleven   b. 529 plan
   c. 4-4-5 Calendar   d. Term structure of interest rates

Chapter 42. Hedging Interest-Rate Risk with Term-Structure Factor Models

6. In finance, a _____ is a debt security, in which the authorized issuer owes the holders a debt and, depending on the terms of the _____, is obliged to pay interest (the coupon) and/or to repay the principal at a later date, termed maturity.

Thus a _____ is a loan: the issuer is the borrower, the _____ holder is the lender, and the coupon is the interest. _____s provide the borrower with external funds to finance long-term investments, or, in the case of government _____s, to finance current expenditure.

a. Puttable bond
b. Catastrophe bonds
c. Convertible bond
d. Bond

7. _____ is a fee paid on borrowed assets. It is the price paid for the use of borrowed money, or, money earned by deposited funds. Assets that are sometimes lent with _____ include money, shares, consumer goods through hire purchase, major assets such as aircraft, and even entire factories in finance lease arrangements.

a. A Random Walk Down Wall Street
b. Insolvency
c. Interest
d. AAB

8. An _____ is the price a borrower pays for the use of money they do not own, and the return a lender receives for deferring the use of funds, by lending it to the borrower. _____s are normally expressed as a percentage rate over the period of one year.

_____s targets are also a vital tool of monetary policy and are used to control variables like investment, inflation, and unemployment.

a. ABN Amro
b. Interest rate
c. A Random Walk Down Wall Street
d. AAB

9. In finance, _____ is the risk involved in using models to value financial securities. Rebonato considers alternative definitions including:

1) After observing a set of prices for the underlying and hedging instruments, different but identically calibrated models might produce different prices for the same exotic product. 2) Losses will be incurred because of an 'incorrect' hedging strategy suggested by a model.

a. Price-to-book ratio
b. Duty of loyalty
c. Takeover
d. Model risk

10. _____ is the discipline of identifying, monitoring and limiting risks. In some cases the acceptable risk may be near zero. Risks can come from accidents, natural causes and disasters as well as deliberate attacks from an adversary.

a. 4-4-5 Calendar
b. FIFO
c. Penny stock
d. Risk management

11. In mathematics, the _____ is a representation of a function as an infinite sum of terms calculated from the values of its derivatives at a single point. It may be regarded as the limit of the Taylor polynomials. _____ are named after English mathematician Brook Taylor.

a. Taylor series
b. Flat interest rate
c. The Glass-Steagall Act of 1933
d. BootStrap Method

12. _____ involves a mathematical procedure that transforms a number of possibly correlated variables into a smaller number of uncorrelated variables called principal components. The first principal component accounts for as much of the variability in the data as possible, and each succeeding component accounts for as much of the remaining variability as possible. Depending on the field of application, it is also named the discrete Karhunen-Lo>ève transform (KLT), the Hotelling transform or proper orthogonal decomposition (POD.)

a. 4-4-5 Calendar
b. 7-Eleven
c. 529 plan
d. Principal component analysis

13. In finance, the _____ is a mathematical model describing the evolution of interest rates. It is a type of 'one-factor model' (short rate model) as it describes interest rate movements as driven by only one source of market risk. The model can be used in the valuation of interest rate derivatives, and has also been adapted for credit markets.

a. Bed Bath ' Beyond Inc.
b. The Hong Kong Securities Institute
c. Double-declining-balance method
d. Vasicek model

Chapter 43. Introduction to Bond Portfolio Management

1. In finance, a _____ is a debt security, in which the authorized issuer owes the holders a debt and, depending on the terms of the _____, is obliged to pay interest (the coupon) and/or to repay the principal at a later date, termed maturity.

Thus a _____ is a loan: the issuer is the borrower, the _____ holder is the lender, and the coupon is the interest. _____s provide the borrower with external funds to finance long-term investments, or, in the case of government _____s, to finance current expenditure.

a. Bond
b. Puttable bond
c. Convertible bond
d. Catastrophe bonds

2. _____ refers to a portfolio management strategy where the manager makes specific investments with the goal of outperforming an investment benchmark index. Investors or mutual funds that do not aspire to create a return in excess of a benchmark index will often invest in an index fund that replicates as closely as possible the investment weighting and returns of that index; this is called passive management. _____ is the opposite of passive management, because in passive management the manager does not seek to outperform the benchmark index.

a. ABN Amro
b. A Random Walk Down Wall Street
c. AAB
d. Active management

3. In finance, _____ is a catch-all term that describes strategies employed to outperform traditional indexing. _____ attempts to generate modest excess returns compared to index funds and other passive management techniques.

_____ combines elements of passive management and active management.

a. ABN Amro
b. AAB
c. A Random Walk Down Wall Street
d. Enhanced indexing

4. _____ is the provision of resources (such as granting a loan) by one party to another party where that second party does not reimburse the first party immediately, thereby generating a debt, and instead arranges either to repay or return those resources (or material(s) of equal value) at a later date. The first party is called a creditor, also known as a lender, while the second party is called a debtor, also known as a borrower.

Movements of financial capital are normally dependent on either _____ or equity transfers.

a. Warrant
b. Clearing house
c. Comparable
d. Credit

5. _____ is the risk of loss due to a debtor's non-payment of a loan or other line of credit (either the principal or interest (coupon) or both)

Most lenders employ their own models (credit scorecards) to rank potential and existing customers according to risk, and then apply appropriate strategies. With products such as unsecured personal loans or mortgages, lenders charge a higher price for higher risk customers and vice versa. With revolving products such as credit cards and overdrafts, risk is controlled through careful setting of credit limits.

a. Market risk
b. Transaction risk
c. Credit risk
d. Liquidity risk

6. A _____ is a variable associated with an increased risk of disease or infection. They are correlational and not necessarily causal, because correlation does not imply causation. For example, being young cannot be said to cause measles, but young people are more at risk as they are less likely to have developed immunity during a previous epidemic.
   a. 4-4-5 Calendar
   b. 7-Eleven
   c. 529 plan
   d. Risk factor

7. _____ in finance is a risk management technique, related to hedging, that mixes a wide variety of investments within a portfolio. Because the fluctuations of a single security have less impact on a diverse portfolio, _____ minimizes the risk from any one investment.

A simple example of _____ is the following: On a particular island the entire economy consists of two companies: one that sells umbrellas and another that sells sunscreen.

   a. 529 plan
   b. 7-Eleven
   c. 4-4-5 Calendar
   d. Diversification

8. In economics, business, and accounting, a _____ is the value of money that has been used up to produce something, and hence is not available for use anymore. In business, the _____ may be one of acquisition, in which case the amount of money expended to acquire it is counted as _____. In this case, money is the input that is gone in order to acquire the thing.
   a. Fixed costs
   b. Sliding scale fees
   c. Marginal cost
   d. Cost

9. _____ is the price at which an asset would trade in a competitive Walrasian auction setting. _____ is often used interchangeably with open _____, fair value or fair _____, although these terms have distinct definitions in different standards, and may differ in some circumstances.

International Valuation Standards defines _____ as 'the estimated amount for which a property should exchange on the date of valuation between a willing buyer and a willing seller in an arm'e;s-length transaction after proper marketing wherein the parties had each acted knowledgeably, prudently, and without compulsion.'

_____ is a concept distinct from market price, which is 'e;the price at which one can transact'e;, while _____ is 'e;the true underlying value'e; according to theoretical standards.

   a. Wrap account
   b. T-Model
   c. Debt restructuring
   d. Market value

10. _____, refers to consumption opportunity gained by an entity within a specified time frame, which is generally expressed in monetary terms. However, for households and individuals, '_____ is the sum of all the wages, salaries, profits, interests payments, rents and other forms of earnings received... in a given period of time.' For firms, _____ generally refers to net-profit: what remains of revenue after expenses have been subtracted.

Chapter 43. Introduction to Bond Portfolio Management

a. Accrual
c. Annual report
b. OIBDA
d. Income

11. In finance, the _____ of a financial asset measures the sensitivity of the asset's price to interest rate movements, expressed as a number of years. The reason for expressing this sensitivity in years is that the time that will elapse until a cash flow is received allows more interest to accumulate. Therefore the price of an asset with long term cashflows has more interest rate sensitivity than an asset with cashflows in the near future.

a. Duration
c. 4-4-5 Calendar
b. Macaulay duration
d. Yield to maturity

12. _____ is a legal entity that develops, registers and sells securities for the purpose of financing its operations. _____s may be domestic or foreign governments, corporations or investment trusts. _____s are legally responsible for the obligations of the issue and for reporting financial conditions, material developments and any other operational activities as required by the regulations of their jurisdictions.

a. Arbitrage
c. Initial margin
b. Efficient-market hypothesis
d. Issuer

13. _____ are government bonds issued by the United States Department of the Treasury through the Bureau of the Public Debt. They are the debt financing instruments of the U.S. Federal government, and they are often referred to simply as Treasuries or Treasurys. There are four types of marketable _____: Treasury bills, Treasury notes, Treasury bonds, and Treasury Inflation Protected Securities (TIPS.)

a. Treasury Inflation-Protected Securities
c. Treasury Inflation Protected Securities
b. 4-4-5 Calendar
d. Treasury securities

14. A _____ or market-based mechanism is any of a wide variety of ways to match up buyers and sellers.

An example of a _____ uses announced bid and ask prices. Generally speaking, when two parties wish to engage in a trade, the purchaser will announce a price he is willing to pay (the bid price) and seller will announce a price he is willing to accept (the ask price).

a. Price mechanism
c. 529 plan
b. 4-4-5 Calendar
d. 7-Eleven

15. The _____ for securities is the difference between the price quoted by a market maker for an immediate sale and an immediate purchase The size of the bid-offer spread in a given commodity is a measure of the liquidity of the market.

The trader initiating the transaction is said to demand liquidity, and the other party to the transaction supplies liquidity.

a. Capital outflow
c. Defined contribution plan
b. Trade-off
d. Bid/offer spread

16. A _____ is a bond issued by a corporation. The term is usually applied to longer-term debt instruments, generally with a maturity date falling at least a year after their issue date. (The term 'commercial paper' is sometimes used for instruments with a shorter maturity.)

a. Serial bond
c. Corporate bond
b. Government bond
d. Brady bonds

17. A _____ is a fungible, negotiable instrument representing financial value. They are broadly categorized into debt securities (such as banknotes, bonds and debentures), and equity securities; e.g., common stocks. The company or other entity issuing the _____ is called the issuer.
   a. Tracking stock
   c. Securities lending
   b. Book entry
   d. Security

18. _____ is a term normally applied to stock market trading patterns. In this context, a sector is understood to mean a group of stocks representing companies in similar lines of business.

For example, an investor or trader may describe the current market movements as favoring basic material stocks over semiconductor stocks by calling the environment a _____ from semiconductors to basic materials.

   a. Conglomerate merger
   c. Refunding
   b. Commercial finance
   d. Sector rotation

19. A _____ is a bond bought at a price lower than its face value, with the face value repaid at the time of maturity. It does not make periodic interest payments, or have so-called 'coupons,' hence the term _____. Investors earn return from the compounded interest all paid at maturity plus the difference between the discounted price of the bond and its par value.
   a. Zero-coupon bond
   c. Corporate bond
   b. Clean price
   d. Bond fund

20. _____ is a type of bond that allows the issuer of the bond to retain the privilege of redeeming the bond at some point before the bond reaches the date of maturity. In other words, on the call dates, the issuer has the right, but not the obligation, to buy back the bonds from the bond holders at the call price. Technically speaking, the bonds are not really bought and held by the issuer but cancelled immediately.
   a. Bond fund
   c. Callable bond
   b. Gilts
   d. Coupon rate

21. _____ or Investment _____ is a set of techniques that performance analysts use to explain why a portfolio's performance differed from the benchmark. This difference between the portfolio return and the benchmark return is known as the active return. The active return is the component of a portfolio's performance that arises from the fact that the portfolio is actively managed.
   a. Delta neutral
   c. Central Securities Depository
   b. Convertible arbitrage
   d. Performance attribution

Chapter 44. Quantitative Management of Benchmarked Portfolios 209

1. In finance, a _____ is a debt security, in which the authorized issuer owes the holders a debt and, depending on the terms of the _____, is obliged to pay interest (the coupon) and/or to repay the principal at a later date, termed maturity.

Thus a _____ is a loan: the issuer is the borrower, the _____ holder is the lender, and the coupon is the interest. _____s provide the borrower with external funds to finance long-term investments, or, in the case of government _____s, to finance current expenditure.

   a. Puttable bond
   b. Convertible bond
   c. Catastrophe bonds
   d. Bond

2. In business and accounting, _____s are everything of value that is owned by a person or company. The balance sheet of a firm records the monetary value of the _____s owned by the firm. The two major _____ classes are tangible _____s and intangible _____s.
   a. Accounts payable
   b. Income
   c. Asset
   d. EBITDA

3. A _____ is an asset-backed security whose cash flows are backed by the principal and interest payments of a set of mortgage loans. Payments are typically made monthly over the lifetime of the underlying loans.
   a. Mortgage-backed security
   b. Conforming loan
   c. Home equity line of credit
   d. Shared appreciation mortgage

4. _____ is the process of setting or keeping the delta of a portfolio as close to zero as possible.

Mathematically, delta is the partial derivative [x]> of the instrument or portfolio's fair value with respect to the price of the underlying security.

Therefore, if a position is delta neutral (or, instantaneously delta-hedged) its instantaneous change in value, for an infinitesimal change in the value of the underlying, will be zero; see Hedge (finance.)

   a. Convertible arbitrage
   b. Central Securities Depository
   c. Financial services
   d. Delta hedging

5. In finance, the _____ of a financial asset measures the sensitivity of the asset's price to interest rate movements, expressed as a number of years. The reason for expressing this sensitivity in years is that the time that will elapse until a cash flow is received allows more interest to accumulate. Therefore the price of an asset with long term cashflows has more interest rate sensitivity than an asset with cashflows in the near future.
   a. Macaulay duration
   b. Duration
   c. 4-4-5 Calendar
   d. Yield to maturity

6. A _____ is a fungible, negotiable instrument representing financial value. They are broadly categorized into debt securities (such as banknotes, bonds and debentures), and equity securities; e.g., common stocks. The company or other entity issuing the _____ is called the issuer.
   a. Security
   b. Securities lending
   c. Book entry
   d. Tracking stock

7. In finance, a _____ is a derivative in which two counterparties agree to exchange one stream of cash flows against another stream. These streams are called the legs of the _____.

The cash flows are calculated over a notional principal amount, which is usually not exchanged between counterparties.

a. Volatility arbitrage
c. Local volatility

b. Volatility swap
d. Swap

8. In finance, the term _____ describes the amount in cash that returns to the owners of a security. Normally it does not include the price variations, at the difference of the total return. _____ applies to various stated rates of return on stocks (common and preferred, and convertible), fixed income instruments (bonds, notes, bills, strips, zero coupon), and some other investment type insurance products (e.g. annuities.)

a. Yield to maturity
c. Yield

b. 4-4-5 Calendar
d. Macaulay duration

9. _____ is the provision of resources (such as granting a loan) by one party to another party where that second party does not reimburse the first party immediately, thereby generating a debt, and instead arranges either to repay or return those resources (or material(s) of equal value) at a later date. The first party is called a creditor, also known as a lender, while the second party is called a debtor, also known as a borrower.

Movements of financial capital are normally dependent on either _____ or equity transfers.

a. Comparable
c. Warrant

b. Clearing house
d. Credit

10. _____ is the risk of loss due to a debtor's non-payment of a loan or other line of credit (either the principal or interest (coupon) or both)

Most lenders employ their own models (credit scorecards) to rank potential and existing customers according to risk, and then apply appropriate strategies. With products such as unsecured personal loans or mortgages, lenders charge a higher price for higher risk customers and vice versa. With revolving products such as credit cards and overdrafts, risk is controlled through careful setting of credit limits.

a. Transaction risk
c. Liquidity risk

b. Credit risk
d. Market risk

11. _____ in finance is a risk management technique, related to hedging, that mixes a wide variety of investments within a portfolio. Because the fluctuations of a single security have less impact on a diverse portfolio, _____ minimizes the risk from any one investment.

A simple example of _____ is the following: On a particular island the entire economy consists of two companies: one that sells umbrellas and another that sells sunscreen.

Chapter 44. Quantitative Management of Benchmarked Portfolios

a. 7-Eleven
c. 529 plan

b. 4-4-5 Calendar
d. Diversification

12. In probability theory and statistics, _____ is a measure of how much two variables change together (variance is a special case of the _____ when the two variables are identical.)

If two variables tend to vary together (that is, when one of them is above its expected value, then the other variable tends to be above its expected value too), then the _____ between the two variables will be positive. On the other hand, when one of them is above its expected value the other variable tends to be below its expected value, then the _____ between the two variables will be negative.

a. Probability distribution
c. Frequency distribution

b. Covariance
d. Stratified sampling

13. In statistics and probability theory, the _____ is a matrix of covariances between elements of a vector. It is the natural generalization to higher dimensions of the concept of the variance of a scalar-valued random variable.

If entries in the column vector

$$X = \begin{bmatrix} X_1 \\ \vdots \\ X_n \end{bmatrix}$$

are random variables, each with finite variance, then the _____ Σ is the matrix whose (i, j) entry is the covariance

$$\Sigma_{ij} = \operatorname{cov}(X_i, X_j) = \operatorname{E}\big[(X_i - \mu_i)(X_j - \mu_j)\big]$$

where

$$\mu_i = \operatorname{E}(X_i)$$

is the expected value of the ith entry in the vector X.

a. Covariance matrix
c. 7-Eleven

b. 4-4-5 Calendar
d. 529 plan

14. In finance, _____ is that risk which is common to an entire market and not to any individual entity or component thereof. It should be distinguished from systemic risk which is the risk that the entire financial system will collapse as a result of some catastrophic event.

Risks can be reduced in four main ways: Avoidance, Reduction, Retention and Transfer.

Chapter 44. Quantitative Management of Benchmarked Portfolios

a. Capital surplus
b. Primary market
c. Conglomerate merger
d. Systematic risk

15. _____ refers to the use of formal econometric techniques to determine the aggregate risk in a financial portfolio. _____ is one of many subtasks within the broader area of financial modeling.

_____ uses a variety of techniques including market risk, Value-at-Risk (VaR), Historical Simulation (HS), or Extreme Value Theory (EVT) in order to analyze a portfolio and make forecasts of the likely losses that would be incurred for a variety of risks.

a. Risk adjusted return on capital
b. Risk premium
c. Value at risk
d. Risk modeling

16. _____ most frequently refers to the standard deviation of the continuously compounded returns of a financial instrument with a specific time horizon. It is often used to quantify the risk of the instrument over that time period. _____ is typically expressed in annualized terms, and it may either be an absolute number ($5) or a fraction of the mean (5%).
a. Portfolio insurance
b. Currency swap
c. Seasoned equity offering
d. Volatility

17. _____ is a process of analyzing possible future events by considering alternative possible outcomes (scenarios.) The analysis is designed to allow improved decision-making by allowing consideration of outcomes and their implications.

For example, in economics and finance, a financial institution might attempt to forecast several possible scenarios for the economy (e.g. rapid growth, moderate growth, slow growth) and it might also attempt to forecast financial market returns (for bonds, stocks and cash) in each of those scenarios.

a. 4-4-5 Calendar
b. 529 plan
c. Detection Risk
d. Scenario analysis

18. _____ or Investment _____ is a set of techniques that performance analysts use to explain why a portfolio's performance differed from the benchmark. This difference between the portfolio return and the benchmark return is known as the active return. The active return is the component of a portfolio's performance that arises from the fact that the portfolio is actively managed.
a. Performance attribution
b. Convertible arbitrage
c. Central Securities Depository
d. Delta neutral

19. A _____ is a financial contract whose value is derived from the value of something else (known as the underlying.) The underlying on which a _____ is based can be an asset, weather conditions bonds or other forms of credit.
a. 7-Eleven
b. Derivative
c. 529 plan
d. 4-4-5 Calendar

20. In statistics, _____ is a method of sampling from a population.

Chapter 44. Quantitative Management of Benchmarked Portfolios

When sub-populations vary considerably, it is advantageous to sample each subpopulation (stratum) independently. Stratification is the process of grouping members of the population into relatively homogeneous subgroups before sampling.

    a. Mean
    c. Kurtosis
    b. Correlation
    d. Stratified sampling

21. A _____ is a credit derivative contract between two counterparties. The buyer makes periodic payments (premium leg) to the seller, and in return receives a payoff (protection or default leg) if an underlying financial instrument defaults. _____ contracts have been incorrectly compared with insurance, because the buyer pays a premium and, in return, receives a sum of money if a specified event occurs.

    a. Stock market index future
    c. Credit default swap
    b. Commodity tick
    d. Futures contract

22. In finance, _____ occurs when a debtor has not met its legal obligations according to the debt contract, e.g. it has not made a scheduled payment, or has violated a loan covenant (condition) of the debt contract. _____ may occur if the debtor is either unwilling or unable to pay their debt. This can occur with all debt obligations including bonds, mortgages, loans, and promissory notes.

    a. Vendor finance
    c. Credit crunch
    b. Debt validation
    d. Default

23. A _____ is an option granting its owner the right but not the obligation to enter into an underlying swap. Although options can be traded on a variety of swaps, the term '_____' typically refers to options on interest rate swaps.

There are two types of _____ contracts:

- A payer _____ gives the owner of the _____ the right to enter into a swap where they pay the fixed leg and receive the floating leg.
- A receiver _____ gives the owner of the _____ the right to enter into a swap where they will receive the fixed leg, and pay the floating leg.

The buyer and seller of the _____ agree on:

- the premium (price) of the _____
- the strike rate (equal to the fixed rate of the underlying swap)
- length of the option period (which usually ends two business days prior to the start date of the underlying swap),
- the term of the underlying swap,
- notional amount,
- amortization, if any
- frequency of settlement of payments on the underlying swap

The participants in the _____ market are predominantly large corporations, banks, financial institutions and hedge funds. End users such as corporations and banks typically use _____s to manage interest rate risk arising from their core business or from their financing arrangements.

a. Bear call spread
c. Put option
b. Straddle
d. Swaption

24. In finance, a _____ (non-investment grade bond, speculative grade bond or junk bond) is a bond that is rated below investment grade at the time of purchase. These bonds have a higher risk of default or other adverse credit events, but typically pay higher yields than better quality bonds in order to make them attractive to investors.

a. Volatility
c. Sharpe ratio
b. Private equity
d. High yield bond

25. _____ is the risk of an asset or portfolio of assets moving more than 3 standard deviation from its current price in a probability density function, this is often under estimated using normal statistical methods for calculating the probability of changes in the price of financial assets.

The normal distribution which can be used for calculating the probability of sudden asset price changes is particularly prone to this type of error, however many if not most types of analysis are prone to this error to a lesser scale.

a. Commodity Pool Operator
c. Revenue recognition
b. Tail risk
d. Regulation Fair Disclosure

Chapter 45. Financing Positions in the Bond Market

1. _____ are a type of structured asset-backed security (ABS) whose value and payments are derived from a portfolio of fixed-income underlying assets. _____s are assigned different risk classes, or tranches, whereby 'senior' tranches are considered the safest securities. Interest and principal payments are made in order of seniority, so that junior tranches offer higher coupon payments (and interest rates) or lower prices to compensate for additional default risk.
   a. Senior debt
   b. Zero coupon bond
   c. Municipal bond
   d. Collateralized debt obligations

2. In finance, _____ (or gearing) is borrowing money to supplement existing funds for investment in such a way that the potential positive or negative outcome is magnified and/or enhanced. It generally refers to using borrowed funds, or debt, so as to attempt to increase the returns to equity. Deleveraging is the action of reducing borrowings.
   a. Pension fund
   b. Limited partnership
   c. Leverage
   d. Financial endowment

3. A _____ is an exchange of promises between two or more parties to do an act which is enforceable in a court of law. It is where an unqualified offer meets a qualified acceptance and the parties reach Consensus ad Idem. The parties must have the necessary capacity to _____ and the _____ must not be either trifling, indeterminate, impossible or illegal.
   a. 7-Eleven
   b. 4-4-5 Calendar
   c. 529 plan
   d. Contract

4. _____ is that which is owed; usually referencing assets owed, but the term can cover other obligations. In the case of assets, _____ is a means of using future purchasing power in the present before a summation has been earned. Some companies and corporations use _____ as a part of their overall corporate finance strategy.
   a. Partial Payment
   b. Cross-collateralization
   c. Credit cycle
   d. Debt

5. A _____ is a financial contract whose value is derived from the value of something else (known as the underlying.) The underlying on which a _____ is based can be an asset, weather conditions bonds or other forms of credit.
   a. Derivative
   b. 4-4-5 Calendar
   c. 529 plan
   d. 7-Eleven

6. The official bank rate has existing in various forms since 1694 and has ranged from 0.5% to 17%. The name of this key interest rate has changed over the years. The current name 'Official Bank Rate' was introduced in 2006 and replaced the previous title '_____' (repo is short for repurchase agreement) in 1997.
   a. Cash accumulation equation
   b. Repo rate
   c. London Interbank Bid Rate
   d. London Interbank Offered Rate

7. A _____ allows a borrower to use a financial security as collateral for a cash loan at a fixed rate of interest. In a repo, the borrower agrees to immediately sell a security to a lender and also agrees to buy the same security from the lender at a fixed price at some later date. A repo is equivalent to a cash transaction combined with a forward contract.
   a. Total return swap
   b. Contango
   c. Volatility arbitrage
   d. Repurchase agreement

8. _____ is the provision of resources (such as granting a loan) by one party to another party where that second party does not reimburse the first party immediately, thereby generating a debt, and instead arranges either to repay or return those resources (or material(s) of equal value) at a later date. The first party is called a creditor, also known as a lender, while the second party is called a debtor, also known as a borrower.

Movements of financial capital are normally dependent on either _____ or equity transfers.

a. Warrant
c. Comparable
b. Credit
d. Clearing house

9. _____ is the risk of loss due to a debtor's non-payment of a loan or other line of credit (either the principal or interest (coupon) or both)

Most lenders employ their own models (credit scorecards) to rank potential and existing customers according to risk, and then apply appropriate strategies. With products such as unsecured personal loans or mortgages, lenders charge a higher price for higher risk customers and vice versa. With revolving products such as credit cards and overdrafts, risk is controlled through careful setting of credit limits.

a. Market risk
c. Transaction risk
b. Credit risk
d. Liquidity risk

10. In finance, a _____ is collateral that the holder of a position in securities, options, or futures contracts has to deposit to cover the credit risk of his counterparty (most often his broker.) This risk can arise if the holder has done any of the following:

- borrowed cash from the counterparty to buy securities or options,
- sold securities or options short, or
- entered into a futures contract.

The collateral can be in the form of cash or securities, and it is deposited in a _____ account. On U.S. futures exchanges, '_____' was formally called performance bond.

_____ buying is buying securities with cash borrowed from a broker, using other securities as collateral.

a. Margin
c. Credit
b. Procter ' Gamble
d. Share

11. In the United States, _____ are overnight borrowings by banks to maintain their bank reserves at the Federal Reserve. Banks keep reserves at Federal Reserve Banks to meet their reserve requirements and to clear financial transactions. Transactions in the _____ market enable depository institutions with reserve balances in excess of reserve requirements to lend reserves to institutions with reserve deficiencies.

a. Regulation T
c. 4-4-5 Calendar
b. Federal funds rate
d. Federal funds

12. In the United States, the _____ is the interest rate at which private depository institutions (mostly banks) lend balances (federal funds) at the Federal Reserve to other depository institutions, usually overnight. Changing the target rate is one form of open market operations that the Chairman of the Federal Reserve uses to regulate the supply of money in the U.S. economy.

U.S. banks and thrift institutions are obligated by law to maintain certain levels of reserves, either as reserves with the Fed or as vault cash.

 a. 4-4-5 Calendar   b. Regulation T
 c. Federal funds rate   d. Taylor rule

13. A _____ is similar to a repurchase agreement. The investor sells a mortgage-backed security for settlement on one date and buys it back for settlement at a later date. The investor gives up the principal and interest payments during the roll period but can invest the proceeds and usually is able to buy back the mortgage for a lower price than the sale price.
 a. Freight derivative   b. Dollar roll
 c. Commodity tick   d. Delivery month

14. In economics, business, and accounting, a _____ is the value of money that has been used up to produce something, and hence is not available for use anymore. In business, the _____ may be one of acquisition, in which case the amount of money expended to acquire it is counted as _____. In this case, money is the input that is gone in order to acquire the thing.
 a. Fixed costs   b. Cost
 c. Sliding scale fees   d. Marginal cost

15. _____ or financing is to provide capital (funds), which means money for a project, a person, a business or any other private or public institutions.

Those funds can be allocated for either short term or long term purposes. The health fund is a new way of _____ private healthcare centers.

 a. Proxy fight   b. Product life cycle
 c. Funding   d. Synthetic CDO

16. The _____ is the financial market where previously issued securities and financial instruments such as stock, bonds, options, and futures are bought and sold. The term '_____' is also used refer to the market for any used goods or assets, or an alternative use for an existing product or asset where the customer base is the second market

With primary issuances of securities or financial instruments, or the primary market, investors purchase these securities directly from issuers such as corporations issuing shares in an IPO or private placement, or directly from the federal government in the case of treasuries.

 a. Secondary market   b. Delta neutral
 c. Financial market   d. Performance attribution

17. _____ is a legal term where specific property rights ('use and title') in equity belong to a person even though legal title of the property belongs to another person.
 a. Covenant   b. National Securities Markets Improvement Act of 1996
 c. Personal property   d. Beneficial owner

18. _____ is buying securities with cash borrowed from a broker, using other securities as collateral. This has the effect of magnifying any profit or loss made on the securities. The securities serve as collateral for the loan.
    a. SPI 200 futures contract
    b. Risk-neutral measure
    c. Triple witching hour
    d. Margin buying

19. In financial accounting, the term _____ is most commonly used to describe any part of shareholders' equity, except for basic share capital. Sometimes, the term is used instead of the term provision; such a use, however, is inconsistent with the terminology suggested by International Accounting Standards Board. For more information about provisions, see provision (accounting.)
    a. Treasury stock
    b. Reserve
    c. FIFO and LIFO accounting
    d. Closing entries

20. A _____ is a fungible, negotiable instrument representing financial value. They are broadly categorized into debt securities (such as banknotes, bonds and debentures), and equity securities; e.g., common stocks. The company or other entity issuing the _____ is called the issuer.
    a. Book entry
    b. Tracking stock
    c. Securities lending
    d. Security

21. In finance, _____ or stock lending refers to the lending of securities by one party to another. The terms of the loan will be governed by a '_____ Agreement', which, under U.S. law, requires that the borrower provides the lender with collateral, in the form of cash, government securities, or a Letter of Credit of value equal to or greater than the loaned securities. As payment for the loan, the parties negotiate a fee, quoted as an annualized percentage of the value of the loaned securities.
    a. Tracking stock
    b. Securities lending
    c. Marketable
    d. Book entry

22. In finance, a _____ is the party in a loan agreement which receives money or other instrument from a lender and promises to repay the lender in a specified time.
    a. Cash credit
    b. Debt management plan
    c. Line of credit
    d. Borrower

23. The _____ requirement is the amount required to be collateralized in order to open a position. Thereafter, the amount required to be kept in collateral until the position is closed is the maintenance requirement. The maintenance requirement is the minimum amount to be collateralized in order to keep an open position.
    a. Arbitrage
    b. Initial margin
    c. Issuer
    d. Efficient-market hypothesis

24. The _____ is the amount required to be collateralized in order to open a position. Thereafter, the amount required to be kept in collateral until the position is closed is the maintenance requirement. The maintenance requirement is the minimum amount to be collateralized in order to keep an open position.
    a. A Random Walk Down Wall Street
    b. AAB
    c. Initial margin requirement
    d. ABN Amro

25. The variation margin or _____ is not collateral, but a daily offsetting of profits and losses. Futures are marked-to-market every day, so the current price is compared to the previous day's price. The profit or loss on the day of a position is then paid to or debited from the holder by the futures exchange.

Chapter 45. Financing Positions in the Bond Market

a. SPI 200 futures contract
c. Delivery month

b. Total return swap
d. Maintenance margin

26. The _____, sometimes called the maintenance margin requirement, is the ratio set for:

- (Stock Equity - Leveraged Dollars) to Stock Equity

- Stock Equity being the stock price * no. of stocks bought and Leveraged Dollars being the amount borrowed in the margin account.

- E.g. An investor bought 1000 shares of ABC company each priced at $50. If the initial margin requirement were 60%:

- Stock Equity: $50 * 1000 = $50,000

- Leveraged Dollars or amount borrowed: ($50 * 1000)* (1-60%) = $20,000

So the maintenance margin requirement uses the above variables to form a ratio that investors have to abide by in order to keep the account active.

The point is, let's say the maintenance margin requirement is reduced from 60% to 25% - At what price would the investor be getting a margin call? Let P be the price, so 1000P in our case is the Stock Equity.

- (Stock Equity - Leveraged Dollars) divided by Stock Equity = 25%

- (1000P - $20,000)/1000P = 0.25

- (1000P - $20,000) = 250P

- P = $26.67

So if the stock price drops from $50 to $26.67, investors will be called to add additional funds to the account to make up for the loss in stock equity.

Margin requirements are reduced for positions that offset each other.

a. Minimum margin requirement
c. 7-Eleven

b. 4-4-5 Calendar
d. 529 plan

Chapter 46. Global Credit Bond Portfolio Management

1. An _____ is a security whose value and income payments are derived from and collateralized (or 'backed') by a specified pool of underlying assets. The pool of assets is typically a group of small and illiquid assets that are unable to be sold individually. Pooling the assets allows them to be sold to general investors, a process called securitization, and allows the risk of investing in the underlying assets to be diversified because each security will represent a fraction of the total value of the diverse pool of underlying assets.
   a. ABN Amro
   b. Asset-backed security
   c. A Random Walk Down Wall Street
   d. AAB

2. _____ are a type of bond commonly issued in American security markets. They are a type of mortgage-backed security backed by mortgages on commercial rather than residential real estate. CMBS issues are usually structured as multiple tranches, similar to CMOs, rather than typical residential 'passthroughs.'

   Many American CMBSs carry less prepayment risk than other MBS types, thanks to the structure of commercial mortgages.

   a. Stock market index
   b. Contract for difference
   c. Stop order
   d. Commercial mortgage-backed securities

3. _____ is the provision of resources (such as granting a loan) by one party to another party where that second party does not reimburse the first party immediately, thereby generating a debt, and instead arranges either to repay or return those resources (or material(s) of equal value) at a later date. The first party is called a creditor, also known as a lender, while the second party is called a debtor, also known as a borrower.

   Movements of financial capital are normally dependent on either _____ or equity transfers.

   a. Credit
   b. Comparable
   c. Warrant
   d. Clearing house

4. A _____ is an asset-backed security whose cash flows are backed by the principal and interest payments of a set of mortgage loans. Payments are typically made monthly over the lifetime of the underlying loans.
   a. Home equity line of credit
   b. Conforming loan
   c. Shared appreciation mortgage
   d. Mortgage-backed security

5. In business and accounting, _____s are everything of value that is owned by a person or company. The balance sheet of a firm records the monetary value of the _____s owned by the firm. The two major _____ classes are tangible _____s and intangible _____s.
   a. Income
   b. EBITDA
   c. Asset
   d. Accounts payable

6. A _____ is a fungible, negotiable instrument representing financial value. They are broadly categorized into debt securities (such as banknotes, bonds and debentures), and equity securities; e.g., common stocks. The company or other entity issuing the _____ is called the issuer.
   a. Security
   b. Book entry
   c. Securities lending
   d. Tracking stock

Chapter 46. Global Credit Bond Portfolio Management

7. _____ is a risk-adjusted measure of the so-called active return on an investment. It is the return in excess of the compensation for the risk borne, and thus commonly used to assess active managers' performances. Often, the return of a benchmark is subtracted in order to consider relative performance, which yields Jensen's _____.

    a. Annuity   b. Option
    c. Alpha   d. Amortization

8. _____ is the method by which one calculates the creditworthiness of a business or organization. The audited financial statements of a large company might be analyzed when it issues or has issued bonds. Or, a bank may analyze the financial statements of a small business before making or renewing a commercial loan.

    a. Credit crunch   b. Capital note
    c. Credit report monitoring   d. Credit analysis

9. The _____ on a portfolio of investments takes into account not only the capital appreciation on the portfolio, but also the income received on the portfolio. The income typically consists of interest, dividends, and securities lending fees. This contrasts with the price return, which takes into account only the capital gain on an investment.

    a. Global tactical asset allocation   b. Profitability index
    c. Capitalization rate   d. Total return

10. The _____ is that part of the capital markets that deals with the issuance of new securities. Companies, governments or public sector institutions can obtain funding through the sale of a new stock or bond issue. This is typically done through a syndicate of securities dealers.

    a. Peer group analysis   b. Sector rotation
    c. Primary market   d. Volatility clustering

11. A _____ is a documented investigation of a Market that is used to inform a firm's planning activities particularly around decision of: inventory, purchase, work force expansion/contraction, facility expansion, purchases of capital equipment, promotional activities, and many other aspects of a company.

Not all managers are asked to conduct a _____, but all managers must make decisions using _____ data and understand how the data was derived. So all managers need a reasonable understanding of the tools most used for making sales forecasts and analyzing markets.

    a. 529 plan   b. 4-4-5 Calendar
    c. 7-Eleven   d. Market analysis

12. _____ is a life of security. It may also refer to the final payment date of a loan or other financial instrument, at which point all remaining interest and principal is due to be paid.

1, 3, 6 months _____ band can be calculated by using 30-day per month periods.

    a. Maturity   b. False billing
    c. Primary market   d. Replacement cost

13. _____ is a measure of the ability of a debtor to pay their debts as and when they fall due. It is usually expressed as a ratio or a percentage of current liabilities.

For a corporation with a published balance sheet there are various ratios used to calculate a measure of liquidity.

    a. Operating profit margin
    b. Accounting liquidity
    c. Invested capital
    d. Operating leverage

14. In finance, the term _____ describes the amount in cash that returns to the owners of a security. Normally it does not include the price variations, at the difference of the total return. _____ applies to various stated rates of return on stocks (common and preferred, and convertible), fixed income instruments (bonds, notes, bills, strips, zero coupon), and some other investment type insurance products (e.g. annuities.)

    a. Macaulay duration
    b. 4-4-5 Calendar
    c. Yield to maturity
    d. Yield

15. In finance, the _____ is the difference between the quoted rates of return on two different investments, usually of different credit quality.

It is a compound of yield and spread.

The '_____ of X over Y' is simply the percentage return on investment (ROI) from financial instrument X minus the percentage return on investment from financial instrument Y (per annum.)

    a. Portfolio insurance
    b. Duty of loyalty
    c. Debtor-in-possession financing
    d. Yield spread

16. _____ is the balance of the amounts of cash being received and paid by a business during a defined period of time, sometimes tied to a specific project. Measurement of _____ can be used

- to evaluate the state or performance of a business or project.
- to determine problems with liquidity. Being profitable does not necessarily mean being liquid. A company can fail because of a shortage of cash, even while profitable.
- to generate project rate of returns. The time of _____s into and out of projects are used as inputs to financial models such as internal rate of return, and net present value.
- to examine income or growth of a business when it is believed that accrual accounting concepts do not represent economic realities. Alternately, _____ can be used to 'validate' the net income generated by accrual accounting.

_____ as a generic term may be used differently depending on context, and certain _____ definitions may be adapted by analysts and users for their own uses. Common terms include operating _____ and free _____.

Chapter 46. Global Credit Bond Portfolio Management

_____s can be classified into:

1. Operational _____s: Cash received or expended as a result of the company's core business activities.
2. Investment _____s: Cash received or expended through capital expenditure, investments or acquisitions.
3. Financing _____s: Cash received or expended as a result of financial activities, such as interests and dividends.

All three together - the net _____ - are necessary to reconcile the beginning cash balance to the ending cash balance. Loan draw downs or equity injections, that is just shifting of capital but no expenditure as such, are not considered in the net _____.

a. Cash flow
b. Shareholder value
c. Real option
d. Corporate finance

17. _____ is a term normally applied to stock market trading patterns. In this context, a sector is understood to mean a group of stocks representing companies in similar lines of business.

For example, an investor or trader may describe the current market movements as favoring basic material stocks over semiconductor stocks by calling the environment a _____ from semiconductors to basic materials.

a. Conglomerate merger
b. Commercial finance
c. Sector rotation
d. Refunding

18. A _____ is an option granting its owner the right but not the obligation to enter into an underlying swap. Although options can be traded on a variety of swaps, the term '_____' typically refers to options on interest rate swaps.

There are two types of _____ contracts:

- A payer _____ gives the owner of the _____ the right to enter into a swap where they pay the fixed leg and receive the floating leg.
- A receiver _____ gives the owner of the _____ the right to enter into a swap where they will receive the fixed leg, and pay the floating leg.

The buyer and seller of the _____ agree on:

- the premium (price) of the _____
- the strike rate (equal to the fixed rate of the underlying swap)
- length of the option period (which usually ends two business days prior to the start date of the underlying swap),
- the term of the underlying swap,
- notional amount,
- amortization, if any
- frequency of settlement of payments on the underlying swap

The participants in the _____ market are predominantly large corporations, banks, financial institutions and hedge funds. End users such as corporations and banks typically use _____s to manage interest rate risk arising from their core business or from their financing arrangements.

a. Put option
b. Bear call spread
c. Swaption
d. Straddle

19. In finance, a _____ is a debt security, in which the authorized issuer owes the holders a debt and, depending on the terms of the _____, is obliged to pay interest (the coupon) and/or to repay the principal at a later date, termed maturity.

Thus a _____ is a loan: the issuer is the borrower, the _____ holder is the lender, and the coupon is the interest. _____s provide the borrower with external funds to finance long-term investments, or, in the case of government _____s, to finance current expenditure.

a. Puttable bond
b. Catastrophe bonds
c. Convertible bond
d. Bond

20. In finance, a _____ is a derivative in which two counterparties agree to exchange one stream of cash flows against another stream. These streams are called the legs of the _____.

The cash flows are calculated over a notional principal amount, which is usually not exchanged between counterparties.

a. Local volatility
b. Volatility arbitrage
c. Volatility swap
d. Swap

21. _____ means regulating, adapting or settling in a variety of contexts:

In commercial law, _____ means the settlement of a loss incurred on insured goods. The calculation of the amounts of compensation to be paid by or to the several interests is a complicated matter. It involves much detail and arithmetic, and requires a full and accurate knowledge of the principles of the subject.

Chapter 46. Global Credit Bond Portfolio Management

a. Adjustment
c. Asset recovery
b. Equity method
d. Intelligent investor

22. _____ is the flat spread over the treasury yield curve required to discount a security payment to match its market price. This concept can be applied to mortgage-backed security (MBS), Options, Bonds and any other interest-rate Derivative.

In contrast to the simple 'yield curve spread' measurement of bond premium over a pre-determined cash-flow model, the _____ describes the market premium over a model including two types of volatility:

- Variable interest rates
- Variable prepayment rates.

Designing such models in the first place is complicated because prepayment variations are a behavioural function of the stochastic interest rate. (They tend to go up as interest rates come down.)

a. ABN Amro
c. AAB
b. A Random Walk Down Wall Street
d. Option adjusted spread

23. A _____ is a bond bought at a price lower than its face value, with the face value repaid at the time of maturity. It does not make periodic interest payments, or have so-called 'coupons,' hence the term _____. Investors earn return from the compounded interest all paid at maturity plus the difference between the discounted price of the bond and its par value.

a. Zero-coupon bond
c. Clean price
b. Corporate bond
d. Bond fund

Chapter 47. Bond Immunization: An Asset/Liability Optimization Strategy

1. In finance, a _____ is a debt security, in which the authorized issuer owes the holders a debt and, depending on the terms of the _____, is obliged to pay interest (the coupon) and/or to repay the principal at a later date, termed maturity.

Thus a _____ is a loan: the issuer is the borrower, the _____ holder is the lender, and the coupon is the interest. _____s provide the borrower with external funds to finance long-term investments, or, in the case of government _____s, to finance current expenditure.

a. Puttable bond
b. Convertible bond
c. Bond
d. Catastrophe bonds

2. _____ are government bonds issued by the United States Department of the Treasury through the Bureau of the Public Debt. They are the debt financing instruments of the U.S. Federal government, and they are often referred to simply as Treasuries or Treasurys. There are four types of marketable _____: Treasury bills, Treasury notes, Treasury bonds, and Treasury Inflation Protected Securities (TIPS.)

a. Treasury securities
b. 4-4-5 Calendar
c. Treasury Inflation-Protected Securities
d. Treasury Inflation Protected Securities

3. A _____ is a bond bought at a price lower than its face value, with the face value repaid at the time of maturity. It does not make periodic interest payments, or have so-called 'coupons,' hence the term _____. Investors earn return from the compounded interest all paid at maturity plus the difference between the discounted price of the bond and its par value.

a. Zero-coupon bond
b. Corporate bond
c. Bond fund
d. Clean price

4. The institution most often referenced by the word '_____' is a public or publicly traded _____, the shares of which are traded on a public stock exchange (e.g., the New York Stock Exchange or Nasdaq in the United States) where shares of stock of _____s are bought and sold by and to the general public. Most of the largest businesses in the world are publicly traded _____s. However, the majority of _____s are said to be closely held, privately held or close _____s, meaning that no ready market exists for the trading of shares.

a. Protect
b. Federal Home Loan Mortgage Corporation
c. Corporation
d. Depository Trust Company

5. _____ is the action of bringing a portfolio of investments that has deviated away from one's target asset allocation back into line. Under-weighted securities can be purchased with newly saved money; alternatively, over-weighted securities can be sold to purchase under-weighted securities.

The investments in a portfolio will perform according to the market.

a. Market timing
b. Rebalancing
c. Security market line
d. Divestment

6. In probability and statistics, the _____ of a collection of numbers is a measure of the dispersion of the numbers from their expected (mean) value. It can apply to a probability distribution, a random variable, a population or a data set. The _____ is usually denoted with the letter σ (lowercase sigma).

a. Sample size
c. Standard deviation
b. Mean
d. Kurtosis

7. In finance, the _____ of a financial asset measures the sensitivity of the asset's price to interest rate movements, expressed as a number of years. The reason for expressing this sensitivity in years is that the time that will elapse until a cash flow is received allows more interest to accumulate. Therefore the price of an asset with long term cashflows has more interest rate sensitivity than an asset with cashflows in the near future.

a. 4-4-5 Calendar
c. Macaulay duration
b. Yield to maturity
d. Duration

8. A _____ is a pool of assets forming an independent legal entity that are bought with the contributions to a pension plan for the exclusive purpose of financing pension plan benefits.

_____s are important shareholders of listed and private companies. They are especially important to the stock market where large institutional investors like the Ontario Teachers' Pension Plan dominate.

a. Pension fund
c. Leveraged buyout
b. Limited liability company
d. Leverage

9. In finance, a _____ is a standardized contract, to buy or sell a specified commodity of standardized quality at a certain date in the future, at a market determined price (the futures price.)

The price is determined by the instantaneous equilibrium between the forces of supply and demand among competing buy and sell orders on the exchange at the time of the purchase or sale of the contract.

In many cases, the items may be such non-traditional 'commodities' as foreign currencies, commercial or government paper [e.g., bonds], or 'baskets' of corporate equity ['stock indices'] or other financial instruments.

a. Repurchase agreement
c. Financial future
b. Futures contract
d. Heston model

Chapter 48. Dedicated Bond Portfolios

1. In finance, a _____ is a debt security, in which the authorized issuer owes the holders a debt and, depending on the terms of the _____, is obliged to pay interest (the coupon) and/or to repay the principal at a later date, termed maturity.

Thus a _____ is a loan: the issuer is the borrower, the _____ holder is the lender, and the coupon is the interest. _____s provide the borrower with external funds to finance long-term investments, or, in the case of government _____s, to finance current expenditure.

   a. Catastrophe bonds
   c. Puttable bond
   b. Convertible bond
   d. Bond

2. A _____ is a pool of assets forming an independent legal entity that are bought with the contributions to a pension plan for the exclusive purpose of financing pension plan benefits.

_____s are important shareholders of listed and private companies. They are especially important to the stock market where large institutional investors like the Ontario Teachers' Pension Plan dominate.

   a. Limited liability company
   c. Pension fund
   b. Leverage
   d. Leveraged buyout

3. In the most general sense, a _____ is anything that is a hindrance, or puts individuals at a disadvantage.

Before we discuss the financial terms, we should note that a _____ can also have a much more important slang meaning.

This is best described in an example.

   a. McFadden Act
   c. Covenant
   b. Liability
   d. Limited liability

4. _____ or financing is to provide capital (funds), which means money for a project, a person, a business or any other private or public institutions.

Those funds can be allocated for either short term or long term purposes. The health fund is a new way of _____ private healthcare centers.

   a. Synthetic CDO
   c. Funding
   b. Product life cycle
   d. Proxy fight

Chapter 49. International Bond Portfolio Management

1. In finance, a _____ is a debt security, in which the authorized issuer owes the holders a debt and, depending on the terms of the _____, is obliged to pay interest (the coupon) and/or to repay the principal at a later date, termed maturity.

   Thus a _____ is a loan: the issuer is the borrower, the _____ holder is the lender, and the coupon is the interest. _____s provide the borrower with external funds to finance long-term investments, or, in the case of government _____s, to finance current expenditure.

   a. Convertible bond
   b. Puttable bond
   c. Catastrophe bonds
   d. Bond

2. _____s are deposits denominated in United States dollars at banks outside the United States, and thus are not under the jurisdiction of the Federal Reserve. Consequently, such deposits are subject to much less regulation than similar deposits within the United States, allowing for higher margins. There is nothing 'European' about _____ deposits; a US dollar-denominated deposit in Tokyo or Caracas would likewise be deemed _____ deposits.

   a. Eurodollar
   b. ABN Amro
   c. A Random Walk Down Wall Street
   d. AAB

3. A _____ is a pool of assets forming an independent legal entity that are bought with the contributions to a pension plan for the exclusive purpose of financing pension plan benefits.

   _____s are important shareholders of listed and private companies. They are especially important to the stock market where large institutional investors like the Ontario Teachers' Pension Plan dominate.

   a. Pension fund
   b. Limited liability company
   c. Leverage
   d. Leveraged buyout

4. In finance, _____, also known as return on investment is the ratio of money gained or lost on an investment relative to the amount of money invested. The amount of money gained or lost may be referred to as interest, profit/loss, gain/loss, or net income/loss. The money invested may be referred to as the asset, capital, principal, or the cost basis of the investment.

   a. Stock or scrip dividends
   b. Doctrine of the Proper Law
   c. Composiition of Creditors
   d. Rate of return

5. A _____ is a bond issued by a national government denominated in the country's own currency. Bonds issued by national governments in foreign currencies are normally referred to as sovereign bonds. The first ever _____ was issued by the British government in 1693 to raise money to fund a war against France.

   a. Municipal bond
   b. Collateralized debt obligations
   c. Zero-coupon bond
   d. Government Bond

6. The _____ is a measure of the excess return (or Risk Premium) per unit of risk in an investment asset or a trading strategy it is defined as:

$$S = \frac{R - R_f}{\sigma} = \frac{E[R - R_f]}{\sqrt{\mathrm{var}[R - R_f]}},$$

where R is the asset return, R_f is the return on a benchmark asset, such as the risk free rate of return, $E[R - R_f]$ is the expected value of the excess of the asset return over the benchmark return, and σ is the standard deviation of the asset excess return.

Note, if R_f is a constant risk free return throughout the period,

$$\sqrt{\operatorname{var}[R - R_f]} = \sqrt{\operatorname{var}[R]}.$$

The _____ is used to characterize how well the return of an asset compensates the investor for the risk taken. When comparing two assets each with the expected return E[R] against the same benchmark with return R_f, the asset with the higher _____ gives more return for the same risk.

a. Sharpe ratio
c. Receivables turnover ratio
b. Current ratio
d. P/E ratio

7. _____ is the provision of resources (such as granting a loan) by one party to another party where that second party does not reimburse the first party immediately, thereby generating a debt, and instead arranges either to repay or return those resources (or material(s) of equal value) at a later date. The first party is called a creditor, also known as a lender, while the second party is called a debtor, also known as a borrower.

Movements of financial capital are normally dependent on either _____ or equity transfers.

a. Clearing house
c. Comparable
b. Credit
d. Warrant

8. _____ is the risk of loss due to a debtor's non-payment of a loan or other line of credit (either the principal or interest (coupon) or both)

Most lenders employ their own models (credit scorecards) to rank potential and existing customers according to risk, and then apply appropriate strategies. With products such as unsecured personal loans or mortgages, lenders charge a higher price for higher risk customers and vice versa. With revolving products such as credit cards and overdrafts, risk is controlled through careful setting of credit limits.

a. Market risk
c. Transaction risk
b. Liquidity risk
d. Credit risk

9. The _____ is a financial market where participants buy and sell debt securities, usually in the form of bonds. As of 2006, the size of the international _____ is an estimated $45 trillion, of which the size of the outstanding U.S. _____ debt was $25.2 trillion.

Nearly all of the $923 billion average daily trading volume in the U.S. _____ takes place between broker-dealers and large institutions in a decentralized, over-the-counter market.

Chapter 49. International Bond Portfolio Management

a. Bond market
b. Fixed income
c. 4-4-5 Calendar
d. 529 plan

10. The term _____ is used to describe a nation's social, or business activity in the process of rapid industrialization. _____ are generally less-wealthy than the developed world, and are wealthier (or the wealthiest of) the developing world. According to The Economist many people find the term dated, but a new term has yet to gain much traction.

   a. A Random Walk Down Wall Street
   b. AAB
   c. ABN Amro
   d. Emerging markets

11. A _____ is a person who makes investment decisions using money other people have placed under his or her control. In other words, it is a financial career involved in investment management. They work with a team of analysts and researchers, and are ultimately responsible for establishing an investment strategy, selecting appropriate investments and allocating each investment properly for a fund- or asset-management vehicle.

   a. Day trader
   b. Financial analyst
   c. Purchasing manager
   d. Portfolio manager

12. _____ is a security analysis discipline for forecasting the future direction of prices through the study of past market data, primarily price and volume. In its purest form, _____ considers only the actual price and volume behavior of the market or instrument. Technical analysts may employ models and trading rules based on price and volume transformations, such as the relative strength index, moving averages, regressions, inter-market and intra-market price correlations, cycles or, classically, through recognition of chart patterns.

   a. Point and figure
   b. Dow theory
   c. Support and resistance
   d. Technical analysis

13. _____ is a risk-adjusted measure of the so-called active return on an investment. It is the return in excess of the compensation for the risk borne, and thus commonly used to assess active managers' performances. Often, the return of a benchmark is subtracted in order to consider relative performance, which yields Jensen's _____.

   a. Annuity
   b. Option
   c. Amortization
   d. Alpha

14. In finance, the _____ of a financial asset measures the sensitivity of the asset's price to interest rate movements, expressed as a number of years. The reason for expressing this sensitivity in years is that the time that will elapse until a cash flow is received allows more interest to accumulate. Therefore the price of an asset with long term cashflows has more interest rate sensitivity than an asset with cashflows in the near future.

   a. Yield to maturity
   b. Macaulay duration
   c. 4-4-5 Calendar
   d. Duration

15. _____ is the investment strategy where an investor buys a financial instrument denominated in a foreign currency, and hedges his foreign exchange risk by selling a forward contract in the amount of the proceeds of the investment back into his base currency. The proceeds of the investment are only known exactly if the financial instrument is risk-free and only pays interest once, on the date of the forward sale of foreign currency. Otherwise, some foreign exchange risk remains.

   a. Floating exchange rate
   b. Triangular arbitrage
   c. Currency future
   d. Covered interest arbitrage

Chapter 49. International Bond Portfolio Management

16. _____ is a fee paid on borrowed assets. It is the price paid for the use of borrowed money, or, money earned by deposited funds. Assets that are sometimes lent with _____ include money, shares, consumer goods through hire purchase, major assets such as aircraft, and even entire factories in finance lease arrangements.

   a. AAB
   b. Insolvency
   c. Interest
   d. A Random Walk Down Wall Street

17. An _____ is the price a borrower pays for the use of money they do not own, and the return a lender receives for deferring the use of funds, by lending it to the borrower. _____ s are normally expressed as a percentage rate over the period of one year.

   _____ s targets are also a vital tool of monetary policy and are used to control variables like investment, inflation, and unemployment.

   a. ABN Amro
   b. A Random Walk Down Wall Street
   c. AAB
   d. Interest rate

18. In economics and finance, _____ is the practice of taking advantage of a price differential between two or more markets: striking a combination of matching deals that capitalize upon the imbalance, the profit being the difference between the market prices. When used by academics, an _____ is a transaction that involves no negative cash flow at any probabilistic or temporal state and a positive cash flow in at least one state; in simple terms, a risk-free profit.

   a. Initial margin
   b. Issuer
   c. Efficient-market hypothesis
   d. Arbitrage

19. An _____ is a contract written by a seller that conveys to the buyer the right -- but not the obligation -- to buy (in the case of a call _____) or to sell (in the case of a put _____) a particular asset, such as a piece of property such as, among others, a futures contract. In return for granting the _____, the seller collects a payment (the premium) from the buyer.

   For example, buying a call _____ provides the right to buy a specified quantity of a security at a set strike price at some time on or before expiration, while buying a put _____ provides the right to sell.

   a. Option
   b. Annuity
   c. Amortization
   d. AT'T Mobility LLC

20. The _____ is the weighted-average most likely outcome in gambling, probability theory, economics or finance.

   In gambling and probability theory, there is usually a discrete set of possible outcomes. In this case, _____ is a measure of the relative balance of win or loss weighted by their chances of occurring.

   a. ABN Amro
   b. A Random Walk Down Wall Street
   c. AAB
   d. Expected return

21. The _____ for an investment is a calculated annual yield for an investment, which may not pay out yearly. This allows investments which payout with different frequencies to be compared.

a. 529 plan
b. 7-Eleven
c. 4-4-5 Calendar
d. Bond equivalent yield

22. In finance, the term _____ describes the amount in cash that returns to the owners of a security. Normally it does not include the price variations, at the difference of the total return. _____ applies to various stated rates of return on stocks (common and preferred, and convertible), fixed income instruments (bonds, notes, bills, strips, zero coupon), and some other investment type insurance products (e.g. annuities.)

a. Macaulay duration
b. 4-4-5 Calendar
c. Yield to maturity
d. Yield

23. In economics and business, specifically cost accounting, the _____ is the point at which cost or expenses and revenue are equal: there is no net loss or gain, and one has 'broken even'. A profit or a loss has not been made, although opportunity costs have been paid, and capital has received the risk-adjusted, expected return.

For example, if the business sells less than 200 tables each month, it will make a loss, if it sells more, it will be a profit.

a. Fixed asset turnover
b. Market microstructure
c. Defined contribution plan
d. Break-even point

Chapter 50. Transition Management

1. The _____ duty is a legal relationship of confidence or trust between two or more parties, most commonly a _____ or trustee and a principal or beneficiary. One party, for example a corporate trust company or the trust department of a bank, holds a _____ relation or acts in a _____ capacity to another, such as one whose funds are entrusted to it for investment. In a _____ relation one person justifiably reposes confidence, good faith, reliance and trust in another whose aid, advice or protection is sought in some matter.
   a. Financial Institutions Reform Recovery and Enforcement Act
   b. Legal tender
   c. General obligation
   d. Fiduciary

2. _____ are dollar-denominated bonds, issued mostly by Latin American countries in the 1980s, named after U.S. Treasury Secretary Nicholas Brady.

_____ were created in March 1989 in order to convert bonds issued by mostly Latin American countries into a variety or 'menu' of new bonds after many of those countries defaulted on their debt in the 1980's. At that time, the market for sovereign debt was small and illiquid, and the standardization of emerging-market debt facilitated risk-spreading and trading.

   a. Coupon rate
   b. Municipal bond
   c. Nominal yield
   d. Brady bonds

3. A _____ is an international bond that is denominated in a currency not native to the country where it is issued. It can be categorised according to the currency in which it is issued. London is one of the centers of the _____ market, but _____s may be traded throughout the world - for example in Singapore or Tokyo.
   a. Interest rate option
   b. Education production function
   c. Economic entity
   d. Eurobond

4. _____s are deposits denominated in United States dollars at banks outside the United States, and thus are not under the jurisdiction of the Federal Reserve. Consequently, such deposits are subject to much less regulation than similar deposits within the United States, allowing for higher margins. There is nothing 'European' about _____ deposits; a US dollar-denominated deposit in Tokyo or Caracas would likewise be deemed _____ deposits.
   a. A Random Walk Down Wall Street
   b. Eurodollar
   c. ABN Amro
   d. AAB

5. A _____ is a legal pledge in United States municipal finance, in which an entity pledges its full faith and credit to repay its debt, typically a _____ bond.
   a. Letter of credit
   b. General obligation
   c. Covenant
   d. Financial Institutions Reform Recovery and Enforcement Act

6. In finance, a _____ (non-investment grade bond, speculative grade bond or junk bond) is a bond that is rated below investment grade at the time of purchase. These bonds have a higher risk of default or other adverse credit events, but typically pay higher yields than better quality bonds in order to make them attractive to investors.
   a. Private equity
   b. Sharpe ratio
   c. Volatility
   d. High yield bond

Chapter 50. Transition Management

7. In finance, a _____ is a debt security, in which the authorized issuer owes the holders a debt and, depending on the terms of the _____, is obliged to pay interest (the coupon) and/or to repay the principal at a later date, termed maturity.

Thus a _____ is a loan: the issuer is the borrower, the _____ holder is the lender, and the coupon is the interest. _____s provide the borrower with external funds to finance long-term investments, or, in the case of government _____s, to finance current expenditure.

a. Puttable bond
b. Bond
c. Convertible bond
d. Catastrophe bonds

8. In financial accounting, _____s are precautions for which the amount or probability of occurrence are not known. Typical examples are _____s for warranty costs and _____ for taxes the term reserve is used instead of term _____; such a use, however, is inconsistent with the terminology suggested by International Accounting Standards Board.

a. Money measurement concept
b. Provision
c. Petty cash
d. Momentum Accounting and Triple-Entry Bookkeeping

9. In economics, business, and accounting, a _____ is the value of money that has been used up to produce something, and hence is not available for use anymore. In business, the _____ may be one of acquisition, in which case the amount of money expended to acquire it is counted as _____. In this case, money is the input that is gone in order to acquire the thing.

a. Marginal cost
b. Fixed costs
c. Sliding scale fees
d. Cost

10. _____ is a measure of the ability of a debtor to pay their debts as and when they fall due. It is usually expressed as a ratio or a percentage of current liabilities.

For a corporation with a published balance sheet there are various ratios used to calculate a measure of liquidity.

a. Operating leverage
b. Operating profit margin
c. Invested capital
d. Accounting liquidity

11. _____ is the corporate management term for the act of reorganizing the legal, ownership, operational, or other structures of a company for the purpose of making it more profitable or better organized for its present needs. Alternate reasons for restructing include a change of ownership or ownership structure, demerger repositioning debt _____ and financial _____.

a. Cross-border leasing
b. Day trading
c. Concentrated stock
d. Restructuring

12. In business and accounting, _____s are everything of value that is owned by a person or company. The balance sheet of a firm records the monetary value of the _____s owned by the firm. The two major _____ classes are tangible _____s and intangible _____s.

a. Accounts payable b. EBITDA
c. Income d. Asset

13. _____ is the provision of resources (such as granting a loan) by one party to another party where that second party does not reimburse the first party immediately, thereby generating a debt, and instead arranges either to repay or return those resources (or material(s) of equal value) at a later date. The first party is called a creditor, also known as a lender, while the second party is called a debtor, also known as a borrower.

Movements of financial capital are normally dependent on either _____ or equity transfers.

a. Comparable b. Clearing house
c. Warrant d. Credit

14. _____ is the risk of loss due to a debtor's non-payment of a loan or other line of credit (either the principal or interest (coupon) or both)

Most lenders employ their own models (credit scorecards) to rank potential and existing customers according to risk, and then apply appropriate strategies. With products such as unsecured personal loans or mortgages, lenders charge a higher price for higher risk customers and vice versa. With revolving products such as credit cards and overdrafts, risk is controlled through careful setting of credit limits.

a. Transaction risk b. Liquidity risk
c. Market risk d. Credit risk

15. _____ is the discipline of identifying, monitoring and limiting risks. In some cases the acceptable risk may be near zero. Risks can come from accidents, natural causes and disasters as well as deliberate attacks from an adversary.
a. FIFO b. 4-4-5 Calendar
c. Risk management d. Penny stock

16. _____ refers to any type of investment that yields a regular (or fixed) return.

For example, if you lend money to a borrower and the borrower has to pay interest once a month, you have been issued a fixed-income security. When a company does this, it is often called a bond or corporate bank debt (although preferred stock is also sometimes considered to be _____).

a. Bond market b. Fixed income
c. 529 plan d. 4-4-5 Calendar

17. _____, refers to consumption opportunity gained by an entity within a specified time frame, which is generally expressed in monetary terms. However, for households and individuals, '_____ is the sum of all the wages, salaries, profits, interests payments, rents and other forms of earnings received... in a given period of time.' For firms, _____ generally refers to net-profit: what remains of revenue after expenses have been subtracted.
a. Annual report b. Accrual
c. OIBDA d. Income

Chapter 51. Introduction to Interest-Rate Futures and Options Contracts

1. A _____ is a financial contract whose value is derived from the value of something else (known as the underlying.) The underlying on which a _____ is based can be an asset, weather conditions bonds or other forms of credit.
   a. 4-4-5 Calendar
   b. Derivative
   c. 7-Eleven
   d. 529 plan

2. In finance, a _____ is a standardized contract, to buy or sell a specified commodity of standardized quality at a certain date in the future, at a market determined price (the futures price.)

   The price is determined by the instantaneous equilibrium between the forces of supply and demand among competing buy and sell orders on the exchange at the time of the purchase or sale of the contract.

   In many cases, the items may be such non-traditional 'commodities' as foreign currencies, commercial or government paper [e.g., bonds], or 'baskets' of corporate equity ['stock indices'] or other financial instruments.

   a. Repurchase agreement
   b. Heston model
   c. Financial future
   d. Futures contract

3. In economics and finance, _____ is the practice of taking advantage of a price differential between two or more markets: striking a combination of matching deals that capitalize upon the imbalance, the profit being the difference between the market prices. When used by academics, an _____ is a transaction that involves no negative cash flow at any probabilistic or temporal state and a positive cash flow in at least one state; in simple terms, a risk-free profit.
   a. Arbitrage
   b. Efficient-market hypothesis
   c. Initial margin
   d. Issuer

4. A _____ is an exchange of promises between two or more parties to do an act which is enforceable in a court of law. It is where an unqualified offer meets a qualified acceptance and the parties reach Consensus ad Idem. The parties must have the necessary capacity to _____ and the _____ must not be either trifling, indeterminate, impossible or illegal.
   a. 529 plan
   b. 7-Eleven
   c. 4-4-5 Calendar
   d. Contract

5. A _____ is an agreement between two parties to buy or sell an asset at a specified point of time in the future. The price of the underlying instrument, in whatever form, is paid before control of the instrument changes. This is one of the many forms of buy/sell orders where the time of trade is not the time where the securities themselves are exchanged.
   a. Derivatives markets
   b. Loan Credit Default Swap Index
   c. Constant maturity credit default swap
   d. Forward contract

6. _____ is the provision of resources (such as granting a loan) by one party to another party where that second party does not reimburse the first party immediately, thereby generating a debt, and instead arranges either to repay or return those resources (or material(s) of equal value) at a later date. The first party is called a creditor, also known as a lender, while the second party is called a debtor, also known as a borrower.

   Movements of financial capital are normally dependent on either _____ or equity transfers.

   a. Clearing house
   b. Credit
   c. Warrant
   d. Comparable

Chapter 51. Introduction to Interest-Rate Futures and Options Contracts

7. _____ is the risk of loss due to a debtor's non-payment of a loan or other line of credit (either the principal or interest (coupon) or both)

Most lenders employ their own models (credit scorecards) to rank potential and existing customers according to risk, and then apply appropriate strategies. With products such as unsecured personal loans or mortgages, lenders charge a higher price for higher risk customers and vice versa. With revolving products such as credit cards and overdrafts, risk is controlled through careful setting of credit limits.

- a. Liquidity risk
- b. Market risk
- c. Transaction risk
- d. Credit risk

8. Days to Cover (DTC) is a numerical term that describes the relationship between the amount of shares in a given equity that have been short sold and the number of days of typical trading that it would require to 'cover' all _____ outstanding. For example, if there are ten million shares of XYZ Inc. that are currently short sold and the average daily volume of XYZ shares traded each day is one million, it would require ten days of trading for all _____ to be covered (10 million / 1 million.)
- a. Stock or scrip dividends
- b. Cash budget
- c. Guaranteed investment contracts
- d. Short positions

9. A _____ is a financial contract between two parties, the buyer and the seller of this type of option. Often it is simply labeled a 'call'. The buyer of the option has the right, but not the obligation to buy an agreed quantity of a particular commodity or financial instrument (the underlying instrument) from the seller of the option at a certain time (the expiration date) for a certain price (the strike price.)
- a. Call option
- b. Bear spread
- c. Bear call spread
- d. Bull spread

10. In options, the _____ is a key variable in a derivatives contract between two parties. Where the contract requires delivery of the underlying instrument, the trade will be at the _____, regardless of the spot price (market price) of the underlying instrument at that time.

Definition - The fixed price at which the owner of an option can purchase, in the case of a call in the case of a put, the underlying security or commodity.

- a. Strike price
- b. Moneyness
- c. Naked put
- d. Swaption

11. An _____ is a contract written by a seller that conveys to the buyer the right -- but not the obligation -- to buy (in the case of a call _____) or to sell (in the case of a put _____) a particular asset, such as a piece of property such as, among others, a futures contract. In return for granting the _____, the seller collects a payment (the premium) from the buyer.

For example, buying a call _____ provides the right to buy a specified quantity of a security at a set strike price at some time on or before expiration, while buying a put _____ provides the right to sell.

Chapter 51. Introduction to Interest-Rate Futures and Options Contracts

a. AT'T Mobility LLC
c. Amortization
b. Option
d. Annuity

12. The _____ is the price the buyer of the options contract pays for the right to buy or sell a security at a specified price in the future.
   a. ABN Amro
   c. Option premium
   b. AAB
   d. A Random Walk Down Wall Street

13. A _____ is a financial contract between two parties, the seller (writer) and the buyer of the option. The put allows its buyer the right but not the obligation to sell a commodity or financial instrument (the underlying instrument) to the writer (seller) of the option at a certain time for a certain price (the strike price.) The writer (seller) has the obligation to purchase the underlying asset at that strike price, if the buyer exercises the option.
   a. Bear call spread
   c. Bear spread
   b. Debit spread
   d. Put option

14. _____ are government bonds issued by the United States Department of the Treasury through the Bureau of the Public Debt. They are the debt financing instruments of the U.S. Federal government, and they are often referred to simply as Treasuries or Treasurys. There are four types of marketable _____: Treasury bills, Treasury notes, Treasury bonds, and Treasury Inflation Protected Securities (TIPS.)
   a. Treasury Inflation-Protected Securities
   c. Treasury Inflation Protected Securities
   b. Treasury securities
   d. 4-4-5 Calendar

15. In finance, a _____ is a debt security, in which the authorized issuer owes the holders a debt and, depending on the terms of the _____, is obliged to pay interest (the coupon) and/or to repay the principal at a later date, termed maturity.

Thus a _____ is a loan: the issuer is the borrower, the _____ holder is the lender, and the coupon is the interest. _____s provide the borrower with external funds to finance long-term investments, or, in the case of government _____s, to finance current expenditure.

   a. Catastrophe bonds
   c. Puttable bond
   b. Convertible bond
   d. Bond

16. The institution most often referenced by the word '_____' is a public or publicly traded _____, the shares of which are traded on a public stock exchange (e.g., the New York Stock Exchange or Nasdaq in the United States) where shares of stock of _____s are bought and sold by and to the general public. Most of the largest businesses in the world are publicly traded _____s. However, the majority of _____s are said to be closely held, privately held or close _____s, meaning that no ready market exists for the trading of shares.
   a. Protect
   c. Federal Home Loan Mortgage Corporation
   b. Depository Trust Company
   d. Corporation

17. _____s are deposits denominated in United States dollars at banks outside the United States, and thus are not under the jurisdiction of the Federal Reserve. Consequently, such deposits are subject to much less regulation than similar deposits within the United States, allowing for higher margins. There is nothing 'European' about _____ deposits; a US dollar-denominated deposit in Tokyo or Caracas would likewise be deemed _____ deposits.

a. ABN Amro
b. AAB
c. A Random Walk Down Wall Street
d. Eurodollar

18. _____ mature in one year or less. Like zero-coupon bonds, they do not pay interest prior to maturity; instead they are sold at a discount of the par value to create a positive yield to maturity. Many regard _____ as the least risky investment available to U.S. investors.

a. 4-4-5 Calendar
b. Treasury securities
c. Treasury Inflation Protected Securities
d. Treasury bills

19. In finance, a _____ is a derivative in which two counterparties agree to exchange one stream of cash flows against another stream. These streams are called the legs of the _____.

The cash flows are calculated over a notional principal amount, which is usually not exchanged between counterparties.

a. Volatility swap
b. Local volatility
c. Volatility arbitrage
d. Swap

20. In the United States, _____ are overnight borrowings by banks to maintain their bank reserves at the Federal Reserve. Banks keep reserves at Federal Reserve Banks to meet their reserve requirements and to clear financial transactions. Transactions in the _____ market enable depository institutions with reserve balances in excess of reserve requirements to lend reserves to institutions with reserve deficiencies.

a. 4-4-5 Calendar
b. Federal funds rate
c. Regulation T
d. Federal funds

21. A _____ is an order to buy a security at no more (or sell at no less) than a specific price. This gives the customer some control over the price at which the trade is executed, but may prevent the order from being executed ('filled'.)

A buy _____ can only be executed by the broker at the limit price or lower.

a. Commercial mortgage-backed securities
b. Limit order
c. Block premium
d. Common stock

22. A _____ is a buy or sell order to be executed by the broker immediately at current market prices. As long as there are willing sellers and buyers, _____s are filled.

A _____ is the simplest of the order types.

a. Block premium
b. Market order
c. Stockholder
d. Trading curb

23. A _____ is an order to buy (or sell) a security once the price of the security has climbed above (or dropped below) a specified stop price. When the specified stop price is reached, the _____ is entered as a market order (no limit.)

With a _____, the customer does not have to actively monitor how a stock is performing.

Chapter 51. Introduction to Interest-Rate Futures and Options Contracts

a. Share price
c. Stop order
b. Stock split
d. Wash sale

24. A _____ combines the features of a stop order and a limit order. Once the stop price is reached, the _____ becomes a limit order to buy (or to sell) at no more (or less) than a specified price. As with all limit orders, a _____ doesn't get filled if the security's price never reaches the specified limit price.
   a. Wash sale
   c. Box spread
   b. Stop-limit order
   d. Stop price

25. In banking and finance, _____ denotes all activities from the time a commitment is made for a transaction until it is settled. _____ is necessary because the speed of trades is much faster than the cycle time for completing the underlying transaction.

In its widest sense _____ involves the management of post-trading, pre-settlement credit exposures, to ensure that trades are settled in accordance with market rules, even if a buyer or seller should become insolvent prior to settlement.

   a. Procter ' Gamble
   c. Clearing house
   b. Share
   d. Clearing

26. The _____ requirement is the amount required to be collateralized in order to open a position. Thereafter, the amount required to be kept in collateral until the position is closed is the maintenance requirement. The maintenance requirement is the minimum amount to be collateralized in order to keep an open position.
   a. Issuer
   c. Initial margin
   b. Arbitrage
   d. Efficient-market hypothesis

27. The variation margin or _____ is not collateral, but a daily offsetting of profits and losses. Futures are marked-to-market every day, so the current price is compared to the previous day's price. The profit or loss on the day of a position is then paid to or debited from the holder by the futures exchange.
   a. Delivery month
   c. Maintenance margin
   b. Total return swap
   d. SPI 200 futures contract

28. In finance, a _____ is collateral that the holder of a position in securities, options, or futures contracts has to deposit to cover the credit risk of his counterparty (most often his broker.) This risk can arise if the holder has done any of the following:

   - borrowed cash from the counterparty to buy securities or options,
   - sold securities or options short, or
   - entered into a futures contract.

The collateral can be in the form of cash or securities, and it is deposited in a _____ account. On U.S. futures exchanges, '_____' was formally called performance bond.

_____ buying is buying securities with cash borrowed from a broker, using other securities as collateral.

242 Chapter 51. Introduction to Interest-Rate Futures and Options Contracts

a. Credit
c. Procter ' Gamble
b. Margin
d. Share

29. _____ refers to any type of investment that yields a regular (or fixed) return.

For example, if you lend money to a borrower and the borrower has to pay interest once a month, you have been issued a fixed-income security. When a company does this, it is often called a bond or corporate bank debt (although preferred stock is also sometimes considered to be _____).

a. 529 plan
c. Fixed income
b. 4-4-5 Calendar
d. Bond market

30. _____, refers to consumption opportunity gained by an entity within a specified time frame, which is generally expressed in monetary terms. However, for households and individuals, '_____ is the sum of all the wages, salaries, profits, interests payments, rents and other forms of earnings received... in a given period of time.' For firms, _____ generally refers to net-profit: what remains of revenue after expenses have been subtracted.

a. OIBDA
c. Income
b. Annual report
d. Accrual

31. The _____ or forward rate is the agreed upon price of an asset in a forward contract. Using the rational pricing assumption, we can express the _____ in terms of the spot price and any dividends etc., so that there is no possibility for arbitrage.

The _____ is given by:

where

F is the _____ to be paid at time T
e^x is the exponential function
r is the risk-free interest rate
q is the cost-of-carry
S_0 is the spot price of the asset (i.e. what it would sell for at time 0)
D_i is a dividend which is guaranteed to be paid at time t_i where $0 < t_i < T$.

The two questions here are what price the short position (the seller of the asset) should offer to maximize his gain, and what price the long position (the buyer of the asset) should accept to maximize his gain?

At the very least we know that both do not want to lose any money in the deal.

a. Biweekly Mortgage
c. Financial Gerontology
b. Security interest
d. Forward price

Chapter 51. Introduction to Interest-Rate Futures and Options Contracts 243

32. In finance, a _____ is a forward contract in which one party pays a fixed interest rate, and receives a floating interest rate equal to a reference rate (the underlying rate.) The payments are calculated over a notional amount over a certain period, and netted, i.e. only the differential is paid. It is paid on the effective date.

   a. Local volatility
   b. Triple witching hour
   c. PAUG
   d. Forward rate agreement

33. In economics, _____ describes the state of a market with respect to competition.

   - Perfect competition, in which the market consists of a very large number of firms producing a homogeneous product.
   - Monopolistic competition where there are a large number of independent firms which have a very small proportion of the market share.
   - Oligopoly, in which a market is dominated by a small number of firms which own more than 40% of the market share.
   - Oligopsony, a market dominated by many sellers and a few buyers.
   - Monopoly, where there is only one provider of a product or service.
   - Natural monopoly, a monopoly in which economies of scale cause efficiency to increase continuously with the size of the firm. A firm is a natural monopoly if it is able to serve the entire market demand at a lower cost than any combination of two or more smaller, more specialized firms.
   - Monopsony, when there is only one buyer in a market.

The imperfectly competitive structure is quite identical to the realistic market conditions where some monopolistic competitors, monopolists, oligopolists, and duopolists exist and dominate the market conditions. The elements of _____ include the number and size distribution of firms, entry conditions, and the extent of differentiation.

These somewhat abstract concerns tend to determine some but not all details of a specific concrete market system where buyers and sellers actually meet and commit to trade.

   a. Fixed exchange rate
   b. Gross domestic product
   c. Human capital
   d. Market structure

Chapter 52. Pricing Futures and Portfolio Applications

1. In finance, a _____ is a standardized contract, to buy or sell a specified commodity of standardized quality at a certain date in the future, at a market determined price (the futures price.)

The price is determined by the instantaneous equilibrium between the forces of supply and demand among competing buy and sell orders on the exchange at the time of the purchase or sale of the contract.

In many cases, the items may be such non-traditional 'commodities' as foreign currencies, commercial or government paper [e.g., bonds], or 'baskets' of corporate equity ['stock indices'] or other financial instruments.

 a. Heston model
 c. Financial future
 b. Futures contract
 d. Repurchase agreement

2. The _____ is an economic law stated as: 'In an efficient market all identical goods must have only one price.'

The intuition for this law is that all sellers will flock to the highest prevailing price, and all buyers to the lowest current market price. In an efficient market the convergence on one price is instant.

Commodities can be traded on financial markets, where there will be a single offer price, and bid price.

 a. Letter of credit
 c. Liability
 b. Law of one price
 d. Personal property

3. In economics and finance, _____ is the practice of taking advantage of a price differential between two or more markets: striking a combination of matching deals that capitalize upon the imbalance, the profit being the difference between the market prices. When used by academics, an _____ is a transaction that involves no negative cash flow at any probabilistic or temporal state and a positive cash flow in at least one state; in simple terms, a risk-free profit.

 a. Initial margin
 c. Arbitrage
 b. Efficient-market hypothesis
 d. Issuer

4. A _____ is an exchange of promises between two or more parties to do an act which is enforceable in a court of law. It is where an unqualified offer meets a qualified acceptance and the parties reach Consensus ad Idem. The parties must have the necessary capacity to _____ and the _____ must not be either trifling, indeterminate, impossible or illegal.

 a. 529 plan
 c. 7-Eleven
 b. 4-4-5 Calendar
 d. Contract

5. The _____ of an asset is the return obtained from holding it (if positive), or the cost of holding it (if negative)

For instance, commodities are usually negative _____ assets, as they incur storage costs, but in some circumstances, commodities can be positive _____ assets as the market is willing to pay a premium for availability.

This can also refer to a trade with more than one leg, where you earn the spread between borrowing a low _____ asset and lending a high _____ one.

Chapter 52. Pricing Futures and Portfolio Applications

a. Cramdown
c. Financial assistance
b. Bankruptcy remote
d. Carry

6. In economics, business, and accounting, a _____ is the value of money that has been used up to produce something, and hence is not available for use anymore. In business, the _____ may be one of acquisition, in which case the amount of money expended to acquire it is counted as _____. In this case, money is the input that is gone in order to acquire the thing.

a. Fixed costs
c. Sliding scale fees
b. Marginal cost
d. Cost

7. The _____ is the cost of 'carrying' or holding a position. If long, the _____ is the cost of interest paid on a margin account. Conversely, if short, the _____ is the cost of paying dividends, or opportunity cost the cost of purchasing a particular security rather than an alternative.

a. Delta hedging
c. Spot price
b. Cost of carry
d. Secondary market

8. _____ or financing is to provide capital (funds), which means money for a project, a person, a business or any other private or public institutions.

Those funds can be allocated for either short term or long term purposes. The health fund is a new way of _____ private healthcare centers.

a. Proxy fight
c. Product life cycle
b. Synthetic CDO
d. Funding

9. In finance, the _____ of a financial asset measures the sensitivity of the asset's price to interest rate movements, expressed as a number of years. The reason for expressing this sensitivity in years is that the time that will elapse until a cash flow is received allows more interest to accumulate. Therefore the price of an asset with long term cashflows has more interest rate sensitivity than an asset with cashflows in the near future.

a. Yield to maturity
c. 4-4-5 Calendar
b. Macaulay duration
d. Duration

10. The official bank rate has existing in various forms since 1694 and has ranged from 0.5% to 17%. The name of this key interest rate has changed over the years. The current name 'Official Bank Rate' was introduced in 2006 and replaced the previous title '_____' (repo is short for repurchase agreement) in 1997.

a. London Interbank Offered Rate
c. London Interbank Bid Rate
b. Cash accumulation equation
d. Repo rate

11. In economics and business, specifically cost accounting, the _____ is the point at which cost or expenses and revenue are equal: there is no net loss or gain, and one has 'broken even'. A profit or a loss has not been made, although opportunity costs have been paid, and capital has received the risk-adjusted, expected return.

For example, if the business sells less than 200 tables each month, it will make a loss, if it sells more, it will be a profit.

a. Fixed asset turnover
c. Defined contribution plan
b. Market microstructure
d. Break-even point

12. _____ is the rate of return of borrowing money to buy an asset in the spot market and delivering it in the futures market where the notional is used to repay the loan.

$\boxed{\times}$ >

dayBase is 365 or 360

To determine the cheapest bond in a basket of deliverable bonds against a futures contract, _____ is computed for each bond; the bond with the highest repo rate is the cheapest. It is the cheapest because it has the lowest initial value to yield a higher return provided it is delivered with the stated futures price.

a. AAB
c. ABN Amro
b. Implied Repo rate
d. A Random Walk Down Wall Street

13. In business and accounting, _____s are everything of value that is owned by a person or company. The balance sheet of a firm records the monetary value of the _____s owned by the firm. The two major _____ classes are tangible _____s and intangible _____s.
a. Income
c. EBITDA
b. Accounts payable
d. Asset

14. _____ is a term used to refer to how an investor distributes his or her investments among various classes of investment vehicles (e.g., stocks and bonds.)

A large part of financial planning is finding an _____ that is appropriate for a given person in terms of their appetite for and ability to shoulder risk. This can depend on various factors; see investor profile.

a. Investment performance
c. Investing online
b. Alternative investment
d. Asset allocation

15. A _____ is a fungible, negotiable instrument representing financial value. They are broadly categorized into debt securities (such as banknotes, bonds and debentures), and equity securities; e.g., common stocks. The company or other entity issuing the _____ is called the issuer.
a. Book entry
c. Tracking stock
b. Securities lending
d. Security

16. In finance, the term _____ describes the amount in cash that returns to the owners of a security. Normally it does not include the price variations, at the difference of the total return. _____ applies to various stated rates of return on stocks (common and preferred, and convertible), fixed income instruments (bonds, notes, bills, strips, zero coupon), and some other investment type insurance products (e.g. annuities).
a. 4-4-5 Calendar
c. Yield
b. Macaulay duration
d. Yield to maturity

Chapter 52. Pricing Futures and Portfolio Applications

17. In finance, a _____ is a position established in one market in an attempt to offset exposure to the price risk of an equal but opposite obligation or position in another market -- usually, but not always, in the context of one's commercial activity. Hedging is a strategy designed to minimize exposure to such business risks as a sharp contraction in demand for one's inventory, while still allowing the business to profit from producing and maintaining that inventory. A typical hedger might be a farmer with 2000 acres of unharvested wheat in the ground, who would rather tend his crop without the distraction of uncertain prices.

   a. 529 plan
   b. 4-4-5 Calendar
   c. Hedge
   d. 7-Eleven

18. _____ is a risk-adjusted measure of the so-called active return on an investment. It is the return in excess of the compensation for the risk borne, and thus commonly used to assess active managers' performances. Often, the return of a benchmark is subtracted in order to consider relative performance, which yields Jensen's _____.

   a. Amortization
   b. Option
   c. Annuity
   d. Alpha

19. The term _____ is often used to refer to the investment management of collective investments, (not necessarily) whilst the more generic fund management may refer to all forms of institutional investment as well as investment management for private investors. Investment managers who specialize in advisory or discretionary management on behalf of (normally wealthy) private investors may often refer to their services as wealth management or portfolio management often within the context of so-called 'private banking'.

   The provision of 'investment management services' includes elements of financial analysis, asset selection, stock selection, plan implementation and ongoing monitoring of investments.

   a. A Random Walk Down Wall Street
   b. ABN Amro
   c. AAB
   d. Asset management

20. _____ in finance is the risk associated with imperfect hedging using futures. It could arise because of the difference between the asset whose price is to be hedged and the asset underlying the derivative, or because of a mismatch between the expiration date of the futures and the actual selling date of the asset.

   Under these conditions, the spot price of the asset, and the futures price, do not converge on the expiration date of the future.

   a. Liquidity risk
   b. Basis risk
   c. Currency risk
   d. Credit risk

21. The _____ is a daily reference rate based on the interest rates at which banks borrow unsecured funds from banks in the London wholesale money market (or interbank market.) It is roughly comparable to the U.S. Federal funds rate.

   During 1984 it became apparent that an increasing number of banks were trading actively in a variety of relatively new market instruments, notably interest rate swaps, foreign currency options and forward rate agreements.

   a. Shanghai Interbank Offered Rate
   b. Risk-free interest rate
   c. Fixed interest
   d. London Interbank Offered Rate

Chapter 52. Pricing Futures and Portfolio Applications

22. _____ is an investment management term which refers to the return of an investment manager who has intentionally and completely eliminated his market risk, or beta. The return of such a portfolio will only represent the manager's skill in selecting investments within the market, and will be independent of the direction or magnitude of the market's movement. The elimination of market risk can be accomplished through use of futures, swaps, options, or short selling.
   a. Certificate in Investment Performance Measurement
   b. Rebalancing
   c. Market timing
   d. Portable alpha

Chapter 53. Treasury Bond Futures Mechanics and Basis Valuation

1. _____ are government bonds issued by the United States Department of the Treasury through the Bureau of the Public Debt. They are the debt financing instruments of the U.S. Federal government, and they are often referred to simply as Treasuries or Treasurys. There are four types of marketable _____: Treasury bills, Treasury notes, Treasury bonds, and Treasury Inflation Protected Securities (TIPS.)
 a. Treasury Inflation-Protected Securities   b. 4-4-5 Calendar
 c. Treasury securities   d. Treasury Inflation Protected Securities

2. In finance, a _____ is a debt security, in which the authorized issuer owes the holders a debt and, depending on the terms of the _____, is obliged to pay interest (the coupon) and/or to repay the principal at a later date, termed maturity.

Thus a _____ is a loan: the issuer is the borrower, the _____ holder is the lender, and the coupon is the interest. _____s provide the borrower with external funds to finance long-term investments, or, in the case of government _____s, to finance current expenditure.

 a. Bond   b. Catastrophe bonds
 c. Puttable bond   d. Convertible bond

3. A _____ is an exchange of promises between two or more parties to do an act which is enforceable in a court of law. It is where an unqualified offer meets a qualified acceptance and the parties reach Consensus ad Idem. The parties must have the necessary capacity to _____ and the _____ must not be either trifling, indeterminate, impossible or illegal.
 a. 7-Eleven   b. 4-4-5 Calendar
 c. 529 plan   d. Contract

4. In finance, a _____ is a standardized contract, to buy or sell a specified commodity of standardized quality at a certain date in the future, at a market determined price (the futures price.)

The price is determined by the instantaneous equilibrium between the forces of supply and demand among competing buy and sell orders on the exchange at the time of the purchase or sale of the contract.

In many cases, the items may be such non-traditional 'commodities' as foreign currencies, commercial or government paper [e.g., bonds], or 'baskets' of corporate equity ['stock indices'] or other financial instruments.

 a. Repurchase agreement   b. Financial future
 c. Heston model   d. Futures contract

5. An _____ or bill is a commercial document issued by a seller to the buyer, indicating the products, quantities, and agreed prices for products or services the seller has provided the buyer. An _____ indicates the buyer must pay the seller, according to the payment terms.

In the rental industry, an _____ must include a specific reference to the duration of the time being billed, so rather than quantity, price and discount the invoicing amount is based on quantity, price, discount and duration.

 a. ABN Amro   b. AAB
 c. A Random Walk Down Wall Street   d. Invoice

Chapter 53. Treasury Bond Futures Mechanics and Basis Valuation

6. _____ are dollar-denominated bonds, issued mostly by Latin American countries in the 1980s, named after U.S. Treasury Secretary Nicholas Brady.

_____ were created in March 1989 in order to convert bonds issued by mostly Latin American countries into a variety or 'menu' of new bonds after many of those countries defaulted on their debt in the 1980's. At that time, the market for sovereign debt was small and illiquid, and the standardization of emerging-market debt facilitated risk-spreading and trading.

   a. Nominal yield
   c. Coupon rate
   b. Municipal bond
   d. Brady bonds

7. A _____ is an international bond that is denominated in a currency not native to the country where it is issued. It can be categorised according to the currency in which it is issued. London is one of the centers of the _____ market, but _____s may be traded throughout the world - for example in Singapore or Tokyo.
   a. Eurobond
   c. Interest rate option
   b. Economic entity
   d. Education production function

8. _____s are deposits denominated in United States dollars at banks outside the United States, and thus are not under the jurisdiction of the Federal Reserve. Consequently, such deposits are subject to much less regulation than similar deposits within the United States, allowing for higher margins. There is nothing 'European' about _____ deposits; a US dollar-denominated deposit in Tokyo or Caracas would likewise be deemed _____ deposits.
   a. Eurodollar
   c. ABN Amro
   b. A Random Walk Down Wall Street
   d. AAB

9. A _____ is a legal pledge in United States municipal finance, in which an entity pledges its full faith and credit to repay its debt, typically a _____ bond.
   a. Letter of credit
   c. General obligation
   b. Covenant
   d. Financial Institutions Reform Recovery and Enforcement Act

10. In finance, a _____ (non-investment grade bond, speculative grade bond or junk bond) is a bond that is rated below investment grade at the time of purchase. These bonds have a higher risk of default or other adverse credit events, but typically pay higher yields than better quality bonds in order to make them attractive to investors.
    a. High yield bond
    c. Private equity
    b. Sharpe ratio
    d. Volatility

11. _____ is the rate of return of borrowing money to buy an asset in the spot market and delivering it in the futures market where the notional is used to repay the loan.

x >

dayBase is 365 or 360

Chapter 53. Treasury Bond Futures Mechanics and Basis Valuation

To determine the cheapest bond in a basket of deliverable bonds against a futures contract, _____ is computed for each bond; the bond with the highest repo rate is the cheapest. It is the cheapest because it has the lowest initial value to yield a higher return provided it is delivered with the stated futures price.

   a. A Random Walk Down Wall Street
   b. ABN Amro
   c. AAB
   d. Implied repo rate

12. In financial accounting, _____s are precautions for which the amount or probability of occurrence are not known. Typical examples are _____s for warranty costs and _____ for taxes the term reserve is used instead of term _____; such a use, however, is inconsistent with the terminology suggested by International Accounting Standards Board.

   a. Money measurement concept
   b. Momentum Accounting and Triple-Entry Bookkeeping
   c. Petty cash
   d. Provision

13. The official bank rate has existing in various forms since 1694 and has ranged from 0.5% to 17%. The name of this key interest rate has changed over the years. The current name 'Official Bank Rate' was introduced in 2006 and replaced the previous title '_____' (repo is short for repurchase agreement) in 1997.

   a. London Interbank Bid Rate
   b. London Interbank Offered Rate
   c. Cash accumulation equation
   d. Repo rate

14. The _____ of an asset is the return obtained from holding it (if positive), or the cost of holding it (if negative)

For instance, commodities are usually negative _____ assets, as they incur storage costs, but in some circumstances, commodities can be positive _____ assets as the market is willing to pay a premium for availability.

This can also refer to a trade with more than one leg, where you earn the spread between borrowing a low _____ asset and lending a high _____ one.

   a. Bankruptcy remote
   b. Cramdown
   c. Carry
   d. Financial assistance

15. An _____ is a contract written by a seller that conveys to the buyer the right -- but not the obligation -- to buy (in the case of a call _____) or to sell (in the case of a put _____) a particular asset, such as a piece of property such as, among others, a futures contract. In return for granting the _____, the seller collects a payment (the premium) from the buyer.

For example, buying a call _____ provides the right to buy a specified quantity of a security at a set strike price at some time on or before expiration, while buying a put _____ provides the right to sell.

   a. Annuity
   b. Amortization
   c. AT'T Mobility LLC
   d. Option

Chapter 53. Treasury Bond Futures Mechanics and Basis Valuation

16. In finance, the term _____ describes the amount in cash that returns to the owners of a security. Normally it does not include the price variations, at the difference of the total return. _____ applies to various stated rates of return on stocks (common and preferred, and convertible), fixed income instruments (bonds, notes, bills, strips, zero coupon), and some other investment type insurance products (e.g. annuities.)

   a. Macaulay duration
   c. 4-4-5 Calendar
   b. Yield to maturity
   d. Yield

17. In finance, the _____ is the difference between the quoted rates of return on two different investments, usually of different credit quality.

It is a compound of yield and spread.

The '_____ of X over Y' is simply the percentage return on investment (ROI) from financial instrument X minus the percentage return on investment from financial instrument Y (per annum.)

   a. Portfolio insurance
   c. Debtor-in-possession financing
   b. Duty of loyalty
   d. Yield spread

18. A _____ is a financial contract between two parties, the buyer and the seller of this type of option. Often it is simply labeled a 'call'. The buyer of the option has the right, but not the obligation to buy an agreed quantity of a particular commodity or financial instrument (the underlying instrument) from the seller of the option at a certain time (the expiration date) for a certain price (the strike price.)

   a. Bear spread
   c. Bear call spread
   b. Call option
   d. Bull spread

19. A _____ is a financial contract between two parties, the seller (writer) and the buyer of the option. The put allows its buyer the right but not the obligation to sell a commodity or financial instrument (the underlying instrument) to the writer (seller) of the option at a certain time for a certain price (the strike price.) The writer (seller) has the obligation to purchase the underlying asset at that strike price, if the buyer exercises the option.

   a. Bear call spread
   c. Bear spread
   b. Put option
   d. Debit spread

Chapter 54. The Basics of Interest-Rate Options

1. An _____ is a contract written by a seller that conveys to the buyer the right -- but not the obligation -- to buy (in the case of a call _____) or to sell (in the case of a put _____) a particular asset, such as a piece of property such as, among others, a futures contract. In return for granting the _____, the seller collects a payment (the premium) from the buyer.

For example, buying a call _____ provides the right to buy a specified quantity of a security at a set strike price at some time on or before expiration, while buying a put _____ provides the right to sell.

   a. AT'T Mobility LLC   b. Annuity
   c. Amortization   d. Option

2. In options, the _____ is a key variable in a derivatives contract between two parties. Where the contract requires delivery of the underlying instrument, the trade will be at the _____, regardless of the spot price (market price) of the underlying instrument at that time.

Definition - The fixed price at which the owner of an option can purchase, in the case of a call in the case of a put, the underlying security or commodity.

   a. Strike price   b. Naked put
   c. Moneyness   d. Swaption

3. A _____ is a financial contract between two parties, the buyer and the seller of this type of option. Often it is simply labeled a 'call'. The buyer of the option has the right, but not the obligation to buy an agreed quantity of a particular commodity or financial instrument (the underlying instrument) from the seller of the option at a certain time (the expiration date) for a certain price (the strike price.)

   a. Bull spread   b. Bear call spread
   c. Bear spread   d. Call option

4. A _____ is a financial contract between two parties, the seller (writer) and the buyer of the option. The put allows its buyer the right but not the obligation to sell a commodity or financial instrument (the underlying instrument) to the writer (seller) of the option at a certain time for a certain price (the strike price.) The writer (seller) has the obligation to purchase the underlying asset at that strike price, if the buyer exercises the option.

   a. Bear spread   b. Debit spread
   c. Put option   d. Bear call spread

5. In finance, _____ refers to the value of a security which is intrinsic to or contained in the security itself. It is also frequently called fundamental value. It is ordinarily calculated by summing the future income generated by the asset, and discounting it to the present value.

   a. Alpha   b. Intrinsic value
   c. Amortization   d. Accretion

6. In finance, _____ is the process of estimating the potential market value of a financial asset or liability. they can be done on assets (for example, investments in marketable securities such as stocks, options, business enterprises, or intangible assets such as patents and trademarks) or on liabilities (e.g., Bonds issued by a company.) _____s are required in many contexts including investment analysis, capital budgeting, merger and acquisition transactions, financial reporting, taxable events to determine the proper tax liability, and in litigation.

Chapter 54. The Basics of Interest-Rate Options

a. Procter ' Gamble
b. Margin
c. Valuation
d. Share

7. An _____ option has no intrinsic value. A call option is _____ when the strike price is above the spot price of the underlying security. A put option is _____ when the strike price is below the spot price.
   a. A Random Walk Down Wall Street
   b. AAB
   c. ABN Amro
   d. Out-of-the-money

8. In finance, the value of an option consists of two components, its intrinsic value and its _____. Time value is simply the difference between option value and intrinsic value. _____ is also known as theta, extrinsic value, or instrumental value.
   a. Conservatism
   b. Time value
   c. Debt buyer
   d. Global Squeeze

9. _____ most frequently refers to the standard deviation of the continuously compounded returns of a financial instrument with a specific time horizon. It is often used to quantify the risk of the instrument over that time period. _____ is typically expressed in annualized terms, and it may either be an absolute number ($5) or a fraction of the mean (5%).
   a. Seasoned equity offering
   b. Currency swap
   c. Portfolio insurance
   d. Volatility

10. In finance, a _____ is a debt security, in which the authorized issuer owes the holders a debt and, depending on the terms of the _____, is obliged to pay interest (the coupon) and/or to repay the principal at a later date, termed maturity.

    Thus a _____ is a loan: the issuer is the borrower, the _____ holder is the lender, and the coupon is the interest. _____s provide the borrower with external funds to finance long-term investments, or, in the case of government _____s, to finance current expenditure.

    a. Convertible bond
    b. Puttable bond
    c. Catastrophe bonds
    d. Bond

11. _____ is a type of bond that allows the issuer of the bond to retain the privilege of redeeming the bond at some point before the bond reaches the date of maturity. In other words, on the call dates, the issuer has the right, but not the obligation, to buy back the bonds from the bond holders at the call price. Technically speaking, the bonds are not really bought and held by the issuer but cancelled immediately.
    a. Gilts
    b. Coupon rate
    c. Bond fund
    d. Callable bond

12. The _____ of an asset is the return obtained from holding it (if positive), or the cost of holding it (if negative)

    For instance, commodities are usually negative _____ assets, as they incur storage costs, but in some circumstances, commodities can be positive _____ assets as the market is willing to pay a premium for availability.

    This can also refer to a trade with more than one leg, where you earn the spread between borrowing a low _____ asset and lending a high _____ one.

Chapter 54. The Basics of Interest-Rate Options

a. Bankruptcy remote
c. Financial assistance
b. Cramdown
d. Carry

13. _____ is the process of setting or keeping the delta of a portfolio as close to zero as possible.

Mathematically, delta is the partial derivative [ ] > of the instrument or portfolio's fair value with respect to the price of the underlying security.

Therefore, if a position is delta neutral (or, instantaneously delta-hedged) its instantaneous change in value, for an infinitesimal change in the value of the underlying, will be zero; see Hedge (finance.)

a. Delta hedging
c. Financial services
b. Convertible arbitrage
d. Central Securities Depository

14. _____, refers to consumption opportunity gained by an entity within a specified time frame, which is generally expressed in monetary terms. However, for households and individuals, '_____ is the sum of all the wages, salaries, profits, interests payments, rents and other forms of earnings received... in a given period of time.' For firms, _____ generally refers to net-profit: what remains of revenue after expenses have been subtracted.

a. Accrual
c. OIBDA
b. Annual report
d. Income

15. In finance, a _____ is an investment strategy involving the purchase or sale of particular option derivatives that allows the holder to profit based on how much the price of the underlying security moves, regardless of the direction of price movement. The purchase of particular option derivatives is known as a long _____, while the sale of the option derivatives is known as a short _____.

An option payoff diagram for a long _____ position

A long _____ involves going long, i.e., purchasing, both a call option and a put option on some stock, interest rate, index or other underlying.

a. Bear call spread
c. Straddle
b. Moneyness
d. Put option

16. _____ (in a financial context) is the assumption of the risk of loss, in return for the uncertain possibility of a reward. Only if one may safely say that a particular position involves no risk may one say, strictly speaking, that such a position represents an 'investment.' Financial _____ involves the buying, holding, selling, and short-selling of stocks, bonds, commodities, currencies, collectibles, real estate, derivatives, or any valuable financial instrument to profit from fluctuations in its price as opposed to buying it for use or for income via methods such as dividends or interest. _____ represents one of four market roles in Western financial markets, distinct from hedging, long- or short-term investing, and arbitrage.

a. Speculation
c. Market anomaly
b. Central Securities Depository
d. Forward market

17. _____ is compression of the neck that leads to unconsciousness or death by causing an increasingly hypoxic state in the brain. Fatal _____ typically occurs in cases of violence, accidents, and as the mechanism of suicide in hangings. _____ does not have to be fatal; limited or interrupted _____ is practiced in erotic asphyxia, in the choking game, and is an important technique in many combat sports and self-defense systems

   a. 4-4-5 Calendar
   b. Strangling
   c. 7-Eleven
   d. 529 plan

18. In options trading, a _____ is a bullish, vertical spread options strategy that is designed to profit from a moderate rise in the price of the underlying security.

Because of put-call parity, a _____ can be constructed using either put options or call options. If constructed using calls, it is a bull call spread.

   a. Calendar spread
   b. Strike price
   c. Bull spread
   d. Call option

19. In options trading, a _____ is a bearish, vertical spread options strategy that can be used when the options trader is moderately bearish on the underlying security.

Because of put-call parity, a _____ can be constructed using either put options or call options. If constructed using calls, it is a bear call spread.

   a. Bear spread
   b. Barrier option
   c. Bull spread
   d. Net volatility

20. _____ is an insurance policy which compensates lenders or investors for losses due to the default of a mortgage loan. _____ can be either public or private depending upon the insurer. The policy is also known as a mortgage indemnity guarantee (Mortgage insuranceG), particularly in the UK.

   a. Reverse mortgage
   b. Subprime lending
   c. Mortgage-backed security
   d. Mortgage insurance

21. _____ is a method of hedging a portfolio of stocks against the market risk by short selling stock index futures.

This hedging technique is frequently used by institutional investors when the market direction is uncertain or volatile. Short selling index futures can offset any downturns, but it also hinders any gains.

   a. Freight derivative
   b. Delivery month
   c. PAUG
   d. Portfolio Insurance

22. A _____ is a transaction in which the seller of call options already owns the corresponding amount of the underlying instrument, such as shares of a stock or other securities. These owned shares provide the 'cover' as they can be handed over to the buyer of the options when he decides to exercise them, instead of having to buy the optioned shares at unfavorable market prices in the case of 'uncovered' or short call. Thus, the _____ limits the (potentially unlimited) loss that results from a short call when the price of the underlying stock moves above the strike price of the option.

Chapter 54. The Basics of Interest-Rate Options 257

a. 4-4-5 Calendar
c. Covered call

b. 7-Eleven
d. 529 plan

23. An _____ is implemented by combining one or more option positions and possibly an underlying stock position. Options are financial instruments that give the buyer the right to buy (for a call option) or sell (for a put option) the underlying security at some specific point of time in the future (European Option) or until some specific point of time in the future (American Option) for a price (strike price), which is fixed in advance (when the option is bought.)

Calls increase in value as the underlying stock increases in value.

a. Iron condor
c. Options spreads

b. Option screener
d. Option strategy

24. In financial mathematics, the _____ of an option contract is the volatility implied by the market price of the option based on an option pricing model. In other words, it is the volatility that, given a particular pricing model, yields a theoretical value for the option equal to the current market price. Non-option financial instruments that have embedded optionality, such as an interest rate cap, can also have an _____.

a. Interest rate future
c. Equity derivative

b. Interest rate derivative
d. Implied Volatility

25. In finance, a _____ is a standardized contract, to buy or sell a specified commodity of standardized quality at a certain date in the future, at a market determined price (the futures price.)

The price is determined by the instantaneous equilibrium between the forces of supply and demand among competing buy and sell orders on the exchange at the time of the purchase or sale of the contract.

In many cases, the items may be such non-traditional 'commodities' as foreign currencies, commercial or government paper [e.g., bonds], or 'baskets' of corporate equity ['stock indices'] or other financial instruments.

a. Financial future
c. Futures contract

b. Heston model
d. Repurchase agreement

Chapter 55. Interest-Rate Swaps and Swaptions

1. The _____ (or notional principal amount or notional value) on a financial instrument is the nominal or face amount that is used to calculate payments made on that instrument. This amount generally does not change hands and is thus referred to as notional.

Contrast a bond with an interest rate swap:

- In a bond, the buyer pays the principal amount at issue (start), then receives coupons (computed off this principal) over the life of the bond, then receives the principal back at maturity (end.)
- In a swap, no principal changes hands at inception (start) or expiry (end), and in the meantime, interest payments are computed based on a _____, which acts as if it were the principal of a bond, hence the term notional principal amount, abbreviated to notional.

In simple terms the notional principal amount is essentially how much of the asset or bonds a person has. For example, if I bought a premium bond for Â£1 then the notional principal amount would be Â£1. Hence the notional principal amount is the quantity of the assets and bonds.

a. Forward start option
b. Credit derivative
c. Basis trading
d. Notional amount

2. In finance, a _____ is a derivative in which two counterparties agree to exchange one stream of cash flows against another stream. These streams are called the legs of the _____.

The cash flows are calculated over a notional principal amount, which is usually not exchanged between counterparties.

a. Volatility arbitrage
b. Volatility swap
c. Swap
d. Local volatility

3. _____ (Euro OverNight Index Average) is an effective overnight rate computed as a weighted average of all overnight unsecured lending transactions in the interbank market. It has been initiated within the euro area by the contributing panel banks. It is one of the two benchmarks for the money and capital markets in the euro zone (the other one being Euribor.)

a. Exchange Rate Mechanism
b. A Random Walk Down Wall Street
c. Eonia
d. Euro Interbank Offered Rate

4. _____ is the provision of resources (such as granting a loan) by one party to another party where that second party does not reimburse the first party immediately, thereby generating a debt, and instead arranges either to repay or return those resources (or material(s) of equal value) at a later date. The first party is called a creditor, also known as a lender, while the second party is called a debtor, also known as a borrower.

Movements of financial capital are normally dependent on either _____ or equity transfers.

a. Warrant
b. Clearing house
c. Credit
d. Comparable

5. _____ is the risk of loss due to a debtor's non-payment of a loan or other line of credit (either the principal or interest (coupon) or both)

Most lenders employ their own models (credit scorecards) to rank potential and existing customers according to risk, and then apply appropriate strategies. With products such as unsecured personal loans or mortgages, lenders charge a higher price for higher risk customers and vice versa. With revolving products such as credit cards and overdrafts, risk is controlled through careful setting of credit limits.

- a. Liquidity risk
- b. Market risk
- c. Transaction risk
- d. Credit risk

6. A _____ is an exchange of promises between two or more parties to do an act which is enforceable in a court of law. It is where an unqualified offer meets a qualified acceptance and the parties reach Consensus ad Idem. The parties must have the necessary capacity to _____ and the _____ must not be either trifling, indeterminate, impossible or illegal.
- a. 529 plan
- b. 7-Eleven
- c. 4-4-5 Calendar
- d. Contract

7. A _____ is an agreement between two parties to buy or sell an asset at a specified point of time in the future. The price of the underlying instrument, in whatever form, is paid before control of the instrument changes. This is one of the many forms of buy/sell orders where the time of trade is not the time where the securities themselves are exchanged.
- a. Derivatives markets
- b. Constant maturity credit default swap
- c. Loan Credit Default Swap Index
- d. Forward contract

8. _____ is the Sterling OverNight Index Average. Launched in 1997 by the Wholesale Markets Brokers' Association (WMBA), the weighted average is calculated using brokered unsecured overnight trades between banks listed under Section 43 of the Financial Services Act 1986.
- a. London Interbank Offered Rate
- b. SONIA
- c. London Interbank Bid Rate
- d. Repo rate

9. _____ is a securities industry term describing the trading day a trade (bonds, equities, foreign exchange, commodities etc) was conducted. _____ does not necessarily equal the actual calendar date because in many cases (differing from market to market and asset to asset and exchange or OTC) a trade done very early or very late falls on the previous or following _____.

This occurs because in the international market a trade conducted in (e.g.)

- a. No-arbitrage bounds
- b. Volatility clustering
- c. Black-Litterman model
- d. Trade date

10. In finance, _____ is the process of estimating the potential market value of a financial asset or liability. they can be done on assets (for example, investments in marketable securities such as stocks, options, business enterprises, or intangible assets such as patents and trademarks) or on liabilities (e.g., Bonds issued by a company.) _____s are required in many contexts including investment analysis, capital budgeting, merger and acquisition transactions, financial reporting, taxable events to determine the proper tax liability, and in litigation.
- a. Margin
- b. Procter ' Gamble
- c. Share
- d. Valuation

11. A '_____' is a 'Charge' that is paid to obtain the right to delay a payment. Essentially, the payer purchases the right to make a given payment in the future instead of in the Present. The '_____', or 'Charge' that must be paid to delay the payment, is simply the difference between what the payment amount would be if it were paid in the present and what the payment amount would be paid if it were paid in the future.

   a. Risk aversion   b. Value at risk
   c. Risk modeling   d. Discount

12. The _____, P(T), is the number which a future cash flow, to be received at time T, must be multiplied by in order to obtain the current present value. Thus, a fixed annually compounded discount rate is

$$P(T) = \frac{1}{(1+r)^T}$$

For fixed continuously compounded discount rate we have

$$P(T) = e^{-rT}$$

For discounts in marketing, see discounts and allowances, sales promotion, and pricing.

   a. Risk premium   b. Risk modeling
   c. Discount   d. Discount factor

13. The _____ or forward rate is the agreed upon price of an asset in a forward contract. Using the rational pricing assumption, we can express the _____ in terms of the spot price and any dividends etc., so that there is no possibility for arbitrage.

The _____ is given by:

where

       F is the _____ to be paid at time T
       e^x is the exponential function
       r is the risk-free interest rate
       q is the cost-of-carry
       S_0 is the spot price of the asset (i.e. what it would sell for at time 0)
       D_i is a dividend which is guaranteed to be paid at time t_i where $0 < t_i < T$.

The two questions here are what price the short position (the seller of the asset) should offer to maximize his gain, and what price the long position (the buyer of the asset) should accept to maximize his gain?

Chapter 55. Interest-Rate Swaps and Swaptions

At the very least we know that both do not want to lose any money in the deal.

a. Biweekly Mortgage
c. Security interest

b. Forward price
d. Financial Gerontology

14. _____ is the value on a given date of a future payment or series of future payments, discounted to reflect the time value of money and other factors such as investment risk. _____ calculations are widely used in business and economics to provide a means to compare cash flows at different times on a meaningful 'like to like' basis.

The most commonly applied model of the time value of money is compound interest.

a. Present value of benefits
c. Negative gearing

b. Net present value
d. Present value

15. A _____ is an option granting its owner the right but not the obligation to enter into an underlying swap. Although options can be traded on a variety of swaps, the term '_____' typically refers to options on interest rate swaps.

There are two types of _____ contracts:

- A payer _____ gives the owner of the _____ the right to enter into a swap where they pay the fixed leg and receive the floating leg.
- A receiver _____ gives the owner of the _____ the right to enter into a swap where they will receive the fixed leg, and pay the floating leg.

The buyer and seller of the _____ agree on:

- the premium (price) of the _____
- the strike rate (equal to the fixed rate of the underlying swap)
- length of the option period (which usually ends two business days prior to the start date of the underlying swap),
- the term of the underlying swap,
- notional amount,
- amortization, if any
- frequency of settlement of payments on the underlying swap

The participants in the _____ market are predominantly large corporations, banks, financial institutions and hedge funds. End users such as corporations and banks typically use _____s to manage interest rate risk arising from their core business or from their financing arrangements.

a. Put option
c. Straddle

b. Swaption
d. Bear call spread

16. A _____ is a swap that allows the purchaser to fix the duration of received flows on a swap.

The floating leg of an interest rate swap typically resets against a published index. The floating leg of a _____ fixes against a point on the swap curve on a periodic basis.

   a. PAUG
   b. Weather derivatives
   c. Triple witching hour
   d. Constant maturity Swap

17. _____ is a life of security. It may also refer to the final payment date of a loan or other financial instrument, at which point all remaining interest and principal is due to be paid.

1, 3, 6 months _____ band can be calculated by using 30-day per month periods.

   a. Replacement cost
   b. False billing
   c. Primary market
   d. Maturity

18. A _____ is an interest rate swap which involves the exchange of two floating rate financial instruments. A floating-floating interest rate swap under which the floating rate payments is referenced to different bases.

Basis risk occurs for positions that have at least one paying and one receiving stream of cash flows that are driven by different factors and the correlation between those factors are less than one.

   a. Trade date
   b. Basis swap
   c. Creditor
   d. Carrying charge

19. _____ is the term used to describe deposits residing in banks that are located outside the borders of the country that issues the currency the deposit is denominated in. For example a deposit denominated in US dollars residing in a Japanese bank is a _____ deposit, or more specifically a Eurodollar deposit.

Key points are the location of the bank and the denomination of the currency, not the nationality of the bank or the owner of the deposit/loan.

   a. ABN Amro
   b. Eurocurrency
   c. A Random Walk Down Wall Street
   d. AAB

20. In finance, the term _____ describes the amount in cash that returns to the owners of a security. Normally it does not include the price variations, at the difference of the total return. _____ applies to various stated rates of return on stocks (common and preferred, and convertible), fixed income instruments (bonds, notes, bills, strips, zero coupon), and some other investment type insurance products (e.g. annuities.)

   a. Yield to maturity
   b. Yield
   c. 4-4-5 Calendar
   d. Macaulay duration

21. In finance, the _____ is the relation between the interest rate (or cost of borrowing) and the time to maturity of the debt for a given borrower in a given currency. For example, the current U.S. dollar interest rates paid on U.S. Treasury securities for various maturities are closely watched by many traders, and are commonly plotted on a graph such as the one on the right which is informally called 'the _____.' More formal mathematical descriptions of this relation are often called the term structure of interest rates.

Chapter 55. Interest-Rate Swaps and Swaptions

The yield of a debt instrument is the annualized percentage increase in the value of the investment.

a. 529 plan
c. 7-Eleven
b. Yield curve
d. 4-4-5 Calendar

22. _____ most frequently refers to the standard deviation of the continuously compounded returns of a financial instrument with a specific time horizon. It is often used to quantify the risk of the instrument over that time period. _____ is typically expressed in annualized terms, and it may either be an absolute number ($5) or a fraction of the mean (5%).

a. Volatility
c. Portfolio insurance
b. Currency swap
d. Seasoned equity offering

23. In finance, a _____ is a debt security, in which the authorized issuer owes the holders a debt and, depending on the terms of the _____, is obliged to pay interest (the coupon) and/or to repay the principal at a later date, termed maturity.

Thus a _____ is a loan: the issuer is the borrower, the _____ holder is the lender, and the coupon is the interest. _____s provide the borrower with external funds to finance long-term investments, or, in the case of government _____s, to finance current expenditure.

a. Catastrophe bonds
c. Puttable bond
b. Bond
d. Convertible bond

24. _____ is a type of bond that allows the issuer of the bond to retain the privilege of redeeming the bond at some point before the bond reaches the date of maturity. In other words, on the call dates, the issuer has the right, but not the obligation, to buy back the bonds from the bond holders at the call price. Technically speaking, the bonds are not really bought and held by the issuer but cancelled immediately.

a. Callable bond
c. Bond fund
b. Coupon rate
d. Gilts

Chapter 56. Interest-Rate Caps and Floors and Compound Options

1. In finance, the _____ of a derivative is an asset, basket of assets, index, or even another derivative, such that the cash flows of the (former) derivative depend on the value of this _____. There must be an independent way to observe this value to avoid conflicts of interest.

For example, in a stock option to buy 100 shares of Nokia at EUR 50 in September 2006, the _____ is a Nokia share.

a. A Random Walk Down Wall Street
b. Underlying
c. ABN Amro
d. AAB

2. The _____ (or notional principal amount or notional value) on a financial instrument is the nominal or face amount that is used to calculate payments made on that instrument. This amount generally does not change hands and is thus referred to as notional.

Contrast a bond with an interest rate swap:

- In a bond, the buyer pays the principal amount at issue (start), then receives coupons (computed off this principal) over the life of the bond, then receives the principal back at maturity (end.)
- In a swap, no principal changes hands at inception (start) or expiry (end), and in the meantime, interest payments are computed based on a _____, which acts as if it were the principal of a bond, hence the term notional principal amount, abbreviated to notional.

In simple terms the notional principal amount is essentially how much of the asset or bonds a person has. For example, if I bought a premium bond for £1 then the notional principal amount would be £1. Hence the notional principal amount is the quantity of the assets and bonds.

a. Credit derivative
b. Basis trading
c. Notional amount
d. Forward start option

3. _____ are bonds that have a variable coupon, equal to a money market reference rate, like LIBOR or federal funds rate, plus a spread. The spread is a rate that remains constant. Almost all _____ have quarterly coupons, i.e. they pay out interest every three months, though counter examples do exist.

a. Floating rate notes
b. Loan participation
c. CVECAs
d. Gordon growth model

4. In finance, a _____ is a derivative in which two counterparties agree to exchange one stream of cash flows against another stream. These streams are called the legs of the _____.

The cash flows are calculated over a notional principal amount, which is usually not exchanged between counterparties.

a. Volatility swap
b. Local volatility
c. Volatility arbitrage
d. Swap

Chapter 56. Interest-Rate Caps and Floors and Compound Options

5. In finance, a _____ is a debt security, in which the authorized issuer owes the holders a debt and, depending on the terms of the _____, is obliged to pay interest (the coupon) and/or to repay the principal at a later date, termed maturity.

Thus a _____ is a loan: the issuer is the borrower, the _____ holder is the lender, and the coupon is the interest. _____s provide the borrower with external funds to finance long-term investments, or, in the case of government _____s, to finance current expenditure.

  a. Catastrophe bonds
  c. Puttable bond
  b. Convertible bond
  d. Bond

6. A _____ is a financial contract between two parties, the buyer and the seller of this type of option. Often it is simply labeled a 'call'. The buyer of the option has the right, but not the obligation to buy an agreed quantity of a particular commodity or financial instrument (the underlying instrument) from the seller of the option at a certain time (the expiration date) for a certain price (the strike price.)

  a. Bear spread
  c. Bear call spread
  b. Call option
  d. Bull spread

7. An _____ is a contract written by a seller that conveys to the buyer the right -- but not the obligation -- to buy (in the case of a call _____) or to sell (in the case of a put _____) a particular asset, such as a piece of property such as, among others, a futures contract. In return for granting the _____, the seller collects a payment (the premium) from the buyer.

For example, buying a call _____ provides the right to buy a specified quantity of a security at a set strike price at some time on or before expiration, while buying a put _____ provides the right to sell.

  a. AT'T Mobility LLC
  c. Option
  b. Annuity
  d. Amortization

Chapter 57. Controlling Interest-Rate Risk with Futures and Options

1. In finance, a _____ is a standardized contract, to buy or sell a specified commodity of standardized quality at a certain date in the future, at a market determined price (the futures price.)

The price is determined by the instantaneous equilibrium between the forces of supply and demand among competing buy and sell orders on the exchange at the time of the purchase or sale of the contract.

In many cases, the items may be such non-traditional 'commodities' as foreign currencies, commercial or government paper [e.g., bonds], or 'baskets' of corporate equity ['stock indices'] or other financial instruments.

   a. Financial future
   b. Heston model
   c. Repurchase agreement
   d. Futures contract

2. A _____ is an exchange of promises between two or more parties to do an act which is enforceable in a court of law. It is where an unqualified offer meets a qualified acceptance and the parties reach Consensus ad Idem. The parties must have the necessary capacity to _____ and the _____ must not be either trifling, indeterminate, impossible or illegal.
   a. 4-4-5 Calendar
   b. 529 plan
   c. 7-Eleven
   d. Contract

3. A _____ is a unit that is equal to 1/100th of a percentage point. It is frequently used to express percentage point changes of less than 1%. It avoids the ambiguity between relative and absolute discussions about rates.
   a. 529 plan
   b. Basis point
   c. Bond market
   d. 4-4-5 Calendar

4. In finance, the _____ of a financial asset measures the sensitivity of the asset's price to interest rate movements, expressed as a number of years. The reason for expressing this sensitivity in years is that the time that will elapse until a cash flow is received allows more interest to accumulate. Therefore the price of an asset with long term cashflows has more interest rate sensitivity than an asset with cashflows in the near future.
   a. Yield to maturity
   b. 4-4-5 Calendar
   c. Macaulay duration
   d. Duration

5. In finance, a _____ is a debt security, in which the authorized issuer owes the holders a debt and, depending on the terms of the _____, is obliged to pay interest (the coupon) and/or to repay the principal at a later date, termed maturity.

Thus a _____ is a loan: the issuer is the borrower, the _____ holder is the lender, and the coupon is the interest. _____s provide the borrower with external funds to finance long-term investments, or, in the case of government _____s, to finance current expenditure.

   a. Catastrophe bonds
   b. Convertible bond
   c. Bond
   d. Puttable bond

6. In finance, a _____ is a position established in one market in an attempt to offset exposure to the price risk of an equal but opposite obligation or position in another market -- usually, but not always, in the context of one's commercial activity. Hedging is a strategy designed to minimize exposure to such business risks as a sharp contraction in demand for one's inventory, while still allowing the business to profit from producing and maintaining that inventory. A typical hedger might be a farmer with 2000 acres of unharvested wheat in the ground, who would rather tend his crop without the distraction of uncertain prices.

    a. 529 plan
    c. 7-Eleven
    b. 4-4-5 Calendar
    d. Hedge

7. _____ is an economic policy in which a central bank estimates and makes public a projected, or 'target,' inflation rate and then attempts to steer actual inflation towards the target through the use of interest rate changes and other monetary tools.

Because interest rates and the inflation rate tend to be inversely related, the likely moves of the central bank to raise or lower interest rates become more transparent under the policy of _____. Examples:

- if inflation appears to be above the target, the bank is likely to raise interest rates. This usually (but not always) has the effect over time of cooling the economy and bringing down inflation.

- if inflation appears to be below the target, the bank is likely to lower interest rates. This usually (again, not always) has the effect over time of accelerating the economy and raising inflation.

    a. AAB
    c. Inflation accounting
    b. A Random Walk Down Wall Street
    d. Inflation targeting

8. _____ in finance is the risk associated with imperfect hedging using futures. It could arise because of the difference between the asset whose price is to be hedged and the asset underlying the derivative, or because of a mismatch between the expiration date of the futures and the actual selling date of the asset.

Under these conditions, the spot price of the asset, and the futures price, do not converge on the expiration date of the future.

    a. Currency risk
    c. Credit risk
    b. Basis risk
    d. Liquidity risk

9. In finance, the term _____ describes the amount in cash that returns to the owners of a security. Normally it does not include the price variations, at the difference of the total return. _____ applies to various stated rates of return on stocks (common and preferred, and convertible), fixed income instruments (bonds, notes, bills, strips, zero coupon), and some other investment type insurance products (e.g. annuities.)

    a. Yield to maturity
    c. Macaulay duration
    b. 4-4-5 Calendar
    d. Yield

10. In finance, the _____ is the difference between the quoted rates of return on two different investments, usually of different credit quality.

It is a compound of yield and spread.

Chapter 57. Controlling Interest-Rate Risk with Futures and Options

The '_____ of X over Y' is simply the percentage return on investment (ROI) from financial instrument X minus the percentage return on investment from financial instrument Y (per annum.)

   a. Debtor-in-possession financing   b. Duty of loyalty
   c. Portfolio insurance   d. Yield spread

11. A _____ is a transaction in which the seller of call options already owns the corresponding amount of the underlying instrument, such as shares of a stock or other securities. These owned shares provide the 'cover' as they can be handed over to the buyer of the options when he decides to exercise them, instead of having to buy the optioned shares at unfavorable market prices in the case of 'uncovered' or short call. Thus, the _____ limits the (potentially unlimited) loss that results from a short call when the price of the underlying stock moves above the strike price of the option.

   a. Covered call   b. 529 plan
   c. 4-4-5 Calendar   d. 7-Eleven

12. An _____ is a contract written by a seller that conveys to the buyer the right -- but not the obligation -- to buy (in the case of a call _____) or to sell (in the case of a put _____) a particular asset, such as a piece of property such as, among others, a futures contract. In return for granting the _____, the seller collects a payment (the premium) from the buyer.

For example, buying a call _____ provides the right to buy a specified quantity of a security at a set strike price at some time on or before expiration, while buying a put _____ provides the right to sell.

   a. Option   b. Annuity
   c. Amortization   d. AT'T Mobility LLC

13. In options, the _____ is a key variable in a derivatives contract between two parties. Where the contract requires delivery of the underlying instrument, the trade will be at the _____, regardless of the spot price (market price) of the underlying instrument at that time.

Definition - The fixed price at which the owner of an option can purchase, in the case of a call in the case of a put, the underlying security or commodity.

   a. Moneyness   b. Swaption
   c. Naked put   d. Strike price

Chapter 58. Introduction to Credit Derivatives

1. _____ is the provision of resources (such as granting a loan) by one party to another party where that second party does not reimburse the first party immediately, thereby generating a debt, and instead arranges either to repay or return those resources (or material(s) of equal value) at a later date. The first party is called a creditor, also known as a lender, while the second party is called a debtor, also known as a borrower.

Movements of financial capital are normally dependent on either _____ or equity transfers.

   a. Credit
   b. Clearing house
   c. Comparable
   d. Warrant

2. A _____ is a credit derivative contract between two counterparties. The buyer makes periodic payments (premium leg) to the seller, and in return receives a payoff (protection or default leg) if an underlying financial instrument defaults. _____ contracts have been incorrectly compared with insurance, because the buyer pays a premium and, in return, receives a sum of money if a specified event occurs.
   a. Futures contract
   b. Commodity tick
   c. Credit default swap
   d. Stock market index future

3. In finance, a _____ is a derivative whose value derives from the credit risk on an underlying bond, loan or other financial asset. In this way, the credit risk is on an entity other than the counterparties to the transaction itself. This entity is known as the reference entity and may be a corporate, a sovereign or any other form of legal entity which has incurred debt.
   a. Futures contract
   b. STIRT
   c. Derivatives markets
   d. Credit derivative

4. A _____ is a collateralized debt obligation (CDO) in which the underlying credit exposures are taken on using a credit default swap rather than by having a vehicle buy physical assets. _____s can either be single tranche CDOs or fully distributed CDOs. _____s are also commonly divided into balance sheet and arbitrage CDOs, although it is often impossible to distinguish in practice between the two types.
   a. Planning horizon
   b. Synthetic CDO
   c. Market capitalization
   d. Counting house

5. In finance, a _____ is a debt security, in which the authorized issuer owes the holders a debt and, depending on the terms of the _____, is obliged to pay interest (the coupon) and/or to repay the principal at a later date, termed maturity.

Thus a _____ is a loan: the issuer is the borrower, the _____ holder is the lender, and the coupon is the interest. _____s provide the borrower with external funds to finance long-term investments, or, in the case of government _____s, to finance current expenditure.

   a. Convertible bond
   b. Catastrophe bonds
   c. Puttable bond
   d. Bond

6. In finance, a _____ is an OTC-traded financial instrument that facilitates an option to buy or sell a particular bond at a certain date for a particular price. It is similar to a stock option with the difference that the underlying asset is a bond. _____s can be valued using the Black model.
   a. Nominal yield
   b. Municipal bond
   c. Dirty price
   d. Bond option

Chapter 58. Introduction to Credit Derivatives

7. In finance, _____ occurs when a debtor has not met its legal obligations according to the debt contract, e.g. it has not made a scheduled payment, or has violated a loan covenant (condition) of the debt contract. _____ may occur if the debtor is either unwilling or unable to pay their debt. This can occur with all debt obligations including bonds, mortgages, loans, and promissory notes.
   a. Debt validation
   b. Vendor finance
   c. Credit crunch
   d. Default

8. A _____ is a financial contract whose value is derived from the value of something else (known as the underlying.) The underlying on which a _____ is based can be an asset, weather conditions bonds or other forms of credit.
   a. 4-4-5 Calendar
   b. 7-Eleven
   c. 529 plan
   d. Derivative

9. An _____ is a contract written by a seller that conveys to the buyer the right -- but not the obligation -- to buy (in the case of a call _____) or to sell (in the case of a put _____) a particular asset, such as a piece of property such as, among others, a futures contract. In return for granting the _____, the seller collects a payment (the premium) from the buyer.

For example, buying a call _____ provides the right to buy a specified quantity of a security at a set strike price at some time on or before expiration, while buying a put _____ provides the right to sell.

   a. Option
   b. Amortization
   c. AT'T Mobility LLC
   d. Annuity

10. In finance, a _____ is a derivative in which two counterparties agree to exchange one stream of cash flows against another stream. These streams are called the legs of the _____.

The cash flows are calculated over a notional principal amount, which is usually not exchanged between counterparties.

   a. Swap
   b. Volatility swap
   c. Volatility arbitrage
   d. Local volatility

11. In probability theory and statistics, _____ indicates the strength and direction of a linear relationship between two random variables. That is in contrast with the usage of the term in colloquial speech, which denotes any relationship, not necessarily linear. In general statistical usage, _____ or co-relation refers to the departure of two random variables from independence.
   a. Geometric mean
   b. Correlation
   c. Probability distribution
   d. Variance

12. _____ are a type of structured asset-backed security (ABS) whose value and payments are derived from a portfolio of fixed-income underlying assets. _____s are assigned different risk classes, or tranches, whereby 'senior' tranches are considered the safest securities. Interest and principal payments are made in order of seniority, so that junior tranches offer higher coupon payments (and interest rates) or lower prices to compensate for additional default risk.
   a. Senior debt
   b. Zero coupon bond
   c. Municipal bond
   d. Collateralized debt obligations

Chapter 58. Introduction to Credit Derivatives

13. _____ is that which is owed; usually referencing assets owed, but the term can cover other obligations. In the case of assets, _____ is a means of using future purchasing power in the present before a summation has been earned. Some companies and corporations use _____ as a part of their overall corporate finance strategy.
    a. Debt
    b. Credit cycle
    c. Partial Payment
    d. Cross-collateralization

14. _____ is a life of security. It may also refer to the final payment date of a loan or other financial instrument, at which point all remaining interest and principal is due to be paid.

    1, 3, 6 months _____ band can be calculated by using 30-day per month periods.

    a. Replacement cost
    b. Primary market
    c. False billing
    d. Maturity

15. The _____ is a trade organization of participants in the market for over-the-counter derivatives. It is headquartered in New York, and has created a standardized contract (Master Agreement) to enter into derivatives transactions. There are currently two versions of the ISDA Master Agreement: the 1992 edition and the 2002 edition.
    a. Interest rate derivative
    b. Equity swap
    c. Open interest
    d. International Swaps and Derivatives Association

16. _____ is a legally declared inability or impairment of ability of an individual or organization to pay their creditors. Creditors may file a _____ petition against a debtor ('involuntary _____') in an effort to recoup a portion of what they are owed or initiate a restructuring. In the majority of cases, however, _____ is initiated by the debtor (a 'voluntary _____' that is filed by the bankrupt individual or organization.)
    a. 4-4-5 Calendar
    b. Debt settlement
    c. 529 plan
    d. Bankruptcy

17. _____ is the corporate management term for the act of reorganizing the legal, ownership, operational, or other structures of a company for the purpose of making it more profitable or better organized for its present needs. Alternate reasons for restructing include a change of ownership or ownership structure, demerger repositioning debt _____ and financial _____.
    a. Day trading
    b. Concentrated stock
    c. Cross-border leasing
    d. Restructuring

18. A _____ is the financial term used to describe either:

    A general default event related to a legal entity's previously agreed financial obligation. In this case, a legal entity fails to meet its obligation on any significant financial transaction (coupon on a bond it issued or interest rate payment on a swap for example.) The marketplace will recognize this as an event related to the legal entity's credit worthiness.

    a. No-arbitrage bounds
    b. Death spiral financing
    c. Capital surplus
    d. Credit event

Chapter 58. Introduction to Credit Derivatives

19. In finance, _____ is the process of estimating the potential market value of a financial asset or liability. they can be done on assets (for example, investments in marketable securities such as stocks, options, business enterprises, or intangible assets such as patents and trademarks) or on liabilities (e.g., Bonds issued by a company.) _____s are required in many contexts including investment analysis, capital budgeting, merger and acquisition transactions, financial reporting, taxable events to determine the proper tax liability, and in litigation.

   a. Share
   b. Procter ' Gamble
   c. Margin
   d. Valuation

20. The _____ is one of several stock market indices, created by nineteenth-century Wall Street Journal editor and Dow Jones ' Company co-founder Charles Dow. Dow compiled the index to gauge the performance of the industrial sector of the American stock market. It is the second-oldest U.S. market index, after the Dow Jones Transportation Average, which Dow also created.

   a. 4-4-5 Calendar
   b. 529 plan
   c. 7-Eleven
   d. Dow Jones Industrial Average

21. _____ is the brand-name for the family of credit default swap index products covering regions of Europe, Japan and non-Japan Asia. They form a large sector of the overall credit derivative market. The indices are constructed on a set of rules with the overriding criterion being that of liquidity of the underlying Credit Default Swaps (CDS.)

   a. Annualcreditreport.com
   b. Intelliscore
   c. Identity score
   d. ITraxx

22. In structured finance, a _____ is one of a number of related securities offered as part of the same transaction. The word _____ is French for slice, section, series, or portion. In the financial sense of the word, each bond is a different slice of the deal's risk.

   a. Credit enhancement
   b. 4-4-5 Calendar
   c. Tranche
   d. Yield curve spread

23. A _____ is an option granting its owner the right but not the obligation to enter into an underlying swap. Although options can be traded on a variety of swaps, the term '_____' typically refers to options on interest rate swaps.

   There are two types of _____ contracts:

   - A payer _____ gives the owner of the _____ the right to enter into a swap where they pay the fixed leg and receive the floating leg.
   - A receiver _____ gives the owner of the _____ the right to enter into a swap where they will receive the fixed leg, and pay the floating leg.

Chapter 58. Introduction to Credit Derivatives

The buyer and seller of the _____ agree on:

- the premium (price) of the _____
- the strike rate (equal to the fixed rate of the underlying swap)
- length of the option period (which usually ends two business days prior to the start date of the underlying swap),
- the term of the underlying swap,
- notional amount,
- amortization, if any
- frequency of settlement of payments on the underlying swap

The participants in the _____ market are predominantly large corporations, banks, financial institutions and hedge funds. End users such as corporations and banks typically use _____s to manage interest rate risk arising from their core business or from their financing arrangements.

a. Straddle
c. Swaption
b. Bear call spread
d. Put option

24. In finance, _____ refers to the way a corporation finances its assets through some combination of equity, debt, or hybrid securities. A firm's _____ is then the composition or 'structure' of its liabilities. For example, a firm that sells $20 billion in equity and $80 billion in debt is said to be 20% equity-financed and 80% debt-financed.

a. Rights issue
c. Book building
b. Capital structure
d. Market for corporate control

Chapter 59. Convertible Securities and Their Investment Characteristics

1. In finance, a _____ is a type of bond that can be converted into shares of stock in the issuing company, usually at some pre-announced ratio. It is a hybrid security with debt- and equity-like features. Although it typically has a low coupon rate, the holder is compensated with the ability to convert the bond to common stock, usually at a substantial discount to the stock's market value.
   a. Bond fund
   b. Convertible bond
   c. Corporate bond
   d. Gilts

2. In finance, a _____ is a debt security, in which the authorized issuer owes the holders a debt and, depending on the terms of the _____, is obliged to pay interest (the coupon) and/or to repay the principal at a later date, termed maturity.

Thus a _____ is a loan: the issuer is the borrower, the _____ holder is the lender, and the coupon is the interest. _____s provide the borrower with external funds to finance long-term investments, or, in the case of government _____s, to finance current expenditure.

   a. Catastrophe bonds
   b. Bond
   c. Puttable bond
   d. Convertible bond

3. A _____ is a fungible, negotiable instrument representing financial value. They are broadly categorized into debt securities (such as banknotes, bonds and debentures), and equity securities; e.g., common stocks. The company or other entity issuing the _____ is called the issuer.
   a. Securities lending
   b. Book entry
   c. Security
   d. Tracking stock

4. In finance, _____ is the process of estimating the potential market value of a financial asset or liability. they can be done on assets (for example, investments in marketable securities such as stocks, options, business enterprises, or intangible assets such as patents and trademarks) or on liabilities (e.g., Bonds issued by a company.) _____s are required in many contexts including investment analysis, capital budgeting, merger and acquisition transactions, financial reporting, taxable events to determine the proper tax liability, and in litigation.
   a. Procter ' Gamble
   b. Valuation
   c. Margin
   d. Share

5. In finance, _____ refers to the way a corporation finances its assets through some combination of equity, debt, or hybrid securities. A firm's _____ is then the composition or 'structure' of its liabilities. For example, a firm that sells $20 billion in equity and $80 billion in debt is said to be 20% equity-financed and 80% debt-financed.
   a. Market for corporate control
   b. Rights issue
   c. Capital structure
   d. Book building

6. _____ or financing is to provide capital (funds), which means money for a project, a person, a business or any other private or public institutions.

Those funds can be allocated for either short term or long term purposes. The health fund is a new way of _____ private healthcare centers.

   a. Funding
   b. Product life cycle
   c. Proxy fight
   d. Synthetic CDO

Chapter 59. Convertible Securities and Their Investment Characteristics

7. In economics and finance, _____ is the practice of taking advantage of a price differential between two or more markets: striking a combination of matching deals that capitalize upon the imbalance, the profit being the difference between the market prices. When used by academics, an _____ is a transaction that involves no negative cash flow at any probabilistic or temporal state and a positive cash flow in at least one state; in simple terms, a risk-free profit.
   a. Issuer
   b. Arbitrage
   c. Initial margin
   d. Efficient-market hypothesis

8. In finance, a _____ is a position established in one market in an attempt to offset exposure to the price risk of an equal but opposite obligation or position in another market -- usually, but not always, in the context of one's commercial activity. Hedging is a strategy designed to minimize exposure to such business risks as a sharp contraction in demand for one's inventory, while still allowing the business to profit from producing and maintaining that inventory. A typical hedger might be a farmer with 2000 acres of unharvested wheat in the ground, who would rather tend his crop without the distraction of uncertain prices.
   a. 529 plan
   b. 7-Eleven
   c. 4-4-5 Calendar
   d. Hedge

9. A _____ is a person who makes investment decisions using money other people have placed under his or her control. In other words, it is a financial career involved in investment management. They work with a team of analysts and researchers, and are ultimately responsible for establishing an investment strategy, selecting appropriate investments and allocating each investment properly for a fund- or asset-management vehicle.
   a. Portfolio manager
   b. Purchasing manager
   c. Day trader
   d. Financial analyst

10. In finance, the term _____ describes the amount in cash that returns to the owners of a security. Normally it does not include the price variations, at the difference of the total return. _____ applies to various stated rates of return on stocks (common and preferred, and convertible), fixed income instruments (bonds, notes, bills, strips, zero coupon), and some other investment type insurance products (e.g. annuities.)
    a. 4-4-5 Calendar
    b. Macaulay duration
    c. Yield to maturity
    d. Yield

11. In economics and business, specifically cost accounting, the _____ is the point at which cost or expenses and revenue are equal: there is no net loss or gain, and one has 'broken even'. A profit or a loss has not been made, although opportunity costs have been paid, and capital has received the risk-adjusted, expected return.

For example, if the business sells less than 200 tables each month, it will make a loss, if it sells more, it will be a profit.

   a. Defined contribution plan
   b. Fixed asset turnover
   c. Market microstructure
   d. Break-even point

12. The _____ or forward rate is the agreed upon price of an asset in a forward contract. Using the rational pricing assumption, we can express the _____ in terms of the spot price and any dividends etc., so that there is no possibility for arbitrage.

The _____ is given by:

$$F > $$

where

F is the _____ to be paid at time T
e^x is the exponential function
r is the risk-free interest rate
q is the cost-of-carry
S_0 is the spot price of the asset (i.e. what it would sell for at time 0)
D_i is a dividend which is guaranteed to be paid at time t_i where $0 < t_i < T$.

The two questions here are what price the short position (the seller of the asset) should offer to maximize his gain, and what price the long position (the buyer of the asset) should accept to maximize his gain?

At the very least we know that both do not want to lose any money in the deal.

a. Forward price
b. Security interest
c. Financial Gerontology
d. Biweekly Mortgage

13. In business and accounting, _____s are everything of value that is owned by a person or company. The balance sheet of a firm records the monetary value of the _____s owned by the firm. The two major _____ classes are tangible _____s and intangible _____s.
  a. EBITDA
  b. Income
  c. Accounts payable
  d. Asset

14. In finance, the _____ of a financial asset measures the sensitivity of the asset's price to interest rate movements, expressed as a number of years. The reason for expressing this sensitivity in years is that the time that will elapse until a cash flow is received allows more interest to accumulate. Therefore the price of an asset with long term cashflows has more interest rate sensitivity than an asset with cashflows in the near future.
  a. Yield to maturity
  b. Duration
  c. Macaulay duration
  d. 4-4-5 Calendar

15. A _____ is the price of a single share of a no. of saleable stocks of the company. Once the stock is purchased, the owner becomes a shareholder of the company that issued the share.
  a. Stock split
  b. Trading curb
  c. Share price
  d. Whisper numbers

Chapter 59. Convertible Securities and Their Investment Characteristics

16. The term _____ refers to three closely related concepts:

    - The _____ model is a mathematical model of the market for an equity, in which the equity's price is a stochastic process.
    - The _____ PDE is a partial differential equation which (in the model) must be satisfied by the price of a derivative on the equity.
    - The _____ formula is the result obtained by solving the _____ PDE for a European call option.

Fischer Black and Myron Scholes first articulated the _____ formula in their 1973 paper, 'The Pricing of Options and Corporate Liabilities.' The foundation for their research relied on work developed by scholars such as Jack L. Treynor, Paul Samuelson, A. James Boness, Sheen T. Kassouf, and Edward O. Thorp. The fundamental insight of _____ is that the option is implicitly priced if the stock is traded.

Robert C. Merton was the first to publish a paper expanding the mathematical understanding of the options pricing model and coined the term '_____' options pricing model.

a. Modified Internal Rate of Return
c. Perpetuity

b. Black-Scholes
d. Stochastic volatility

17. An _____ is a contract written by a seller that conveys to the buyer the right -- but not the obligation -- to buy (in the case of a call _____) or to sell (in the case of a put _____) a particular asset, such as a piece of property such as, among others, a futures contract. In return for granting the _____, the seller collects a payment (the premium) from the buyer.

For example, buying a call _____ provides the right to buy a specified quantity of a security at a set strike price at some time on or before expiration, while buying a put _____ provides the right to sell.

a. Option
c. AT'T Mobility LLC

b. Amortization
d. Annuity

Chapter 60. Convertible Securities and Their Valuation

1. In finance, the _____ of a derivative is an asset, basket of assets, index, or even another derivative, such that the cash flows of the (former) derivative depend on the value of this _____. There must be an independent way to observe this value to avoid conflicts of interest.

For example, in a stock option to buy 100 shares of Nokia at EUR 50 in September 2006, the _____ is a Nokia share.

   a. AAB
   b. ABN Amro
   c. A Random Walk Down Wall Street
   d. Underlying

2. In finance, the _____ of a financial asset measures the sensitivity of the asset's price to interest rate movements, expressed as a number of years. The reason for expressing this sensitivity in years is that the time that will elapse until a cash flow is received allows more interest to accumulate. Therefore the price of an asset with long term cashflows has more interest rate sensitivity than an asset with cashflows in the near future.
   a. Duration
   b. 4-4-5 Calendar
   c. Macaulay duration
   d. Yield to maturity

3. An _____ is a contract written by a seller that conveys to the buyer the right -- but not the obligation -- to buy (in the case of a call _____) or to sell (in the case of a put _____) a particular asset, such as a piece of property such as, among others, a futures contract. In return for granting the _____, the seller collects a payment (the premium) from the buyer.

For example, buying a call _____ provides the right to buy a specified quantity of a security at a set strike price at some time on or before expiration, while buying a put _____ provides the right to sell.

   a. Amortization
   b. AT'T Mobility LLC
   c. Annuity
   d. Option

4. In finance, a _____ is a type of bond that can be converted into shares of stock in the issuing company, usually at some pre-announced ratio. It is a hybrid security with debt- and equity-like features. Although it typically has a low coupon rate, the holder is compensated with the ability to convert the bond to common stock, usually at a substantial discount to the stock's market value.
   a. Corporate bond
   b. Convertible bond
   c. Gilts
   d. Bond fund

5. In business and accounting, _____s are everything of value that is owned by a person or company. The balance sheet of a firm records the monetary value of the _____s owned by the firm. The two major _____ classes are tangible _____s and intangible _____s.
   a. Accounts payable
   b. Income
   c. EBITDA
   d. Asset

6. An _____ is an exchange of tangible assets for intangible assets or vice versa. Since it is a swap of assets, the procedure takes place on the active side of the balance sheet and has no impact on the latter in regards to volume. As an example, a company may sell equity and receive the value in cash thus increasing liquidity.
   a. ABN Amro
   b. Asset swap
   c. A Random Walk Down Wall Street
   d. AAB

Chapter 60. Convertible Securities and Their Valuation

7. _____ are a type of structured asset-backed security (ABS) whose value and payments are derived from a portfolio of fixed-income underlying assets. _____s are assigned different risk classes, or tranches, whereby 'senior' tranches are considered the safest securities. Interest and principal payments are made in order of seniority, so that junior tranches offer higher coupon payments (and interest rates) or lower prices to compensate for additional default risk.
   a. Senior debt
   b. Collateralized debt obligations
   c. Municipal bond
   d. Zero coupon bond

8. _____ is that which is owed; usually referencing assets owed, but the term can cover other obligations. In the case of assets, _____ is a means of using future purchasing power in the present before a summation has been earned. Some companies and corporations use _____ as a part of their overall corporate finance strategy.
   a. Cross-collateralization
   b. Partial Payment
   c. Debt
   d. Credit cycle

9. In finance, _____ occurs when a debtor has not met its legal obligations according to the debt contract, e.g. it has not made a scheduled payment, or has violated a loan covenant (condition) of the debt contract. _____ may occur if the debtor is either unwilling or unable to pay their debt. This can occur with all debt obligations including bonds, mortgages, loans, and promissory notes.
   a. Debt validation
   b. Default
   c. Credit crunch
   d. Vendor finance

10. A _____ is a fungible, negotiable instrument representing financial value. They are broadly categorized into debt securities (such as banknotes, bonds and debentures), and equity securities; e.g., common stocks. The company or other entity issuing the _____ is called the issuer.
    a. Tracking stock
    b. Securities lending
    c. Book entry
    d. Security

11. In finance, a _____ is a derivative in which two counterparties agree to exchange one stream of cash flows against another stream. These streams are called the legs of the _____.

The cash flows are calculated over a notional principal amount, which is usually not exchanged between counterparties.

   a. Volatility arbitrage
   b. Volatility swap
   c. Local volatility
   d. Swap

12. A _____ is a private or public market for the trading of company stock and derivatives of company stock at an agreed price; these are securities listed on a stock exchange as well as those only traded privately.

The size of the world _____ is estimated at about $36.6 trillion US at the beginning of October 2008 . The world derivatives market has been estimated at about $480 trillion face or nominal value, 12 times the size of the entire world economy.

   a. Adolph Coors
   b. Stock market
   c. Andrew Tobias
   d. Anton Gelonkin

Chapter 60. Convertible Securities and Their Valuation

13. _____ is a measurement of corporate or economic size equal to the share price times the number of shares outstanding of a public company. As owning stock represents owning the company, including all its equity, capitalization could represent the public opinion of a company's net worth and is a determining factor in stock valuation. Likewise, the capitalization of stock markets or economic regions may be compared to other economic indicators.

   a. Synthetic CDO
   b. Just-in-time
   c. Proxy fight
   d. Market capitalization

14. The coupon or _____ of a bond is the amount of interest paid per year expressed as a percentage of the face value of the bond.

For example if you hold $10,000 nominal of a bond described as a 4.5% loan stock, you will receive $450 in interest each year (probably in two installments of $225 each.)

Not all bonds have coupons.

   a. Zero-coupon bond
   b. Revenue bonds
   c. Puttable bond
   d. Coupon rate

15. A '_____' is a 'Charge' that is paid to obtain the right to delay a payment. Essentially, the payer purchases the right to make a given payment in the future instead of in the Present. The '_____', or 'Charge' that must be paid to delay the payment, is simply the difference between what the payment amount would be if it were paid in the present and what the payment amount would be paid if it were paid in the future.

   a. Discount
   b. Risk aversion
   c. Risk modeling
   d. Value at risk

16. In finance, the term _____ describes the amount in cash that returns to the owners of a security. Normally it does not include the price variations, at the difference of the total return. _____ applies to various stated rates of return on stocks (common and preferred, and convertible), fixed income instruments (bonds, notes, bills, strips, zero coupon), and some other investment type insurance products (e.g. annuities.)

   a. 4-4-5 Calendar
   b. Macaulay duration
   c. Yield
   d. Yield to maturity

17. _____ is a life of security. It may also refer to the final payment date of a loan or other financial instrument, at which point all remaining interest and principal is due to be paid.

1, 3, 6 months _____ band can be calculated by using 30-day per month periods.

   a. Primary market
   b. Replacement cost
   c. False billing
   d. Maturity

18. In finance, a _____ is a debt security, in which the authorized issuer owes the holders a debt and, depending on the terms of the _____, is obliged to pay interest (the coupon) and/or to repay the principal at a later date, termed maturity.

Chapter 60. Convertible Securities and Their Valuation

Thus a _____ is a loan: the issuer is the borrower, the _____ holder is the lender, and the coupon is the interest. _____s provide the borrower with external funds to finance long-term investments, or, in the case of government _____s, to finance current expenditure.

a. Convertible bond
b. Bond
c. Puttable bond
d. Catastrophe bonds

19. _____ is the increase in the amount of the goods and services produced by an economy over time. It is conventionally measured as the percent rate of increase in real gross domestic product, or real GDP. Growth is usually calculated in real terms, i.e. inflation-adjusted terms, in order to net out the effect of inflation on the price of the goods and services produced.
   a. Economic growth
   b. ABN Amro
   c. A Random Walk Down Wall Street
   d. AAB

20. _____, adopted pursuant to the U.S. Securities Act of 1933, as amended (the 'Securities Act') provides a safe harbor from the registration requirements of the Securities Act of 1933 for certain private resales of restricted securities to QIBs (qualified institutional buyers), which generally are large institutional investors with over $100 million in investable assets. When a broker or dealer is selling securities in reliance on _____, it is subject to the condition that it may not make offers to persons other than those it reasonably believes to be QIBs.

Since its adoption, _____ has greatly increased the liquidity of the securities affected.

   a. Securities Investor Protection Corporation
   b. Prudent man rule
   c. SIPC
   d. Rule 144A

21. In finance, _____ is the process of estimating the potential market value of a financial asset or liability. they can be done on assets (for example, investments in marketable securities such as stocks, options, business enterprises, or intangible assets such as patents and trademarks) or on liabilities (e.g., Bonds issued by a company.) _____s are required in many contexts including investment analysis, capital budgeting, merger and acquisition transactions, financial reporting, taxable events to determine the proper tax liability, and in litigation.
   a. Procter ' Gamble
   b. Share
   c. Margin
   d. Valuation

22. _____ in business and economics refers to the period of time required for the return on an investment to 'repay' the sum of the original investment. For example, a $1000 investment which returned $500 per year would have a two year _____. It intuitively measures how long something takes to 'pay for itself.' _____ is widely used due to its ease of use despite recognized limitations.
   a. Financial Gerontology
   b. Seasoned equity offering
   c. Consignment stock
   d. Payback period

23. _____ is one of the authors of the Black-Scholes equation. In 1997 he was awarded the Nobel Memorial Prize in Economic Sciences for 'a new method to determine the value of derivatives'. The model provides the fundamental conceptual framework for valuing options, such as calls or puts, and is referred to as the Black-Scholes model, which has become the standard in financial markets globally.

Chapter 60. Convertible Securities and Their Valuation

a. Andrew Tobias
b. Adolph Coors
c. Robert James Shiller
d. Myron Samuel Scholes

24. _____ is the provision of resources (such as granting a loan) by one party to another party where that second party does not reimburse the first party immediately, thereby generating a debt, and instead arranges either to repay or return those resources (or material(s) of equal value) at a later date. The first party is called a creditor, also known as a lender, while the second party is called a debtor, also known as a borrower.

Movements of financial capital are normally dependent on either _____ or equity transfers.

a. Credit
b. Warrant
c. Comparable
d. Clearing house

25. _____ most frequently refers to the standard deviation of the continuously compounded returns of a financial instrument with a specific time horizon. It is often used to quantify the risk of the instrument over that time period. _____ is typically expressed in annualized terms, and it may either be an absolute number ($5) or a fraction of the mean (5%).

a. Portfolio insurance
b. Currency swap
c. Seasoned equity offering
d. Volatility

26. In finance, the _____ between two currencies specifies how much one currency is worth in terms of the other. For example an _____ of 102 Japanese yen to the United States dollar means that JPY 102 is worth the same as USD 1. The foreign exchange market is one of the largest markets in the world.

a. Exchange rate
b. A Random Walk Down Wall Street
c. ABN Amro
d. AAB

27. A _____ is a financial contract whose value is derived from the value of something else (known as the underlying.) The underlying on which a _____ is based can be an asset, weather conditions bonds or other forms of credit.

a. 7-Eleven
b. Derivative
c. 4-4-5 Calendar
d. 529 plan

28. In mathematics, a _____ of a function of several variables is its derivative with respect to one of those variables with the others held constant (as opposed to the total derivative, in which all variables are allowed to vary.) _____s are useful in vector calculus and differential geometry.

The _____ of a function f with respect to the variable x is written as f'_x, $\partial_x f$, or $\partial f/\partial x$.

a. 529 plan
b. 7-Eleven
c. 4-4-5 Calendar
d. Partial derivative

29. _____ is a parameter used in the calculation of economic capital or regulatory capital under Basel II for a banking institution. This is an attribute of a bank's client.

The _____ is the likelihood that a loan will not be repaid and will fall into default.

Chapter 60. Convertible Securities and Their Valuation

a. Deposit insurance
c. Probability of default
b. Variable rate mortgage
d. Credit bureau

30. In financial mathematics, the _____ of an option contract is the volatility implied by the market price of the option based on an option pricing model. In other words, it is the volatility that, given a particular pricing model, yields a theoretical value for the option equal to the current market price. Non-option financial instruments that have embedded optionality, such as an interest rate cap, can also have an _____.

a. Interest rate derivative
c. Equity derivative
b. Interest rate future
d. Implied volatility

31. _____ is a process of analyzing possible future events by considering alternative possible outcomes (scenarios.) The analysis is designed to allow improved decision-making by allowing consideration of outcomes and their implications.

For example, in economics and finance, a financial institution might attempt to forecast several possible scenarios for the economy (e.g. rapid growth, moderate growth, slow growth) and it might also attempt to forecast financial market returns (for bonds, stocks and cash) in each of those scenarios.

a. Scenario analysis
c. 529 plan
b. Detection Risk
d. 4-4-5 Calendar

32. A _____ is a financial contract between two parties, the seller (writer) and the buyer of the option. The put allows its buyer the right but not the obligation to sell a commodity or financial instrument (the underlying instrument) to the writer (seller) of the option at a certain time for a certain price (the strike price.) The writer (seller) has the obligation to purchase the underlying asset at that strike price, if the buyer exercises the option.

a. Debit spread
c. Bear spread
b. Bear call spread
d. Put option

33. In finance, a _____ is a position established in one market in an attempt to offset exposure to the price risk of an equal but opposite obligation or position in another market -- usually, but not always, in the context of one's commercial activity. Hedging is a strategy designed to minimize exposure to such business risks as a sharp contraction in demand for one's inventory, while still allowing the business to profit from producing and maintaining that inventory. A typical hedger might be a farmer with 2000 acres of unharvested wheat in the ground, who would rather tend his crop without the distraction of uncertain prices.

a. 7-Eleven
c. 529 plan
b. 4-4-5 Calendar
d. Hedge

34. A _____ is a private investment fund open to a limited range of investors that is permitted by regulators to undertake a wider range of activities than other investment funds and also pays a performance fee to its investment manager. Each fund will have its own strategy which determines the type of investments and the methods of investment it undertakes. _____s as a class invest in a broad range of investments extending over shares, debt, commodities and beyond.

a. 4-4-5 Calendar
c. 7-Eleven
b. 529 plan
d. Hedge fund

35. A _____ is a credit derivative contract between two counterparties. The buyer makes periodic payments (premium leg) to the seller, and in return receives a payoff (protection or default leg) if an underlying financial instrument defaults. _____ contracts have been incorrectly compared with insurance, because the buyer pays a premium and, in return, receives a sum of money if a specified event occurs.

a. Commodity tick

b. Credit default swap

c. Futures contract

d. Stock market index future

ANSWER KEY

Chapter 1
1. a	2. c	3. b	4. b	5. c	6. a	7. d	8. d	9. d	10. a
11. a	12. d	13. a	14. d	15. a	16. b	17. d	18. d	19. a	20. c
21. d	22. b	23. b	24. b	25. a	26. b	27. b	28. d	29. b	30. c
31. d	32. c	33. d	34. d	35. b	36. d	37. c	38. d	39. a	40. d
41. c	42. c	43. c	44. d	45. b	46. a	47. b	48. c	49. d	50. d
51. d	52. c	53. c	54. b	55. c	56. d				

Chapter 2
1. d	2. d	3. d	4. a	5. d	6. c	7. d	8. d	9. a	10. d
11. d	12. d	13. d	14. a	15. d	16. d	17. d	18. c	19. d	20. a
21. a	22. d	23. c	24. d	25. d	26. d	27. d	28. b	29. b	

Chapter 3
1. a	2. b	3. d	4. c	5. d	6. a	7. b	8. d	9. d	10. d
11. a	12. c	13. d	14. b	15. a	16. d	17. d	18. d	19. a	20. b
21. d	22. d	23. d	24. c	25. a	26. b	27. d	28. d	29. d	30. b
31. d	32. d	33. b	34. c	35. a	36. c				

Chapter 4
1. a	2. a	3. b	4. d	5. d	6. a	7. a	8. d	9. d	10. c
11. c	12. d	13. b	14. d						

Chapter 5
1. d	2. d	3. b	4. a	5. d	6. b	7. c	8. a	9. d	10. d
11. c	12. a	13. b	14. d	15. d	16. d	17. c	18. d	19. d	20. d
21. d	22. b	23. d	24. b	25. b	26. d	27. d	28. d	29. d	30. c
31. d	32. d	33. d	34. b	35. d	36. b	37. b	38. b		

Chapter 6
1. b	2. a	3. b	4. d	5. c	6. d	7. d	8. d	9. d	10. d
11. d	12. d	13. d	14. d	15. d	16. d	17. b	18. d	19. d	20. b
21. d	22. a	23. b							

Chapter 7
1. c	2. d	3. b	4. b	5. d	6. b	7. d	8. a	9. d	10. a
11. d	12. a	13. a	14. d	15. a	16. d	17. b	18. d	19. d	20. d
21. d	22. d	23. d	24. d	25. c	26. c	27. d	28. a	29. c	30. a
31. d	32. a	33. d	34. b	35. d	36. d				

Chapter 8
1. a	2. d	3. c	4. d	5. d	6. a	7. a	8. d	9. d	10. c
11. d	12. a	13. b	14. a	15. c	16. d	17. a	18. c	19. d	20. a
21. d	22. d	23. d	24. d	25. d	26. d				

Chapter 9

1. a	2. d	3. c	4. b	5. b	6. c	7. d	8. d	9. d	10. d
11. a	12. d	13. d	14. d	15. d	16. d	17. d	18. d	19. a	20. a
21. d	22. d	23. d	24. d						

Chapter 10

1. a	2. d	3. c	4. d	5. d	6. a	7. d	8. c	9. d	10. c
11. a	12. c	13. d	14. a	15. a	16. a	17. b	18. c	19. d	20. d
21. c	22. d	23. c	24. d	25. c	26. c	27. c	28. b	29. a	

Chapter 11

1. d	2. b	3. c	4. d	5. d	6. a	7. d	8. d	9. d	10. c
11. b	12. a	13. d	14. d	15. b	16. c	17. d	18. b	19. d	20. d
21. a	22. d	23. d	24. a	25. d	26. d	27. d	28. a	29. d	30. a
31. d	32. a	33. d	34. c	35. d	36. d	37. d	38. d	39. d	40. d
41. b	42. d								

Chapter 12

1. d	2. a	3. b	4. d	5. c	6. d	7. c	8. a	9. b	10. a
11. d	12. d	13. d	14. d	15. d	16. a	17. a	18. d	19. d	20. d
21. d	22. d	23. b	24. c	25. d	26. d	27. d			

Chapter 13

1. d	2. d	3. c	4. b	5. a	6. c	7. d	8. d	9. b	10. b
11. b	12. d	13. d	14. a	15. c	16. c	17. c	18. d	19. a	20. c
21. b	22. b	23. c	24. d	25. a	26. b	27. b	28. b	29. b	30. d
31. d	32. d	33. a	34. c	35. d	36. d	37. b	38. d	39. c	40. d
41. b	42. b								

Chapter 14

| 1. b | 2. d | 3. d | 4. d |

Chapter 15

1. d	2. a	3. c	4. c	5. d	6. b	7. a	8. d	9. b	10. d
11. c	12. d	13. a	14. d	15. b	16. b	17. d	18. b	19. c	20. d
21. a									

Chapter 16

| 1. a | 2. d | 3. d | 4. b | 5. d | 6. d | 7. d | 8. b | 9. b | 10. c |
| 11. b | 12. d | 13. c | | | | | | | |

Chapter 17

| 1. d | 2. d |

ANSWER KEY

Chapter 18
1. d   2. c   3. c   4. d   5. d   6. a   7. d   8. d   9. a   10. d
11. d   12. b   13. d   14. c

Chapter 19
1. d   2. d   3. b   4. b   5. d   6. c   7. d   8. c   9. b   10. d
11. c   12. d   13. d   14. d   15. d   16. a   17. a   18. d   19. d   20. b
21. d   22. b   23. b   24. d

Chapter 20
1. d   2. b   3. b   4. a   5. d   6. b   7. d   8. c   9. d   10. c
11. a   12. d   13. b   14. d   15. d   16. d   17. d   18. d   19. c   20. d
21. d   22. d   23. d   24. a   25. d   26. c   27. d

Chapter 21
1. d   2. d   3. d   4. c   5. d   6. a   7. d   8. d   9. d   10. d
11. d   12. d   13. d   14. c   15. c   16. d   17. b   18. c   19. d

Chapter 22
1. b   2. a   3. c   4. d   5. a   6. b   7. b   8. d   9. d   10. c
11. d   12. d   13. c   14. d   15. d   16. b   17. a   18. a   19. b   20. d
21. a

Chapter 23
1. d   2. a   3. d   4. d   5. a   6. b   7. a   8. b   9. d   10. a
11. d   12. d   13. d   14. d   15. a   16. d   17. d   18. d   19. c   20. b
21. a   22. c   23. d   24. a   25. a   26. a   27. b   28. d   29. d   30. c

Chapter 24
1. b   2. d   3. c   4. d   5. b   6. d   7. a   8. d   9. d   10. d
11. c   12. c   13. d   14. d   15. c   16. b   17. d   18. d   19. d   20. d
21. d   22. b   23. d   24. d   25. b   26. d   27. b   28. d   29. a   30. a
31. d   32. d   33. b   34. d

Chapter 25
1. a   2. d   3. a   4. d   5. a   6. d   7. b   8. b   9. a   10. c
11. d   12. d

Chapter 26
1. d   2. d   3. d   4. a   5. d   6. d   7. d   8. b   9. d   10. d
11. d   12. a   13. d   14. c   15. a   16. b   17. c   18. a   19. d   20. d
21. b   22. d   23. d   24. d

Chapter 27
1. a 2. d 3. c 4. d 5. c 6. d 7. d 8. a 9. c 10. a
11. d 12. d 13. a 14. d

Chapter 28
1. c 2. b 3. d 4. d 5. d 6. d 7. c 8. d 9. d 10. d
11. c

Chapter 29
1. d 2. d 3. d 4. d 5. b 6. d 7. d 8. d 9. b 10. c
11. b 12. b 13. d 14. a 15. a 16. c 17. d 18. d 19. d 20. d
21. c 22. d

Chapter 30
1. b 2. d 3. a 4. d 5. d 6. d 7. a 8. d 9. d 10. b
11. c 12. c 13. a 14. b 15. b

Chapter 31
1. b 2. b 3. d 4. b 5. d 6. a 7. b 8. c 9. d 10. d
11. a 12. d 13. b 14. b 15. b 16. a 17. b 18. a 19. c 20. d
21. a 22. d 23. a 24. c 25. d 26. a 27. a

Chapter 32
1. d 2. d 3. b 4. b 5. d 6. a 7. b 8. b 9. d 10. d
11. a 12. d 13. c 14. b 15. c 16. a 17. a 18. c 19. d 20. a
21. d 22. b 23. b 24. a 25. b 26. c 27. c 28. a 29. d 30. a
31. d 32. c 33. a 34. d 35. d 36. c 37. c 38. c 39. d 40. b
41. b

Chapter 33
1. d 2. d 3. d 4. a 5. d 6. a 7. a 8. b 9. a 10. b
11. d 12. a

Chapter 34
1. c 2. d 3. c 4. d 5. d 6. d 7. d 8. d 9. a 10. d
11. d 12. b 13. b 14. d 15. b 16. d 17. d 18. a 19. c 20. d

Chapter 35
1. b 2. a 3. d 4. d 5. d 6. d 7. d 8. a 9. d 10. d
11. b

Chapter 36
1. d 2. a 3. d 4. d 5. a 6. c 7. a 8. d 9. d 10. a
11. d 12. d 13. d 14. d 15. d 16. c 17. d 18. d 19. d

ANSWER KEY

Chapter 37
1. d 2. a 3. d 4. b 5. d 6. b 7. a 8. d 9. d 10. b
11. b 12. c 13. d 14. c 15. d 16. a 17. d

Chapter 38
1. d 2. d 3. d 4. c 5. c 6. d 7. d 8. b 9. c 10. b
11. b 12. a 13. d 14. d 15. d

Chapter 39
1. d 2. a 3. b 4. d 5. c 6. d 7. d

Chapter 40
1. d 2. d 3. a 4. b 5. b 6. d 7. d 8. d 9. c 10. a
11. c 12. a 13. d 14. c 15. c 16. c 17. d

Chapter 41
1. d 2. c 3. d 4. a 5. d 6. d 7. c 8. b 9. d 10. d
11. a 12. d 13. a 14. b 15. d 16. a 17. a 18. d 19. d 20. d
21. d 22. c 23. b 24. c 25. d 26. d

Chapter 42
1. b 2. a 3. c 4. b 5. d 6. d 7. c 8. b 9. d 10. d
11. a 12. d 13. d

Chapter 43
1. a 2. d 3. d 4. d 5. c 6. d 7. d 8. d 9. d 10. d
11. a 12. d 13. d 14. a 15. d 16. c 17. d 18. d 19. a 20. c
21. d

Chapter 44
1. d 2. c 3. a 4. d 5. b 6. a 7. d 8. c 9. d 10. b
11. d 12. b 13. a 14. d 15. d 16. d 17. d 18. a 19. b 20. d
21. c 22. d 23. d 24. d 25. b

Chapter 45
1. d 2. c 3. d 4. d 5. a 6. b 7. d 8. b 9. b 10. a
11. d 12. c 13. b 14. b 15. c 16. a 17. d 18. b 19. b 20. d
21. b 22. d 23. b 24. c 25. d 26. a

Chapter 46
1. b 2. d 3. a 4. d 5. c 6. a 7. c 8. d 9. d 10. c
11. d 12. a 13. b 14. d 15. d 16. a 17. c 18. c 19. d 20. d
21. a 22. d 23. a

Chapter 47
1. c 2. a 3. a 4. c 5. b 6. c 7. d 8. a 9. b

Chapter 48
1. d 2. c 3. b 4. c

Chapter 49
1. d 2. a 3. a 4. d 5. d 6. a 7. b 8. d 9. a 10. d
11. d 12. d 13. d 14. d 15. d 16. c 17. d 18. d 19. a 20. d
21. d 22. d 23. d

Chapter 50
1. d 2. d 3. d 4. b 5. b 6. d 7. b 8. b 9. d 10. d
11. d 12. d 13. d 14. d 15. c 16. b 17. d

Chapter 51
1. b 2. d 3. a 4. d 5. d 6. b 7. d 8. d 9. a 10. a
11. b 12. c 13. d 14. b 15. d 16. d 17. d 18. d 19. d 20. d
21. b 22. b 23. c 24. b 25. d 26. c 27. c 28. b 29. c 30. c
31. d 32. d 33. d

Chapter 52
1. b 2. b 3. c 4. d 5. d 6. d 7. b 8. d 9. d 10. d
11. d 12. b 13. d 14. d 15. d 16. c 17. c 18. d 19. d 20. b
21. d 22. d

Chapter 53
1. c 2. a 3. d 4. d 5. d 6. d 7. a 8. a 9. c 10. a
11. d 12. d 13. d 14. c 15. d 16. d 17. d 18. b 19. b

Chapter 54
1. d 2. a 3. d 4. c 5. b 6. c 7. d 8. b 9. d 10. d
11. d 12. d 13. a 14. d 15. c 16. a 17. b 18. c 19. a 20. d
21. d 22. c 23. d 24. d 25. c

Chapter 55
1. d 2. c 3. c 4. c 5. d 6. d 7. d 8. b 9. d 10. d
11. d 12. d 13. b 14. d 15. b 16. d 17. d 18. b 19. b 20. b
21. b 22. a 23. b 24. a

Chapter 56
1. b 2. c 3. a 4. d 5. d 6. b 7. c

ANSWER KEY

Chapter 57
1. d   2. d   3. b   4. d   5. c   6. d   7. d   8. b   9. d   10. d
11. a   12. a   13. d

Chapter 58
1. a   2. c   3. d   4. b   5. d   6. d   7. d   8. d   9. a   10. a
11. b   12. d   13. a   14. d   15. d   16. d   17. d   18. d   19. d   20. d
21. d   22. c   23. c   24. b

Chapter 59
1. b   2. b   3. c   4. b   5. c   6. a   7. b   8. d   9. a   10. d
11. d   12. a   13. d   14. b   15. c   16. b   17. a

Chapter 60
1. d   2. a   3. d   4. b   5. d   6. b   7. b   8. c   9. b   10. d
11. d   12. b   13. d   14. d   15. a   16. c   17. d   18. b   19. a   20. d
21. d   22. d   23. d   24. a   25. d   26. a   27. b   28. d   29. c   30. d
31. a   32. d   33. d   34. d   35. b

www.ingramcontent.com/pod-product-compliance
Lightning Source LLC
Chambersburg PA
CBHW080545230426
43663CB00015B/2707